Anthony Curtis

The Penguin Book of the Car

Penguin Books

Penguin Books Ltd, Harmondsworth, Middlesex, England
Viking Penguin Inc., 40 West 23rd Street, New York, New York 10010, U.S.A.
Penguin Books Australia Ltd, Ringwood, Victoria, Australia
Penguin Books Canada Ltd, 2801 John Street, Markham, Ontario, Canada L3R 1B4
Penguin Books (N.Z.) Ltd, 182–190 Wairau Road, Auckland 10, New Zealand

First published 1985

Typeset, printed and bound in Great Britain by
Hazell Watson & Viney Limited,
Member of BPCC Ltd,
Aylesbury, Bucks
Set in 8/10pt Univers Light

Penguin Handbooks
The Penguin Book of the Car

Anthony Curtis was born in 1935 in Surbiton, and is Editor of
the weekly magazine *Motor*. He was educated at Stowe
School and at the Imperial College of Science. After completing his national service in the army during the mid fifties, he
spent three years as a corrosion engineer, working on the
cathodic protection of buried structures. His working life since
then has been largely devoted to the written communication
of technical information of one sort or another. For some
years he helped to prepare manuals on aircraft and guided
missiles for such companies as Elliott Automation, but in 1965
he joined the staff of *Motor* as a road-tester and writer of
technical articles. His speciality was attempting to make the
engineering and scientific principles of the car as clear and
simple as possible to his readers. In 1971 he was appointed
Technical Editor, and was Editor from 1978 to 1984. He is
married, has three children, lives in Cobham, Surrey, and likes
classical music.

Contents

Acknowledgements

We wish to thank the following for permission to reproduce illustrations:

AE Autoparts Ltd, Bradford (29,31); ATE (279); Austin-Morris Ltd (72); Automotive Products Ltd (169, 313); Bosch Ltd (88, 89); Robert Bosch GmbH (147); BP Ltd (42); British Leyland (34); Champion Sparking Plug Co. Ltd (156, 158); TI Crypton Ltd (130, 131, 132, 134); AC Delco (44); Dunlop (237, 238, 239, 247); Girling (283); Hobourne Eaton Ltd (32); Lockheed (272, 278); Joseph Lucas Ltd (85, 133, 143, 145); *Motor* (16,17,18,19,23,24,25,27,35,52,59,61,62,65,66,78, 96,97,98,99,173,174,207,246,247,282,286,287,289); Renold Ltd (38); SEV(UK) Ltd (167); Shell Research Ltd (51); Weber Carburetters (79)

one The Basic Elements

The major assemblies

This book is about the basic scientific and engineering principles that lie behind the intricate workings of the modern motorcar. Its basic purpose is to answer the questions 'Why?' and 'How?'. So it will not tell you, for example, how to set the ignition timing of your own particular car – any maintenance manual can do that – but it will tell you why ignition timing is needed in the first place. Similarly, it will tell you why some engines vibrate more than others, and why body roll is the enemy of cornering power; it will tell you how a carburetter sucks fuel out of its float chamber, and how antilock brakes make it possible to steer and stop at the same time on slippery surfaces – and it will tell you a host of other things besides.

I am going to assume, however, that you already know at least the most basic facts about the car. You know, for example, that it is propelled by the chemical energy stored in a liquid fuel which is carried in a tank and burned inside an engine. Because the fuel burns *inside* it, the engine is said to be of the **internal combustion** type – as opposed to a steam engine, for example, which works by **external combustion**. You probably also know that the engine usually, though not always, incorporates cylinders containing pistons which move back and forth (reciprocate).

But there are a few more facts about the engine which you need to know, even at this stage. In nearly all passenger cars, for example, an electric spark is used to ignite the fuel employed, usually petrol (called gasoline in the States) and the engine thus fed is known as a **spark ignition** unit. Occasion-ally, however, a gaseous fuel is used instead of petrol.

Some cars, too, are fitted with **compression-ignition** engines which need a special fuel – diesel. In these engines combustion is initiated solely by the high temperatures created when the air in the cylinders is greatly compressed.

In a few models reciprocating pistons are replaced by rotors executing a complex but purely rotational form of motion within a **rotary engine**. Many experimental forms of rotary power unit have been evolved, but the only type so far to be fitted to production cars is the **Wankel** engine, named after its inventor, Felix Wankel.

By far the most common engine, however, has four pistons moving up and down inside four cylinders which are arranged in a row – hence the term **in-line four** – and water-cooled. For the moment we can regard the power unit as a box from which a rotating output shaft protrudes – we will explore its mysteries thoroughly in later chapters.

There are, however, three further things we need to know about it. The first is that it will not run at all below a certain minimum speed. An automotive internal combustion engine will **stall** or cease to generate any power whatever – until restarted in a special manner – if its output shaft is forced to stop rotating. Since cars are often forced to stop moving, especially in modern traffic conditions, some means of decoupling the engine from the driven wheels is essential. The simplest form of decoupling device is called a **clutch** (fig. 1) and is controlled by a floor-mounted pedal. In principle it consists of two rotating plates; each faced with a hardwearing friction material so as to grip the other

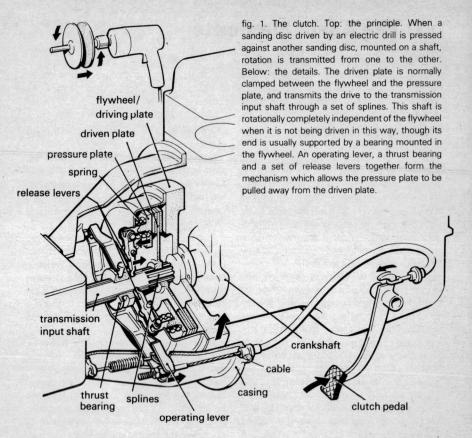

fig. 1. The clutch. Top: the principle. When a sanding disc driven by an electric drill is pressed against another sanding disc, mounted on a shaft, rotation is transmitted from one to the other. Below: the details. The driven plate is normally clamped between the flywheel and the pressure plate, and transmits the drive to the transmission input shaft through a set of splines. This shaft is rotationally completely independent of the flywheel when it is not being driven in this way, though its end is usually supported by a bearing mounted in the flywheel. An operating lever, a thrust bearing and a set of release levers together form the mechanism which allows the pressure plate to be pulled away from the driven plate.

flywheel/
driving plate

driven plate

pressure plate

spring

release levers

transmission
input shaft

crankshaft

cable

thrust
bearing

splines

casing

operating lever

clutch pedal

strongly. The two are clamped together by a powerful spring, but provided with a release mechanism by which they can be separated. When the two plates are pressed together by the spring, the rotational drive, twisting effort or **torque** is transmitted from one to the other, but when the release mechanism is actuated the discs are forced apart and the engine output shaft is decoupled from the input shaft of the **transmission** system, the system which conveys the power to the driven wheels.

In practice, a clutch is rather more complicated, and it usually begins at the **flywheel**, which is simply a disc with a heavy rim, fixed to the output shaft or **crankshaft** of the

engine to smooth out the fluctuations in the torque it generates. This flywheel forms the **driving plate** of the clutch. Sandwiched between the flywheel or driving plate and a spring-loaded **pressure plate** is the **driven plate** of the clutch which has friction material on both sides. The driven plate is fixed, rotationally speaking, to the transmission input shaft but has some freedom to move axially along it. When the clutch pedal is depressed and the pressure plate is forced away from the driving plate against its spring, the driven plate is free to float and no longer transmits any torque from the engine to the transmission system. When the pedal is released again, the driven plate is clamped between the pressure and driving plates and transmits torque to the transmission. The required combination of rotational attachment yet axial freedom is conferred by flutes or grooves called **splines** in the transmission input shaft, which mate with corresponding splines in the bush or bearing collar on which the driven clutch plate is carried.

The second characteristic of the power unit which we need to recognize at this stage is that the turning effort or torque which it produces is not at all matched to the torque needed to drive the car along. At a standstill, for example, a car needs a very high torque delivered at low revolutions per minute (rpm). To match these conflicting requirements, the rotational equivalent of a lever is needed, a lever, what's more, that can be varied in length.

One rotational equivalent of a lever is a system composed of two gears of different sizes meshing together. Imagine, for example, a gear fitted to the transmission input shaft (fig. 2) and driving another gear of the same size attached to an offset auxiliary shaft or **layshaft**. Now imagine a small gear on the end of this shaft driving a second transmission gear three times larger in diameter and with three times as many teeth. The transmission input shaft is then forced to rotate three times faster than the transmission output shaft, but is only called upon to exert one third of the torque to overcome a given resistance. In just the same way, if a boulder is moved by a crowbar exerting a

fig. 2. The gearbox. The pair of gears on the right simply transfer the rotation from the input shaft to the lower shaft of the gearbox. The pair of gears on the left give a reduction ratio of 3:1 – a typical value for first gear. Above: an alternative to the clutch – a simple fluid coupling in which liquid flung from one vaned bowl to another transmits the torque. Most automatic gearboxes incorporate a more sophisticated form of fluid coupling.

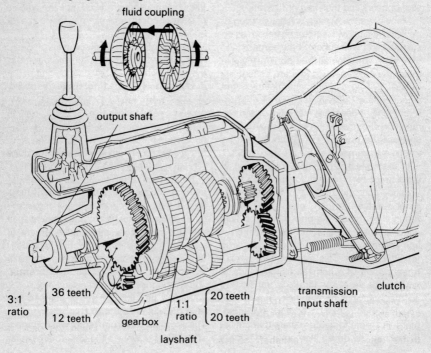

fluid coupling

output shaft

3:1 ratio { 36 teeth / 12 teeth

gearbox

layshaft

1:1 ratio { 20 teeth / 20 teeth

transmission input shaft

clutch

3:1 leverage, the force to be exerted will be one third of the boulder's weight but for every inch the boulder is lifted, the other end of the crowbar has to be moved three inches. Looking at it another way, the two gears have multiplied the engine's torque by three.

The gearing arrangement just described is the sort of thing needed to match the engine to the car when accelerating away from a standstill but is not enough to cope with all the other conditions encountered in normal driving. Not one, but several pairs of gears are needed, and the assembly which meets this requirement is called a **gearbox**; its further function is to provide a reverse gear so that the car can be driven backwards. In most European and Japanese cars the gearbox is controlled manually by the driver, generally (these days) through a floor-mounted lever, using the clutch to decouple the engine each time a change is made. Manual gearboxes have either four or five sets of gears and thus four or five ratios.

Many of you, however, will have driven or travelled in cars with automatic transmission systems and will wonder if the same principles apply. In general they do: most automatic transmission systems are essentially manual gearboxes with automatic control added, though usually they employ a different kind of gear train and have only three ratios. And in place of a clutch they have a special **fluid coupling** in which the driving torque is transmitted by the motion of a fluid.

In its simplest form, a fluid coupling (fig. 2) consists of two rotating bowls filled with a fluid and containing sets of radial dividers or vanes – rather like partitioned cake stands. Rotation of the driving bowl flings the fluid within it outwards and into the driven bowl immediately opposite, which is thus also forced to rotate. This arrangement constitutes a form of automatic clutch, since at low speeds very little torque is transmitted so the engine is free to idle, but as the engine speed rises above about 1000 rpm, more and more torque is transmitted until at higher rpm the driven element is effectively almost locked to the driving element, there being no more than 3–4 per cent of slip between them. However, modern automatic gearboxes use a more complex form of fluid coupling which itself gives some torque multiplication and is called a **torque converter**.

So far we have seen that the transmission system must incorporate a clutch or fluid coupling and a gearbox, manual or automatic, but two further components are necessary. The first is made essential by a car engine's third basic characteristic. This is its working range of rotational speed, which differs from that of the road wheels. Although the engine may not stall until its speed has been reduced to around 500 rpm, it generally will not idle satisfactorily much below 850 rpm, giving a typical speed range of 850–5500 rpm, though some high-performance engines will run at over 7000 rpm. The road-wheel speed range, however, is about 0–1300 rpm for a small family saloon, though at 150 mph the wheels of a high-performance car may rotate at over 2000 rpm.

Accordingly, an additional pair of gears must be interposed between the output of the gearbox and the shafts connected to the driven wheels. These **final drive** gears vary in ratio from nearly 5:1 for small, low-powered cars, to less than 3:1 for cars with very large engines, though in all cases the purpose is the same: to allow the engine to run at any speed from nearly five to not quite three times faster than the driven wheels.

The second of the two additional components mentioned has a quite different function: it is required because in any corner the outer driven wheel has to rotate faster than the inner one. The special arrangement of gears which permits this relative speed difference, while continuing to transmit torque to both driven wheels, is called a **differential** and will be fully described elsewhere.

We are now in a better position to see how the various parts of a car fit together. The simplest, and at one time most common, arrangement involves (fig. 3) a four-cylinder

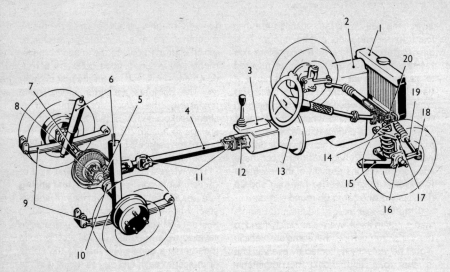

fig. 3. The basic parts of a simple front-engined car:

1 Cooling radiator
2 Front-mounted, four-cylinder, in-line water-cooled engine
3 Manual gearbox
4 Propeller shaft
5 Crown wheel and pinion
6 Dampers
7 Half-shaft
8 Differential
9 Leaf springs
10 Live rear axle
11 Universal joints
12 Splined connection
13 Clutch
14 Upper wishbone
15 Lower wishbone
16 Hub carrier
17 Upper swivel pin
18 Steering arm
19 Track rod
20 Rack and pinion

in-line watercooled engine mounted at the front with its cylinders vertical and in alignment with the longitudinal axis of the car, and its **cooling radiator** located in front of it. Immediately behind it lies the clutch, and behind that in turn is a manual gearbox. This manual gearbox drives a **propeller shaft** extending to the rear of the car where it is coupled to a rear axle. Since the rear axle moves up and down on its springs – more about that in a minute – the propeller shaft has a **universal joint** at each end to permit the relative movement, as well as being splined into the gearbox output shaft to allow in-and-out displacement.

In the centre of the rear axle are the final drive gears in the form of a **crown wheel and pinion**, two **bevel gears** which perform the additional function of turning the drive through a right angle – necessary, since the driven rear wheels, obviously, rotate about a transverse axis through the car, whereas the engine's output shaft or crankshaft rotates about a longitudinal axis. Mounted on the crown wheel is the differential which passes the power to a pair of **half-shafts** extending to the rear wheels.

These half-shafts complete the transmission system which in its entirety is generally composed of a clutch or torque converter, a gearbox, a propeller shaft (not needed, as we shall see, for some cars) final drive gears, a differential and the half-shafts themselves.

For our car of simple and conventional

layout the half-shafts are encased in tubes fixed to the housing of the central final drive/differential gears, so the complete axle forms a single, rigid entity. It is often referred to as a **live rear axle**, 'live' because it transmits power, as opposed to a 'dead' axle which simply connects a pair of undriven wheels. Unfortunately, when one wheel of a live rear axle is deflected by a bump in the road, the other is also. This is its basic defect, which unless carefully controlled can have adverse effects on the ability of these wheels to transmit their power to the road and on the ability of the car to go round corners.

If the live rear axle, in addition to being a rigid entity in itself, were also rigidly fixed to the car's framework, the complete vehicle would be violently deflected by every bump in the road and would be intolerably uncomfortable if not downright dangerous. For this reason **springs** are interposed between the axle and the car, and it is the function of these springs to absorb the shocks created by road surface irregularities. This they do very well, but as so often there is a side effect: in exchange for greatly reducing the upward and downward forces on the body due to imperfections in the road, the springs create a strong tendency for the body to oscillate or bounce up and down upon them like the pan of a heavily loaded weighing machine. Indeed, unless something is done about it, a severe bump could cause the body to execute half a dozen or more complete but gradually diminishing up-and-down cycles before the motion dies away. The only reason why it does not go on for ever is that it is cut down or damped by the friction in the various suspension linkages involved and inside the spring itself.

Internal friction is not enough, however; hence to control these cyclical movements in a more effective way each spring is provided with a device called a **damper**, one end of which is fixed to the axle and the other to the car's frame. Usually a damper is telescopic in action, and consists essentially of a piston pierced by a small hole which is forced through a cylinder of oil by the movements of the axle. It offers a resistance which is proportional to the speed of movement, and when in good condition damps down any oscillation within the first cycle or so. The dampers are often called, quite mistakenly, the 'shock absorbers', but as already explained it is the function of the springs to absorb the shocks, whereas the task of the dampers is to curb the oscillations of the body on the springs.

The live rear axle of the simplest kind of car is mounted on leaf springs. A **leaf spring** is a set of slightly curved blades of special steel which has been tempered to make it resilient and springy rather than malleable or liable to deform. These blades are clamped together in a bundle and fixed to the frame of the car at each end and to the axle in the middle. The component thus formed not only provides springing but also serves as a crude means of locating the axle: it permits vertical movement in response to the irregularities of the road but prevents the axle from moving (much) sideways, keeps the rear wheels roughly parallel to the longitudinal axis of the car and resists the tendency of the axle to rotate about itself under braking and acceleration.

Until the late thirties, the suspension system fitted to the front of most cars closely resembled that at the back. A **dead** or **beam axle** ran across the car, linking the two front wheels, and was mounted on a pair of leaf springs which served to locate it. This arrangement, however, though still used for commercial vehicles and light vans, has now been almost entirely abandoned for private cars. The front wheels of virtually all modern cars are now independently sprung; that means, so arranged that the up-and-down movement of one wheel does not affect the movement of the other. Several kinds of linkage are used to accomplish this, one of the most common being known as the **double wishbone** type because its two principal elements on each side of the car resemble the wishbone of a fowl when viewed in plan; the **hub carrier** which supports the wheel is attached at its upper and lower ends to the apices of the wishbones, the widely spaced inner ends of which pivot on the frame of the car. Coil springs are frequently used and they often encircle telescopic dampers.

We have now very briefly discussed the engine, the transmission, the springs and suspension, but at least two other basic systems are essential to the car: one to make it steer and another to make it stop. Cars are steered firstly by swivelling the hub carrier of each front wheel about an axis which is roughly vertical and meets the ground at the centre of the tyre or not far from it – just how close to the vertical or near to the tyre centre constitutes one of the subtleties of steering and suspension geometry which will be explained in later chapters. Originally the swivelling mechanism generally consisted of an upper and a lower **kingpin** rotating in special load-bearing bushes inserted into the ends of the beam axle or pair of wishbones. Nowadays, however, **ball joints**, like the ball-and-socket joints of the human body, are normally used, though the terms kingpins or **swivel pins** are still employed.

To couple these two swivelling hub carriers together and to allow them to be turned to the left or the right, a steering mechanism is required, and one of the simplest and most elegant of these is also very widely used today. This is the **rack-and-pinion** system: a small pinion on the end of the shaft turned by the steering wheel meshes with a toothed rack which is rather like a gearwheel rolled out flat. To each end of the rack is coupled, via a ball joint, a **track rod**, the outer ends of each of these being coupled through further ball joints to levers fixed to the hub carriers called **steering** or **track-rod arms**. Thus rotation of the steering wheel displaces the rack from side to side across the car, swivelling the wheels through the track rods and steering arms.

So much for steering; we will now con-

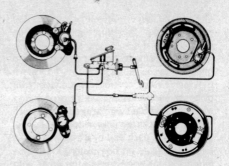

fig. 4. A typical modern braking system. Disc brakes (left) are fitted at the front, drum brakes (right) at the rear, and all four brakes are operated hydraulically. There is a separate cable-operated parking brake.

sider stopping. In a typical modern car, **disc brakes** are fitted to the front wheels and **drum brakes** to the rear ones. In such a system (fig. 4) the major element of each front brake is, as the name suggests, a steel disc which rotates with the wheel and is mounted on its hub. The edge of each disc is partially enclosed by a **caliper**, a sort of G-clamp affair by which **brake pads** of a special friction material can be forced against each side of the disc, opposing its rotation and slowing the car. Bicycle brakes use the same principle, though the rims of the wheels themselves form the discs. As both sides of the disc are exposed to the air, the heat generated by the friction is easily dissipated – most important, since the whole art of braking is to translate the car's speed energy or **kinetic** energy into heat energy as rapidly and efficiently as possible.

The older type of drum brake dissipates heat less readily but often suffices for the rear wheels where there is less work to be done. A drum brake is composed of a rotating drum inside which lies a pair of **brake shoes** curved to match its cylindrical inner surface and faced with **brake linings**. One end of each shoe is usually pivoted on a fixed **backplate** attached to the rear axle, but the other end can be forced outwards to press the linings against the drum and create the braking force.

At one time the foot-operated brakes were operated by cables or rods, but nowadays they are always controlled hydraulically. In place of each rod or cable is a pressure-resistant tube filled with **brake fluid** – which like all liquids is virtually incompressible – and sealed at each end by a piston. When a force is exerted on one piston, it is transferred through the liquid to the other with very little frictional wastage of effort. A hydraulic system, moreover, is virtually self-balancing: it automatically ensures that the braking force on one side of the car is the same as that on the other, greatly reducing the tendency to slew or skid compared with the old fully mechanical arrangements. By law, all cars these days must also be fitted with an auxiliary and completely independent **parking brake** or **handbrake** working on any pair of wheels; this is nearly always mechanically operated.

There remains one further basic feature of the car still to be considered: the structure which holds all its parts together, its frame or **chassis**. Before the Second World War, the chassis generally consisted of two heavy steel girders running the full length of the car on either side and bridged by a number of cross-members. To this was bolted a separate body which made little contribution to the overall stiffness of the resultant combination. Such a body was frequently described as being **coachbuilt**, for even when the car was made in large numbers, its body – often having steel panels on a wooden framework – was constructed by methods not dissimilar to those employed by the coachbuilders of the eighteenth century, involving much manual craftsmanship. Few bodies are coachbuilt these days. Some cars, mostly American ones – and those with glass fibre bodies which are built in small numbers – still feature separate chassis, though these have long been abandoned for nearly all mass-produced Euro-

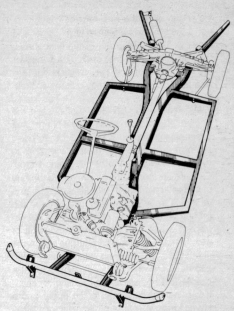

fig. 5. A separate chassis as used for the Triumph Herald/Vitesse/Spitfire range of cars. It is essentially of the backbone type, most of the bending and torsional loads being taken by the central members. Outriggers support the body.

pean and Japanese cars. One relatively recent exception was the Triumph Spitfire (fig. 5), now out of production. The Range-Rover also has a separate chassis, as have the cars of Lotus, Bristol and Morgan.

Separate chassis (the word remains unchanged in the plural) were largely abandoned because of their inefficiency: the rigidity or stiffness they provide is very poor in relation to the weight of steel employed – and stiffness is the most vital requirement for the structure of a car. For modern cars, therefore, the lighter and more efficient **unitary** or **integral** form of construction is nearly always used. In place of a chassis formed from a relatively small area of thick steel, there is a **platform** (fig. 6) fabricated from relatively large areas of thin steel in a complex assembly of numerous panels welded together. With its enclosed or **box-**

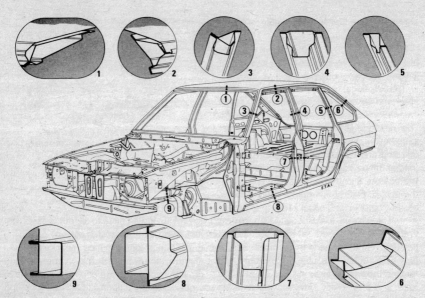

fig. 6. Most modern cars now have integral chassis/bodyshells. This one belongs to the Talbot Alpine. Note the extensive use of box-section structural members to achieve the required stiffness.

section side members called **sills**, the platform does resemble the old chassis to some extent, though it usually differs in having a built-up assembly ahead of the instrument panel called the **scuttle**, which adds greatly to the overall stiffness.

To this platform the body – also a stiff steel assembly – is welded rather than bolted, forming an integral part of the structure and adding significantly to its overall rigidity. Indeed, it is often difficult to say where the platform ends and the body begins, or which makes the bigger contribution to the overall stiffness. The result is a structure far lighter and stiffer than is possible with a separate chassis, eliminating creaks and rattles and providing a stable framework which is essential to modern standards of roadholding. Nowadays, too, the structure also has to meet modern safety requirements, which means providing a rigid central compartment to protect the passengers, with progressively crushable ends to absorb impacts in the manner least harmful to them. A unitary body/chassis, however, does require careful protection against corrosion.

Refinements and simplifications

In the early days of the motorcar, at the beginning of this century, many different arrangements of the engine, transmission and driven wheels were tried, but the simple layout just described soon became by far the most common. Nearly every car had an engine mounted lengthwise at the front, with a gearbox behind it driving through a propeller shaft to a live rear axle mounted on leaf springs. Nowadays many other ways of arranging the engine and transmission system and driven wheels are used, but before considering these, it is worth taking a look at some of the refinements possible with the simple basic layout.

Perhaps the first is to retain a live rear axle but to locate it accurately with a system of links – which generally work in conjunction with coil springs – and which minimize bump steer and some of the other handling faults inherently associated with the live rear axle. The next stage is to fit independent rear suspension. When this is done, the final drive/differential assembly – equivalent to the central part of a live rear axle – is fixed to the chassis and the rear wheels are driven through a pair of swinging **drive-shafts**, usually exposed and usually having universal joints at each end. In this way the **unsprung weight** is decreased, a reduction which helps to improve the ride comfort. Sometimes, to reduce the unsprung weight still further, **inboard brakes** are also fitted at the rear, and these act on the rear wheels through the drive-shafts.

Some designers believe that the front-engined, rear-wheel drive car can be further improved by locating the clutch and gearbox as well as the final drive and differential at the rear of the car. The aim is not to save space – if anything the arrangement wastes it – but to obtain a more even distribution of weight, so that with the car standing on level ground, the load on the rear wheels is almost exactly the same as the load on the front wheels. This condition, they consider, helps to improve handling and roadholding. The Lancia Aurelias and Flaminias of the fifties had their complete transmission systems – often called **transaxles** in this context – located at the rear, while current models arranged in this way are the Alfa Romeo Alfetta and the Porsche 924 (fig. 7) and 928. Although the extra weight on the driving wheels may give them better traction, there is little evidence that cars with this layout handle any better than those with other layouts.

There is another way in which the basic front-engined type of car can be made more complex, but for a different purpose. This is

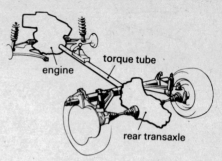

fig. 7. A rear transaxle is a basic feature of the Porsche 924.

to provide it with drive to all four wheels, not just two, for improved **traction**, or driving grip. For high-performance cars like the Audi Quattro, the purpose may simply be to provide especially safe and sure handling in wet and dry conditions as well as on ice and snow, but in many cases the aim is to provide the facility for off-road driving on soft ground. The Land-Rover has thus had four-wheel drive since 1948 and the system used for the newer Range-Rover, introduced in 1970, is a typical one.

In many ways the Range-Rover has the same layout as our basic car. Its engine (which has eight cylinders laid out in V-formation) is mounted at the front and drives through a manual gearbox behind it. But the gearbox (fig. 8) is coupled to a two-speed **transfer gearbox** (which provides an additional range of very low gears for rough going) and central differential. From this transfer gearbox and central differential one propeller shaft runs backwards to a live rear axle and another forwards to a second but special live axle designed to allow the front wheels to steer. In this way all four wheels can be driven simultaneously.

Driving to all four wheels or mounting the complete transmission system at the rear are two ways in which, for different purposes, the basic front-engined car can be made more complex, but it can also be simplified by dispensing with one of its four

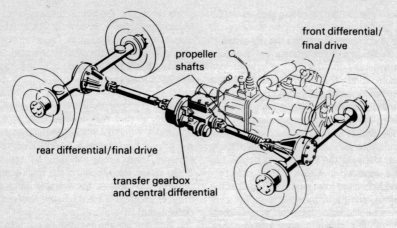

fig. 8. Four-wheel drive – the Range-Rover arrangement.

wheels. Thus modern three-wheelers like the Reliant have a single, steered front wheel, and, also at the front, an engine driving through a manual gearbox to a live rear axle. The Morgan three-wheeler had two front wheels and a single driven rear wheel, and almost every possible arrangement has been used from time to time.

Although in Britain the three-wheeler has a faithful band of users (qualified motorcyclists can legally drive it without having to pass the car driving test) it has very little to recommend it. The elimination of a wheel has hardly any effect on its construction costs, since it needs all the usual expensive major assemblies such as a steering system, a gearbox and a rear axle. Moreover, it is extremely difficult to give the three-wheeler a comfortable ride and safe, stable handling.

Different layouts

At about the time of the First World War, when the front engine/live rear axle arrangement had become almost universal, designers began to have second thoughts about it. It was wasteful of space, they

argued, to have one part of the transmission system, the final drive gears and differential, completely separated from the other, the gearbox. And it was absurd, they said, to drive the rear wheels through a propeller shaft which ran almost the full length of the car and which required a hump in the floor (called the **transmission tunnel**) to accommodate it, a hump wasting still more space. It would be much more logical to group engine and transmission together in one compact unit and to locate it near the driven wheels so that its weight would help to improve the traction, or the forward driving force, on slippery surfaces.

One possible answer would be to drive the front wheels. But this calls for a pair of drive shafts with sophisticated universal joints, capable not merely of accommodating normal up-and-down suspension movements, but also of transmitting power to wheels that steer. At the time that these ideas were being put forward, this requirement was not easily met.

A better solution, it was felt, was to combine the engine and the complete transmission system and to mount it at the rear of the car to drive the rear wheels. The best-known example of this philosophy was the

Volkswagen Beetle, designed in 1935 (fig. 9a). In this car, typical of the rear-engined type, the engine overhangs the rear wheels, which like the front wheels are independently suspended, and drives forward to a gearbox and final drive unit mounted between them. But even though over 20 million Beetles have been built, its layout never quite lived up to its promise.

One defect of the rear-engined car is its surprisingly wasteful use of space. This is partly because the back seat generally has to be displaced towards the front of the car – and hence the front seat also – to clear the gearbox, and partly because the front compartment accommodates an engine comfortably, but makes a poor luggage boot, even if the car has not been given a low bonnet line to improve its wind resistance. The **footwell** which provides room for the legs of the driver and front passenger protrudes into it, much space is taken up by the front wheels, which need room for both steering and suspension movements, and more by the spare wheel. And if, as in some rear-engined cars (like the Volkswagen Beetle) the waste space behind the rear seat has been used to create an auxiliary rear luggage compartment, it is generally rather inaccessible and much smaller than the front compartment, so the total luggage space remains much less than in a front-wheel-drive car of the same overall length or even than in a conventionally laid-out car – compare the Beetle (fig. 9a) with the Lada (fig. 9e).

But a rear-engined car has a further and perhaps more serious defect due to its rearward weight bias, which creates **handling** or road-behaviour faults. One of these is a greater sensitivity to deflection by sidewinds than is typical of front-engined cars.

More important, though, is the way a rear-engined car behaves on corners. The trouble, crudely speaking, is that in a sudden manoeuvre or when near the limit of adhesion, the tail tends to wag the dog: the back wheels are liable to lose their grip on the road much more easily than the front ones, allowing the car to spin bodily around. Although a few rear-engined cars – the Porsche 911 and the Hillman Imp, for example – have been made to handle well, this tendency is inherent and very difficult to compensate for. Mounting the engine and transmission system transversely helps to improve matters a little, but the two basic defects remain.

It was perhaps the astonishing success of the Beetle which for a long time blinded many engineers to its basic defects, for these did not become fully and widely appreciated until the late sixties. But right from the conception of the rear-engined car there were other designers who did not concede its worth. The proper place for the engine, in their view, was at the front, driving the front wheels, and if this arrangement introduced driveshaft problems, it was a challenge to be met. Citroën were one company to meet this challenge, introducing the front-wheel drive 7CV, forerunner of the Light Fifteen, in 1934. In those days before the Second World War, when materials, labour and petrol were cheap, the compactness possible with a front-wheel drive design was less important to those involved than the good handling and traction which they believed to be a product of the layout. Time has confirmed the correctness of this belief.

In most early front-wheel drive cars, the gearbox, final drive and differential were mounted ahead of the engine, and the same

---

fig. 9. Packaging: how mechanical layout affects interior space. Legroom dimensions are in inches; boot capacity in cubic feet of suitcases as measured by *Motor* magazine; each car is approximately 160 in long. Front wheel drive, preferably with a transverse engine, gives the most roomy interior for a given overall length, while the mid-engine layout – used for the Lotus Esprit – wastes space but helps to improve handling. The Renault 14 doesn't have the biggest boot, but it is around 4 in (10 cm) shorter than rivals such as the Citroën GS and the Lada.

	Legroom (ins.)			Luggage Space (cu.ft)		
	Front	Rear	Total	Front	Rear	Total
(a) VW Beetle	38·5	21·25	59·75	2·6	4·7	7·3
(b) Citroën GS	40·3	26·0	66·3		10·4	10·4
(c) Renault 14	40·0	24·5	64·5		9·5	9·5
(d) Lotus Esprit	40·0	–	40·0		3·5	3·5
(e) Lada	38·5	26·0	64·5		10·7	10·7

layout has been used for many more recent cars including four Renault models, the R4, R5, R6 and R16. In other modern front-wheel drive cars such as the Citroën GS (fig. 9b) and the Volkswagen Passat/Audi 80, the transmission system is located behind the engine. In virtually all front-wheel drive cars the front wheels are independently suspended and driven through a pair of exposed drive-shafts having universal joints at each end.

But the master stroke in front-wheel drive design was executed by Alec Issigonis, of what was then known as the British Motor Corporation (now British Leyland) when in 1959 he created the Mini. Like many front-wheel drive cars this is powered by a water-cooled in-line four-cylinder engine, but one which is mounted transversely rather than longitudinally. This transverse orientation of the engine – and its associated transmission system which lies immediately behind and beneath it – releases a very high percentage of the interior space to the passengers and luggage, making the car very compact indeed. In particular, it allows a great saving in the overall length, which is the most important external dimension, since cars vary in width only from around 5 ft (1.5 m) to around 6 ft (1.85 m), but in length from 10 ft (3 m) to 20 ft (6 m). For the Mini, therefore, the proportion of usable interior volume to total exterior volume is almost certainly the highest ever achieved for any car, though it may be closely rivalled by one or two other models using the same layout, such as the BL Metro or the Fiat Panda. But there is no other car which is only 10 ft (3 m) long and yet has enough space inside for a little luggage and four adults in tolerable comfort – an achievement not always conceded by its users, due to the poor design of early seats and the lack of fore-and-aft adjustment for the driver's seat.

But these are detail faults which in no way negate the basic brilliance of the design. For a car of such compactness has many advantages: it sometimes attracts low rates on ferries, it fits into small garages, it is easily manoeuvred in heavy traffic and it can be parked without difficulty in spaces too small for its rivals. Most of all, its small size means lightness, less unnecessary metal for the engine to haul around and hence good fuel consumption.

Strictly speaking Sir Alec Issigonis was not the first to design a transverse-engined front-wheel drive car, as it was a feature of another car called the Christie which was built experimentally in 1904. But mere invention is a relatively minor achievement: it is the development into something of value which really matters, and Sir Alec deserves every credit for being the first to exploit fully the advantages of this layout for mass-produced cars. So many of the world's major motor manufacturers have imitated his design that there are too many transverse-engined front-wheel drive cars currently in production to list in full here. Apart from BL's own family of front-wheel drive models, there is the Citroën CX, the Talbot Alpine, the Datsun Cherry, the Fiat 127 and Panda, the Honda Civic and Accord, the Lancia Beta, the Peugeot 104, 304 and 305, and the Volkswagen Golf and Polo.

But the transverse-engine front-wheel drive layout by no means exhausts all the possible ways of arranging the power unit, the transmission system and the driven wheels. There is at least one further arrangement of importance, though its goal is not the saving of space but the improvement of handling and roadholding. This is rather mis-leadingly called the mid-engined layout – misleadingly because the engine is not located right in the middle of the car.

Its purpose is to obtain the advantages of a rear-mounted engine without the disadvantages. The first advantage is that the high proportion of the overall weight on the driven wheels confers good traction, and this is especially important for a sports or high-performance car. The second advantage is that the correspondingly low proportion of the weight on the front wheels means that it is easy to fit fat tyres to them for good roadholding without making the steering heavy. As already mentioned, the big disadvantage is a tendency towards 'tail-happy' handling.

In a mid-engined car, however, the power unit (sometimes transversely, sometimes longitudinally mounted) is located just ahead of the rear wheels and drives to a gearbox and final drive assembly immediately behind it (fig. 9d). Often the arrangement may physically look little different from that of a rear-engined car, but the forward shift of the centre of gravity confers a vital improvement in handling: it permits the good traction and light steering to be combined with much more stable behaviour on corners. There are generally two luggage compartments and space is wasted – which is why the layout is generally employed for two-seaters – but the sacrifice is quite acceptable for the sake of the precision handling, high cornering power and stability expected of a good sports car.

two **The Conventional Petrol Engine**

The vast majority of all cars are powered by the reciprocating petrol engine. Because of its importance, all of this chapter and the next one are devoted to its workings. Advanced forms of reciprocating petrol engine are described in Chapter 4, together with the diesel; rotary engines in Chapter 5. Chapter 6 deals with the much-vaunted 'alternatives' to the conventional engine – the gas turbine, the electric motor, the Stirling and so on – which we might see in the car of the year 2000.

The simple petrol engine

The basic workings of a reciprocating petrol engine are not difficult to understand if we start by looking at a single-cylinder engine (fig. 10) of the type often fitted to motor-

cycles. All car engines have at least two cylinders, usually four, sometimes six and occasionally eight or even twelve, but they are more complex only in detail, not principle.

A petrol engine starts with a crankshaft, which for a single-cylinder unit has one stepped or eccentric section called a **crank-throw** fitting inside the **big-end** or lower part of a **connecting rod**. The upper part or **small-end** of this connecting rod encircles a **wrist pin** or **gudgeon pin** which runs diametrically across a piston sliding inside a cylinder. Special sprung **piston rings**, usually made of cast iron, encircle the aluminium piston and seal in the hot gases of combustion. Rotation of the crankshaft moves the piston up and down in the cylinder.

The upper part of the cylinder is enclosed by a **combustion chamber** into which the **sparking plug** protrudes. This is the device with which the fuel is ignited; essentially it is a gap in an electrical circuit across which a spark can be made to jump when required.

In the roof of the combustion chamber are two circular holes sealed by mushroom-shaped **poppet valves** which are held against their sealing surfaces or **seats** by powerful helical **valve springs**. These valves can be nudged open by **rockers** swinging about fixed pivots and actuated by **push-rods**. One valve, the **inlet valve**, admits the mixture of air and fine droplets of fuel which is supplied by a **carburetter** and controlled by a **throttle** or **butterfly valve**; the other,

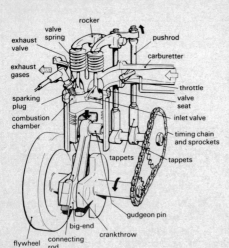

fig. 10. A single-cylinder four-stroke petrol engine. For simplicity, the electrical, cooling and lubrication systems have not been included.

the **exhaust valve**, allows the hot gases to escape when combustion is complete. The lower ends of the pushrods rest on **tappets** which are moved up and down by a **camshaft**, a shaft with lobes or bulges in it. The camshaft runs at half the speed of the crankshaft from which it is driven by a **timing chain** and pair of **sprockets**. The engine is completed by a flywheel which smooths out the impulses created by the successive explosions of the air/fuel mixture. Not shown are the structural details, the lubrication system, the cooling system, the fuel supply system or the arrangements for producing the spark.

The four-stroke cycle

The engine's components are made to work together to produce useful power in a sequence of events called the **four-stroke** or **Otto** cycle (fig. 11) after the man who in 1876 first introduced an engine working on this principle.

1. In the first stroke of this cycle the piston moves from **top dead centre** (tdc) or the upper limit of its travel down to **bottom dead centre** (bdc) or the lower limit of its travel, the crankshaft turning through 180°. As it does so, the inlet valve is open, so the piston acts as a pump, drawing in a charge of air/fuel mixture supplied by the carburetter. This is called the **induction stroke**.

2. Next follows the **compression stroke**, during which both the exhaust and the inlet valves remain closed and the crankshaft turns through another 180°, forcing the piston up to tdc again. The resultant compression of the unburned mixture has an important bearing on the efficiency of the engine to which we will return later.

3. When the mixture has been fully compressed, a spark is made to jump between the **electrodes** or bare terminals of the

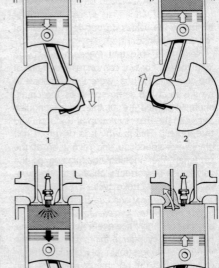

fig. 11. The four-stroke cycle: 1, induction; 2, compression; 3, combustion; 4, exhaust.

sparking plug, the mixture of fuel and air is ignited, and the resultant explosion forces the piston downwards towards bdc on its **combustion stroke**. It is only during this stroke – when the crankshaft again turns through 180° – that the engine develops its useful power and ability to work against an external resistance.

4. The cycle is completed by an **exhaust stroke** during which the exhaust valve is held open and the piston moves upwards towards tdc for the second time, expelling

the hot gases created by the combustion process.

The first point to observe is that this sequence is an idealized description of the true state of affairs. In a real engine, for example, the valves do not open exactly at top and bottom centre.

Next, take note that the complete cycle lasts for 720 ° or two complete revolutions of the crankshaft. Thus, were the camshaft to be driven at the same speed as the crankshaft, it would be unable to distinguish between the first revolution of the cycle and the second. This is why it is driven at half crankshaft speed: in one revolution of the camshaft the opening and closing of the valves can be correctly phased for the two-revolution four-stroke cycle.

As there is only one combustion stroke in each complete cycle, a single-cylinder engine fires only once every two revolutions. For a multi-cylinder engine, therefore, the number of firing strokes per crankshaft revolution is half the number of cylinders: one for a two-cylinder engine, two for a four-cylinder engine, three for a six-cylinder engine, four for an eight-cylinder engine and so on.

If we look more closely at the four-stroke cycle we can see that useful power is only generated over a short part of it, and that some power – though a much smaller amount – is absorbed during the remainder. This power is absorbed partly by friction, partly by the pumping effort associated with the drawing in of the fresh charge and partly by the energy needed to compress it. The inertia of the flywheel helps to keep the engine turning during this non-productive part of the cycle and also to smooth out the firing impulses. But the process is essentially discontinuous: if anything causes the crankshaft to come to a dead stop, the cycle is broken and the engine cannot generate useful power – hence the need for a clutch as described in Chapter 1. In this respect reciprocating internal combustion engines differ from other sources of motive power such as steam engines or electric motors, which can continue to exert a twisting effort or torque even when their output shafts are at a standstill. And to restart a reciprocating internal combustion engine, it must be turned at a minimum cranking speed – about 75 rpm – before its cycle becomes self-supporting.

Capacity and compression ratio

There is another characteristic of the internal combustion engine which is now easy to understand. The power it generates obviously depends upon the quantity of air and fuel that it can draw in during any given period of time: the more air and fuel drawn in, the bigger the explosion that follows and the greater the amount of heat energy released to be converted into useful mechanical work. This in turn is clearly determined, in part at least, by the volume of the cylinder. In fact it is not the complete volume of the cylinder that counts, including (fig. 12) the

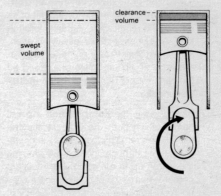

fig. 12. The swept volume of an engine ultimately determines the amount of power it can develop.

Compression ratio =
$$\frac{\text{clearance volume} + \text{swept volume}}{\text{clearance volume}}$$

clearance volume at the top, but only the **swept volume** traversed by the piston from tdc to bdc, since this is what determines an engine's ability to draw in air and fuel. All other things being equal, then, the power developed by an engine is proportional to the total swept volume of all its cylinders, or its **capacity**. This is usually quoted in cubic centimetres, though sometimes in cubic inches. Small, twin-cylinder engines such as those of the Fiat 126 and Citroën 2CV have capacities of around 600 cc (37 cu in); large engines, such as the 12-cylinder unit of the Jaguar XJS or the V-8 of the Aston Martin have capacities of around 5500 cc, 5.5 litres or 336 cu in. The Rolls-Royce engine has a capacity of 6750 cc (412 cu in), while some American cars have been powered by engines with capacities greater than 7 litres.

A further feature of an engine's basic geometry – its compression ratio – has, for reasons too complex to give in this book, an important influence on its efficiency. The compression ratio is the ratio of the volume above the piston at bottom dead centre – the swept volume plus the clearance volume – to the volume above the piston at top dead centre – the clearance volume alone. The larger the value of this ratio the greater the efficiency.

The compression ratios of current petrol engines range from about 7.0:1 to around 12:1 and for diesels the range is 16:1 to 22:1 (which is one reason why they are more efficient than petrol engines). For petrol engines the limiting factor is a phenomenon called **detonation** or **knock**: if the compression ratio is raised too much, the mixture, instead of burning smoothly, tends to go off with a violent and damaging bang, emitting a noise known as **pinking**. For any given design of combustion chamber the maximum usable compression ratio is determined by a quality of the fuel, its **octane rating** – the higher the octane rating the higher the compression ratio that can be employed without fear of detonation.

The two-stroke cycle

The four-stroke cycle is not the only system by which fuel and air can be drawn in, compressed, ignited, expanded and exhausted. These processes can also be correctly sequenced by the two-stroke cycle, now wholly abandoned for cars but still used for motorcycles, lawnmower engines, outboards and the like.

In its simplest form a two-stroke engine (fig. 13) has apertures or ports in its cylinder

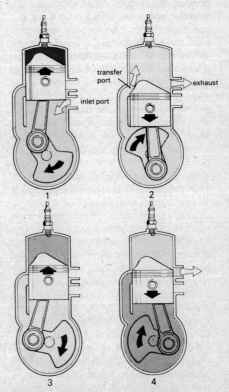

fig. 13. The two-stroke cycle. A fuel/air mixture is drawn in underneath the piston, then pumped from the crankcase to the combustion chamber through a transfer port. 1, induction beneath piston; 2, transfer; 3, compression; 4, combustion and exhaust. The cycle is completed within one revolution of the crankshaft.

walls in place of valves and a sealed crank-case which forms part of the induction system in conjunction with the underside of the piston. As a result of this arrangement it is generally necessary to mix the lubricating oil with the fuel.

The two-stroke sequence begins with the piston rising from bottom dead centre, creating a partial vacuum in the crankcase until it exposes an **inlet port** and a fresh charge of air and fuel is drawn in. After rising to top dead centre the piston descends again, compressing the mixture in the crankcase until a **transfer port** is exposed and the mixture is transferred into the cylinder, the hump in the piston crown deflecting it away from the **exhaust port** which lies opposite. Further upward movement of the piston compresses the mixture still more, until it is ignited – by a sparking plug in the same way as for a four-stroke engine – and the downward power stroke begins. Towards the end of this downward movement the exhaust port is exposed, completing the cycle above the piston, while a fresh charge for the next one is being compressed beneath the piston. Thus the engine is able to execute a power stroke for every revolution of the crankshaft.

Such a characteristic should theoretically make the two-stroke twice as powerful as a four-stroke of the same capacity, but this promise has seldom been realized in practice. Two-strokes do have smoother torque curves, though, and the three-cylinder 850 cc Saab unit did develop around 50 per cent more power than similar four-stroke engines in the early 1960s. Another advantage of the two-stroke is its mechanical simplicity.

Against that must be set the inconvenience of being required to mix the lubricating oil with the fuel in certain proportions, a narrower power range and unstable running under light loads. The two-stroke's major disadvantage, however, is its poor fuel consumption. With its two-stroke engine, for example, the Saab 96 returned an overall consumption of 21.6 mpg during a *Motor* road test, but of 28.5 mpg when fitted with the more powerful 1498 cc Ford V-4 four-stroke engine which replaced it.

This poor fuel consumption springs from the two-stroke's inherently low efficiency. One cause is the high pumping losses associated with the long and tortuous path followed by the incoming fuel and air during the induction part of the cycle. But the main problem is the poor control over the induction and exhaust processes provided by ports compared with valves. The **scavenging** or clearing-out of the cylinder at the end of the exhaust stroke, for example, depends basically on exhaust-gas pressure and derives no help from piston movement as in a four-stroke. And if the fresh charge is used for scavenging purposes, it is very difficult to prevent a certain proportion of it from passing wastefully straight through the engine into the exhaust pipe as, during the exhaust stroke, the exhaust port communicates directly with the transfer port. (This is much less important for a two-stroke diesel which can be scavenged by air alone, rather than by a mixture of air and fuel.) The faults of this layout can to some extent be alleviated by the clever use of exhaust-gas pulsations or by complicating the design with valves, but it remains a basic drawback which makes it all but impossible to cut the pollutants in a two-stroke's exhaust gases to the levels imposed on cars by current worldwide legislation.

Torque and power

So far the exact meanings of such terms as torque and power have not been carefully defined, but to understand the internal combustion engine properly we must be much more precise. Let us start, though, by merely assuming the meaning of the word **force**. We all know intuitively more or less what a force is: it is what sets objects moving or what brings them to rest, it is what bends or breaks them if they are not free to move.

Scientists and engineers use a more exact definition, but this basic idea will do.

The size of a force is easily defined in terms of the Earth's gravity. Thus a force of 50 pounds weight is the force required to lift a weight of 50 lb against the gravitational pull of the Earth. In practice, the word 'weight' is usually omitted, and we speak of a force being so many pounds in magnitude. The pound is, as we shall see, still used as a unit of force in connection with cars and their engines. Its nearest metric equivalent is the kilogram weight abbreviated kg, kgf or kp, which is 2.2 times bigger than a pound weight. And of course there is the SI (Système International) unit, the **newton** (after Sir Isaac) and abbreviated N; it is smaller than a kilogram weight: 1 kg = 9.81 N, or 1 N = 0.102 kg.

Torque or twisting effort is the next quantity to be defined: it is simply the force exerted on a shaft or structure multiplied by the distance at which it acts from the centre of rotation of the shaft or the axis about which the structure is being twisted. A force of 50 lb, for example, exerted at a distance of 1 ft (fig. 14) creates a torque of 50 **pounds-feet** or lb ft. It can be balanced, for example, by a 100 lb weight hanging from a rope which acts at a distance of 6 in or ½ ft from the centre of the shaft, giving a resultant torque of 100 × ½ = 50 lb ft. Note that the distance involved has to be the distance from the axis

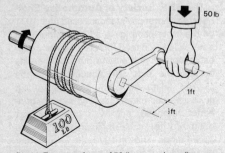

fig. 14. Torque: a force of 50 lb exerted at a distance of 1 foot creates the same torque as a force of 100 lb exerted at a distance of 6 in.

of twist measured at *right angles* to the line of action of the force. A torque which creates a twisting effect but does not cause a shaft to rotate is generally called a **moment**. A metric unit of torque still used in connection with cars is the **metre-kilogram**, mkg, which is equal to 7.23 lb ft. Often the **Newton-metre** (Nm) is used instead, and this is 0.102 mkg.

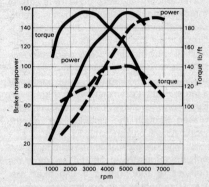

fig. 15. Typical power and torque curves – shown here for the 3.5-litre Rover V-8 engine (solid line) and the 2-litre four-cylinder Lotus engine. The two engines have approximately the same maximum power, but the larger-capacity Rover unit develops a good deal more torque and at lower rpm.

Let us now look at the torque characteristics of a typical reciprocating petrol engine. To measure these, the throttle or butterfly valve, which controls the amount of air and fuel drawn in, is held wide open and the engine's output shaft is restrained by a special brake (in which a lot of heat is dissipated as a result). First the engine is held at 1000 rpm, then at 1500 rpm, and so on. The torque does not increase continuously with engine speed (fig. 15) but rises to a maximum roughly half-way up the engine's rev range before tailing off again at very high rpm. (So little torque is developed at low rotational speeds, incidentally, that it is rarely plotted below 1000 rpm.)

Torque, though, tells only half the story.

To complete it, further ideas must be intro-duced. First there is the concept of **work**, which engineers define as the force exerted, multiplied by the distance through which it is exerted. If we lift a 50 lb weight a distance of 10 ft, for instance, we will have done 500 units of work – described in this case as **foot-pounds** or ft lb to distinguish them from pounds-feet or lb ft, which, as we have just learned, are the units of torque.

The amount of work done by a steady torque in one revolution of a shaft is directly proportional to that torque. (Numerically it is simply the force which creates the torque multiplied by the circumference of the circle through which it is displaced in one revolu-tion. Suppose the torque, T, is the product of a force, F, acting at a distance r. Then $T = rF$. But in one revolution the force F will have moved through the distance $2\pi r$, so the work, W, will be $2\pi rF$ or $2\pi T$.)

But the basic capability of an engine can only be completely defined if we know the number of foot-pounds it can exert per second or minute – its **power**, or the rate at which it will do work. Since the work done during each crankshaft revolution is propor-tional to the torque, the rate at which work is done in turn is proportional to the torque multiplied by the engine's rotational speed in rpm. (Numerically, the power, $P = 2\pi T \times \text{rpm}$.)

In practice, power is not quoted in foot-pounds per minute but in **horsepower**. In Imperial units one horsepower is 550 ft lb per second or 33,000 ft lb per minute – because experiments conducted more than a hundred years ago established this as the rate at which a (perhaps rather energetic) carthorse could briefly work. Thus the horsepower of an engine can be calculated from the formula $P = \dfrac{2\pi T \times \text{rpm}}{33,000}$

A metric horsepower, defined in terms of Newton-metres per second, is equal to 0.986 Imperial horsepower – a difference small enough to be ignored. Note that in Continen-tal countries the abbreviations for horse-power are generally derived directly from translations of the words 'horse' and 'power' or 'vapour' from the original association with steam engines. Thus in German the abbre-viation is PS from Pferde-Stärke; in French CV from Cheval Vapeur, and in Italian CV also, from Cavallo Vapore.

Another measure of power output coming increasingly into use these days is the **Watt**, W, or its multiple the kilowatt, kW; 1 kW = 1000W; 1 hp = 746W.

In most cases the power developed by an engine is quoted not merely as horsepower but as **brake horsepower** or bhp. This is to distinguish true horsepower, as actually determined from brake or **dynamometer** measurements, from **fiscal** horsepower which in some countries is calculated for taxation purposes only from some arbitrary formula based on the cylinder dimensions of the engine. In France, for example, the engines of cars are assigned for taxation purposes ratings ranging from 2CV for a 602 cc Citroën to 54CV for a 6750 cc Rolls-Royce.

Brake horsepower, furthermore, is meas-ured under specified conditions in accord-ance with some standard procedure. The most usual and useful of these is the West German **DIN** (Deutsche Industrie Norm) standard which gives a good indication of the true net bhp of the engine as installed in the car, the horsepower that is genuinely available to the owner.

The **SAE, Society of Automotive Engi-neers** (of America), standard used until 1971 on the other hand, gave a gross rather than a net value – indeed, an unrealistically high estimation of true engine output. This was because the tests were conducted with the silencer taken off, with power-absorbing auxiliaries such as the cooling fan and gen-erator removed, and with other settings optimized for each measurement in the speed range. Thus in 1970, the SAE output of a 5897 cc Dodge V-8 engine was quoted as 259 bhp in a standard work of reference, 46 per cent more than the DIN figure which was only 177 bhp. In 1971 the SAE introduced a new net specification giving results close to the DIN values, and a more realistic – though still generous – gross specification. Whenever possible rely on DIN figures if you wish to make a meaningful comparison between one engine and another.

Consider now the shapes of typical power curves (fig. 15) and the way they are related to engine speed and power. A torque curve tends to droop at each end, because engines become inefficient at very low and very high revs. In consequence the power curves – effectively obtained by multiplying the torque by the rpm – are not straight lines though they are often very nearly so over the middle part of an engine's speed range. At very high rpm, though, nearly all engines become so very inefficient that the power reaches a maximum and then tails off very rapidly. Often the basic limitation is a carburetter too small to admit air and fuel at the rate needed for more power. Even if the power does not fall off rapidly, there is always a safe maximum rpm which should not be exceeded if damage to the engine is to be avoided.

The distinction between power and torque is very important. Engineers and journalists often write about power units being **flexible** or **torquey** or having 'good low-speed pull'. What they really mean by all these expressions is that the engine in question not only develops a lot of torque in relation to its power, but also that it develops useful torque at low rpm, giving good response when the accelerator is pressed, reducing the need to change gear for overtaking.

Imagine, for example, driving in top gear along a level road at a moderate speed, with the accelerator only lightly depressed, in a car powered by the Rover 3.5-litre V-8 engine and having ratios of 1:1 and 1.5:1 for top and third gears respectively. The engine is running, say at 2500 rpm, so that when you floor the accelerator to clear a minor emergency nearly the full 198 lb ft of its torque (fig. 15) is available to accelerate the car. Now consider what would happen if

exactly the same car with exactly the same gearbox and final drive ratios were powered by the 2-litre Lotus engine. At 2500 rpm it develops only 115 lb ft of torque, so to obtain the same acceleration as before, third gear must be selected and the engine speed brought up to 3500 rpm when the torque is 132 lb ft, becoming 198 lb ft when multiplied by 1.5, the ratio of a third. The significant difference is that the driver of the car with the larger engine is able to achieve the same result without the fuss and bother of changing gear. In outright performance, though, there will be little to choose between the two cars: their maximum speeds and standing-start acceleration times should be much the same because these depend on power, not torque, and the two engines have almost the same maximum power output. Generally both power and torque increase with engine size, but the larger the capacity the greater the torque available at low rpm.

Balance and geometry

One of the most important requirements of any piece of machinery from a windmill to a watch is that its rotating parts should be in balance. The centrifugal force created by a revolving component which is not perfectly balanced about its axis of rotation can be very large and can impose a heavy side-load on the bearings which support it. In a piston engine the most important revolving component and potential source of such large unwanted forces is the crankshaft, each throw of which is inherently unsymmetrical and unbalanced about its axis of rotation.

Rotational imbalance, however, is only part of the problem: very large out-of-balance forces are also generated by the reciprocating motion of the pistons which are constantly being accelerated up to speed in mid-stroke, momentarily brought to a standstill at top and bottom centre, then accelerated away again in the opposite direction.

But both kinds of imbalance create forces which increase with the square of the engine speed and have two basic effects. The first is not merely to put heavy side-loads on bearings but to create unnecessary stresses within the structure of the engine itself, stresses which tend to make the crankcase and cylinder block flex and bend. The second effect is to cause the complete engine to vibrate as an entity. This vibration is transmitted to the bodyshell, causing discomfort to the driver and passengers at least, and at worst damage to some part of the car.

Balancing a revolving part is in principle easy: all you do is attach to the shaft concerned another weight of the same magnitude as the first one, diametrically opposite and at the same distance from the centre of rotation. In practice it is seldom possible to fit a balance weight in the same plane as the mass to be balanced – you cannot balance a **crankpin**, for example, by giving the crankshaft a false and additional diametrically opposed crankpin; it would foul the connecting rod. In any case the **webs** which support the crankpin must also be balanced, as well as the big-end which revolves with the crankpin and part of the connecting-rod **shank** which can be considered as rotating rather than reciprocating.

The solution is to extend the crankpin webs to the far side of the crankshaft centreline (fig. 16). The two extended webs are not in the same plane as the resultant out-of-balance weight, which acts in the centre of the crankpin, but the two twisting efforts or moments they exert cancel each other out, and in this case there is no force left over either to be resisted by the main bearings or to cause vibration. The criterion for balance is that the size of the out-of-balance weight multiplied by the distance of its centre of gravity from the crankshaft centreline must be equal to the sum of the sizes of the balance weights multiplied by the distances of their centres of gravity from the crankshaft centreline.

For a complete crankshaft one crankthrow

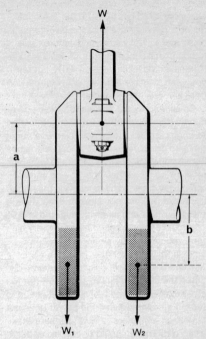

fig. 16. Rotational balance: the crankpin, big-end and rotating part of the con-rod can all be balanced by extending the crankthrow webs so that $b(W_1 + W_2) = aW$.

fig. 17. For a multi-cylinder engine, one crankthrow can be used to balance another 180 degrees away from it, so long as the resultant rotating moment is balanced out by that from another pair of crankthrows.

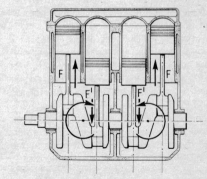

can be used to balance another displaced 180° from it, so long as the unbalanced rotating moment (twisting force) created by the two together is cancelled out by the unbalanced rotating moment created by another pair of crankthrows. The crankshaft of a four-cylinder in-line engine has the necessary symmetry (fig. 17) as does that of an in-line six, but other types of crankshaft – such as that of a V-4 engine, for example – do not.

Achieving balance of the reciprocating parts is more difficult. When a piston is pulled downwards, its inertia (fig. 18) makes

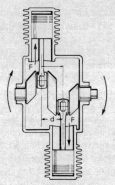

fig. 19. In a twin-cylinder horizontally opposed engine, the inerti forces on one piston are balanced by those on the other – though the offset between them creates a yawing moment or couple.

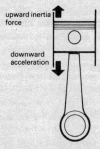

upward inertia force

downward acceleration

fig. 18. Inertia forces: the downward acceleration of the piston creates an upward inertia force in the con-rod; similarly upward acceleration of the piston imposes a downward force on the con-rod.

it reluctant to be accelerated, creating an upward force on the crankshaft and stretching the connecting rod. Hold an object above your head and pull it rapidly downwards and your arm will be subjected to the same sort of force. Similarly, during the upward part of the stroke the inertia force acts downwards, tending to compress the connecting rod.

For many engines, however, the reciprocating forces are quite easily balanced: so long as there is one piston moving up for every piston that moves down, and so long as the couples created are in balance, no external vibration is created (though large internal stresses still exist). This situation exists (fig. 19) in a twin-cylinder **boxer** or **horizontally opposed** engine, for instance,

though the inevitable offset between the centrelines of the two cylinders, creating oscillations about a vertical axis, creates a small residual unbalanced **yawing moment** or **couple**. An in-line four-cylinder engine, though, has complete inherent balance of this sort.

A single rotating weight cannot normally balance a reciprocating force, but it can balance the reciprocating forces in a 90° V-twin: if the size of the weight (fig. 20) is correctly chosen, the **component** or part of

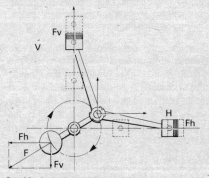

fig. 20. A single rotating weight cannot normally balance a reciprocating force, but it can balance the reciprocating forces in a 90° V-twin.

the centrifugal force acting along one cylinder axis will always exactly balance the inertia force on the associated piston, while the component at 90° will exactly balance the force on the other. Such power units are not fitted to cars, but the principle has relevance to a V-8 engine which is effectively composed of four V-twins.

In other types of engines the designer may not be so lucky, but a further technique exists by which he can be helped. This is the use (fig. 21) of a pair of contra-rotating balance weights running at crankshaft speed. When the two weights are in their lowermost

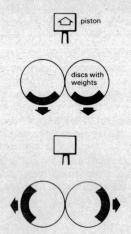

fig. 21. A single piston or out-of-balance reciprocating force can be balanced by a pair of contra-rotating weighted discs.

positions, the centrifugal forces on them balance the upward inertia force on the piston; when the weights are in their uppermost positions they balance the downward force, and when the piston is at mid-stroke and exerting no inertia force at all (because it has no acceleration) the two weights are in opposition and exert forces which cancel each other out.

This system is used for the Ford V-4 engine. One set of balance weights is mounted on the crankshaft itself, the other on a special balance shaft geared to it and

running at the same speed but in the opposite direction. In this way unwanted reciprocating forces which act horizontally are cancelled out (revolving imbalance in the crankshaft also has to be taken care of). More often, however, the reciprocating forces and couples can be balanced out using the 'mirror image' principle already discussed.

Unfortunately, all that has been said so far refers only to **primary** imbalance and there is another sort to be reckoned with: **secondary** imbalance. This exists because the connecting rod is not of infinite length. When a piston is pulled down from top dead centre, for example, by a connecting rod which is short compared to the crankshaft throw (fig. 22) it is displaced further (distance x) than if the connecting rod were long (distance y) because the sideways movement of the bottom end of the connecting rod increases the vertical displacement. Similarly, when the piston is moved upwards from bottom dead centre by a short connecting rod, the swing of the connecting rod is to some extent neutralized by the swing of the crankshaft, and the vertical displacement of the piston is less than would occur with a long connecting rod. Thus the acceleration downwards is not quite the same as

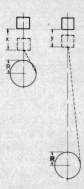

fig. 22. Secondary imbalance occurs because the con-rod is not infinitely long. The short con-rod displaces the piston further from top dead centre than the long one.

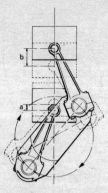

fig. 23. The finite length of the con-rod means that when a pair of pistons lie on the same side of the crankshaft, the motion of one is not exactly the same as that of the other. This creates secondary imbalance.

the acceleration upwards, which means that the accelerations of opposed pairs of pistons do not quite cancel each other out (fig. 23) for an in-line engine in which all the pistons are on the same side of the crankshaft. But in a horizontally opposed engine with the pistons on both sides of the crankshaft, the motion of one piston is exactly duplicated (fig. 24) by its opposite, giving complete balance of the secondary forces. Complete balance not merely of the primary and secondary forces, but of the primary and secondary couples can theoretically be achieved in a horizontally opposed four, but only with a layout in which all four pistons are simultaneously at top dead centre. Since at least

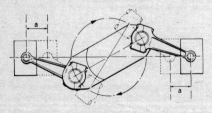

fig. 24. In a horizontally opposed engine, the motion of one piston is exactly duplicated by that of its opposite.

two pistons would arrive together at the end of their compression strokes, the cylinders would fire in pairs at 360° instead of at 180° intervals and the arrangement would be no smoother than an opposed twin. Most horizontally opposed fours – such as the Volkswagen Beetle unit, for example – therefore use a slightly different layout (fig. 26e) despite some residual secondary imbalance.

The secondary reciprocating force differs from the primary in two important respects, of which the first is that it oscillates at twice the frequency (fig. 25), reaching two peaks

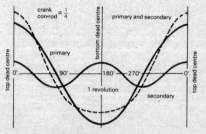

fig. 25. The secondary unbalanced forces are smaller than primary forces in proportion to the crankthrow/con-rod length ratio and oscillate at twice the frequency.

and two troughs during each crankshaft revolution. It is also smaller than the primary – its relative size is proportional to the crankthrow/connecting rod length ratio – but still increases with the square of the speed and so becomes large enough at high revs to be troublesome.

In some engines such as the V-8, these secondary forces are in balance, but not for the in-line four in which they act in the plane of the cylinders and are one of the main sources of vibration at high revs. To absorb residual vibrations, both primary and secondary, all power units are mounted on pads of rubber, but if these are too soft the engine will shake about as the car passes over bumps in the road surface. The situation is eased for in-line engines if they are inclined, as is the **slant four** type, since the mountings of such units can be made relatively stiff

Primary vibrating
force or couple

Secondary vibrating
force or couple

fig. 26. Various four-stroke engines showing their crankshaft layout, typical firing order and state of balance: (a) vertical twin – crankthrows in line; (b) horizontally opposed twin – crankthrows at 180°; (c) three-cylinder in-line – three crankthrows at 120° (the Daihatsu three-cylinder unit has engine speed balance shaft which cancels the primary pitching couple); (d) in-line 4 – crankthrows in line or at 180°; (e) horizontally opposed four – crankthrows in line or at 180°; (f) 60° V-4 with balance shaft for primary

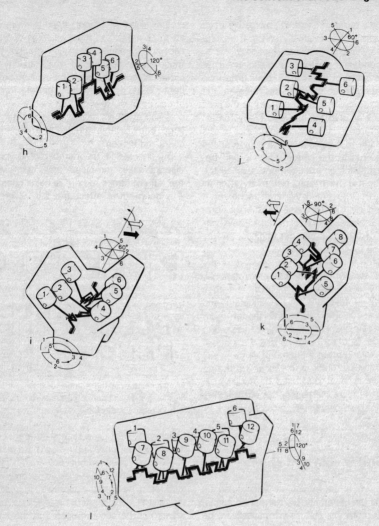

rotational and reciprocating forces – the crank-throws are at 120° and 60°; (g) in-line 5 – crankthrows are spaced at 72°; (h) in-line 6 – crankthrows are spaced at 120°; (i) 60° V-6 – crankthrows spaced at 60°; (j) flat 6 – crankthrows spaced at 60°; (k) V-8 with two-plane crankthrows spaced at 90°; (l) 60° V-12 – crankthrows spaced at 120°.

vertically to resist excitation by road surface irregularities but relatively soft in the plane of the cylinders to absorb vibration.

Secondary forces can also be balanced out by a system of two contra-rotating balance weights similar to that applicable to the primary forces and incorporated into the Ford V-4 power unit. For the secondary forces, the difference is that the two balance shafts are made to revolve at twice engine speed and so run at the correct phasing and frequency. Such an arrangement is called the **Lanchester harmonic balancer**, after its inventor, Dr Frederick William Lanchester. It is used by the Japanese Mitsubishi company, makers of Colt cars, for certain versions of their four-cylinder engines, and by Porsche for their 944 engine.

Such a mechanism is not needed for the in-line six, which has inherent rotational, primary and secondary balance and thus remains a favourite of the engineer and connoisseur. The V-6 engine, though more compact in shape, does not have this perfect balance. Figure 26 summarizes the state of balance (and other features) of all the types of engine currently in use including the in-line five-cylinder kind used by Audi and in diesel form by Mercedes, but not the very rare (for road use) flat-12 arrangement.

Cylinder size and shape

Even when an engine is fully balanced against the generation of external vibrations, its structure will still, as we have seen, be subjected to very large internal forces and moments. These can to some extent be minimized by correctly choosing the shape and the number of cylinders used, as was shown more than fifty years ago in a theory invented again by Dr Lanchester. His argument was that the mass of a piston goes up more rapidly with increasing cylinder diameter or **bore** size than does the bearing

area available to support it, so the stresses on the big-end and main bearings of large-capacity cylinders are much greater than those on the bearings of small-capacity cylinders having the same ratio of stroke to bore. Thus it is definitely better, from a stress point of view, to use a large number of small cylinders than a small number of large ones, within the limits imposed by costs and friction.

But increasing the number of cylinders also increases the piston area, even when the ratio of stroke to bore remains constant – a geometrical effect (fig. 27) which, as

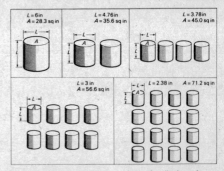

fig. 27. Increasing the number of cylinders for a given capacity and stroke/bore ratio (in this case 1:1) increases the piston area, A.

Lanchester wrote in a slightly different context, might be 'looked upon as a mere matter of common sense, but like many other matters of common sense, it is only one step removed from the abstruse'. Increasing the piston area in turn means that large valves can be accommodated in the combustion chamber allowing more air and fuel to be drawn in each minute, and thus more power to be developed than from engines with the same capacity but less piston area. On the other hand, small cylinders have a greater **surface-to-volume** ratio than large ones and so allow heat to leak away more readily, which is bad for efficiency. Moreover, cost and friction losses rise rapidly as the number of cylinders is increased, so the final choice of the number to be used for any given application is a compromise, as is so often the case in engineering.

But Lanchester also showed that the stresses imposed on bearings and the internal structure of the engine further depend on the piston speed which falls as the stroke is reduced. Hence an engine with a stroke which is short in relation to its bore will run safely to higher rpm than a long-stroke engine. It was this thinking which led to a new generation of Ford engines, starting with the 105E unit introduced in 1960, most of which were highly **oversquare** – that is, had strokes much shorter than their bores – at a time when most engines were slightly **undersquare**. But less advantage – as far as stress reduction is concerned – is obtained from shortening the stroke than from increasing the number of cylinders, since too short a stroke leads once more to a large, heavy and stress-inducing piston. Current thinking is that very short-stroke engines are poor from an exhaust emissions point of view – and perhaps for low-speed torque also – and that the best results are achieved when the stroke is roughly equal to the bore or the engine is approximately **square**.

Firing intervals and order

Another advantage of an engine with many cylinders is its **smoothness** which is partly a consequence of its state of balance but partly of the lack of fluctuation in its torque output. For the torque curve clearly becomes more and more smooth as the number of cylinders is increased. And since the power strokes last for 180° of crankshaft rotation, these begin to overlap when there are more than two such strokes per revolution – i.e. in engines of more than four cylinders.

For all engines the designer's aim is to space the firing strokes at regular intervals, which are usually 360° for the twin-cylinder engine, 180° for the four, 120° for the six and 90° for the eight. In some cases, though, this is not possible. The firing intervals for one type of V-6 engine, with 90° between cylinder banks, are 150° and 90°. The order in which the cylinders are made to fire is usually partly chosen to alternate between a crank-throw on one side of the crankshaft centre-line and a crankthrow on the other side, so as to even out the twisting or torsional stresses imposed on the crankshaft. It is also general practice to distribute the firing strokes between the front and the back of the engine and between the left and right cylinder blocks of flat or vee engines. Thus a typical firing order for a four-cylinder engine is 1, 3, 4, 2 (using the numbering system shown in fig. 26) though an alternative is 1, 2, 4, 3 while for a six-cylinder unit the usual firing orders are 1, 5, 3, 6, 2, 4 or 1, 4, 2, 6, 3, 5.

Friction and lubrication

We do not need to have tried to light a fire, boy-scout style, by rubbing two sticks together, to appreciate that when one surface slides on another, several things happen. First, their relative motion is resisted by the force of friction. Engineers know that this is proportional to the **coefficient of friction**, a basic characteristic of the two surfaces, and to the force pressing them together (fig. 28). Thus if the compressive force is 100 lb and the coefficient of friction is 0.7, then the frictional force resisting motion will be 100×0.7=70 lb. The second consequence of one surface sliding on another is the generation of heat. And if the two surfaces are dry, the third is rapid wear.

Since a petrol engine abounds in sliding surfaces of different sorts, some means of drastically reducing the effect of friction is

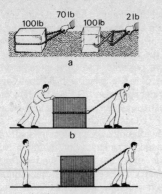

fig. 28. The force exerted by friction is proportional (a) to the load forcing the two sliding surfaces together, and to their coefficient of friction – 0.7 and 0.02 for the blocks of rubber and ice shown sliding on concrete. The initial static friction or stiction (b) is higher than the sliding friction.

needed. This means is the lubricating oil, the molecules of which slide freely over each other but cling to metal surfaces. The function of the lubricating oil is to keep the moving surfaces apart so that they do not touch at all and oil slides on oil rather than metal on metal. By doing this it is able to reduce both friction and wear drastically.

An effect known as **hydrodynamic lubrication** helps to keep the surfaces apart even when they are squeezed together by very large forces. This occurs if the gap or **clearance** between the surfaces has the correct, very small value (a few thousandths of an inch or hundredths of a millimetre), if it is continuously supplied with oil and if the speed of relative movement is sufficiently large. When all these conditions are satisfied, the two surfaces tend to converge towards a point of closest approach into which the sliding layers of oil are pumped by the relative motion. The pressure in the wedge of oil which forms in this region is many times higher than in the oil of surrounding areas and successfully keeps the two surfaces apart.

This mechanism is especially applicable to the **plain bearings** – straightforward tubes of bearing material – used for the more important parts of a modern engine such as the crankshaft and big-ends. (**Ball bearings** or **roller bearings** are seldom used within an engine itself – they are noisy and expensive – though they may be found in an auxiliary component such as the generator.) When the shaft involved is at rest inside such a plain bearing (fig. 29) it falls to the bottom, making contact with it at point A, but when the shaft is rotating it tends to climb up the bearing and to assume an eccentric position within it. The rotation of the shaft pumps oil from the low-pressure region, B, where the clearance is relatively large, to the high-pressure region or wedge at the point of closest approach, C, where the two shafts are kept apart yet the clearance between them is very small, perhaps as little as 0.0002–0.0004 in (0.005–0.01 mm) compared to about 0.0025–0.003 in (0.06–0.08 mm) which is the typical total clearance for a 2 in (50 mm) diameter journal.

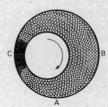

fig. 29. Wedge lubrication in a plain bearing – the pressure in the area of closest approach is much higher than elsewhere.

Lubricating oils

Unfortunately this hydrodynamic lubrication mechanism works best when the bearing is steadily loaded, whereas the crankshaft and big-end bearings are subjected to violently oscillating explosion and inertia shock loads which for brief periods during each revolution may squeeze the wedge of oil away almost entirely. Here a second kind of lubrication, **boundary lubrication**, comes to the rescue. It depends on an important but difficult to define property of lubricants, known (don't laugh) as their 'oiliness'. The oiliness of a lubricant is its tendency to form an electro-chemical bond with the metal surfaces to which it is applied and to deposit on those surfaces a 'boundary' layer only two or three molecules thick which cannot be removed by washing.

But engine lubrication is largely hydro-dynamic, which means that instead of metal being forced to slide on metal, the molecular layers of oil in each bearing must be made to slide over one another. This sliding action creates its own friction, very much less than dry friction, but appreciable nonetheless. Considerable heat is generated in the bear-ings, for example – particularly the main and big-end bearings – so an important secon-dary function of the lubricating oil and the system which circulates it through the engine is to carry this heat away – as well as some combustion heat from the undersides of the pistons. For this reason some cars are fitted with oil coolers.

Just as two sliding surfaces have a char-acteristic coefficient of friction, so every liquid offers a characteristic resistance to the sliding of the molecular layers within it, and this resistance is known as its **viscosity**. Viscosity defines resistance to flow – indeed the time taken for a certain quantity of liquid to flow out of a vessel under specified conditions is one measure of viscosity. A lubricating oil's viscosity is one of its most important properties: if it is too high exces-sive drag will be created, if too low the thin films of lubricant will break down and the bearings will seize. Moreover, viscosity falls as temperature rises, so the heat generated by the friction within the oil itself may lower its viscosity to a dangerous level.

Lubricating oil viscosities are universally classified by a system of numbers devised in the 1920s by the SAE (p. 30). The larger the number the more viscous or 'thick' is the oil, and for engines typical grades are 10, 20, 30, 40 or 50. These specify a *minimum* viscosity at a normal running temperature (210°F, or 99°C). In other words, the oils must not get 'thinner' than certain specified levels of viscosity under these conditions.

But these ratings apply to oils intended for use in summer or where ambient tempera-tures are high. The gradings applied to oils used in winter carry a 'W' suffix and are defined in a different way. Thus a 10W oil must not have more than a certain *maximum* viscosity at 0°F (−18°C), i.e. must not be 'thicker' than a certain amount.

Many years ago all oils used for car engines were specified by single gradings of this sort. The big drawback of a single-grade oil, however, is that its viscosity varies enor-mously with temperature. Thus the viscosity of a 30 grade oil in an engine started up at 32°F (0°C) is 150 units, falling to 10 units at 212°F (100°C), a typical winter running tem-perature.

In the early fifties, therefore, **multigrade** oils were introduced containing **viscosity index improvers** which reduce, but by no means eliminate, the change in viscosity with temperature (fig. 30). Oils of this sort are classified by two grading numbers such as 10W/30, meaning no thicker than a 10 grade oil at 0°F and no thinner than a 30 grade oil at 210°F. This particular grade was

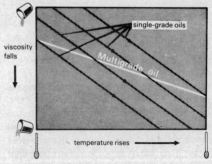

fig. 30. The viscosity of a multigrade oil drops less with rising temperature than does the viscosity of a single-grade oil.

the one most popular at first, but due to the more severe conditions imposed by the expanding motorway network the 20W/50 grade which stays thicker in hot weather became more frequently specified. But the frictional losses created by a relatively viscous oil have a significant adverse effect on fuel consumption during the first few miles after start-up in cold weather, so thinner 10W/30 grades of oil are increasingly being recommended.

A viscosity index improver is only one of several additives found in a modern engine oil. These include a **dispersing agent** which retains carbon from combustion in suspension so that it can be removed from the engine at the oil change, and prevents the build-up of sludge deposits. As the carbon in suspension is too fine to be filtered out, the oil quickly turns black, but this is a good sign, not a bad one. An **anti-oxidant** is another common constituent, its purpose being the prevention of deterioration at high temperatures. Modern oils operate satisfactorily at 195–305°F (90–150°C) but the maximum temperature reached can be 104°F (40°C), higher than is registered by the oil temperature gauge if fitted. Most oils also contain **anti-corrosion additives** to neutralize the effects of contamination by the corrosive products of combustion, and **anti-wear** additives which make the addition of a proprietory anti-wear additive unnecessary, perhaps positively harmful.

Bearing materials

Since an engine's rotating shafts touch the bearings which support them when starting up and sometimes when running too, the bearing material is of vital importance. It must satisfy several basic requirements apart from that of a low lubricated coefficient of friction with the journal. One of these is **compatibility**, since incompatible materials tend to 'pick up' material from each other and to **seize** or weld together even when well lubricated. Another is **conformability**, the capacity to accommodate slight misalignments without failing, even though the local loading in some part of the bearing may be high. A third is **embeddability** – the ability to absorb tiny pieces of grit and swarf so that they do not abrade the journal. Load-bearing capacity and resistance to wear, corrosion and fatigue (failure due to repeated changes of load) are further requirements.

The first modern bearing material, patented by Babbitt in 1839, was an alloy of tin, antimony and copper known as white metal or Babbitt metal; some later variants were based on lead. In pre-war cars this was cast into the bearing bore, sometimes using the bearing housing as a mould in conjunction with the shaft which was afterwards removed so that the bearing could be hand-scraped to provide the necessary clearance.

But all modern cars use **shell bearings** – strips of steel carrying a layer of a special bearing material and bent into half-circles. The bearing materials employed vary, but may be white metal alloys – though these have relatively low fatigue resistance by modern standards – or one of the more up-to-date aluminium–tin or copper–lead alloys which are capable of giving a long life despite high loads and operating temperatures. Nowadays it is extremely rare for main or big-end bearings to fail prematurely and a commonplace for them to last 60–80,000 miles (95–130,000km) even in the smallest and cheapest engines.

How engines are constructed

Lubrication system

The modern engine largely owes its ability to run continuously at high speeds and power outputs to the adoption of **pressure lubrication** systems involving a pump force-feed-

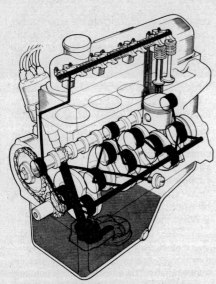

fig. 31. A typical pressure lubrication system.

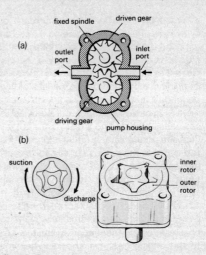

fig. 32. Engine oil pumps: (a) gear type; (b) rotor type.

ing oil to its bearings. Early engines relied merely on splash or 'spit and hope' lubrication.

A typical modern lubrication system (fig. 31) begins at the bottom of the engine where there is a **sump**, often made of sheet steel, but sometimes of finned aluminium, into which the oil is returned after circulation. A **pickup pipe** with a wire gauze filter at its mouth extends nearly to the bottom of the lowermost part of the sump and is connected to the inlet side of the oil pump. Sometimes the pump is mounted close to the end of the pickup pipe beneath the surface of the oil, sometimes it is mounted higher up in the engine or externally on the crankcase. Often the oil pump lies at the bottom of a shaft driven from the camshaft by **skew gears** at the top end of which the **contact breaker** which triggers the electrical spark is mounted, together with the distributor. But the oil pump drive arrangements vary a great deal from engine to engine.

A common form of oil pump (fig. 32a) is the **gear** type which consists of two gear wheels meshing together within a casing which fits closely around them. Oil in the region of the inlet port is drawn into the pump, carried round between the gear teeth and the casing, and then ejected through the outlet port. Another kind of pump is the **rotor** type (fig. 32b). It is composed of a driving inner gear wheel with one fewer teeth or lobes than an internally lobed driven outer wheel. The space between the two wheels increases in volume near the inlet port, drawing in oil which is then carried round to the outlet port where the space available contracts, expelling the oil.

The oil pump outlet pipe incorporates a **pressure relief valve** consisting of a spring loaded ball, plate or plunger. When the pressure rises above the prescribed value, the relief valve opens, returning surplus oil back to the inlet side of the pump.

The cleanliness of the oil is of the utmost importance, and the removal from it of abrasive particles of grit, even when very small, is essential to long engine life. In most modern engines, therefore, all the oil delivered by the pump is passed to a **filter** which is generally cylindrical in shape and usually mounted on the side of the crankcase or elsewhere outside the engine so that it can easily be detached and replaced. Inside the filter is an element of porous paper, heavily pleated to increase both its surface area and its rigidity, and supported by meshes of fine perforated metal. Such a modern filter element is capable of filtering out particles as small as 0.00004 in (0.001 mm). But as deposits accumulate, it offers an increasing resistance to the passage of oil and so must be replaced at specified intervals, sometimes 5–6000 miles (8–10,000 km), though for more and more cars these days it is 10–12,000 miles (16–20,000 km). The filter is provided with its own internal relief valve to ensure an emergency supply of unfiltered oil to the engine bearings should it become choked through neglect. Some engines incorporate an auxiliary centrifugal filter on the end of the crankshaft, others use a partial-flow system in which a small proportion only of the oil is filtered before being passed to the bearings. Many engines now have magnetic sump drain plugs to remove particles of iron or steel from circulation.

From the filter the oil is generally passed to the crankshaft which can be lubricated in one of two ways. In the first (and least common) system the crankshaft is pierced from end to end by angled drillings, oil is introduced at the front and flows to the back lubricating all main and big-end bearings in turn.

In the alternative system (fig. 31) the oil is passed from the filter to a main gallery in the crankcase casting which runs along the side of the engine. Oil from this gallery is directed via further passages to the main bearings through small holes in the upper shell bearings. Crankshaft cross-drillings registering with grooves in these bearing shells pass the oil from a main bearing to adjacent big-end bearings. Sometimes only the upper bearing shell is grooved – to increase the load-bearing capacity of the complete bearing – in which case the crankshaft journal is drilled across its diameter to ensure a continuous supply of oil to the adjacent big-ends.

Subsidiary galleries carry the oil to the camshaft bearings, which may similarly be lubricated separately or through the camshaft itself. Very often the oil which escapes from the sides of the camshaft bearing is trapped in a small bath which lubricates the lobes of the cams where they make contact with the tappets. The rockers may be lubricated through drillings in a hollow **rocker shaft**, and to minimize oil consumption the supply to this is sometimes made through a small rotating cross-drilling in the end of the camshaft.

When the engine runs, the pressure in its crankcase rises a little above the atmospheric level, partly because of the leakage of the blow-by gases during the combustion strokes and partly because of the pumping and churning action of the crankshaft and pistons. If not relieved, this pressure would speedily force all the oil out of the engine through any convenient orifice such as the dipstick tube. Thus all engines have a ventilation system, air usually being drawn in through a combined oil filler/breather cap incorporating a wire mesh filter to keep dust out of the engine. The high-pressure crankcase air, contaminated by the **blow-by gases**, is generally ejected through a breather pipe connected to the side of the crankcase and incorporating a baffle to retain oil mist. Since 1971 engines have been legally required to consume their own crankcase blow-by gases because these tend to pollute the atmosphere. Nowadays, therefore, the breather pipe is always connected to the carburetter air intake system for combustion (p. 54).

But there is more to keeping the oil within an engine than merely relieving the crankcase pressure, for there are two major potential sources of leakage – where the ends of the rotating crankshaft pass through the crankcase walls. Each end is sealed in a similar way, but the problem is more difficult at the flywheel end than at the other end where some of the oil leaking from the end

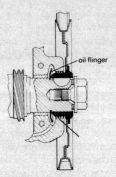

fig. 33. A crankshaft oil sealing system incorporating a flinger, and an oil-return thread.

cooler is often included in the circuit. Because the oil picked up has become frothy and difficult to handle in its passage through the engine, two scavenge pumps are sometimes fitted, each considerably larger in capacity than the pressure pump. The Porsche 911 and some Ferrari and Maserati models are the only road cars to be fitted with a dry sump lubrication system.

Crankshaft and connecting rods

Each of the main bearings is split into two halves (fig. 34) so that the crankshaft can be

main bearing can be used to lubricate the timing chain or gears (if fitted); a **toothed rubber timing belt** needs no lubrication. Generally the first line of defence (fig. 33) is a **flinger**, a small saucer-shaped disc which catches any oil running along the crankshaft and flings it outwards and backwards into the engine by centrifugal force. This may be followed by an oil-return screw with a coarse thread which tends to drive escaping oil back into the engine. More often, though, there is a rubber **lip seal** with a lightly spring-loaded flange which wipes oil away from the cylindrical sealing surface.

A conventional lubrication system has two basic defects which assume some importance in a car of very high performance. One is that even when the sump is heavily baffled, violent acceleration and deceleration may make the oil surge away from or towards the pump, causing alternate starvation and flooding of the bearings. The other is the depth taken up by the conventional sump, which may make it difficult to fit an engine into a low engine compartment.

Both these faults can be eliminated by fitting a dry sump lubrication system. In such a system oil is delivered by a pressure pump immersed in a separate oil reservoir – which may be located anywhere in the engine compartment – and returned to this reservoir by scavenge pumps in the engine, which has only the most vestigial of sumps; an oil

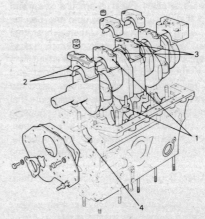

fig. 34. A crankshaft, its connecting rods and bearings: 1, big-end shell bearing halves and caps; 2, lower main shell bearing halves and caps; 3, thrust washers; 4, upper main shell bearing halves.

installed and removed if required. The upper halves fit into main bearing saddles formed in strong ribs which run across the crankcase and brace it. It is of the utmost importance that the crankcase and these ribs together form a very stiff structure to keep any flexure to a minimum – excessive flexure means a **rough** or vibratory engine and a short bearing life. For the same reason it is essential that the detachable **main bearing caps** into which the lower shell bearings fit should bolt up absolutely square to the main bearing saddles. Hence the main bearing caps are usually provided with pegs or dowels to ensure accurate location. In modern engines such as the Peugeot–Renault–Volvo V-6 unit, it is increasingly becoming the practice to join the main bearing caps into a one-piece 'ladder' to ensure the utmost rigidity.

Several important features are incorporated into the shell bearings. Generally each is provided with a hole to admit lubricating oil under pressure and a groove registering with a cross-drilling in the crankshaft journal to distribute it to adjacent big-end bearings. Each has a lug to ensure its accurate location in the bearing housing, each is slightly flattened or given a certain amount of **spread** so that it can be sprung into the bearing housing and then retained there while other parts are being prepared; and when in position, each stands proud of its housing by a few thousandths of an inch (hundredths of a millimetre). This last feature is called **nip** or **crush** and its purpose is to make sure that the two shells are a tight fit in their housing when the main bearing bolts are tightened, so that there is no chance of them rotating, and the intimate contact they make with the housing allows the very considerable amount of heat generated by the friction within them to be carried away.

The crankshaft needs axial as well as radial location, especially against the large forces which tend to press the flywheel into the engine when the clutch is released. These are usually resisted by a set of semicircular **thrust washers**, similar in material and design to the shell bearings and installed each side of one of the main bearings. Alternatively, one pair of the shell bearings may be provided with integral flanges.

A modern crankshaft is a pretty strong and rigid affair, made generally either of forged steel or of a special cast iron, a material pioneered for this use by Ford. The relatively short strokes still fashionable these days (p. 39) mean a small crankthrow radius, which in conjunction with the large journal diameters currently used, leads to useful

overlap between the crankpins and main journals. Plenty of support is provided, too: for many years it has been general practice to place a main bearing on either side of every crankthrow for in-line engines. Each crankpin carries a single connecting rod in most engines, but two connecting rods in V-8 units. In-line fours generally but not always have five main bearings, as do V-8 engines, while V-6 units usually have four, and flat-six and in-line six engines normally have seven bearings.

But the use of a large number of main bearings – particularly seven for the crankshaft of an in-line six – can introduce problems. For the longer a crankshaft becomes the more easily it can be excited by the combustion impulses into twisting or **torsional oscillation** which can cause breakages unless controlled. Effectively, the crankshaft and flywheel act like the torsional equivalent of two weights, with freedom to slide back and forth in a tube, which are connected together by a spring (fig. 35). If

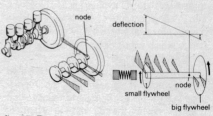

fig. 35. Torsional oscillations in a crankshaft. The point of highest stress lies between the node and the flywheel.

the two weights are pulled apart and released they will oscillate towards and away from each other at the same frequency. Similarly, the crankshaft–flywheel system is equivalent to a pair of weights connected by a spring. One weight is the flywheel itself, the other is the smaller flywheel equivalent to all the crankthrows lumped together and the spring is the crankshaft between them. When this system is set into torsional oscillation, therefore, the flywheel makes little twisting movements in one direction about a **node** or point of no deflection, while on the other side the remainder of the crankshaft twists in the opposite direction. This crankshaft torsional oscillation has a certain natural or **resonant** frequency which may be excited by a particular (usually high) engine speed. If the crankshaft is subject to this sort of treatment for too long, it may well break at the point of highest stress which lies between the node and the flywheel.

The cure is to fit a **torsional damper**, usually just a small flywheel, and often doing double duty as an auxiliaries drive pulley, which is bonded through a rubber torsional spring to the crankshaft nose and tuned to the natural frequency of the crankshaft itself to absorb its vibrations.

At its other end the crankshaft usually terminates in a small flange to which the flywheel is securely attached by a ring of bolts. The flywheel is simply a disc with a heavy rim giving a high rotational inertia to smooth out the combustion impulses. It carries the ring gear driven by the starter motor and a friction face for the clutch, or, if automatic transmission is fitted, one element of the torque converter.

Techniques and shell bearings similar to those used for the crankshaft journals are also employed for the connecting rod big-

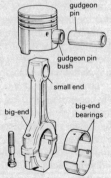

end bearings (fig. 36). The shell bearings are similar in design and the bearing caps are frequently serrated or stepped to ensure their accurate location. Often the big-end is split at an angle so that the connecting rod can be passed through the cylinder bore.

Small-end bearings are usually rather different. Generally, these days, the small end of the connecting rod is formed into a continuous eye with no split, and in one common system this contains a bush, often having a hard lead–bronze bearing material with a steel backing. Through this bush, and free to rotate within it, passes the gudgeon pin which links the steel connecting rod to the aluminium alloy piston. The gudgeon pin, retained in position by **circlips**, is in this arrangement also free to rotate in the piston and so is described as **fully floating**, the rotation required as the piston moves up and down being shared between the small-end bush and the piston bearings. In an alternative arrangement the gudgeon pin is said to be **semi-floating** because it is clamped in the small-end and rotates only in the piston bosses.

The **shank** which joins the small-end of the connecting rod to the big-end nearly always has an I-shaped cross-section which confers the maximum rigidity for the minimum weight. Usually alloy steel forgings, the connecting rods need to be generously radiused in areas of high stress such as the **shoulders** into which the clamping bolts are threaded, in just the same way as the crankshaft must have large **fillet radii** where the crankpins and main journals join the webs. In both cases the reason is the same: stress tends to concentrate at any sharp change in shape or surface discontinuity.

gudgeon pin

gudgeon pin bush

small end

big-end

big-end bearings

fig. 36. A connecting rod showing big-end, big-end shell bearings, small-end and fully floating gudgeon pin.

Pistons and cylinders

Almost always made of aluminium alloy, a piston has several functions which include transmitting the combustion forces to the connecting rod, absorbing the side-thrust created by its angularity and sealing in the

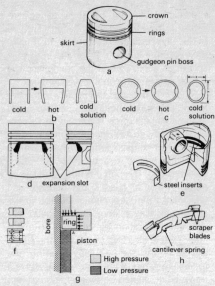

fig. 37. Modern piston design: (a) The basic parts of a piston; (b) and (c) shaping to reduce expansive distortion; (d) an expansion slot – this is the Hepolite W-type which blocks heat flow from the piston crown and gives the skirt flexibility; (e) nowadays a more common method of controlling expansion is to use steel inserts; (f) a sectional view through the three piston rings usually fitted; (g) how a piston ring works – the gas pressure does the sealing; (h) a typical oil control ring – the two blades or rails have been cut away to show the springs which force them against the cylinder walls.

hot gases liberated by the burning of the fuel. The upper part of a piston (fig. 37a) is called its **crown** and in many engines is flat, though in others it may have a marked upward bulge to reduce the clearance volume at the top of the stroke and thus increase the compression ratio; such a bulge may also have the auxiliary purpose of improving combustion by promoting **swirl** or **turbulence** (p. 59) in the burning gases. Alternatively, the piston crown may be flat with **cut-outs** to clear the valves when they are fully open, or may be deeply recessed to form a **bowl-in-piston** or **Heron** type of combustion chamber of the kind used for the range of Ford Kent engines. Beneath the crown lies a set of grooves, usually three, in the walls of the piston accommodating the **piston rings** which act as seals. Beneath the grooves and rings in turn are the strong bosses which surround the gudgeon pin bearings, and below them lies the **skirt** which is a close fit in the cylinder and helps to guide the piston.

Since the connecting rod lies at a small angle to the cylinder axis except at top and bottom centre, a side-thrust is created during the combustion stroke, a side-thrust which is significant because the explosion force on the piston is so large. A smaller side-thrust is also exerted during the compression stroke, but on the other side of the piston. To accommodate these forces, a piston is often unsymmetrical in design – sometimes the gudgeon pin is slightly offset towards the thrust side. Hence the piston skirt is usually marked F (for front) to ensure that it is fitted the correct way round.

A large part of piston design is concerned with compensation for expansion, since the aluminium alloys used expand at about twice the rate of the cast iron cylinders into which they are generally required to fit – for cylinder liners of this material are almost always employed even when the engine itself is made of aluminium.

To accommodate the expansion involved, a piston is in the first instance very carefully contoured to assume the correct shape when hot. In side view (fig. 37b) it is very slightly tapered, being smaller in diameter at the crown where it becomes very hot, than at the bottom of the skirt where it runs significantly cooler. In plan view (fig. 37c) it is given a tiny degree of ovality, being smaller in diameter when cold along the gudgeon pin axis, where there is a large mass of metal to expand, than across the more lightly constructed thrust faces.

All pistons incorporate a further means of accommodating expansion, of which one is the inclusion of specially designed slots.

Sometimes these are located close to the piston bosses and run parallel and near to the lower ring groove often forming part of it with the purpose of blocking the flow of heat to the thrust faces (fig. 37d). Nearly vertical slots near the bosses may serve a similar purpose. An alternative arrangement is the provision of a horizontal slot on the minor thrust face connected to a second, long and near vertical slot which closes up to accommodate the expansion of the skirt. In older designs this slot extended right to the bottom of the skirt – hence the expression **split skirt** piston.

A more common approach is to cast steel alloy inserts into the piston on either side of its bosses (fig. 37e). These act as bimetallic strips with the aluminium which surrounds them, bowing the piston outwards along the gudgeon pin axis and contracting it along the thrust axis so that it assumes a truly circular shape and becomes a close fit in the cylinder at its correct running temperature.

As important as compensation for expansion is the design of a piston's rings. Each of these is interrupted by a small gap, partly so that it can be expanded over the piston into its groove and partly to exert an initial spring pressure on the cylinder walls. Contrary to popular belief, there is no significant leakage through these gaps and it does not matter how they are spaced during assembly, since the rings slowly rotate when the engine runs. Piston rings are generally made of cast iron, a hard and wear-resistant material which retains good elasticity at high temperatures, though it also tends to be brittle.

There are usually three rings (fig. 37f), the top two being called **compression rings** because they do nearly all the sealing work. Both compression rings rely on the outward spring force they exert for sealing at very low engine speeds only (fig. 37g). At higher speeds (or throttle openings) the ring is forced outwards by the gas pressure which in this way is itself made to do the work of sealing. The upper compression ring is generally rectangular in section with a coating of chrome or molybdenum to reduce wear. It must be light in weight or in spite of combustion pressure, downward acceleration of the piston during the firing stroke will press it hard against the top of the groove. In this case the gas pressure cannot get behind the ring which then collapses inwards, increasing blow-by.

Conditions are less arduous for the second compression ring which either has a tapered face or a tilted section so that its bottom edge alone contacts the cylinder wall during the induction, compression and exhaust strokes. With this form of contact its action is to scrape the oil film away from the combustion chamber during the induction stroke, but to ride over it during the compression and exhaust strokes, thus minimizing oil consumption. During the combustion stroke the gas pressure forces this ring against the cylinder wall in the same way as for the upper compression ring.

The third and lowest, the **oil control** ring, measures out and distributes the oil delivered by the lubrication system on to the cylinder walls. Oil control rings are often complex, composite assemblies, composed of several interlocking parts, but generally involve (fig. 37h) two blades forced outwards by springs and thin enough to exert a high wiping pressure on the cylinder walls and separated by a strip incorporating drainage slots through which surplus oil is returned to the sump.

Almost all pistons run in cylinders made of cast iron, bored true and honed to a high state of surface finish. Only in the General Motors Vega, the Porsche 928 and 944 and the lightweight Mercedes V-8 engines do aluminium pistons run in aluminium cylinders for which a special high silicon alloy is used. Generally the complete engine is made of iron and the cylinder bores are cast into it, but in some cases detachable **liners** are used, and these are described as **wet liners** when they form the outer wall of the water jacket surrounding each cylinder. If the upper part of the water jacket is open to the air when the cylinder head is removed, the cylinder block casting is simplified and is said to be of the **open deck** type. Cast iron cylinders are also nearly always used for aircooled engines, either as complete cylinder barrels incorporating integral cooling fins, or as liners to finned barrels of aluminium alloy.

Valvegear

The camshafts of modern engines are occasionally driven by gears, sometimes by toothed belts, but more often by chains, especially in the pushrod system already briefly mentioned (p. 24). These chains

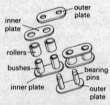

fig. 38. The parts of a roller timing or valvegear chain.

(fig. 38) are generally of the **roller** type which is designed to promote rolling rather than sliding motion between its links and the teeth of the sprockets with which they engage. One of these sprockets (fig. 10) is attached to the front end of the crankshaft, while the other, which is fixed to the end of the camshaft, is twice the diameter to give the required 2:1 speed reduction ratio. To accommodate the apparent stretch occasioned by wear in the links, an adjustable spring-loaded rubber-faced pad or **tensioner** usually bears on the chain in the centre of the slack side of its run. Sometimes the spring loading is augmented by hydraulic pressure derived from the lubrication system.

In a pushrod system the camshaft rotated by a chain drive mechanism of this sort is generally located low down in the side of the cylinder block. To allow it to be inserted into

its bearings from one end, its journals are often larger in diameter than the major diameters of the cams. The function of each cam is to open one of the engine's valves at exactly the required point in the four-stroke cycle, to hold it open for the designed period, and finally to allow its spring to close it at another carefully chosen point in the cycle. Because the correct phasing is so important, the two camshaft drive sprockets are provided with **timing marks** which must be aligned when the chain is fitted. Special keys or dowel pins ensure that the sprockets in turn can only be fitted to their respective shafts in one position.

When the nose of the cam bears on its associated tappet or **cam follower**, it applies the maximum deflection, via the pushrod and rocker, to the tip of the valve which is thus fully opened. Conversely, when the **base circle** part of the cam is in contact with the tappet, the valve is not deflected at all and remains fully closed. The nose of the cam is linked to the base circle by a pair of curves which control how gently or violently the valve is opened or closed. Determining the shapes of these curves, and indeed of the cam as a whole, is a complex mathematical art.

Above the cams lie barrel tappets incorporating seatings for the lower ends of the pushrods. The tappet surface is usually given a slightly convex shape to prevent the cam from digging into it – as can happen if camshaft and tappet are not completely parallel. In addition, the cam is generally offset from the centre of the tappet and has a face which is slightly inclined axially. The combined effect of these two features is to force the tappet to rotate, distributing wear more evenly over its surface.

Generally the lower end of the pushrod which engages with the tappet is formed into a ball, while the upper end is formed into a cup. Into this cup fits another ball, on the end of a rod which screws into the rocker and can be clamped by a locknut. This arrangement allows a clearance to be set between the tip of the **valve stem** and the other end of the rocker to allow for the expansion of the valve train components relative to the cylinder block. If the adjuster works loose and the clearance closes up, the valve will remain slightly open when it should be closed, its sealing face will soon become damaged by excessive exposure to the hot gases of combustion – and, of course, the engine will run at much reduced efficiency.

Some engines, notably American V-8 units, are provided with **hydraulic tappets** which automatically take up the clearances and compensate for any wear in the valve mechanism. A hydraulic tappet (fig. 39) essentially consists of a piston and a closed cylinder forced apart by the pressure of the lubricating oil which is supplied through a small hole when the valve is closed. When the cam begins to lift the valve, this supply duct no longer registers with the tappet so that the trapped incompressible oil inside it acts as a rigid strut – though there is some controlled leakage to make sure that the valve always returns fully to its seating as the tappet meets the base circle of the cam. But at very high engine speeds – above about 6000 rpm, say – it is difficult to prevent hydraulic tappets from remaining permanently pumped up, which is why they are seldom used for engines of exceptionally high output.

The difference between a cam's base circle radius and the radius at its nose determines the maximum **lift** applied to the valve. Usually, though, this is magnified by about 1.5:1 by leverage in the rocker to reduce the displacements imposed on the relatively heavy tappets and pushrods – and hence also the accelerations and inertia forces acting on them. The normal valve lift is about one quarter of the valve head diameter, because at this value the area of the annulus or ring between the open valve and its seat is the same as the area of the valve opening itself – so increasing the lift still further will do little to ease the flow of gases into or out of the combustion chamber.

The valve itself is a mushroom-shaped device with a long stem and a circular head which seals the opening in the combustion chamber. To perform its sealing function efficiently, it is provided with a conical **facing** which mates with a similar seating in the cylinder head. Each valve must be mated to its seat by a **grinding-in** process using a fine abrasive paste. Some years ago, it was often necessary to repeat this process at 20–40,000-mile intervals to maintain engine efficiency, but modern power units do not need such attention, though it is advisable to regrind the valves if the cylinder head has to be removed for any other reason.

Both the inlet and the exhaust valves are subjected to very high mechanical and thermal stresses, the exhaust valve particularly, since its head runs red-hot at about 900°C. Accordingly, modern exhaust valves are often made of high-chromium stainless steels and sometimes are additionally faced with an even harder and heat-resistant alloy called Stellite. The exhaust valves used by Alfa Romeo are unusual in being filled with sodium which becomes liquid at the running temperature and improves the transfer of heat to the cooling system.

The more lightly stressed inlet valves may have chromium-plated as well as aluminium-coated facings to reduce wear, but are made of lower-grade alloys.

The valve stem passes through a **valve guide** in the cylinder head with a working

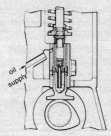

fig. 39. A hydraulic tappet. Oil is pumped between the small piston and cylinder to take up the valve clearance.

clearance of a few thousandths of an inch (hundredths of a millimetre) – more for the hotter exhaust valve. When the cylinder head is made of cast iron, the valve guide is generally machined directly in it, as is the valve seat, but inserts of a more durable material may be used for both – and generally are if the cylinder head is made of aluminium alloy.

Just below the tip of the valve stem is a groove for the **collets** which retain a cap. This in turn retains (fig. 10) the powerful coil spring which returns the valve to its seat. The slight twisting action of the spring with compression and relaxation helps, it is said, to rotate the valve, distributing its wear more evenly, though other designers believe that engine vibration is responsible for valve rotation. Some engines incorporate devices specifically designed to ensure valve rotation.

In some engines two valve springs are fitted, the rubbing action between them helping to damp out **valve surge**. This can occur if the frequency of valve operation coincides with the resonant frequency of the spring, inducing compression and extension waves in it which interfere badly with the proper motion of the valve. Even if valve surge does not occur, valve **float** or **bounce** may do so at very high rpm when the inertia of the valve tends to hold it more or less permanently open against the force of the spring. Valve bounce creates a sharp power cut-off at high rpm – accompanied by an alarming noise – though many modern engines 'run out of breath' before this point is reached: their inlet systems aren't big enough to pass sufficient fuel and air for the valve bounce point to be reached.

These deficiencies of a conventional valve mechanism led some engineers to believe that valves should not be closed by a spring but by positive mechanical means. The resultant arrangement, grandly known as a **desmodromic** form of valve actuation (fig. 40), is not used in road cars, though it was briefly used by Mercedes for racing in the fifties. The advantages of such a system

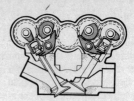

fig. 40. Desmodromic valves – closed positively rather than by spring. Right: the principle; left: a practical arrangement.

seem marginal, however, especially as modern Grand Prix engines use valve springs in the ordinary way yet will run to more than 12,000 rpm.

But the pushrod valve operation system on which description has so far concentrated does have some deficiencies which are both more serious and more easily cured. The first deficiency is the excessive inertia of the tappet, pushrod and rocker; the second is the flexibility of these components, particularly the last two. In combination these two characteristics mean that the motion represented by the shape of the cam is not transmitted at all faithfully to the valve. In fact investigations with high-speed sensors have shown that a pushrod-operated valve spends a lot of its time just waving about rather than opening and closing in the required manner.

A partial solution is to mount the camshaft high in the cylinder block to shorten the valve train as was done for the pre-war Riley engines. A similar arrangement, involving short, stubby pushrods, is to be found in certain Opel engines.

A better answer, though, is a **single overhead camshaft** (sohc) which can operate through rockers if the exhaust valves are inclined to the inlet valves as they are in many designs. Still more inertia and complication is removed if the valves are in line and directly actuated by a camshaft just above them through inverted **bucket tappets** enclosing the upper parts of the valve stems. The simplicity and efficiency of such an arrangement has been apparent for so long that its neglect by designers until relatively recently is surprising.

The bucket tappets are subject to the same sort of design principles as barrel tappets – they are usually made to rotate, for example – but are more highly stressed and must incorporate some form of valve clearance adjustment. In one such form of adjustment, the manufacturer makes available a set of small discs or **shims** in a wide range of standard thicknesses so that a shim can be inserted into or under the tappet of the total thickness giving the clearance required. In another system used by Vauxhall for their (now obsolescent) sohc four-cylinder engines, the tappet incorporates an inclined screw with a flat machined in its flank which is in contact with the valve stem; each full turn of the screw moves the tappet closer to or further from the valve.

Double overhead camshaft (dohc) engines are also used for road cars, Jaguar's six-cylinder unit being one of the best-known, though Aston Martin, Ferrari, Fiat, Lamborghini, Lotus, Maserati and Mercedes make engines of the same type. In power units of this kind the designer has ample freedom to design the best possible inlet and exhaust systems, but the two separate camshafts do add cost, complication, weight and bulk.

The overhead camshafts of many modern engines are driven neither by gears nor by chains but by toothed rubber belts (fig. 41). Reinforced by internal glass fibre cords, these are light, long-lasting and quiet running; moreover they require no lubrication. Their only disadvantage is that their width of about an inch may add a little to the overall length of the engine.

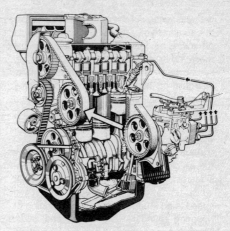

fig. 41. An overhead camshaft driven by a toothed rubber belt – this one forms part of the Volkswagen Golf diesel engine, and also drives the fuel injection pump.

Induction and fuel system

Induction system layout

Air is essential to any ordinary form of combustion and an internal combustion engine inhales large quantities of it. It does so through what is often one of the most prominent objects under the bonnet of a car – the **air cleaner**. Air cleaners vary a great deal in size and shape, but the most common type looks like an inverted frying pan, the handle of which is the pipe admitting the air. Often this pipe can be swivelled, so that in summer it draws in cool air from the front of the car and in winter it can be set to take in air warmed by the exhaust system. Sometimes the connections to the two sources of air are permanent and there is a flap or slide to effect the changeover from one to the other. It is becoming increasingly common to fit a thermostatically controlled inlet air temperature system (p. 108) which blends the air from these two sources automatically.

At one time the incoming air was often filtered by an oil-wetted wire mesh element, often working in conjunction with an oil bath beneath it. Nowadays, however, modern engines are nearly always provided with a dry paper air filter element, usually shaped like a ring, which needs replacing roughly every 10,000 miles (16,000 km). This filter provides vital protection against excessive wear, especially of the cylinders and pistons, due to abrasive particles of dust that would otherwise be drawn into the engine. Unless the weather is particularly dry and dusty, no serious harm is likely to result in most parts of Britain or the Continent if the air cleaner element is absent for a week or so, though its removal may upset the carburation. But as a long-term defence against wear, it is essential.

Another important function performed by the air cleaner is the silencing of the considerable noise made by the incoming air which tends to make a sharp hiss at idling speeds and loud low-frequency thudding or booming sounds at higher rpm and loads. The air-cleaning element itself and the shape and angle of the entrance pipe help to suppress the first kind of noise. The second is suppressed using the principle of resonance. The large cavity formed by the air cleaner body is capable of resonating in several different ways at several different frequencies, and by the correct choice of its size and shape these can be tuned to coincide with – and thus absorb – the most objectionable frequencies generated by the rush of the incoming air.

After flowing through the air cleaner, the incoming air passes to the device which mixes fuel with it in the correct proportions. Usually this device relies on a suction effect to draw the fuel in a fine spray from a special **jet**, and is called a carburetter; often it is located immediately beneath the air cleaner and it nearly always incorporates the throttle valve which controls the flow of air and fuel. When partially closed the throttle valve offers significant resistance to the flow of air and fuel which increases the pumping effort required of the engine and leads to a drop in the pressure on its downstream side in the **inlet manifold**. This drop in pressure is referred to as the **manifold depression**. The principle of the carburetter is described in the next section, but for some engines – usually those of the more expensive or high-performance sort – the fuel may be supplied

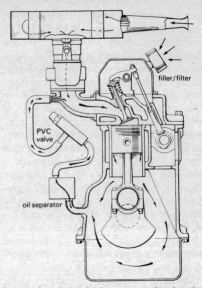

fig. 42. A typical induction system showing the air cleaner, inlet manifold, port and valve. The crankcase fumes are drawn into the inlet manifold via a pressure control valve or PCV; in this instance the arrangement is such that the flow of fumes is restricted when the manifold depression is high.

in an alternative and fundamentally different way. This alternative is **fuel injection** and involves squirting the fuel into the engine under pressure rather than allowing it to be draw in by suction. In such a system the air usually passes from the air cleaner through a throttle valve and into a collector box or **plenum chamber**. This is in turn connected to long induction pipes leading to the cylinders, the **injectors** which supply the fuel lying inside these pipes close to the valves.

In addition to being coupled to the carburetter, the air cleaner is also connected to the crankcase vent, usually by a small-diameter rubber hose. At one time this connection was often a direct one, but nowadays it is more usual for crankcase ventilation to be assisted by inlet manifold depression using a **pressure control valve** or **PCV**. The action of this valve is such that at normal speeds and loads, most of the crankcase ventilating air is drawn through the air cleaner, but it is differently routed during idling and on the **overrun**, a condition similar to coasting in which the throttle is closed and the engine is being turned by the momentum of the car. During both these modes of engine operation the inlet manifold depression is high and the ventilating air is drawn directly into the inlet manifold, allowance for this by-passing being made in the setting of the carburetter. In some engines the crankcase fumes are drawn directly into the inlet manifold, a different form of control valve being used to restrict the flow when the manifold depression is high.

The inlet manifold itself is generally a system of branched pipes which connect the carburetter to the cylinders. Sometimes there is more than one carburetter; occasionally there is effectively a separate carburetter for each cylinder. The cross-sectional area, shape and length of the inlet manifold pipes have a profound influence on the ability of the engine to 'breathe' freely and hence on its efficiency. The last part of the inlet passage to each cylinder, the part usually formed in the cylinder head itself and located close to the valve, is called the **port**.

The principle of the carburetter

Some readers may have seen a lighted cigarette being extinguished by rapid immersion in an open can of petrol. The point of this showy and highly dangerous experiment – please do not try it for yourself – is that there's more to combustion than an inflammable material. To make something burn well, it must not merely be in the presence of air – which contains the oxygen essential to combustion – but must also present a large surface area to that air. If the combustion reaction is to flourish, the substance involved must be in what chemists describe as a finely divided state. Solid magnesium, for example, often used for wheels, will not readily burn, but magnesium powder or fine strip burns very easily indeed.

And for efficient combustion in a petrol engine, the fuel must be not just finely divided, but vaporized.

A basic problem of the motorcar, therefore, is how to put the liquid fuel into the appropriate finely divided state and how to mix it evenly with the incoming air. Both these tasks are usually – but not always – performed by a carburetter.

Nearly all modern carburetters depend for their operation on the principle of the **venturi**, or **choke**, a smooth and streamlined constriction (fig. 43) in the tube through

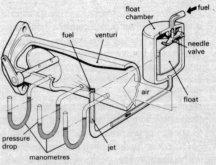

fig. 43. The principle of the carburetter: the low pressure in the constriction or venturi sucks the fuel out of the jet.

which the incoming air is drawn by the suction created when the piston descends on the induction stroke. This constriction or venturi, incidentally, is always outboard of, or upstream of, the throttle.

Now imagine a stream of air flowing steadily along the choke tube. Because the flow is steady, and the air is neither piling up in one place nor accelerating in another, the amount passing any given point in the tube in a given time must be the same as the amount passing any other point in the same time. Hence when the air gets to the venturi, it is forced to speed up to maintain the same flow rate. Now here comes the difficult bit: when it speeds up, its pressure does not rise as many people imagine it should, but instead falls. This is because the energy in the air has to remain constant, so if it gains some kinetic energy it must lose some pressure energy.

If this seems puzzling, think of a gas-tight box containing a small quantity of air. The molecules of air move about in an entirely random way and at very high speeds which depend on the temperature: the higher the temperature the greater the speeds. The random high-speed motion of the molecules means that they are constantly colliding with each other and bombarding the walls of the box and this bombardment is what creates pressure. Thus if the air is heated until its pressure is above atmospheric pressure, and if the box is then punctured, the heated air will rush out through the hole and the pressure in the box will fall. For the organized, unidirectional kinetic energy in the stream of escaping air can only be obtained by robbing the gas in the box of some of its random pressure energy. In just the same way, when the venturi forces the gas flowing through it to speed up, the pressure of that gas falls.

This pressure drop can easily be measured with a **manometer** which is simply a U-tube filled with a liquid, say water. If the pressure is measured at a number of points in the system, and if the venturi is smoothly shaped, the pressure downstream of it will be found to rise very nearly to the pressure upstream of it. There will be a small loss through friction since no streamlining can be perfect. If the venturi is replaced by a sharp-edged orifice, there will still be a pressure drop in its vicinity, but the downstream pressure recovery will be much less complete due to the high losses introduced by the violent eddying of the gases.

In a carburetter the pressure-drop effect is utilized through a small vertical tube called a jet which protrudes into the air stream from the floor of the venturi at its narrowest part. This jet is connected to a **float chamber** which is vented to atmosphere and kept full of petrol at a level just below the top of the jet by a float-controlled valve, in principle just like the ball valve of a cistern. The system is completed, of course, by a fuel pump, sometimes electrically operated, sometimes mechanically driven off the camshaft, which draws fuel from the tank and delivers it to the carburetter float chamber.

When the engine is at rest, therefore, no fuel flows from the carburetter jet. When the engine runs, however, the pressure above the jet falls below the atmospheric pressure above the float chamber. Hence the fuel is sucked out of the jet in a fine spray and drawn into the engine with the air. The subsequent vaporization of the fine droplets of fuel in the air stream and in contact with the hot manifold walls has an important bearing on the cleanness and completeness of combustion: the greater the vaporization the greater the combustion efficiency.

But supplying the engine with fuel in a finely divided state is not enough: it must also be **metered** or very precisely apportioned to the incoming air. The air/fuel mixture will not burn if it is either too **rich** or too **weak**, the theoretically correct strength for complete combustion being fifteen parts by weight of air to one part of fuel.

This is where the carburetter is so simple and ingenious, for the physics of the venturi effect are such that in theory the weight of fuel sucked through the jet is always exactly proportional to the weight of air drawn in, provided that the air density remains constant. By correctly choosing, therefore, the size of the jet in relation to the size of the venturi, it is theoretically possible to deliver a mixture which at all times remains constant in strength. Unfortunately theory is not borne out by practice, so real carburetters are more complex. They also incorporate a cold starting system (the **choke**) and arrangements for enriching the mixture during acceleration, but all these matters are discussed in Chapter 3.

Fuel pump and tank

The fuel is carried in a tank, usually fabricated from sheet steel, which ranges in size from around 5 gallons (23 litres) for a small car to over 20 gallons (91 litres) for a large one. It is generally located remotely from the engine – which for most cars means at the back. Nowadays it is becoming common practice to mount the fuel tank in such a position that it is unlikely to become damaged in a severe crash – ahead of the rear wheels, for example, in a front-engined car.

Fuel tanks are generally provided with baffles so that when the car accelerates and corners, the petrol does not surge away from the outlet pipe, which reaches nearly to the bottom – but not quite, to prevent sediment from being sucked up by the pump. Even so, avoid running out of petrol if you can, because when you do, sediment often *is* drawn into the carburetter, stopping the car or making it run very badly. Watch the fuel gauge, which gets its information from a pivoted float mechanism in the tank.

Most tanks are fitted with air vent pipes and filler caps incorporating small vent valves so that air can enter the tank freely as the fuel level falls and be readily expelled as it is filled. It is most important that these vents do not become obstructed; if they do the fuel pump is powerful enough to reduce the pressure in the tank by 2–3 lb/sq in (13,800–20,700 Pa) which is enough for it to be collapsed by atmospheric pressure acting on its outer surface. Due to legal requirements limiting the overflow of fuel and its evaporation into the atmosphere, vent pipes nowadays are often deliberately small in size so that it is very difficult to fill the tank right to the top; thus space is left for the expansion of the fuel in hot weather. Similarly, the vent pipe (and carburetter float chamber) may be connected to a canister of vapour-absorbing activated charcoal forming part of an **evaporative loss** control system (p. 99) in which the fumes given off by the petrol are eventually drawn back into the engine.

Fuel is transferred from the tank to the carburetter float chamber by a pump, often mechanically operated by an **eccentric** or off-centre disc on the camshaft. A typical pump (fig. 44) consists of a small chamber

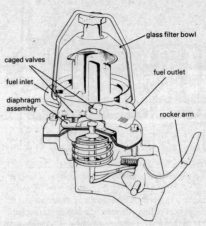

glass filter bowl

caged valves

fuel inlet

fuel outlet

diaphragm assembly

rocker arm

fig. 44. A mechanical fuel pump. The large spring exerts the pumping force and determines the fuel pressure, and when this reaches its preset value a cunning linkage allows the rocker arm to freewheel.

sealed by a flexible diaphragm and two non-return valves working in opposite senses. When the diaphragm is pulled out, the outlet valve closes, the inlet valve opens and fuel is drawn into the chamber; when the diaphragm is pressed in, the inlet valve closes, the outlet valve opens and fuel is forced out of the pump towards the carburetter. The diaphragm is pulled and pushed by a cunning linkage which fulfils two conditions. Firstly, although it pulls the diaphragm out, it does not press it in: this is done by a spring which thus determines the pressure in the system – usually 3.5–7.0 lb/sq in (24–48,000 Pa). Secondly, if the fuel pressure balances the spring pressure, the diaphragm remains in its lowermost position and the linkage disengages from it or freewheels until the output pressure falls again. In this way the carburetter float valve is not subjected to an excessive pressure.

An electrical fuel pump (fig. 45) works in a similar way, except that the diaphragm is displaced by a solenoid and contact-breaker mechanism. Some cars are fitted with electrical rotary impeller pumps, fully submerged at the bottom of the fuel tank. Pumps of a

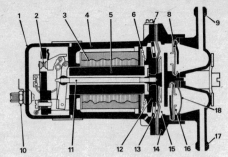

fig. 45. The SU electric fuel pump. 1, contact breaker cover; 2, contact breaker points; 3, magnet coil; 4, magnet housing; 5, magnet core; 6, return spring; 7, earth connection; 8, outlet valve; 9, outlet connection; 10, electrical supply connection; 11, pushrod; 12, magnet armature; 13, diaphragm assembly; 14, pump body; 15, pumping chamber; 16, inlet valve; 17, inlet connection; 18, filter.

different sort are generally used for fuel injection systems (p. 114).

The exhaust system

The section of the exhaust duct leading from each combustion chamber which lies within the cylinder head and close to the valve is called the **exhaust port**, and each exhaust port is connected to the branch of an **exhaust manifold** (fig. 46). Unlike the inlet manifold, though, which is often made of aluminium alloy, the exhaust manifold is always cast in iron, fabricated from steel tubing and sheet or made from some even more heat-resistant material because of the high temperatures it must withstand. When the engine runs continuously at full power, for example, the exhaust manifold often glows red hot.

The **exhaust pipe** to which it is connected, normally also a steel tube, is joined to one or more **silencers** which greatly reduce the noise made by the hot escaping gases – details are given in Chapter 3. The outer end of the final silencer is connected to a short **tailpipe** which usually emerges at the rear of the car so that the exhaust gases are released away from the car's occupants.

Although the exhaust manifold should last the life of the car, the remainder of the exhaust system is generally very vulnerable to corrosion, both from water, dirt and salt splashed on its outer surfaces and from the acidic products of combustion which attack from within. An unprotected exhaust system, therefore, may last no more than

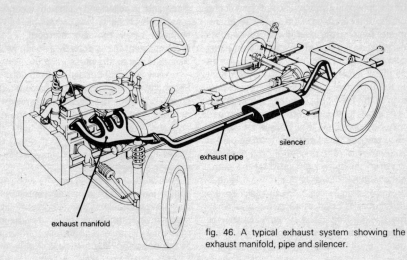

silencer

exhaust pipe

exhaust manifold

fig. 46. A typical exhaust system showing the exhaust manifold, pipe and silencer.

15–20,000 miles – clearly an unsatisfactory state of affairs. Accordingly, some cars are now fitted with exhaust systems made of aluminized steel and a few with systems made of stainless steel – which are additionally becoming available as replacements for many cars from independent suppliers.

The electrical system

Igniting the mixture of fuel and air inside the cylinder is a taxing problem. The first difficulty lies in the design of the sparking plug (fig. 47), the small component which screws into a hole in the combustion chamber and incorporates the small gap across which the spark jumps to ignite the air/fuel mixture. The **electrodes** which form this gap, for example, must be capable of withstanding chemical attack for long periods as well as high temperatures – the electrodes of modern plugs run at about 900°C. The ceramic insulator which separates them is also

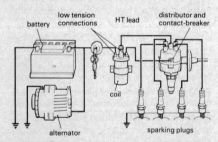

low tension connections

battery

HT lead

distributor and contact-breaker

coil

alternator

sparking plugs

fig. 47. The main electrical components are a coil ignition system, the battery which energizes it and the alternator which charges the battery (via rectifying circuits not shown).

exposed to the same unfriendly environment and the whole assembly must be gas-tight against peak combustion pressures of one thousand lb /sq in (around 70 bar).

Next there is the task of generating a voltage high enough to jump the gap. At least 15,000 V is needed, more if there is

turbulence in the mixture – violent eddying movements designed to improve the mixing of the fuel with the air. But unfortunately the voltage freely available is very much lower than this – most car batteries develop only 12 V, for example.

For many years this discrepancy has been resolved in most cars by a **coil** type of ignition system. Such a system relies upon the principle of the induction coil which essentially consists of two coils of wire, insulated from each other but wound on a common former about a core made of ferrous material to intensify the magnetic fields generated. There is a **primary** or **low** tension (LT) coil of relatively few turns which carries a large current and so is made of thick wire, and there is a **secondary** or **high** tension (HT) coil of many turns carrying a very small current and so wound in fine wire.

The primary coil is connected to the 12 V battery supply via a switch which is constantly turned on and off. This switch is called the **contact breaker** and consists of a stationary contact and a spring-loaded moving contact operated by the lobes of a cam attached to a shaft, which, like the camshaft, runs at half engine speed. Each time the contacts open, a large voltage is induced in the primary coil by the very rapid collapse of its own magnetic field. Due to the transformer effect, this voltage is further multiplied in proportion to the secondary: primary turns ratio – to about 20,000 V. This high voltage creates the spark that ignites the fuel.

One end of the primary coil is connected (usually) to the positive terminal of the battery, the contact-breaker being wired between the other end and **earth** – the vehicle's steel structure which is used as a handy return line. The circuit is completed by similarly earthing the negative terminal of the battery, so that when the **points** of the contact-breaker close, the primary coil is supplied with current. To produce the correct number of sparks per revolution, the number of lobes on the contact-breaker cam is equal to the number of cylinders. Thus a four-cylinder engine has a four-lobe cam which, since it is running at half engine speed, creates two sparks per turn of the crankshaft – the correct number for an engine of that type.

Above the contact-breaker lies the **distributor** which distributes the spark to each cylinder in turn. As for the primary coil, one end of the secondary is earthed through the vehicle's steel structure but the 'live' end is connected to a terminal post in the centre of a **distributor cap** made of insulating plastic. A carbon brush connects this terminal post to a rotating brass electrode forming part of a rotor arm which also turns at half engine speed. As this electrode revolves, its tip passes in succession a further set of electrodes spaced around the distributor cap and connected to the sparking plugs of the individual cylinders. The spark is able to jump, without significant wastage of electrical energy, across the small gap between the rotor arm tip and the distributive electrode.

But the ignition circuit is only one of several systems which draw electric current from the battery. Next in importance is the **starter motor** which turns the engine to start it and is disengaged when it fires. Other essential systems or devices requiring electrical power are the lights and windscreen wipers. Then there are those near-essential luxuries which contribute so much to the comfort of modern motoring, such as the heater fan and the rear window demister, plus other items like the cigar lighter and radio.

Clearly the energy stored in a battery will not last long if subjected to all these demands, so it is provided with a charging system driven by the engine. Until relatively recently, the essential component of this was a **direct current dynamo** usually driven from the nose of the crankshaft by a pulley and belt system. It was provided with a **voltage regulator** to maintain an output responsive to demand yet largely independent of variations in engine speed, and with

a **cut-out** which prevented the battery from feeding current back into it when the engine was at rest.

Dynamos are still used for some of the smaller and cheaper cars, but have been largely superseded by the **alternator**. The disadvantage of this is that the **alternating current** it generates has to be converted by **rectifiers** to direct current before it can be used to charge the battery and elsewhere. In return, however, alternators can safely be run to higher speeds and develop a greater output for their size and weight than direct-current dynamos, especially at low engine revs.

Cooling

All car engines are provided with cooling systems to dissipate surplus heat to the surrounding air. Such systems are needed because the materials used in the engine have their limitations. The combustion temperature of petrol is about 2500°C, yet the hottest part of the engine which is the exhaust valve must be kept down to temperatures in the 700–900°C range, and the piston crown to the 200–300°C region. At higher temperatures, quite apart from the possibility of an exhaust valve or cylinder head failure, the incoming air/fuel mixture is heated up so much that the **volumetric efficiency** (the ratio of the actual weight of mixture drawn in to the weight that would fill the cylinder at the outside air temperature and pressure) suffers badly and the engine loses power. In addition, hot spots in the combustion chamber begin to glow red-hot, causing pre-ignition and a further reduction in efficiency. For these reasons, it's always worth stopping to investigate if your engine starts to lose power or run roughly, since faults in the cooling system do not always make themselves immediately obvious in other ways (such as the production of clouds of steam). A cooling system is also needed to preserve the lubricating oil, which transfers quite a lot of heat from the undersides of the pistons to the crankcase and should be maintained at below about 150°C if its qualities are to be maintained and if its chemical deterioration is to be avoided.

There are three basic facts about cooling which need to be assimilated before considering the different systems in common use. Firstly, all cooling systems are fundamentally aircooling systems: in watercooled engines the heat is merely transferred to the cooling water first, before being passed to the outside air. Secondly, the rate of loss of heat from a hot surface to the air – the amount of heat lost per square inch per minute – is approximately proportional to the temperature difference between the air and the hot surfaces. Thus if 10 units of heat per square inch per minute are lost from a surface which is 20°C above the air temperature, 5 will be lost at 10°C above the air temperature. Thirdly, and similarly, the rate of loss of heat from a hot surface increases as the speed of the air flow over it is increased.

The majority of car engines produced today are cooled with the help of water rather than by air alone. The main disadvantages of a watercooling system are the weight of its waterjacket and radiator plus the risk of leakages and freezing in cold weather. An aircooled engine lacks these disadvantages, but has disadvantages of its own, though some are more imagined than real. An aircooled engine is often said to be more noisy than a watercooled engine, for example, but this view is not confirmed by such aircooled units as the Citroën flat-four which powers the GS range. Similarly, the cooling fan of an aircooled engine might be thought likely to absorb more power than that of a watercooled engine (especially when this is electrically driven) but there is no evidence for this belief in the Porsche flat-six engine and the good fuel consumption in relation to performance returned by the 911 range of cars that it powers. But an aircooled engine does have one very definite disadvantage: the poor performance and constantly fluctuating output of its heater, and this alone is enough to condemn it in the eyes of many designers and users – comfort being a highly important factor these days.

Watercooling

A watercooled engine (fig. 48) is provided with passages in its cylinder block and cylinder head through which water – or more precisely, a mixture of water and anti-freeze chemicals – is circulated under pressure by a pump to an external heat-exchanger called a **radiator**. The outside air is drawn through this radiator by a **cooling** fan.

Most water pumps are driven from the crankshaft by a V-belt and pulley system and run on the same spindle as the cooling fan, if this is engine driven, and lying behind it. Nearly all are of the centrifugal type, composed of a bladed impeller, often made of aluminium, rotating within a snail-shaped or circular housing, sometimes formed in the front of the cylinder block. Cool water from the bottom of the radiator is drawn into the central eye of the impeller and flung out-

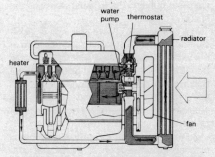

fig. 48. A watercooling system showing the radiator, fan, water pump, heater and thermostat. The latter controls the flow of water both to the radiator and through the by-pass pipe just above the water pump. When the engine is cold the main flow to the radiator is shut off completely and the water circulates straight back to the pump as shown by the dotted arrow.

wards by centrifugal force into the delivery passage. To prevent leakage of coolant along the spindle, special seals are provided, often composed of a fixed element formed from a carbon-based material spring-loaded against a rotating steel element, and in some designs the output pressure developed in the water delivered by the pump is used to squeeze the two sealing elements together and thus assist the spring loading.

From the pump the coolant is directed into the lower part of the cylinder block and generally passes through a ducting system which apportions roughly equal amounts to the spaces surrounding each of the cylinders. Usually each cylinder bore or liner is completely surrounded by a water jacket, but in some engines, especially those which have been increased in capacity over the years, the cylinders may be **siamesed**, that is, their outer walls may touch or join together where they are closest to each other.

Gathering heat, the water passes upwards, often through small holes at the top of the cylinder block, into the cylinder head. To prevent pockets of steam developing and to create a scouring action which improves heat transfer, baffles or nozzles speed up the flow and direct it at the vital areas surrounding the exhaust valve and the sparking plugs.

The water next flows through a jacket surrounding the inlet manifold, if this form of mixture heating is used, before emerging from the engine at an outlet point where the **thermostat** housing is located. Generally a common thermostat and housing is employed when there are two banks of cylinders.

Some twenty years ago it was common practice to use a form of thermostat controlled by a brass bellows containing a small amount of alcohol. As the coolant temperature rose, the bellows expanded with the expansion of the vapour inside it, lifting an associated water valve off its seat. But a **bellows thermostat** of this sort is influenced by the system pressure, so nowadays

wax thermostats are almost universally used.

A wax thermostat incorporates a small copper capsule lined with a sleeve of heavy paraffin wax impregnated with copper dust to improve its thermal conductivity. The capsule is linked to the valve seat and penetrated by a stainless steel needle (to which the valve itself is attached) passing through a rubber seal at its top end and surrounded by a rubber sleeve beneath. When the capsule is heated, the wax changes from a solid to a plastic state and expands, squeezing the rubber sleeve, pushing out the needle and opening the valve, a spring returning the needle and the valve when the wax cools again. The action of the capsule is not significantly affected by the pressure so it is ideal for modern cooling systems which run at 5–15 lb/sq in to raise the boiling point of water, to allow a higher working temperature, to increase the heat dissipation rate and to permit the use of a smaller radiator.

A small **jiggle pin** lets in air when the system is being filled but shuts under pump pressure when the engine is running. Some thermostat valves incorporate a small permanent bleed hole to promote flow past the capsule if it tends to remain in a pocket of stagnant water.

In modern engines the thermostat generally controls the flow of water to the radiator in conjunction with a by-pass pipe. When the engine is cold, the thermostat valve remains completely shut so the coolant cannot pass to the radiator but circulates entirely within the cylinder block and head via the by-pass pipe. As the engine temperature rises, more and more water is allowed to pass to the radiator, and the valve opening continuously fluctuates to maintain the system outlet temperature constant. Except under severe conditions, it seldom opens more than 30–40 thousandths of an inch (0.75–1.0 mm). In some engines both the main and the by-pass lines are controlled by a thermostat with a double valve, the by-pass flow gradually being cut off as the main flow increases.

The action of the thermostat profoundly influences the speed with which the engine warms up and hence its fuel consumption: a cold engine means poor fuel consumption. So it is well worth making sure that the thermostat of your car is working properly. Keep an eye on the temperature gauge, if there is one, and become suspicious if it always reads cold – or if the heater doesn't get hot. Thermostats are available in a range of temperature settings, but most cars these days are already fitted with the hottest type practical.

The radiator which is used to dissipate the surplus heat to the surrounding air is nearly always mounted at the front of the car to benefit from the **ram pressure** created by forward motion. Its function is to offer to the water the largest possible surface area in contact with the air. It thus consists of a **matrix** of small tubes through which the coolant passes, which are finned to increase their effective surface area and are separated by small gaps through which the air flows. The details vary, but a common arrangement involves vertical tubes connected by networks of zig-zag fins. Until relatively recently, radiators were made largely of copper because of its high thermal conductivity but owing to the high cost of this metal they are now sometimes made of aluminium – in an assembly of bonded rather than soldered parts.

Generally the water enters the radiator matrix via a **header tank** at its top end which is often sealed by a filler cap incorporating a spring-loaded pressure-relief valve. If the pressure rises above the set level, this valve lifts to vent the system to an overflow pipe. Like the thermostat, it incorporates a jiggle pin to let in air when the system cools down again.

One function of the header tank is to separate air from the water since aerated water is not an efficient cooling medium. In some cars therefore, the header tank is mounted remotely from the radiator at a high level. This arrangement is particularly common with radiators of the **crossflow** type in which the water flows across the unit rather than downwards, allowing a low, wide matrix suited to modern body designs.

Nowadays the overflow pipe is often connected to a vented **expansion bottle** from which water expelled during temporary overload conditions can afterwards be drawn back into the radiator. This creates a permanently sealed system which seldom needs topping up or maintenance, since modern antifreeze mixtures contain corrosion inhibitors and can safely be left in the system for up to four years.

At high speeds the forward motion of the car generally passes enough air through the radiator for adequate cooling even in hot weather. But at lower speeds, in traffic, and when working hard in a low gear, a cooling fan is needed. Often this is driven by the engine and has irregularly spaced blades to break the whining noise it would otherwise tend to generate. Its efficiency is improved if it is enclosed by a cowl.

The disadvantage of an engine-driven fan, however, is that it is generally designed to provide cooling which will cope with the most severe conditions imaginable – say towing a caravan up a steep hill in bottom gear during a heatwave. At most other times it is hardly needed at all, but it consumes a significant amount of power: up to ten per cent of the total output at maximum revs. Various ways of minimizing this wastage are available, one of the most common being the use of a **viscous coupling**. This is filled with a silicone fluid and slips at a certain torque level, limiting fan speed. More refined versions of such couplings additionally incorporate thermostatic control so that the fan does not turn at all when the engine temperature falls below a certain level. Other systems of control generally involve reducing the pitch of the fan blades at high speeds by spring loading against centrifugal force or by controlled flexibility.

But more and more modern cars are being fitted with thermostatically controlled electric fans. These consume little power and run surprisingly infrequently, even in hot weather.

In modern cars some of the cooling water is supplied to the heater, a small secondary heat exchanger, usually located under the facia. This has a matrix of tubes and fins, just like the radiator, but smaller. Air is forced through it to warm the interior either by a separate fan or by ram pressure or by a combination of both. Generally it is supplied with a small proportion of the fully heated water, bled from just before the thermostat, which is returned to the rear of the cylinder block after passing through the heater matrix. A valve regulating the water flow through the heater matrix is often used to govern the temperature of the heated air, though it generally proves an unprogressive and sluggish control device. An **air-blending** system of control, which involves the mixing of hot and cold streams of air, is much more satisfactory.

Nowadays a heater is rightly regarded as one of a car's most vital items of equipment, as much on the grounds of safety as comfort – the two being closely interrelated. Heaters designed to deliver up to 6 kW are not uncommon, which means that in exceptionally cold weather they may provide all the engine cooling needed, allowing the thermostat to remain completely closed. Conversely, running the heater at full blast may offer a useful emergency means of temporarily cooling the engine if the fan fails to work. In luxury cars the heater may work in conjunction with an air conditioning system which refrigerates and dehumidifies the incoming air.

Aircooling

An aircooled engine dissipates heat to the ambient air through an external surface which is artificially increased in area by fins (fig. 49) particularly around the cylinders and

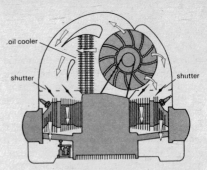

fig. 49. The aircooling system of the Volkswagen Beetle. A thermostatically controlled shutter regulates the flow of air to the cylinders.

cylinder head or heads. Careful design of these fins is needed, not only to ensure adequate overall cooling but also to prevent local overheating and distortion. As the fin temperature is usually about 160°C, the rate of loss of heat from them is nearly double that from the same area of the radiator of a watercooled engine, which generally runs at about 90°C. However, in order to transfer the heat from the inside of the engine to the outside, it is desirable to construct it of aluminium alloy, the thermal conductivity of which is more than three times greater than that of cast iron and more than four times greater than that of steel. Aircooled engines thus often have a double weight advantage over watercooled engines: not only are they lighter through the absence of a waterjacket and radiator, but also from the use of a lighter material, watercooled engines frequently being constructed from cast iron.

To complete the cooling arrangements a powerful fan is required and a system of ducts which allows air to be drawn in from the outside and blown over the finned external surfaces of the engine. Baffle plates deflect the air from the fan to the parts of the engine that would otherwise remain uncooled. The system is usually refined by a thermostatically controlled shutter which cuts off the supply of air when the engine is cold, for rapid warm-up, and thereafter regulates the flow to maintain a constant temperature. Some aircooled engines incorporate oil coolers which give a considerable reduction in temperature in hot weather and heavy load conditions.

As already mentioned, one of the big disadvantages of aircooling lies in the difficulty of using it to provide an efficient heater. The first problem is to extract enough heat, since air is a much poorer heat-transfer medium than water. The usual solution is to pass the incoming air through exhaust-gas heat exchangers as well as over the hot surfaces of the engine, but even with these, separate petrol-burning heaters are often needed for cold climates. Usually the heated air is forced into the interior of the car by the engine cooling fan itself, and this creates the second major problem: a heat output which is highly dependent on engine speed. The use of a separate electric fan mitigates this fault somewhat, but even so the warmth reaching the occupants of the car tends to vary a lot with the traffic conditions because there is no heat reservoir as there is for a watercooling system. This problem alone has been enough to make car manufacturers like Volkswagen and Porsche change over to watercooled engines for their latest models.

three **More About the Petrol Engine**

Conventional fuel

Were it not for a rain of tiny dying organisms on to the beds of ancient seas some hundreds of millions of years ago, the motorcar as we know it would almost certainly not exist. The decomposition of these dead organisms created the fossil fuel which we now know as crude oil. It is found right at the surface of the Earth in some parts of the world, but generally at considerable depths of anything up to several miles beneath it.

Crude oil is a dark, tarry liquid composed of many different substances all of which (except for small quantities of impurities) are compounds of hydrogen and carbon called **hydrocarbons**. These are separated by distillation into a series of products which are characterized by their boiling points, ranging from substances which are gaseous at room temperature to a near-solid bituminous residue. The principal gaseous and liquid fuels used for transport and heating are:

Notice that all these fuels have similar **calorific values**, which means that each one contains roughly the same amount of stored heat energy per pound or kilogram, measured either in BTU (British Thermal Units) per pound – the amount of heat required to warm 1 lb of water by 1°F – or in MJ (mega joules) per kilogram (1 joule = 1 Nm). But this does not make them all equally suitable for the petrol engine. To work well in such an engine, for example, a fuel must have the correct degree of **volatility** or readiness to vaporize. It must be volatile enough to give good cold starting, warm-up performance and fuel economy, but not so volatile as to become prone to carburetter icing in cold, damp conditions or vapour lock in hot weather.

Another highly important factor is a fuel's **octane rating** which determines its resistance to an unwanted phenomenon called knock which tends to take place towards the end of the combustion process. At first the

Fuel	Boiling point range	Calorific value		Raw octane number	Treated octane number
		(BTU/lb)	(MJ/kg)		
LPG (Liquefied Petroleum Gas)	−10–0°C	21,600	48.3	100	—
Petrol (Gasoline)	30–200°C	19,000	42.5	60–70	78–100 for cars
Paraffin (Kerosene)	150–275°C	18,900	42.1	Very low	—
TVO (Tractor Vaporizing Oil)	170–250°C	18,900	42.1	Very low	—
Diesel fuel (Derv or Gas-oil)	225–350°C	18,700	41.8	Very low	—

flame spreads smoothly and relatively slowly outwards from the sparking plug. But then, if conditions are not right, the high pressure and radiated heat generated may cause the remaining unburnt mixture, called the **end-gas**, to burn very suddenly and violently. This very rapid combustion reduces efficiency because it is too swift to generate useful power and can damage the engine if persistent and severe; it creates a knocking or pinking noise.

Knock (sometimes referred to as detonation) is influenced by several factors, but the three most important are the combustion chamber design, the compression ratio and the octane rating of the fuel used. For any given type of combustion chamber (p. 76) there is a limiting compression ratio, the **highest usable compression ratio**, which can be employed before knock begins. This is an important limitation, since the higher the compression ratio the more efficient the engine becomes.

The many different types of hydrocarbon present in crude oil differ widely in their resistance to knock. Indeed, it is from the name of one of these hydrocarbons, **iso-octane** (so called because it has eight atoms of carbon) that the term octane rating is derived. Iso-octane fuel has excellent resistance to knock and so was arbitrarily assigned the octane number 100. Another 'reference' fuel, on the other hand, called **n–heptane**, has very poor knock resistance and is given an octane rating of zero. Thus a fuel with a detonation resistance the same as that, say, of a 75 per cent iso-octane: 25 per cent n–heptane mixture has an octane rating of 75 – and so on.

The resistance to detonation of the fuel being investigated is compared to that of the reference fuel with the help of a special variable compression ratio engine. The compression ratio of this power unit, running under specified **load** (p. 71) and speed conditions is gradually increased until knock – which is detectable in various ways – just begins to occur. Two sets of conditions are used, the most common being specified by the Research Method of measurement and giving rise to **Research Octane Numbers** (RON). These are the numbers usually posted on the pumps of filling stations, and they are largely indicative of resistance to low-speed knock – the sort you get at about 20 mph in top gear (p. 310). The alternative Motor Method of measurement involves more severe conditions and leads to **Motor Octane Numbers** (MON) which are more representative of the less easily detected but far more damaging high-speed knock. For any given fuel, the MON number, usually quoted only in engineering journals or specialist publications, is generally about 10 units lower than the RON number. Thus a 97-octane (RON) fuel will have a MON rating of about 87.

By careful refining of the crude oil, therefore, and careful blending of its constituents, it is possible to increase the octane rating of petrol considerably. But only a limited supply of the required high-octane components is available naturally, so these are augmented by two additional chemical processes: **cracking**, which involves breaking large hydrocarbon molecules into smaller ones, and **reforming**, which involves rearranging molecules to give them different structures.

But even with the help of these processes, it is uneconomic to produce fuels with very high octane ratings. In the late twenties, however, it was discovered that the octane rating of petrol could be easily and markedly raised by adding to it small quantities of certain lead compounds such as **tetra–ethyl lead** (TEL). The increase obtained depends a lot on the base fuel used, but with enough additive to give a lead content of 0.5 g/litre (grams per litre) the RON value is increased by about 6, while with a lead content of 0.9 g/litre (about the most ever used for cars) the RON value is raised by roughly 10. The use of more additive still gives little further improvement in the octane rating.

This discovery led to gradual increases

over the years in the octane ratings of commercially available fuels, and to an associated rise in the average compression ratio of the petrol engine which in turn brought about increased efficiency and improved fuel consumption. Different grades of fuel for engines of different performance were introduced, and the average compression ratio rose from 6.8:1 in 1950 to 9.1:1 in 1970, the culmination of the trend being exemplified by the Audi 100 introduced in 1968 with an engine having a compression ratio of 10.8:1. But the trend came to a halt in the early 1970s: no engines requiring fuel with an octane rating of more than 100 have been introduced in Britain since 1973, and the ratings of the four grades of fuel currently available are slightly lower than they were a few years ago.

This fall was largely brought about by widespread fears that the many thousands of tons of lead from the anti-knock additive released into the atmosphere annually by road vehicles constituted an important health hazard. And in the United States a lead-free grade of petrol has in any case been available for several years, because the catalysts in the exhaust-gas reactors (p. 102) extensively used to cut air pollution are poisoned by the lead in ordinary petrol.

But the elimination of lead from petrol or its reduction below certain levels creates other problems. The difficulties spring from the extreme importance now attached to the conservation of fuel and from the fact that the extensive use of high-compression engines is at present the best known way of doing this. But today's high-compression engines require high-octane fuel, and high-octane/low-lead fuels are not only more expensive to produce but also involve increased consumption of crude oil – the very thing that most countries are trying hard to avoid.

In view of these conflicting tendencies, most governments have so far settled for relatively modest reductions in the lead level. In Britain, for example, the maximum lead level has been voluntarily reduced from 0.84 g/litre in 1972 to 0.45 g/litre in 1978 and current legislation will limit the level to 0.15 g/litre by 1985. In this we are following the example set by West Germany, where the maximum lead levels were reduced from 0.64 g/litre in 1971 to 0.15 g/litre in 1976. For a short period some engine failures after prolonged high-speed motorway running were attributed to this policy, but in general it has had little adverse effect on German cars or their fuel consumption. Quite recently, the British government declared its intention to press for legislation requiring, by 1990 at the latest, lead-free petrol to be mandatory for new cars in all EEC countries.

Alternative fuels

General

One of the most important consequences of the 1973 Middle East war was its effect on politicians, economists and planners. It forced them to take notice of the fact that the world's supply of crude oil is not infinitely large and must eventually run out. At that time, indeed, it seemed that crude oil reserves might be exhausted very rapidly – in a mere thirty years or so. Even in 1976 the world's oil consumption growth rate was still nearly 4 per cent annually, a level of expansion which could only be met by finding a new source about four times larger than the Forties Field every year – hardly likely.

Since then the situation has changed considerably. Firstly, through widespread economies and efficiency improvements in all areas of energy consumption – not least the motor industry – the worldwide demand for oil has become virtually static. In 1982 it was 2,986 million barrels a day, and it is not expected to have increased much by the end of this century. Secondly, many of the panic scenarios of the late seventies ignored the obvious fact that, quite apart from the various 'renewable' sources of energy which are available, including hydro-electric power, there are huge reserves of other kinds of fossil fuel – such as coal, for example. And there is no reason why a proportion of the coal in the Earth's crust cannot be turned into petrol – in South Africa this has been done on a commercial basis for many years.

But from the motorist's point of view, a far more important factor is the existence of enormous, largely untapped, further reserves of crude oil contained in shale (a kind of soft, slate-like rock) and tar sands. So when all the known and estimated further reserves are added together, the probability now is that the Earth's fossil fuels will last anything from 240 years to over 2000 years.

The snag, though, is that despite the petrol-pump price-cutting wars of recent years, these fuels will become progressively more expensive to obtain. The search for new sources will lead to ever more inaccessible and inhospitable places; already it is far more expensive to extract oil from Alaska or the North Sea than it is from the Middle East. And it is much more expensive yet again to extract it from shale or tar sands. Clearly, therefore, the renewed interest, precipitated by the energy crisis, in the reduction of the fuel consumption of the motorcar is certain to intensify in the future.

To make existing supplies last as long as possible, many planners now believe that the use of crude oil should be confined to the purposes for which it is best suited – chemical manufacture and the production of liquid fuels for transport purposes – leaving coal, nuclear reactors and other sources of energy to fulfil the remaining requirements such as domestic heating and the generation of electricity. It is possible that, at some time in the future, almost all energy available will be in the form of electricity, and this could either be used to produce a standard fuel or to power vehicles directly. But the introduction of a satisfactory electrical storage system still seems a long way off. The great bulk and weight of lead–acid batteries (p. 148) serve to highlight the marked advantages of liquid fuels over most alternatives for vehicles.

There are, however, a number of fuels other than petrol itself which may play a part in the years ahead:

Diesel fuel

An existing fossil fuel which is extracted at a lower energy cost than petrol. It can be used very efficiently, due to the high compression ratios (16–23:1) of diesel engines, and other factors. But its widespread adoption would mean a massive change-over from the petrol to the diesel engine which is generally a good deal heavier and more expensive to make, though advanced diesel cars such as Volkswagen's diesel version of the Golf may change the position.

Wide cut distillate

A possible fuel of the future which would still be obtained from crude, but including paraffin, the cruder constituents of petrol and some diesel components. Even more easily and cheaply refined than diesel fuel, it could only be used by advanced stratified charge engines (p. 125), so is not in production yet.

Petrol from coal

A genuine alternative to conventional petrol which was produced in Germany and elsewhere during the Second World War. Its costs would be high, but these could be reduced by combining the manufacture of petrol with that of other products. A viable possibility since known coal reserves are very large, though it is unlikely that more than a small percentage of the total liquid fuel requirement could be satisfied in this way.

Alcohol

Both **methanol** (methyl alcohol) and **ethanol** (ethyl alcohol) are entirely suited to the petrol engine, having octane ratings of around 100. But their calorific values are about half that of petrol, so their use would involve large fuel tanks. They could be used to extend petrol, either by mixing or as a separate additive. Methanol could be produced from coal, but not at much advantage over petrol, though it might find considerable application as a fuel for fuel cells. Ethanol can be manufactured in a number of ways including the fermentation of organic material, and is now being produced in Brazil from sugar cane for automotive use.

LPG

Liquid Petroleum Gas; an existing fossil fuel found in association with crude oil and a low-level by-product of refinery operation. It is easily reduced to a liquid at normal ambient temperatures by low pressure, and in this form (often used for cooking) has roughly the same calorific value as petrol. It also has an octane rating of around 100 and can be made to burn cleanly, giving low levels of exhaust pollution. It is available at present only in small quantities, though future supplies may be substantially greater.

Natural gas

Natural gas or methane is an excellent fuel, but is unlikely to gain wide usage due to storage difficulties: to become liquid it must be kept at $-160°C$. Alternatively, it could be stored at pressures of 3000-5000 lb/sq in ($20-35 \times 10^6$ Pa).

Paraffin

Petrol engines with special inlet systems will run on paraffin, and do run on the very similar TVO – but very inefficiently, since the octane rating is so low that the compression ratio must be limited to about 4:1. Such fuels are not likely to do much better in any foreseeable engine of the future except the gas turbine, and this is unlikely ever to be suited

to cars, though it might prove viable for long-distance buses and trucks.

Hydrogen

A possible fuel, but it can only be extracted from other materials (e.g. water) at a high energy cost and is at present extremely difficult to store.

Combustion – Power and Economy

Mixture strength

The most vital characteristic of an internal combustion engine is the efficiency with which it burns the fuel supplied to it. Many factors influence this efficiency for a petrol engine – the design of the combustion chambers, the compression ratio, etc. – but perhaps the most basic of all is the strength of the air/fuel mixture. A mixture containing 14.7 parts by weight of air to 1 of fuel is said to be chemically correct or **stoichiometric**. When this is ignited, all the carbon in the hydrocarbon fuel should in theory be converted to CO_2 (carbon dioxide) and all the hydrogen to H_2O (water).

But to develop maximum power – or obtain the best possible fuel consumption – completeness of combustion is less important than its speed. The combustion process must not be too rapid, of course – because it then leads to detonation which we have already learned must be avoided. Even so, normal combustion in a modern engine is very rapid, so time is of the utmost importance.

It is important for two basic reasons. The first is that for maximum power the peak of the pressure rise created by combustion must occur soon after top dead centre. The second is that when combustion is slow, the heat energy in the fuel tends to leak away through the cylinder walls as heat, rather than remaining as pressure to be converted into useful mechanical work.

Hence the mixture is normally enriched – more fuel and less air than the stoichiometric proportions – to around a strength of 12–14:1 in order to speed up the combustion process and give maximum power. In addition, the excess fuel acts as an internal coolant, keeping the maximum temperatures attained within bounds and so preventing engine damage by overheating. Futher enrichment of the mixture, however, would reduce the combustion speed, until eventually at a strength of about 8:1 the incoming charge would become so wet that the flame would be extinguished.

As the mixture is weakened from the stoichiometric point, the combustion rate also slows down, reducing the power developed. But at the same time the gradually increasing amounts of air and hence oxygen available mean that combustion becomes more and more complete. Thus if the ignition timing is suitably chosen to compensate for the delays involved, more energy is at first extracted from the fuel until, at a mixture strength of about 17:1 for conventional engines, the fuel consumption in relation to the energy extracted is at its lowest. This quantity is called the **specific fuel consumption** and is the amount of fuel consumed per unit of energy produced. In Imperial units it is measured in pints or pounds of fuel per bhp-hour (sometimes kW-hour) and in metric units in grams or litres of fuel per bhp-hour or kW-hour.

With further weakening of the mixture beyond the maximum economy point, the specific consumption rises. The power developed falls off rapidly, too, partly because the combustion rate slows down as already explained, partly because the amounts of fuel being burned – and hence of energy released – are smaller. Eventually, at an air/fuel ratio of around 18:1 the mixture becomes too weak for a conventional engine to burn at all.

These trends are nicely illustrated by what

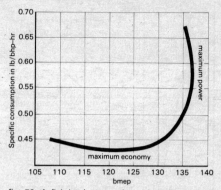

fig. 50. A fish-hook curve shows how bmep – a measure of engine power – varies with the specific fuel consumption. The curve is obtained at full throttle and a constant engine speed by varying the air/fuel ratio.

is known as a **fish-hook curve** (fig. 50) obtained by plotting specific fuel consumption against some convenient measure of engine power, usually the **brake mean effective pressure** which is the mean pressure sustained throughout the combustion stroke (p. 88). Another way of looking at them is to consider graphs (fig. 51) of power and specific fuel consumption plotted against air/fuel ratio. They show that the power falls more quickly when the mixture is weakened than when it is enriched, and illustrate the considerable size of the reduction in power when the specific fuel consumption is at its minimum.

These relationships apply to engines running with the throttle wide open or at full **load**. An engine is said to be fully loaded when it is delivering full power at a given speed – because it is being loaded with the maximum resistance it will overcome at that speed. To overcome that resistance its throttle must of course be fully open, though the power developed will only be the maximum appropriate to the particular engine speed, not the outright maximum. Fortunately for the carburetter designer, the mixture requirements do not vary a lot with engine speed: if an air/fuel ratio of 13:1 is correct for

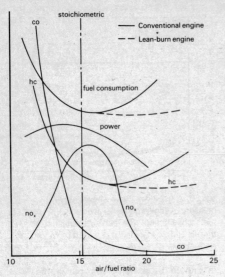

fig. 51. Power and specific fuel consumption versus air/fuel ratio. The power falls more quickly when the mixture is weakened than when it is enriched. Few conventional engines will run on air/fuel ratios leaner than about 18:1, but special lean-burn engines (p. 79) will. The effect of air/fuel ratio on the three major exhaust pollutants (p. 98) is also shown.

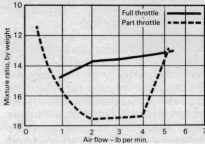

fig. 52. Modern fixed-choke carburetters are designed to deliver a part-throttle weak mixture for improved economy.

full load at 2000 rpm, it will also be almost correct for full load (and power) at, say, 6000 rpm.

In normal driving, however, the accelerator pedal is relatively infrequently pressed hard to the floor to open the throttle wide. Part throttle or part load running therefore takes up a high proportion of total driving time and so is of vital importance. But for various reasons (p. 94) a petrol engine runs very inefficiently under part throttle conditions. The associated deterioration in fuel consumption, though, can be minimized through the use of a special weak mixture.

For during part throttle running the driver by definition does not require full power at the given engine speed – if he did, he would open the throttle fully. The drop in power which accompanies the use of a weak mixture is thus unimportant: what matters is

that the small or moderate amounts of power which are required should be extracted from the engine in return for the minimum possible expenditure of fuel. Most modern carburetters are therefore designed to deliver (fig. 52) two kinds of mixture: a rich mixture for full load running and a special weak economy mixture with an air/fuel ratio of around 16–17:1 for part throttle running.

The slow burning of such a weak economy mixture means that its delivery must be accompanied by additional ignition advance to compensate for the delays involved. Providing that the ignition is advanced in this way, the extra heat released by the slowness of the combustion causes no damage to the engine at moderate proportions of the total output. But to prevent overheating, it is necessary to revert to the full load rich mixture, even when running on part load, at about 80 per cent of maximum power. And if the ignition is not adequately advanced, the extra heat released by the weak mixture, and the prolongation of combustion until the exhaust valve opens, may cause damage.

Ignition timing

So far the importance of the duration of the combustion process has been emphasized, but the equal importance of its correct phasing or timing has only been touched upon. The basic problem is that although combustion does tend to increase speed as the engine revs rise, there is an initial delay which remains roughly constant. Assume, for the moment, that the overall delay between ignition and the peak of the pressure rise is roughly 1/1200 sec. This corresponds to 30° of crankshaft rotation at 6000 rpm, but at 1000 rpm it corresponds to 5° only. As the speed of an engine rises, therefore, some means must be provided of progressively advancing the ignition point or spark so that the peak of the pressure rise always occurs at the optimum point in the cycle – which experience has shown is about 12° after top dead centre. The maximum advance required generally ranges from 10° to 30° before top dead centre.

For this reason most engines are fitted with a **centrifugal advance** mechanism. This mechanism (described fully on p. 165) involves a pair of bob-weights restrained by springs, which, under the influence of centrifugal force, progressively twist round the contact-breaker cam in relation to the shaft driving it, as the engine speeds up. Hence by advancing the point in relation to crankshaft rotation at which the contact-breaker points are forced open, the spark is triggered earlier in the cycle. Increasingly, the mechanized ignition advance device is being replaced by an electronic ignition control system.

If the combustion delay were indeed absolutely constant, the amount of spark advance needed in degrees would be exactly proportional to engine speed and the graph of advance against engine revs would be a straight line. In fact the delay does not remain constant, so a typical optimum advance curve has small peaks and troughs in it.

If the spark is gradually advanced beyond the optimum point the power developed begins to fall off until eventually detonation sets in and damage to the engine may occur. If the ignition is too far retarded, on the other hand, the power again falls off, but more quickly, and the late burning raises the temperature of the exhaust gases, leading to rapid damage to the exhaust valve.

Still more spark advance than that provided centrifugally is required at part throttle to compensate for the slow combustion of the weak economy mixture which many carburetters are designed to deliver under these conditions. Fortunately, when the throttle is only partly open, the pressure in the inlet manifold falls significantly below the atmospheric level – the inlet manifold depression therefore increases – and this reduced pressure can be used to operate the necessary **vacuum advance** mechanism. This essentially consists (full details p. 165) of a spring-loaded flexible diaphragm, exposed to atmospheric pressure on one side and inlet manifold pressure on the other, which is linked to the plate carrying the contact-breaker points. Under part throttle conditions, the inlet manifold depression flexes the diaphragm, rotating the contact-breaker plate with respect to its camshaft, thus advancing the spark.

Load and manifold depression

Inlet manifold depression is a side-effect of throttle opening which has an important bearing on many aspects of engine operation and which varies widely with the conditions. At full load and low rpm, for example, the throttle offers little obstruction to the flow of air and fuel which it meets edgewise, so the depression in the manifold will be small – or in other words its pressure will be nearly atmospheric. At full throttle and high rpm, however, the pressure will be a little lower (that is, the manifold depression will be slightly higher) since even the minor obstructions in the inlet system create a noticeable pressure drop when the flow rate of the air and fuel is high.

The inlet manifold depression rises still further as the throttle opening is reduced, reaching a high value when it is fully closed. In the closed position the throttle shuts off the inlet duct almost completely, being held open a few degrees against an adjustment screw to admit enough fuel and air to keep the engine idling. As soon as the pressure inside the throttle drops to one half or less of the atmospheric pressure outside it, the speed of the incoming mixture rushing through the small gap left open is raised to the speed of sound. This condition exists during idling when the inlet manifold pressure may fall to about 5 lb/sq in (0.35 bar) compared to the 14.7 lb/sq in (1.0 bar) of atmospheric pressure. When **sonic flow** of this sort is established, the very small throttle opening becomes **sonically choked**: the air and fuel can only flow through it at a certain fixed rate determined by the size of the opening no matter how low the pressure in the inlet manifold.

Consider, for example, what happens on the **overrun** – when the throttle is closed and the car is travelling forward under its own momentum, as when descending a hill. The engine then sucks furiously against the almost closed throttle, reducing the inlet manifold pressure still further to about 2 lb/sq in (0.14 bar), but the sonic choking of the very small orifice involved prevents any increase in the flow of fuel and air.

The almost permanent existence in the inlet manifold of a pressure below atmospheric represents a source of potential energy which is often put to good use in **vacuum servos** of various sorts – such as the vacuum ignition timing advance system already mentioned – but particularly for reducing brake pedal effort. And the variations in inlet manifold pressure – easily detected by an inexpensive **vacuum gauge** – provide a useful means of monitoring engine performance.

Idling

When an engine idles, sonic flow across the throttle valve is only one of several special conditions which are brought into existence. One basic cause is that the cylinder tends

already to be partially filled with exhaust gases left over from the previous combustion when fresh mixture is admitted. This is partly because the exhaust gases do not reach a high enough pressure to escape rapidly and completely from the combustion chambers, and partly a result of the **valve overlap** being inappropriate to the very low rpm. Valve overlap is the name given to the universally employed form of timing by which the inlet and exhaust valves are simultaneously held open during the last part of the exhaust stroke and the beginning of the induction stroke (full details on p. 83). During idling, overlap tends to cause the exhaust gases to be pushed right back into the inlet duct at the very end of the exhaust stroke, causing dilution of the incoming charge. Equally overlap also allows some fresh mixture to pass straight through the combustion chamber into the exhaust pipe. Since the exhaust gas residuals are chemically inert, containing little or no oxygen, the air/fuel mixture supplied will only burn if it is very rich, so carburetters generally incorporate special idle delivery systems.

On the overrun, combustion conditions deteriorate still further. The sonic flow effect prevents the supply of fuel and air from being increased, so the engine may receive at 5000 rpm a quantity of mixture which is just sufficient for 500 rpm. Such a small amount of mixture is virtually unburnable and mostly passes straight through to the exhaust system. Slow, weak combustion may occasionally occur, igniting the unburned mixture in the exhaust system and creating a characteristic overrun backfiring and banging which is accentuated if there is a leak which admits additional air. All this has an important bearing on the exhaust emission problems described later in this chapter.

Cold starting

One of the principal defects of nearly all engines is the lack of consistency or homogeneity in the mixture supplied by conventional carburetters. As a result, the **distribution** is often poor: at certain speeds some cylinders tend to receive too much fuel and others too little, whereas at a different engine speed the inequality may be reversed. This lack of homogeneity is in turn largely due to the erratic and unpredictable behaviour of the fuel droplets – behaviour which has been made strikingly visible in experimental engines fitted with glass manifolds. These droplets tend to cling to the walls of the manifold, form puddles in its floor and to negotiate bends with less ease than the air which supports them.

These particular problems disappear if the fuel is completely vaporized. Experiments have demonstrated that not only is the distribution greatly improved, but smoother, cleaner and more efficient combustion results. However, no way of achieving complete vaporization without introducing an unacceptable power loss has yet been developed. Engines running on a wholly gaseous fuel such as LPG, though, are free from mixture distribution problems, to the benefit of exhaust gas cleanliness.

The proper functioning of an ordinary engine depends upon at least a proportion of the liquid fuel being vaporized. It is to improve this vital vaporization that the inlet manifolds of nearly all engines are either heated by a water jacket or by the exhaust gases via a **hotspot**. Yet under many running conditions the inlet manifold walls are partly covered by a thin layer of liquid fuel which is continuously being vaporized by the heat supplied – helped by reductions in pressure when the throttle is fully or partly closed – and continuously being maintained by a supply of fresh fuel.

But when the engine has fully cooled, it may not at first run at all, because the droplets of fuel fall to the manifold floor and are not vaporized – even when the ambient temperature is high – so that very little fuel is drawn into the combustion chambers. Hence to start a cold engine a much enrichened mixture is required, typically having an air/fuel ratio of around 2:1, though the lower the air temperature the richer the initial mixture which must be supplied and the longer the period for which it is required. The carburetter device which supplies this mixture is usually called the **choke** and is fully described later in this chapter (p. 107). Once the engine fires and runs, it begins to warm up and the starting mixture can be gradually weakened. Providing a mixture of the proper richness and no more, progressively weakening it in the correct way, and ensuring rapid warm up can together have a profound influence on the fuel consumption, especially for short journeys. For this reason, the inlet manifolds of some cars nowadays are provided with electrical heaters which are energized during the warm up period to reduce its length.

Acceleration enrichment

The extensive wetting of the inlet manifold wall has its effect on another aspect of engine operation. Imagine that you are cruising along at a steady speed with a fully warmed engine, a significant proportion of the fuel entering the combustion chambers being evaporated from a stable and continuously replenished layer of liquid petrol on the manifold walls. Now suppose that you take your foot off the accelerator pedal to slow down behind a lorry. The throttle closes, creating a high manifold depression or low pressure, and lowering the pressure above a volatile liquid like petrol greatly increases the rate at which it evaporates. The hitherto stable layer of fuel therefore speedily vaporizes away. If you then accelerate to overtake, there will be no source of fuel for vaporization in the inlet manifold, the mixture will momentarily become weak and the car will hesitate. To compensate for this effect, it is generally necessary to provide some temporary enrichment of the mixture when accelerating. This is done in various ways, often by a device in the carburetter called an **accelerator pump** (p. 109).

Combustion chamber design

An engine's compression ratio, we have already learned, is the most important factor influencing its efficiency. The most important factor after the fuel's octane rating which in turn influences the highest usable compression ratio is the design of the combustion chamber. As already mentioned, too, the limiting factor is the onset of detonation. This occurs because the flame, spreading out from the sparking plug, heats the remaining unburned gases by radiation and compression, and may eventually cause them to ignite spontaneously and violently. The greater the distance from the sparking plug to the furthest point in the combustion chamber, the higher will be the final pressure and temperature of the end-gas and the greater the chance of detonation. The first requirement of a good combustion chamber, therefore, is that it should be compact in size, with a centrally located sparking plug

giving roughly equal flame paths to the furthest points. The same requirement is also important for a completely different reason: combustion chamber compactness generally goes with a low surface-to-volume ratio which minimizes wasteful heat losses.

Most early engines were fitted with **side valves** (fig. 53a) which are easy to operate mechanically, for the resultant valve train resembles a pushrod system in which the valves themselves are substituted for the pushrods. But the high surface-to-volume ratio of such chambers and the tortuous path of their associated inlet ducts make them inherently inefficient and they have long been wholly abandoned. Only in the six-cylinder Land-Rover engine used until the late seventies did some trace of the side-valve concept survive, since it had combustion chambers with overhead inlet valves and side exhaust valves (fig. 53b).

All other engines in use since about 1950, however, have had overhead valves, and the

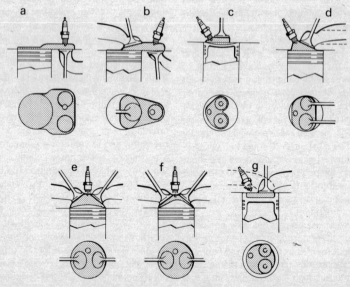

fig. 53. Different types of combustion chamber: (a) side valve; (b) overhead inlet, side exhaust; (c) bathtub; (d) wedge; (e) low-compression hemi-spherical; (f) high-compression hemispherical; (g) Heron or bowl-in-piston.

oldest form of combustion chamber associated with them, still widely used – by B L, for example, in their A series engines – is the **bathtub** type (fig. 53c). It generally has straight sides and semi-circular ends in plan view – B L's is heart-shaped – with slightly arched walls. It is reasonably compact yet allows the valves to be mounted both vertically and in line – again, a simple arrangement mechanically. The sparking plug may be mounted between them, or better still, at an angle in the sidewall and slightly closer to the exhaust valve than the inlet valve so that combustion begins in the hottest part of the chamber and ends in the coolest to inhibit detonation.

Along one axis the bathtub chamber is usually overlapped by the cylinder bores for a reason which is basic to the combustion process. This is the importance of inducing **turbulence** or rapid and random eddying movements in the gases before and during combustion. It is only because a certain degree of turbulence created by the upward movement of the piston on the compression stroke is inherent in all engines that combustion is not merely enough for useful power to be developed but also speeds up as the revs rise, lasting for progressively shorter periods of time but roughly the same angle of crankshaft rotation. (But as already described, on p. 72, there is an initial and roughly constant delay, and it is largely for this that the centrifugal advance system is needed.)

Some of this turbulence is naturally created by the upward, compressive movement of the piston, forcing the mixture into the combustion chamber, but two much more specific processes are also involved. The first of these takes place where the piston overlaps the combustion chamber. At top dead centre this area very closely approaches the flat cylinder head surface, forming a **squish** zone which usually occupies about 25 per cent of the piston crown area. Squish is the word used to describe the violent ejection of the trapped mixture

back into the central part of the combustion chamber, a process which is highly effective in promoting turbulence. At the same time the squish zone also acts as a **quench** area: its large local surface-to-volume ratio cools down the end-gases, inhibiting detonation.

But a major defect of the bathtub combustion chamber is the proximity of its walls to the inlet valve which tends to restrict the inward flow of air and fuel (the exhaust valve is less sensitive to this obstruction to flow). An alternative, less subject to this fault, is the **wedge** type of combustion chamber (fig. 53d) introduced from America in the late thirties and used in a number of current engines including the Rover V-8 units. The inlet valve, mounted in the inclined roof of the chamber beside the exhaust valve, is not constricted when it opens, and the flame paths from the sparking plug – usually mounted on one side – to the remotest parts of the main chamber are short and roughly equal. The overall surface-to-volume ratio, too, is low, but there is an efficient quench/squish zone at the thin end of the wedge.

Most ordinary cars made do with side valves – or at best bathtub combustion chambers with vertical overhead valves – during the years before the Second World War, but a much more advanced form of combustion chamber was devised almost as soon as the advantages of overhead valves were realized. This was the **hemispherical** or part spherical type with inclined valves (fig. 53e) used for racing and high-performance cars, one of the earliest examples being the Grand Prix Peugeot of 1912, designed by a brilliant Swiss engineer, Ernest Henry.

Since a sphere has the smallest possible surface area in relation to its volume, the first advantage of a hemispherical combustion chamber is its low surface-to-volume ratio. And since it has a sparking plug which is centrally mounted in its roof, the flame paths are equal and fairly short. There is no squish area, but to compensate for this the inlet port is usually given a tangential alignment to impart **swirl** to the incoming mixture, a rotary motion about the cylinder axis which like turbulence, helps to keep the combustion process both smooth and rapid.

But a hemispherical combustion chamber's greatest advantage lies with its valves. Not only are these completely free of masking by the chamber walls, but also, being at a marked inclination – 45° or more – to the cylinder axis, can easily be made large and well cooled. Hence the hemispherical combustion chamber is generally used for high-performance power units, one of the best-known British examples being the six-cylinder Jaguar engine, though more recently the arrangement has been adopted for the engines of front-wheel-drive Fords. For some modern versions of the chamber, the roof is not truly hemispherical, but divided into two halves like the roof of a house, such a variant of the basic design being called a **pentroof** combustion chamber.

One drawback of this type of combustion chamber is the cost and complexity of its valve train. Generally this involves twin overhead camshafts, though the inclined valves can be actuated through a single overhead camshaft and rockers, or even by pushrods and rockers.

If the compression ratio is to be reasonably high, another drawback of the hemispherical rather than the pentroof type of chamber is the need for a highly domed piston to reduce the clearance volume. The combustion chamber then assumes a poor 'orange peel' shape with a large surface-to-volume ratio (including the piston crown) and no great efficiency, especially in modern engines with clearance volumes made inherently large by big cylinder bores (fig. 53f).

Even in its classic form, moreover, the hemispherical combustion chamber does not quite conform to its own logic, since for short and equal flame paths the plug should be at the centre of the hemisphere, not on its surface. It was this thinking which led to the **bowl-in-piston** or **Heron** combustion chamber which is effectively a hemispherical chamber turned upside down: in place of a hemisphere over a (hopefully) flat piston, it consists (fig. 53g) of a completely flat cylinder-head face above a bowl formed in the piston crown. In this way the sparking plug is truly located at the centre of the chamber, and by giving the bowl (which need not be hemispherical) a flat rim, a very effective squish/quench area can be provided. This arrangement, a feature of direct-injection diesel engines (p. 124), was used by Rover for their 2000/2200 model and by Ford for their Kent family of four-cylinder in-line engines and for their Essex family of V-4 and V-6 engines.

Most bowl-in-piston combustion chambers, however, are provided with tangential ports to promote swirl. This is accentuated by the upward movement of the depression in the piston crown into which the rotating mixture is compressed, reducing its turning radius and increasing its speed of rotation just as gyrating ballet dancers or ice-skaters speed up when they drop their arms. Unfortunately there is a snag, for the energy absorbed by the swirl is obtained at the expense of increased **pumping losses** and less efficient filling of the cylinder with fresh mixture. Even so, bowl-in-piston engines are capable of very high outputs in relation to their capacities and can run on high compression ratios without risk of detonation.

Nowadays, however, engine designers have to take into account two further vital factors, the first of which is the need to ensure that exhaust pollution levels conform to complex legal requirements (more about this most important subject later in this chapter – see p. 95 onwards). The second is the need to offset the steadily rising cost of fuel by improving petrol consumption. From both these points of view the bowl-in-piston configuration is now judged to be less satisfactory, and it has thus fallen out of favour since the late 1970s.

So important has fuel consumption become since the 1973 energy crisis that the world's motor manufacturers have been spending vast sums each year investigating ways of making the internal combustion engine more efficient. One result has been a significant improvement in the fuel consumption of the typical European-style car merely through attention to the details of carburation, compression ratio, combustion chamber designs, ignition system and so on. (American cars have, proportionately, improved still more because they offered so much scope for reductions in weight and size.) Thus the average fuel consumption of all the new cars registered in Britain was 7.5 per cent better in 1981 than it was in 1978, a mere three years before.

But much more fundamental improvements are being sought. Some engineers feel that a simple change-over (p. 119) from the petrol engine to the inherently more efficient diesel engine, for example, might be the answer. But for the immediate future at least, most of the major car manufacturers are concentrating their efforts on new forms of combustion chamber which will allow high compression ratios of 12:1 or more and very lean mixtures with air/fuel ratios of 20:1 or greater to be used while running on normal four star, three star or even two star fuel. One basic problem is the creation of sufficient turbulence to ensure the complete combustion within the required time of the very slow-burning lean mixtures envisaged for part-throttle economy running. Another is to prevent the very high compression ratio being considered from causing detonation when using the richer mixtures needed for full power.

There is now a general belief that these conflicting requirements can be reconciled, perhaps partly because of the 'Fireball' combustion chamber invented by Swiss engineer Michael May. Adopted by Jaguar for their V-12 engines, this combustion chamber incorporates (fig. 54) an inlet valve lying in a shallow squish area which is connected by a channel to a deeper and bathtub-shaped pocket surrounding the exhaust valve. The upward movement of the piston creates

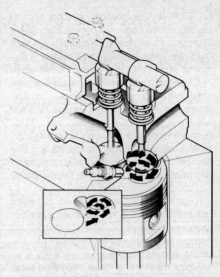

fig. 54. The May Fireball combustion chamber as developed for the Jaguar V-12 engine.

high-velocity swirl and a looping flow pattern which concentrates the charge near the exhaust valve. With Fireball combustion chambers the Jaguar XJS model gained a slight increase in power, a significant reduction in its levels of exhaust gas pollutant emissions and a fuel consumption improvement in the region of 20 per cent. Its fuel consumption for the ECE driving cycle (p. 103) improved from 12.7 mpg to 15.6 mpg, for example, and from 18.6 mpg to 22.5 mpg at a steady 75 mph. Other high-compression, high-turbulence systems are being developed by all the major motor manufacturers.

Influence of electronics

Both the introduction of **lean-burn** high-compression engines of the May type and improvements in the fuel consumption of ordinary power units is being greatly helped by the advent of electronic systems of various sorts, particularly control systems using microchip computers. Normally the first step is to fit a transistorized ignition system (p. 166) which not only ensures that a high-energy spark can be made available to ignite the very weak mixtures demanded, but – just as important – eliminates the deterioration in performance with the passage of time inevitable when a mechanical contact-breaker is fitted. The next stage is often electronic control of the ignition timing. This is far more precise than vacuum/centrifugal control and can be designed to respond to a number of factors additional to engine speed and manifold vacuum such as throttle angle, air flow and coolant temperature.

Since many cars are now fitted with electronically controlled fuel injection systems, and since many of the control variables are the same for both the fuel injection and the timing systems, the current tendency is to combine them into a single integrated **electronic engine management** system (p. 168). One example is the Bosch Motronic system, fitted to various BMW models, which controls both fuel injection and ignition timing.

Further improvements in the fuel consumption of high-compression engines are being made possible by the recent development of 'knock sensors' which allow engines to be run close to their detonation limit without risk of damage.

Breathing and volumetric efficiency

In basic principle an internal combustion engine resembles an air-breathing animal: induction corresponds to breathing, combustion to digestion and excretion to the exhausting of the waste gases. Indeed a poorly designed engine may simultaneously suffer from those three basic maladies, bronchitis, indigestion and constipation! The digestion or combustion part of the process just covered in the preceding few sections is concerned with burning as fully and rapidly as possible the quantities of fuel actually drawn in, and hence with efficiency. Now let us consider the breathing part of the process

which is concerned with making those quantities of fuel (and air) as large as possible, and thus with power. In an engine the breathing is influenced by the design of the exhaust as well as of the induction system, the functioning of the two being closely related.

Success or failure in filling the cylinder with as much fresh mixture as possible is measured by a factor called the **volumetric efficiency**. This is the ratio of the weight of air and fuel actually filling the cylinder to the weight that would fill the cylinder at the outside atmospheric pressure and temperature. Since most of the exhaust gases have escaped when the inlet valve opens, the pressure inside the cylinder is generally several pounds per square inch (several thousand Pa) below atmospheric for a large part of the induction stroke. However, this pressure differential is not large enough to pump more than a relatively modest amount of air into the cylinders. Thus for **naturally aspired** or **unsupercharged** engines in which the air is sucked, not pumped in, the maximum volumetric efficiency attained seldom exceeds 80 per cent, though for a few highly efficient power units it may approach 100 per cent at a certain rotational speed. But for supercharged engines (p. 88) the volumetric efficiency may be much higher.

In either case the volumetric efficiency is influenced by the density of the incoming air which in turn is governed by the barometric pressure and by the temperature. Here the carburetter tends to act as a refrigerator. Normally it is the application of heat which evaporates a liquid – as when water is boiled to create steam – but if the evaporation is made to occur in some other way, the liquid takes the heat required from its surroundings. Some of the fuel sprayed from the carburetter jet is forced to evaporate – by the rapid expansion and reduced pressure to which it is subjected – and thus takes heat from the incoming air. In cold, damp weather this effect can occasionally cause the carburetter to become partially choked with ice, though this has been made a relatively rare occurrence by the **anti-icing additives** which most modern fuels contain and by the general adoption of heated air intakes. In very hot weather, however, the high under-bonnet temperature reached can have a significant adverse effect on volumetric efficiency, especially if the air intake is not correctly set, as well as upon mixture strength (p. 108).

Valve lift and area

Valve lift (p. 51) is one factor affecting volumetric efficiency, but there is little point in this being much more than one quarter of the valve head diameter. The area of the gap between the valve and its seating then becomes equal to the nominal area of the duct or port along which the incoming gases are conveyed, and the actual area is a little smaller due to the obstruction created by the valve guide. The amount of lift possible is in any case restricted by the need to avoid hitting the piston at top dead centre.

A much more important influence is the size of the inlet valve. Here again there are major restrictions, for the combustion chamber surface must also accommodate the sparking plug and the exhaust valve, though this is always a little smaller than the inlet valve (with about 80–85 per cent of the area) since the very high pressure of the exhaust gases makes a large opening relatively unimportant.

Clearly, the larger the diameter of the cylinder the bigger the valves that can be accommodated – which is one reason why more power can be extracted from short-stroke engines than from long-stroke ones. Similarly, still larger valves can be fitted if the surfaces which contain them are inclined to the top of the cylinder rather than parallel to it. Hemispherical or pentroof combustion chambers are therefore particularly popular amongst designers seeking the maximum power possible from an engine of given capacity.

When an engine already has a pentroof combustion chamber and large diameter cylinders, its valve area can be further raised by increasing the number of valves: to a pair of inlet valves and a single exhaust valve, perhaps, but more usually to two inlet valves and two exhaust valves. This is because the total area of the *four* largest valves that can just be squeezed into a surface of given size is considerably greater (fig. 55) than the *two*

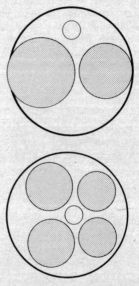

fig. 55. The four-valve concept: the four valves below have the same area as the two above – which would not fit into the combustion chamber.

largest valves that can be squeezed in. For it is always possible to cover a given area (or fill a given volume) more completely with a large number of small objects than with a small number of large objects: the boot of a car, for example, will accommodate a greater volume of table-tennis balls, which fill every nook and cranny, than of suitcases. More area becomes available to cool the valves, and their lower individual inertias makes it possible to reduce valve mechanism stress.

Many racing engines have four-valve cylinder heads, therefore, as does the two-litre Lotus unit, the engine of the Triumph Dolomite Sprint, and other units made by Mercedes and Saab.

Inlet port and manifold

A large valve area will give disappointing results, however, unless it is allied to well-designed inlet ports. Note that in a typical modern engine at maximum power the incoming gases may reach a speed of 600 mph through the valve throat, so a good deal of wasteful friction and eddying is easily induced. Hence the port is usually gently curved (fig. 56) and may be waisted near the

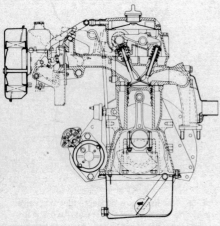

fig. 56. This section through the six-cylinder Rover 2600 engine shows (on the left) its gently curved inlet passage.

valve to about 0.75–0.80 of the valve head diameter. This creates a venturi shape which helps to minimize friction losses as the air/fuel mixture rushes into the cylinder, and to keep the flow smoothly attached to the walls of the port. In such places the air tends to cling to the walls of the port in a stationary boundary layer making surface roughness unimportant. Indiscriminate polishing, there-

fore, may do nothing to improve the power output.

But where the flow is already unstable, it can be very badly disturbed by small surface irregularities such as a casting pimple or a slight misalignment of the inlet manifold/cylinder head joint at the outer end of the port. Smoothing and careful fitting can help here.

There is much less agreement about the design of the inlet manifold. Some engineers rely on extensive heating for vaporization and use a large-volume manifold to reduce gas speeds and hence friction. Others employ less heating and prefer a smaller manifold giving higher gas speeds to promote better mixing and **atomization** or break-up of the fuel droplets. In a design of this sort the joints and bends in the manifold are often deliberately made sharp and angular, as this creates local turbulence which helps the droplets of fuel to evaporate. The **buffer-ended** inlet manifold configuration (fig. 57) has the same purpose.

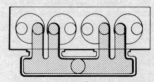

fig. 57. A buffer-ended inlet manifold is designed to create local turbulence for improved vaporization of the fuel droplets.

It is more certain, however, that the carburetter venturi must not be too large, otherwise the pressure drop within it (which depends upon gas speed) will be inadequate to suck fuel from the jet at small flow rates and the engine will not run stably at low revs.

Another inlet manifold design factor to be taken into account is **interference** or the tendency for one cylinder to rob its neighbour of fresh charge during the induction process. Consider, for example, a four-cylinder in-line engine with the firing order 1,3,4,2: the induction stroke of cylinder 2 is immediately followed and slightly overlapped by that of cylinder 1 next door to it, while similarly, induction in cylinder 3 is immediately followed by induction in the adjacent cylinder 4.

fig. 58. Interference is likely to be at its worst when the inlet ports are siamesed.

Thus the beginning of induction in cylinder 1 robs neighbouring cylinder 2 of charge at the critical stage just before its valve closes when the incoming gases have acquired a good deal of momentum which is cramming them into the cylinder. Cylinder 4 robs cylinder 3 in a similar way. The effect is most marked when to simplify the engine the inlet ports are siamesed (fig. 58), the valves being grouped in pairs sharing common ports.

One solution is to link the two parts of the induction system with a bleed pipe so that the cylinder being robbed has access to an alternative source of fresh mixture. A theoretically attractive possibility is to connect the two outer cylinders – the induction strokes of which are well separated in time – to one carburetter and the two inner cylinders to another, though, of course, a single carburetter with two chokes or venturis and a common float chamber can be used instead. In practice, however, this system does not always work well. Interference is a problem in most road-going multi-cylinder engines, and whenever possible the inlet manifold is designed to minimize its effects, the arrangement for a V-8 engine being particularly complex.

Valve timing and overlap

Just as the time taken for the fuel to burn has an important bearing on the combustion process, so time also has an important influence on volumetric efficiency. Here the

reason is the inertia of the gases involved – both inlet and exhaust – which are reluctant to move once stationary and reluctant to stop once moving. It is both to compensate for the resultant effects and to exploit them that the valves do not open exactly at top and bottom centre and that there is an overlap period between the opening of the inlet valve and the closing of the exhaust valve.

In a typical modern engine, for example, the exhaust valve is opened 50–60° before bottom dead centre (fig. 59) to give the hot

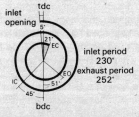

fig. 59. Overlap: to take advantage of the inertia of the incoming and exhaust gases, the inlet and exhaust valves are held simultaneously open at top dead centre at the beginning of the induction stroke.

products of combustion ample time to escape. At that stage in the combustion stroke they have done virtually all the expansive work they can – because the piston has completed most of its travel – yet the pressure inside the cylinder is still around 100 lb/sq in (7 bar). The subsequent upward movement of the piston on the exhaust stroke helps to push the gases out, but the time available for escape is so short that there will still be some left in the cylinder at top dead centre. Moreover, the momentum built up by the outward rush of the gases persists, so for these two reasons the exhaust valve is held open, generally until 15–25° after top dead centre, to ensure that the cylinder becomes as empty as possible. This is essential, for the presence within it of residual exhaust gases at the beginning of the induction stroke has a twofold adverse effect: these gases take up space that would otherwise be occupied by the fresh charge, and they heat up that fresh charge, reducing its density and hence the weight of fuel and air upon which the production of power depends.

To take advantage of the partial vacuum in the cylinder towards the end of the exhaust stroke, the inlet valve is usually opened a little before top dead centre. Thus if the inlet valve opens 5° btdc (before top dead centre) and the exhaust valve shuts 21° atdc (after top dead centre) the total overlap period is 5+21 = 26°. As the induction stroke proceeds, the fresh mixture builds up a good deal of speed and momentum, so the inlet valve is held open for quite a long time after bottom dead centre, 40–70° abdc being a range of typical values. This last part of the valve opening period when the gases continue to flow in against the upward motion of the piston has an important influence on the final filling of the cylinder.

Torque and bmep

In all these processes the important factor is time, so it follows that the valve timing and overlap can only be correct for one particular engine speed. And that engine speed is the one at which the maximum cylinder pressure is developed, for the greater the weight of air and fuel drawn in, the greater the explosive force developed and the higher the pressure on the piston. This pressure ranges from 1–2000 lb /sq in (70–140 bar) near the beginning of the combustion stroke to roughly 100 lb /sq in (70 bar) at the end, but can be represented by an average already referred to (p. 71) called the brake mean effective pressure which can be regarded as acting steadily throughout the combustion stroke from top dead centre to bottom dead centre. The word 'brake' is included to show that this kind of mean effective pressure is one determined through horsepower measurements with a brake or dynamometer and takes into account all frictional losses.

We can usefully relate the brake mean effective pressure to what we already know about power and torque (p. 28). For from the bmep, p, in lb /sq in, the power P, in bhp can easily be calculated. Using Imperial units, if the piston area is A sq in and the stroke is S inches, then:

$$P = \frac{pAS \times number\ of\ firing\ strokes/min}{33,000 \times 12}\ bhp$$

But we already know that the number of firing strokes per revolution is half the number of cylinders or $n/2$, so the number of firing strokes per minute is $n/2$ multiplied by the engine speed, r, in rpm. Hence:

$$P = \frac{pASnr}{33,000 \times 2 \times 12}$$

But the piston area A, multiplied by the stroke, S, multiplied by the number of cylinders, n, is the capacity of the engine, V, in cubic inches. Therefore:

$$P = \frac{pVr}{33,000 \times 2 \times 12} \qquad \text{(Equation 1)}$$

The units employed, however, were chosen to make the principles clear and are not those normally quoted. In practice it will generally be easier to use the following formula:

$$P = \frac{pVr}{12,960}\ bhp \qquad \text{(Equation 2)}$$

Where p = bmep in lb/sq in; V = capacity in litres and r = rpm.

These equations simply mean that power is proportional to bmep multiplied by engine capacity multiplied by revs. Note that bmep is essentially a notional quantity which cannot be measured directly: it is obtained by calculation having first physically measured the horsepower. But it is a very useful quantity for all that, since it is a good measure of an engine's state of tune or of the maximum power being extracted from it, a measure which is independent of capacity and thus allows us to compare small engines with large ones. The bmep is easily calculated from the torque and the capacity, remembering that we have already worked out that power is also proportional to torque multiplied by revs, or:

$$P = \frac{2\pi Tr}{33,000} \text{ bhp}$$

By combining this equation with Equation 1 we find that:

$$2\pi T = pV/2$$

and hence that:

$T = pV/4\pi$ or $p = 4\pi T/V$ where again $p =$ bmep in lb/sq in, $T =$ torque in lb ft and $V =$ capacity in cu in

(once again a more convenient formula to use is $T = 0.40\ SpV$, where $T =$ torque in lb ft, $p =$ bmep in lb/sq in and $V =$ capacity in litres).

This is just another way of saying that torque is proportional to bmep multiplied by capacity, or that bmep is proportional to torque divided by capacity. It is sometimes worth using this relationship to work out the bmep (which is relatively infrequently quoted) from the torque (which is almost invariably given). Thus the bmep figure for a 'cooking' engine fitted to a small car might be as low as 120 lb/sq in (8 bar). For a normally aspirated modern Formula 1 engine like the Cosworth unit, on the other hand, without supercharging or compression of the mixture, a typical figure would be around 225 lb/sq in (16 bar).

Note that when the valve timing and overlap is at an optimum in relation to the engine speed, the volumetric efficiency, bmep and torque are all at a maximum. At lower speeds than this (fig. 15) the bmep falls off as the valve timing becomes progressively inappropriate. And one consequence of inappropriate valve overlap is that the incoming mixture can easily pass straight through the combustion chamber into the exhaust system – which is bad for fuel consumption and even worse for the pollutant levels in the exhaust gases. At rpm higher than the maximum torque speed, the torque falls off once more, partly because the timing and overlap again get out of step with the engine speed, partly because frictional losses increase and partly because the ports and valves are simply not big enough to pass sufficient gas in the time available. The more pronounced the overlap and the longer the periods for which the valves remain open, the more the engine tends to maintain its power at high rpm and the worse it runs at low rpm.

Pulsations and ram tuning

One reason why valve overlap tends to work best at a particular engine speed follows from the way in which the inlet gases move. In fact they have two completely different forms of motion, the first of which is the obvious bulk movement towards the inlet valve. A piston engine, however, doesn't inhale continuously but in separate rhythmic gulps, and these tend to set up very marked pulsations or pressure waves in the incoming mixture which are superimposed on its bulk movement. Although such vibrations involve no large-scale displacement of the gas itself, they do allow the swift transmission (at the speed of sound) of pressure changes in the same way as a shunting engine passes a jolt down a train of goods wagons.

A vibration of this kind is greatly magnified if its frequency coincides with the natural or resonant frequency of the cavity in which it occurs. In just the same way, quite gentle pushes are magnified into large arcs of movement if applied with the correct frequency to a child's garden swing. But a conventional modern inlet manifold is usually capable of 'swinging' at several different natural frequencies which may be excited at different engine speeds by the forcing pulsations in the incoming mixture. Some of these resonant oscillations may have beneficial effects on volumetric efficiency, others may have an adverse influence, but cost and lack of space generally prevent the designer from doing much more than keep the adverse effects within reasonable limits.

But in sophisticated power units the gas pulsations are fully exploited in a way that allows the volumetric efficiency to be improved significantly. The basic aim is to induce a pressure pulse to arrive at the inlet valve just before it shuts so that additional mixture is crammed into the cylinder. The basic method is to give each inlet valve a separate induction pipe of a certain length in which the gases can oscillate predictably and consistently at a known frequency, just as an organ pipe of a given length emits a note of a particular pitch. If carburetters are used, this generally entails the provision of a separate one for each cylinder – or of multi-choke instruments sharing common float chambers – to ensure the necessary independence of the induction pipes.

Nowadays, though, the technique is almost wholly confined to engines fitted with fuel injection (p. 114) which is particularly suited to it. Because separate injectors are used for each cylinder, and because these are both small and located in the inlet ports near the valve, the designer has almost complete freedom to use unobstructed induction pipes of any shape and length he choses. He may decide, for instance, to use short pipes resonating at a high frequency and hence high engine speed to boost maximum power, or to employ longer pipes improving low-speed or mid-range torque. This is the course generally taken, the induction pipes being twenty to thirty-five inches long, giving a fuel-injected engine a characteristic appearance. These pipes are connected to a common plenum chamber which is large enough in volume to prevent the pulses in one pipe from interfering with those in the next, and which allows a single air throttle to be used. The opening of this must, of course, be carefully co-ordinated with the fuel flow to the injectors for the correct mixture strength to be maintained.

Exactly the same ram-pipe principles can be applied to the exhaust manifold, only here the aim is generally to make a wave of low pressure rather than high pressure arrive at the exhaust valve just before it closes, to suck out the last remaining traces of waste gas.

Apart from its prominent plumbing, an engine employing ram-pipe tuning can often additionally be recognized by its torque curve which usually features a distinct hump where the valve timing and pulsation effects combine to bring the volumetric efficiency to a maximum. Equally, there will also be some dips in the curve – though dips which are smaller in size than the hump – for while resonance means amplification at some frequencies, it entails absorption at others. Even so, the method allows a comfortable net gain in power or torque to be obtained.

Exhaust system and silencing

Clearly, the major priority in the design of an exhaust manifold must be to minimize obstruction to the hot escaping gases. An efficient exhaust manifold, therefore, must be large in volume with gently curved pipes, a smooth internal surface and an accurately aligned cylinder head joint.

Interference occurs in an exhaust manifold, just as it does in an inlet manifold, except that one cylinder pressurizes another, pushing exhaust residuals back into it. Thus in an in-line four, number 1 cylinder pressurizes number 2, and number 4 pressurizes number 3. But if sufficient underbonnet space is available, this effect can be eliminated almost entirely by connecting the pipes from the two outer cylinders to a larger-diameter secondary pipe, by similarly coupling the two inner cylinders to another secondary pipe, and by joining, some distance away, the two secondary pipes to a down-pipe still larger in diameter. This continues to the silencers and the rear of the car, completing the system. Similar systems can be devised for other types of engine, though the technique is not practical for a road-going V-8, as it involves cross-connections between the two banks of cylinders. Instead, such power units often have a complete separate system for each bank of cylinders, as do V-6 engines also.

To ram-tune an exhaust system it is not necessary for the pipes from each cylinder to be separate right out to the atmosphere: considerable benefit can be obtained by suitably choosing the length of the down-pipe. For this reason it is a mistake to assume that a car will necessarily go faster if its silencer is removed – modern silencers offer very little obstruction to the passage of the gases – and its removal may actually reduce engine power by altering the carefully worked-out length of the system.

Modern silencers absorb noise in three ways of which the first is by absorption. An **absorption** or **straight-through** silencer (fig. 60) consists of a perforated tube sur-

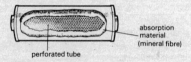

fig. 60. An absorption or straight-through silencer – seldom used on its own, these days.

rounded by absorptive material such as glass wool which soaks up some of the unwanted noise. It is set into vibration by the sound waves and tends to dissipate their energy through its internal friction. Because the absorptive material is acted upon in this way, it tends gradually to be pulled out of its chamber, progressively reducing the efficiency of the silencer.

The second mode of noise reduction is expansion. Imagine a sound pressure wave reaching (fig. 61) the end of a short tube extending into a chamber which is considerably larger in diameter. The front of the wave expands into the chamber and around the entry tube, acquiring a much larger surface with far less energy in each square inch or square centimetre of it. Some of the wave-front actually travels backwards and is subsequently dissipated by the turbulence

created by successive reflections in the expansion chamber. Moreover, only a small portion of the weakened wave-front passes down the outlet tube out of the expansion chamber.

The third way in which noise is reduced in a silencer is by resonance. If a chamber forms a branch in a tube (fig. 62) which is transmitting sound waves, it can be set into resonant vibration, but the vibrations generated are out of phase with those in the tube which are thus cancelled out instead of being transmitted. A perforated tube surrounded by a concentric cylinder (fig. 63) acts in this

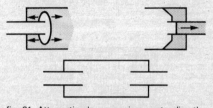

fig. 61. Attenuation by expansion – extending the tubes into the cylinder greatly reduces the noise transmitted.

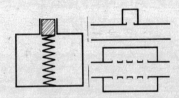

fig. 62. Attenuation by resonance: the side-chamber behaves like a jar sealed with a spring-loaded cork and absorbs sound at its own natural frequency; it is called a Helmholtz resonator.

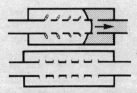

fig. 63. A perforated tube acts both like a series of expansion chambers and as a succession of absorptive resonators.

way – and it also acts as an expansion chamber, the wave-front expanding at each perforation, so the noise is reduced in two ways. Modern silencers generally incorporate a series of expansion chambers and resonators (fig. 64).

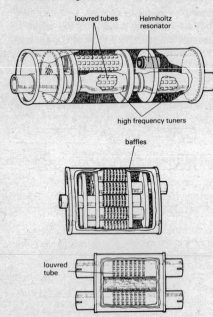

fig. 64. Some typical modern silencers. Top: with louvred tubes, cavities for high frequencies and a Helmholtz resonator. Centre: 'five-pass' system. Bottom: a twin-inlet twin-outlet system.

Supercharging

A supercharger is simply an external pump that crams additional mixture into the engine by brute force. It can either be directly coupled to the engine by a gear or belt drive, or to a small turbine driven by the hot exhaust gases – in which case the combined arrangement is called a **turbocharger**. Positively driven superchargers absorb power and are not particularly efficient, but can raise the

volumetric efficiency to significantly more than 100 per cent from quite low rpm right up to the maximum speed of which the engine is capable, thus imparting a dramatic improvement and flattening to the torque curve as well as creating a big increase in power without any increase in maximum revs. Turbochargers, on the other hand, absorb no power because they use waste energy in the exhaust gases, but provide little boost at low rpm and may respond sluggishly when the throttle is suddenly opened.

The two best-known kinds of positively driven supercharger are the **eccentric drum** (or 'vane') and **Roots** types. An eccentric drum supercharger (fig. 65) contains a cylin-

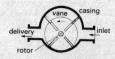

fig. 65. Air is trapped, compressed and passed to the engine between the vanes of an eccentric drum supercharger.

drical rotor turning eccentrically inside a cylindrical casing. The sickle-shaped space between rotor and casing is divided up by a system of vanes between which air is trapped, compressed and passed to the engine.

The more common Roots-type supercharger or ('blower') contains (fig. 66) a system

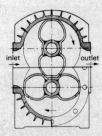

fig. 66. Roots-type superchargers have lobes which mesh together without touching and trap air between them.

of gears driving a pair of specially shaped contra-rotating rotors which trap air and carry it round within the casing of the device to the inlet side of the engine. Because the lobes do not touch but are separated by small clearances, the rotor surfaces need no lubrication and the supercharger tends to be reliable and long-lasting. It is also able to provide a good air delivery for its bulk and is easily balanced for high-speed running.

Both these superchargers must not merely be positively driven by the engine, but are also of the positive-displacement type: within the limits of the small clearances required, they contained sealed chambers within which air is trapped and then compressed.

But there is another kind of supercharger which relies more on the inertia of the air or mixture it handles than on tight clearances and sealed compartments. This is the **centrifugal supercharger**, the basic component of which is a high-speed impeller (fig. 67). Air is drawn in through its centre and flung outwards between its vanes by

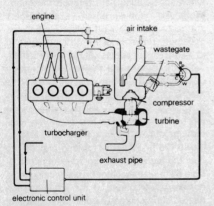

fig. 67. A typical turbocharger layout incorporating a wastegate control to limit boost at high rpm and throttle openings. The arrangement illustrated is the Saab APC (Automatic Performance Control) system; this incorporates an additional electronic control system involving a detonation sensor which automatically compensates for variations in the octane rating of the fuel used.

centrifugal force. Fixed vanes in the surrounding casing form diverging passages to slow down the gas and convert its kinetic energy into pressure energy. Since air is pretty light stuff a centrifugal compressor does not do very much at low revs – generally it needs to run at a minimum of 15,000 rpm – but when its output finally starts to rise, it does so sharply because centrifugal force increases with the square of the rotational speed.

There is no theoretical reason why a centrifugal supercharger should not be positively driven – the famous Rolls-Royce Merlin engine was supercharged in just this way, as was the (unsuccessful) V-16 BRM Formula 1 racing engine of the immediate post-war period and a number of road-going cars of the 1930s. If fitted to a road-going engine, however, a centrifugal supercharger would need to run at five times crankshaft speed at least, and even then would only increase the power output towards the top end of the engine's rev range. It would tend to do so, moreover, rather inefficiently, partly because of frictional losses in the supercharger gearing. And with the impeller rotating at anything between 15,000 and 50,000 rpm, very high inertia loads are imposed on this gearing by changes in engine speed.

Many of these problems disappear if the centrifugal compressor is driven by an exhaust-gas turbine which is easily capable of maintaining the very high rotational speeds required. The gas flow through such a turbine is in the reverse sense to that in the compressor: the exhaust gases are ducted to the periphery of the device and guided by fixed vanes on to the blades of the turbine; they exit at its centre, having given up much of their energy. The exhaust gases form an ideal variable-ratio coupling which allows the compressor to be kept in its required speed range – typically 30–90,000 rpm. In addition, the turbine makes use of energy in the exhaust gases that would otherwise be wasted, so the compressor is driven completely for free, without any power loss. The turbine does create a small additional back pressure in the exhaust system, but this has little adverse effect.

With a turbocharger, therefore, the power of an existing engine can be quickly, easily and efficiently raised by a very considerable amount. This possibility was understood decades ago by engineers in search of more power for the big, slow-revving direct-injection diesel engines of heavy trucks. As a result the turbocharger became a relatively cheap and freely available assembly which was gradually adopted by the designers of petrol engines. With its help, an existing four-cylinder or six-cylinder engine of modest capacity can be given a great deal more power – and hence a new lease of life – at very little development cost and without investing in the hugely expensive tooling that a completely new larger engine would involve. Saab, for example, greatly extended the life of their basic engine – and transformed the appeal of their 99 and 900 models for the better – in just this way.

Nor does the turbocharger carry any significant fuel consumption penalty – a turbocharged engine may well have better fuel consumption than the equivalent normally aspirated unit. The high cylinder pressures generated reduce the importance of friction and lead to more efficient working. Independent road tests certainly show turbocharged cars to have excellent fuel consumption in relation to their performance, even though there is at least one factor which might theoretically be expected to reduce efficiency

This arises because the supercharging process represents an initial stage of compression, and too much compression of the inlet charge before it is ignited leads to detonation and engine damage. So the compression ratio of a supercharged or turbocharged engine generally has to be lower than that of a normally aspirated engine. And although the overall *pressure* ratio may be higher than before, the reduced cylinder compression ratio means a reduced expansion ratio, reduced thermal efficiency and hence an increase in the amount of heat rejected wastefully to the cooling water and exhaust gases.

In practice the losses created by these conditions do not seem to be significant, although some reduction in compression ratio is generally essential. If an engine's compression ratio is more than about 7.5:1 in fact, it is vital that it be reduced if a d-i-y supercharger or turbocharger kit is fitted. The accepted rule is to reduce the compression ratio in proportion to the square root of the inlet pressures. With a boost pressure of 6 lb/sq in (0.4 bar) above the 15 lb/sq in (1.0 bar) of atmospheric pressure, for example, and an unblown compression ratio of 10:1, the blown compression ratio should be no greater than $10\sqrt{15/21} = 8.5$.

If this precaution be taken, a converted engine ought to stand up to supercharging without any trouble. Since the boost pressure is controlled by the throttle opening, full boost is obtained only at full throttle, which in practice mostly means only momentarily when accelerating hard through the gears. Moreover, conversion-kit superchargers invariably have blow-off valves limiting the maximum pressure delivered to 10 lb/sq in (0.7 bar), say, regardless of the revs attained.

On the other hand the greatly increased quantity of mixture being put into the engine means greatly increased heat dissipation, to the danger of gaskets, valves and plugs. So unless the conversion has been very well thought out, it might not be advisable to cruise the boosted car for long periods too near the higher maximum speed made possible by the supercharger. This warning does not apply, of course, to the properly engineered supercharged (usually turbocharged) engines produced by the major motor manufacturers, even though there is an increasing tendency for such engines to run on quite high compression ratios in conjunction with knock sensors which retard the ignition automatically at the onset of detonation to prevent damage.

But while the turbocharged engines offered by the major motor manufacturers seem to be little less reliable than normally aspirated engines, and although they generally offer excellent fuel consumption, they undoubtedly suffer from a couple of characteristic failings. The first is a lack of turbo boost at low rpm, especially when running on part throttle. Below 2000–3000 rpm, in fact, most turbocharged engines behave as if they were naturally aspirated – that is, unsupercharged. And if the throttle is floored at low–moderate rpm, there is generally a lag of 1–2 seconds – the time taken by the turbocharger to spin up to a useful working speed – before the increased torque provided by the additional supply of mixture can be felt.

In these two respects the turbocharger is markedly inferior to the positively driven supercharger which provides useful boost at low rpm without lag.

To minimize lag, modern turbochargers are skilfully integrated into the manifold systems, carefully matched in size to the exhaust gas flow and given turbines and compressor rotors of the smallest possible weight and diameter to reduce rotary inertia. Lag can be further reduced by intelligent design of the control system. Often this involves a **wastegate**, a by-pass valve generally controlled by inlet manifold pressure which diverts the exhaust gases away from the turbine and straight along the downpipe when the required level of boost has been reached. In more sophisticated systems it is sometimes the surplus of incoming compressed air that is diverted from the inlet manifold rather than exhaust gases from the turbine – which is thus kept spinning as fast as is possible so that full boost is available whenever required, with minimum lag.

When a supercharger of any kind compresses the incoming air or mixture it also heats it up, reducing the efficiency of the process; not merely is some of the power absorbed by the supercharger being wastefully dissipated as heat, but the compressed charge becomes less dense than it otherwise would be. This loss can be reduced by fitting a **charge air cooler** or **intercooler** on the outlet side of the supercharger. An intercooler can either be of the water/air type or of the air/air type, but in both cases it consists of a fin-and-tube heat exchanger matrix similar to a watercooled engine's radiator. If it is of the water/air type, then engine coolant is pumped through the tubes, while through the spaces between them is circulated (or vice versa) the compressed air from the supercharger which thus cannot be cooled below the lowest temperature which might be reached by the engine coolant in such a system – say 60°C. But if the intercooler is of the air/air type, its matrix is mounted in the air-stream of the car, usually at its front so that ambient air passes between the tubes of the heat exchanger to cool the compressed air or mixture from the supercharger which is ducted through them. Intercoolers of this kind are fitted to a number of turbocharged road-going cars, including the Renault 18 Turbo and the Porsche 911 Turbo.

Charge heating can also be minimized to some extent if a carburetter is used and if the supercharger is arranged to suck through it rather than to blow into it. More of the latent heat of vaporization of the fuel is extracted than would be the case if the mixture were pressurized, and this helps to lower the temperature and increase the density of the fresh charge before it enters the supercharger and hence the engine. Further advantages of this configuration are that the churning of the fuel droplets inside the blower helps vaporization and distribution, and the carburetter continues to work in the normal way, needing no modifications other than appropriate sizing and jetting.

But the disadvantage of this arrangement is that the presence of a considerable amount of combustible mixture on the engine side of the throttle valve can cause a disconcerting lag when the throttle is closed, so that the engine continues to provide full power for a second or two after the foot has been taken off the accelerator. For this reason, most engineers currently prefer, when a supercharger is fitted, either to use a fuel injection system – which does not introduce lags of this sort – or the alternative pressurized carburetter arrangement. In this configuration the supercharger blows into the carburetter, which must either be sealed or enclosed in an airtight box connected to the supercharger output, since the pressure above the float chamber must be the same as that at the entrance to the carburetter in order to maintain the pressure drop in the venturi which sucks the fuel out of the jets. In addition the fuel delivery pressure must be regulated so that it is always higher than the boost pressure, but not too much higher, otherwise fuel could be forced through the closed needle valve. Furthermore, such an arrangement does not make it easy to ensure a consistently correct mixture, since the carburetter handles air of varying density, for which it cannot correct (p. 108). In practice, however, this theoretical difficulty does not seem to prevent turbocharged engines from returning the excellent fuel consumption already mentioned.

During the past decade increasing interest has been shown in a new type of supercharger which seems potentially almost capable of combining the immediate response and good boost at low rpm provided by the positively driven, positive-displacement supercharger with the zero power requirement of the turbocharger. This is the pressure-wave or Comprex (compression–expansion) supercharger first conceived in 1913, but not taken up until the early 1950s, since which time it has been developed by Brown, Boveri & Co., a Swiss engineering company.

The Comprex supercharger depends upon the creation of pressure waves in the exhaust gases which are used to compress the incoming air. As already mentioned, a pressure wave travels at the speed of sound and involves no bulk movement of the gas

which conducts it. It is analogous, remember, to the 'wave' of jolts that a shunting engine can caused to be passed down a line of stationary railway wagons. The buffer springs of the first wagon compress after being struck by the engine, and then expand, pushing that wagon into the next one, which jerks into the next one and so on. The train as a whole remains stationary, but motion of a very definite sort has been transmitted down it. Moreover, if the far end of the train is in contact with fixed buffers, the wave of jolts will be reflected back towards the engine.

These exhaust-gas pressure waves are formed in a series (fig. 68) of longitudinal holes or cells located in the periphery of a

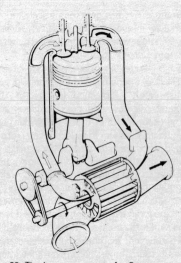

fig. 68. The key component of a Comprex supercharger is a cylinder of longitudinal cells which interrupts both the intake and exhaust systems. The combined effect of the rotation of the cylinder and the pressure waves set up means that slugs of exhaust gas which enter the cells at top right do not pass through to the far end of the cylinder but are carried round to leave the engine through an exit duct. The same pressure waves mean that the incoming mixture which enters at bottom left is reflected out of the cylinder and into the engine at an increased pressure.

rotating cylinder which is enclosed by a casing and driven at some multiple (usually three or four times) of engine speed. A certain area of one end of this cell wheel communicates with a low-pressure air intake, while a smaller area of the same end registers with a high-pressure air outlet pipe. At the other end, there is a small-area high-pressure exhaust gas inlet port and a large-area exhaust gas outlet port.

The action of the supercharger can be understood by imagining the cell wheel to be unrolled (fig. 69) and considering the con-

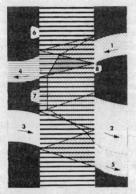

fig. 69. This illustration shows the cell wheel of the Comprex supercharger as if it had been unrolled: the horizontal lines represent the walls of the cells which can be thought of as moving from the top of the drawing to the bottom. 1, exhaust gas from engine; 2, exhaust-gas outlet to atmosphere; 3, incoming ambient air; 4, compressed air to engine inlet manifold; 5, scavenging air; 6, 7, 8, gas pockets to tune wave reflections.

ditions inside one of the longitudinally orientated cells as it travels downwards from its uppermost to its lowermost position. In its uppermost position this cell is filled with air at atmospheric pressure and temperature, but as it travels downwards it moves into registration with the exhaust-gas inlet port at its right-hand end, creating a pressure wave which begins to pass down the cell from right to left and to compress the air within it. A little further downward move-

ment, however, brings the left-hand end of the cell into registration with the high-pressure air outlet port, allowing a pulse of high-pressure air to travel down the outlet pipe to the inlet manifold of the engine. But expansion of this compression wave from the cell into the larger cross-sectional area outlet duct creates another compression wave which begins to travel back through the cell towards its right-hand end, largely preventing mixture of the exhaust gases with the air which has been compressed. By the time it reaches that end, however, it meets a closed face, for the cell has then moved further downwards. Another pressure wave is then reflected back towards the left-hand end of the cell, but by the time it reaches that end, it, too, meets a closed surface, for the cell has moved downwards again.

At this stage in the process, the gases in the cell are stationary but at fairly high pressure and so begin to expand into the low-pressure exhaust outlet duct on the right-hand side when the cell moves still further downwards into registration with it. This movement of gas to the right creates an expansion or rarefaction wave moving from left to right which begins to draw in fresh air from the ambient air intake pipe, thus completing the cycle, which then begins anew.

So far, the Comprex supercharger has only been used experimentally, mostly in conjunction with diesel rather than petrol engines. But published reports confirm that it is capable of providing plenty of boost at any engine speed and without lag, just as its makers claim. Some power is required to drive it, but a small amount – typically about 0.5 per cent of engine output. One disadvantage is that, even when the cells are unevenly spaced to minimize any 'siren' effect, the rotor tends to emit a high-pitched whine audible more from outside the car than from within it. This rotor needs to be a precision casting, but so do the rotors of a turbocharger, and the main obstacle to the adoption of the Comprex supercharger for production seems to be conservatism and doubts about investing in a completely new component.

Efficiency

A bmep figure tells us a lot about the amount of power being extracted from an engine but much less about another highly significant characteristic: its efficiency. What, though, do we mean by efficiency? The word has several meanings when applied to engines, one of which, volumetric efficiency, we have already learned, but amongst the most important is **brake thermal efficiency**. Essentially, this is the proportion of the heat energy stored in each gallon of fuel which is actually converted into useful mechanical work, taking into account the frictional losses within the engine and the power absorbed by auxiliaries such as the generator and cooling fan.

Unfortunately the reciprocating petrol engine, like most practical heat engines, is not very efficient. When running at full throttle and a steady speed, a good engine might have a maximum brake thermal efficiency of 35 per cent, about the same as a jet engine at full power during take-off or an efficient electricity generating station, but less than the 42 per cent of a well-designed direct injection diesel or the 43 per cent of a large coal-fired electricity generating station. And under normal running conditions, when the throttle is only partly open for a high proportion of the time, the thermal efficiency of a typical petrol engine is more like 15 per cent.

The main reason for this low efficiency is that it is impossible to prevent most of the heat energy in the fuel from leaking out of the engine as heat instead of being converted to useful mechanical work. Of the available heat of combustion, about 35 per cent escapes with the exhaust gases, roughly 30 per cent is rejected to the cooling water or air and approximately 5 per cent escapes by convection and radiation from

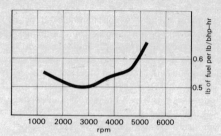

fig. 70. Specific fuel consumption at full throttle falls to a minimum at a point roughly in the middle of the speed range.

the surface of the engine, leaving about 30 per cent to appear as useful mechanical work.

The brake thermal efficiency determines the specific fuel consumption. And if the specific fuel consumption (under full throttle conditions) is plotted against engine revolutions (fig. 70) it can be seen to reach a minimum at a point roughly in the middle of the speed range which is nearly always close to the speed at which the maximum torque/bmep is developed. At low rpm the thermal efficiency tends to be low because plenty of time is available to allow the heat of combustion to leak uselessly away. As the engine speeds up, the leakage reduces at first, bringing the thermal efficiency to a peak, but then the heat losses grow again as the increasingly turbulent motion of the burning gases brings them more into contact with the cylinder walls. Increased frictional losses also tend to reduce the thermal efficiency at high rpm.

Efficiency and throttle opening

Of all the bends, protuberances and obstructions in the inlet system which create frictional losses as the incoming gases flow past them, the greatest is the throttle. The high **pumping losses** associated with the small throttle openings needed for a large part of ordinary driving are big enough to

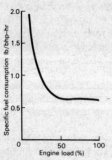

fig. 71. During part-throttle running the petrol engine is very inefficient.

impair efficiency and hence fuel consumption seriously. At small throttle openings, too, the combustion pressures developed are small in proportion to frictional and other losses, making the inefficiency even worse. Thus, efficiency is at its maximum (fig. 71) when the throttle is roughly three-quarters open, but falls off rapidly as the opening is reduced.

This fact also has important implications for economy driving. It means that at any given speed it is nearly always better to run in a high gear with the accelerator pressed roughly three-quarters of the way down to the floor, than in a lower gear with a smaller throttle opening and higher engine speed. Of course there are limits: it is not good practice to go so slowly in top that the engine and transmission system vibrate badly.

Combustion – exhaust emissions

Atmospheric pollution

From the late 1960s onwards, engine designers were forced to take into account a whole range of new factors, largely because the city of Los Angeles, in California, USA, enjoys very peculiar climatic and geographical conditions. It is walled-in by hills and roofed by the San Bernadino inversion, a warm and stagnant overhead layer of air which encloses the district so that for ninety to a hundred days a year pollutants released into the atmosphere cannot easily escape. Long before the area became densely populated, the Indians knew it as the Bay of Smokes because of the almost permanent haze from forest fires trapped above it.

In the early days of this century these conditions merely accentuated the atmospheric pollution due to domestic heating and industrial activity which was – and is – common to almost every highly populated area in the world. But during the late forties and early fifties the pollution in the skies above Los Angeles both changed in character and became very much more intense. In particular, the area became infamous for what is now called photochemical smog: a yellowish mist which reduces visibility, causes eye and respiratory irritation and damage to plant life.

Suspicion fell on the motorcar, since the growth of smog was associated with a huge increase in the road vehicle population. An intensive programme of research confirmed that the car was indeed the culprit, and showed smog to be created by the action of strong sunlight on two major pollutants in automotive exhaust gases: **unburned hydrocarbons** (HC) and **oxides of nitrogen** (NO_x). Another major pollutant, **carbon monoxide** (CO) also gave cause for concern, as it is highly poisonous.

These gases are only emitted because combustion within a motorcar engine is incomplete. If it were complete, the sole products would be water and carbon dioxide, the first being completely harmless and the second being basically inert and directly harmful to man only when present in large concentrations. It is true that more heat from the sun is trapped by the atmosphere if its carbon dioxide content rises, and some scientists feel that this could have a long-term adverse effect on the Earth's climate; others disagree.

Exhaust emission laws

As a result of the discoveries about photochemical smog, the Californian legislature decided in 1959 to enact regulations legally limiting the levels of the three major pollutants – HC, NO_x and CO. The first requirement, effective from 1964 onwards, was relatively simple and easily met. It was that all cars should be fitted with closed crankcase breathing systems (p. 54) as crankcase fumes were known to be responsible for around 25 per cent of the unburned hydrocarbons.

The next step was to tackle the exhaust gases themselves, by deciding how the levels of the three pollutants could be measured and defined. The method adopted was to analyse the exhaust gases of the car under test while subjecting it to a **driving cycle** – a rigidly specified sequence of acceleration, cruising, deceleration and idling. This was devised to simulate a typical pattern of American city driving in which the car spends little time in top gear.

Full-throttle running does not form part of the cycle in either its original or its present form: it is relatively rare in town and generally associated with high-speed cruising, when the pollutants are too highly dispersed to create much harm. At full throttle, in any case, better mixing tends to reduce the pollutant levels. Hence exhaust emission control is almost entirely confined to acceleration, part-throttle running, deceleration and idling.

To obtain a high level of consistency and repeatability, the cycle is followed in a laboratory rather than on a test track, with the car at rest but its driving wheels turning the rollers of a **roller dynamometer**. This is a device which can be used either to measure the horsepower developed at a car's driving wheels or to provide a variable resistance simulating any given driving conditions. The test is often performed with the help of a special moving display visible to the driver who is required to make a pointer indicating the speed of the car follow a graph representing the cycle. With a little practice the cycle can be followed very accurately and repeatably in this way, though an alternative method is to use automatic computer control.

The driving cycle originally evolved by the State of California went through several changes over the years, but was accepted at an early stage by the Environmental Protection Agency (EPA) of the US Federal Government as the standard for exhaust pollution measurement applicable to all the other states in the Union. While other driving cycles, such as that used by Japan, and that adopted by the countries of the ECE (Economic Commission for Europe – Great Britain, West Germany, France, Italy, Holland, Belgium, Sweden, Hungary, Czechoslovakia, Spain, Yugoslavia, Luxembourg, Austria and Switzerland) may differ markedly in the details of their cruising, acceleration, etc. modes, all follow the same general principles as the American one. And all require expensive and elaborate equipment to analyse the exhaust gases which nowadays are collected in huge plastic bags.

The present American EPA driving cycle was laid down in 1975, involves an average speed of 21.2 mph (34.1 kph) and is called the 1975 CVS-CH cycle – all limits quoted in this chapter are expressed in terms of it. The letters CVS stand for the Constant Volume Sampling system of measurement used, in which a pump draws a volume of exhaust gases and dilution air into the sampling bags which remains constant for all the test. The results are expressed in g/mile (grams per mile).

The letters CH stand for Cold–Hot, for the cycle involves both a cold and a hot start. To prepare the car for the test and for its initial cold start, it is put through an elaborate 'preconditioning' procedure culminating in a twelve-hour 'soak' period to ensure that the engine reaches the prescribed temperature range, which is 20–30°C (68–86°F). The first 'cold transient' phase of the cycle begins with the cold start and continues with various acceleration, deceleration, idling and cruising modes, the car reaching 56.7 mph at one point. This runs without a break into a 'cold-stabilized' phase involving rather more stop–start driving. Then, to simulate the hot starts characteristic of American urban driving generally, but in particular that in the Los Angeles area, the engine is restarted after a ten-minute 'soak' at ambient temperature for a third and final phase.

The original aim of the Californian legislators was to choose exhaust emission limits which would bring the pollution in the atmosphere above Los Angeles back to the level of 1940 when there was no significant smog problem. The first limits applied to 1968 model cars and were that the HC emissions should not exceed 6.3 g/mile and that CO emissions should be kept below 52 g/mile. No restriction was at first placed on NO_x emissions. For a typical untreated American engine the emission levels were roughly 15 g/mile for HC, 90 g/mile for CO and 4 g/mile for NO_x.

Evaporation from the fuel tank and carburetter – responsible for another 20 per cent of the unburned hydrocarbons – became the subject of further regulations in 1970. In 1971, limits were imposed on the NO_x emissions permissible, and year by year the standards imposed by the Californian state government became progressively more severe.

The US Federal government followed California in 1968, and using the same driving cycle and test procedures began imposing limits for the remainder of the country which have usually been less severe (Table 2) because smog levels are low in other states.

The ECE standards are based on a special

TABLE 2

	Federal (49 state) standards			California standards		
	HC g/mile	CO g/mile	NO_x g/mile	HC g/mile	CO g/mile	NO_x g/mile
1967 (uncontrolled)	15	90	4–6	The same as federal		
1968	6.3	52	–	6.3	52	–
1969	6.3	52	–	6.3	52	–
1970	4.1	34	–	4.1	34	–
1971	4.1	34	–	4.1	34	4
1972	3.0	28	–	2.8	28	3.2
1973	3.0	28	3.1	2.8	28	3
1974	3.0	28	3.1	2.8	28	2
1975	1.5	15	3.1	0.9	9	2
1976	1.5	15	3.1	0.9	9	2
1977–79	1.5	15	2	0.41	9	1.5
1980	0.41	7	2	0.39*	9	1
1981	0.41	3.4	1	0.39	7	0.7
1982	0.41	3.4	1	0.39	7	0.4
1983	0.41	3.4†	1	0.39	3.4	0.4

* Excluded methane content because methane is considered to be harmless, but is essentially the same as Federal requirement.
† Waived to 7.0 for certain types of vehicle.

European driving cycle – again simulating typical city-centre driving conditions – which involves a maximum speed of 31 mph (50 kph) and an average speed of 12 mph (19 kph). These regulations were adopted on different dates by the member countries; in Britain crankcase emission controls were imposed in 1971 and a limit on the amount of CO emitted at idle since 1972. Limits on CO and HC emitted during the driving cycle have been imposed since 1973, while NO_x limits were additionally included from 1977 when tamperproof carburetters were introduced. The more stringent ECE 15-03 limits were imposed in 1979. Sweden and Switzerland require compliance with the 1973 US regulations, while since 1974 Japan has had very strict limits, similar to California's but based on a different cycle again.

The cures

One of the principal difficulties arises from the way the concentrations of the three main pollutants vary with mixture strength (fig. 51). As might be expected, when the mixture is rich and insufficient oxygen is available, a significant proportion of the hydrocarbons present tend to remain unburned, while combustion in the remainder is incomplete, so the CO level tends to be high also. As the mixture is weakened off, the levels of these two pollutants fall, until at an air/fuel ratio of around 15:1 there is enough oxygen to ensure that much of the CO is oxidized to CO_2. This only means that all the hydrocarbons which burn do so completely, not that there is complete combustion of all the hydrocarbons present: some of these tend to remain unburned due to the quenching effect of the excess air, though with further weakening of the mixture, the unburned hydrocarbons level drops to a minimum while the CO level reaches a minimum at a still weaker mixture.

But both the HC and the CO trends are in opposition to that followed by the NO_x emissions. Here the important factor is temperature: at high combustion temperatures the basically inert nitrogen which makes up around 70 per cent of the air tends to combine with the oxygen present, forming several different oxides, one being nitrogen dioxide (NO_2) which is highly toxic to man and gives smog its yellowish colour. Note that NO_x emission reaches a peak at almost the same air/fuel ratio as that at which the HC emission falls to a minimum – the air/fuel ratio at which the combustion temperature is at its highest. Note, too, that conventional multicylinder engines will not normally run on very weak mixtures having air/fuel ratios in the 18–19:1 region where NO_x emission falls to an acceptable level. One way of reducing the concentration of this pollutant, therefore, is to employ a slightly rich mixture; others are the use of low compression ratios or cool-running combustion chambers with large surface-to-volume ratios – and all of these measures are not merely in complete conflict with those which reduce HC and CO emissions, but also with design trends long established as favourable to efficiency.

To begin with, though, the Californian regulations were not difficult to meet. Many manufacturers were able to comply largely by fitting leaner-running, more precisely calibrated carburetters, the typical metering or apportioning accuracy required being ±3 per cent instead of the ±5 per cent limits deemed adequate for pre-control cars. The American Chrysler Corporation adopted and refined this approach, calling it the Cleaner Air Package or CAP.

Such a system involves particular attention to weakening of the mixture during acceleration, and required modifications to the ignition timing as well as to the carburation during idling and on the overrun. As already mentioned (p. 74) the considerable amounts of exhaust gas left in the combustion chambers at the beginning of the induction stroke during idling call for a rich mixture to maintain combustion, while valve overlap allows some of this rich mixture to escape unburned into the exhaust pipe – immediately loading the waste gases with HC. And on the overrun, remember, the amount of mixture supplied is so small in relation to the engine speed that it is virtually unburnable and again passes straight into the exhaust pipe – once more a highly undesirable state of affairs from the emissions point of view.

One possibility is to cut off the fuel completely, and this solution is increasingly being adopted, though of course it cannot be done when the engine is required to idle. Until recently, however, the problem has been tackled by increasing the amount of both fuel and air supplied. This means better combustion, so a weaker mixture can be used, reducing the levels of HC and CO.

But it also means that more power is developed – it is rather as if the throttle had stuck partly open – and clearly the engine cannot be allowed to roar away at 2000 rpm, say, when the car is standing at the traffic lights – or to develop unwanted power when the driver is trying to slow down. This is prevented by retarding the ignition so that the engine runs very inefficiently and its

idling speed is restored to its normal level. But the delayed combustion also means that the exhaust valve runs hotter and more heat is released to the cooling system.

A similar technique is employed on the overrun. Often the carburetter or its throttle has an overrun valve which opens when the manifold depression is very high to admit more fuel and air. Again it is important that the ignition be retarded to prevent the engine from developing power when – in this case – it is essential that it should not.

Like the initial HC and CO limits, the **evaporative loss** regulations which came into force in 1970 were not too difficult to comply with. A typical system (fig. 72) involves a canister of highly absorbent charcoal which collects vapour from the fuel tank and carburetter float chamber when the car is standing. When the engine runs, fresh air is drawn through the canister and into the inlet manifold.

But significant reductions in the amounts of HC and CO were also required for 1970, and the two major American companies,

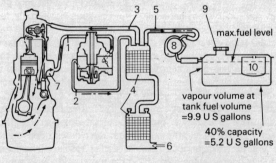

max.fuel level

vapour volume at tank fuel volume =9.9 U S gallons

40% capacity =5.2 U S gallons

⟹ Clean air	3. Canister purge line
→ Mixture of air and fumes	4. Charcoal canisters
–·–→ Fuel and oil fumes	5. Fuel tank vent pipe
	6. Purge air to canisters
	7. Flame arrestor
1. Crankcase purge line	8. Vapour separator
2. Carburetter float chamber vent pipe	9. Sealed cap
	10. Inner expansion tank

fig. 72. An evaporative loss control system incorporating charcoal canisters which absorb fuel vapour. Air and vapour initially trapped in the inner expansion tank prevent the fuel tank from being overfilled and then leak away to leave room for expansion so that fuel does not spill out.

General Motors and Ford, generally adopted a **thermal reactor** or **Thermactor** system. The basic principle is to persuade the exhaust gases to complete their burning in the exhaust system after they have left the cylinders by injecting additional air into the exhaust ports which both oxidizes the CO to CO_2 and consumes the unburned hydrocarbons. This air is provided by a special engine-driven pump. The reaction generates its own heat, but is no longer self-supporting if the temperature of the gases falls below a certain level. Paradoxically, therefore, the air/fuel mixture was generally deliberately made rich in order to 'seed' the oxidation reaction and keep up the temperature. Sometimes the exhaust manifold was merely a little larger and more heavily constructed than a standard assembly, but sometimes a thermal reactor proper was fitted. This was generally heavily insulated with a central reaction chamber pre-heated by the incoming exhaust – again, to keep up the reaction temperature – and it was provided with baffles and a large volume to give the gases the maximum possible time to react.

A practical air injection system generally involves several further complications, the first being a pressure-relief valve which limits pump output at high revs, restraining the violence of the reaction and protecting the exhaust system from excessive heat. Then there is a non-return valve which prevents the exhaust gases from blowing back into the pump. Finally there is usually a **gulp valve** which injects a puff of air into the *inlet* manifold when the car decelerates. This reacts with the fuel suddenly evaporated off the manifold walls by the high manifold depression which exists during deceleration. The extra dose of fuel is thus satisfactorily burned within the cylinders and not in the exhaust system where sudden combustion would again create an overload.

After a short time the atmospheric pollution created by cars became a political issue in the USA and the American industry was accused of being slow to reduce exhaust emissions. Critics of the big three motor manufacturers, General Motors, Ford and Chrysler, led by Senator Muskie, held that the limits in force for 1970 (then the same for California as the other states of the Union) were too easily met, and that little was being done to reduce them further. Accordingly, these limits were regarded as representing datum levels in the Federal Clean Air Act passed that same year which required that by 1976 exhaust emissions from private cars be progressively reduced by at least 90 per cent. This entailed reducing HC emissions from 4.1 g/mile to 0.41 g/mile and CO emissions from 34 g/mile to 3.4 g/mile. At that time there was no NO_x limit, but as already mentioned, the level for a typical American engine was 4 g/mile, so the requirement for 1976 was set at 0.4 g/mile. So low were these limits that many engineers regarded them at that time as being virtually impossible to meet with the technology then known. They have certainly not been easy to comply with: very complex equipment was needed to meet the limits introduced in 1977, for example, yet because of postponements these were significantly less severe than those originally proposed for 1976.

The State of California with its special smog problem required the levels to be lowered more rapidly than the Federal regulations specified, introducing for the first time a limit – 4 g/mile – on NO_x emissions in 1971. This rendered the existing control systems – mainly of the CAP or thermal reaction type – inadequate.

Earlier research had already established that the simplest way of meeting this limit was to reduce peak combustion temperatures by diluting the incoming mixture with up to 15 per cent of recirculated exhaust gases. The amount of exhaust gas fed back to the inlet manifold in such EGR (Exhaust Gas Recirculation) systems (fig. 73) is generally governed by a metering valve which in turn is controlled by manifold vacuum. Little or no exhaust gas is recirculated when the

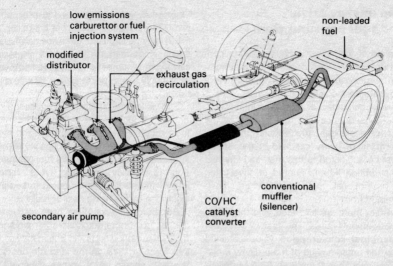

low emissions
carburettor or fuel
injection system

non-leaded
fuel

modified
distributor

exhaust gas
recirculation

conventional
muffler
(silencer)

CO/HC
catalyst
converter

secondary air pump

fig. 73. Exhaust gas recirculation or EGR was introduced to dilute the incoming mixture, reduce combustion temperatures and hence to cut the NO$_x$ emission level. The car shown here also has a catalytic converter to cut CO and HC emissions.

engine idles, for combustion temperatures are then too low for NO$_x$ emission to be significant. Recirculation is at a maximum during acceleration when the NO$_x$ emission is increased by the engine power being used, and during moderate-speed cruising when it is increased by the high combustion temperatures due to the weak mixtures employed. There is usually no recirculation at full throttle for reasons already given (p. 96). By 1973, the Federal regulations also included an NO$_x$ limit, so EGR systems became widely used.

One consequence of this trend was a marked deterioration in fuel economy. The deliberate enriching of the mixture to maintain the clean-up reactions in the exhaust system was partly responsible. Another cause was the use of retarded ignition during the acceleration and cruise modes as well as during deceleration and idling. This helps to minimize emissions because it reduces maximum combustion temperatures as well as raising exhaust gas temperatures, thus encouraging the post-combustion oxidation of HC and CO. A third was the widespread adoption of lower compression ratios to decrease NO$_x$ emissions.

Apart from performance – which also deteriorated significantly – another characteristic to suffer was 'driveability'. This mostly means the smoothness with which a car responds when the driver wishes to accelerate and opens the throttle suddenly. The emission-controlled cars of 1973 did not respond smoothly at all, hesitating badly under such conditions.

These trends together with the growing difficulty of meeting the increasingly stringent limits led to many protests and complaints. All critics of the Environmental Protection Agency, who were responsible for framing the regulations, accepted the need for exhaust emission control, but most felt that the United States motor industry was being asked to do far too much far too quickly. The European motor manufacturers also felt the burden, many of them being highly dependent upon sales in the States.

The energy crisis and fuel consumption

The drawbacks of the exhaust pollution control programme in America – the deterioration in fuel consumption particularly – were brought into focus by the fuel crisis of 1973 which changed the position significantly. One consequence was the creation by the EPA of a standard fuel consumption test. Examples of every car sold in the States must be subjected to this test, and any fuel consumption figures quoted in advertising or promotional material must be those obtained from it.

In fact there are two tests and three fuel consumption figures. The first is the **EPA urban fuel consumption** value obtained from the urban driving of the ordinary emissions cycle. Then there is an **EPA highway fuel consumption** figure obtained from a special highway driving cycle with a much higher average speed. Finally there is a third value: the **EPA combined fuel consumption** value, which is the first two figures combined taking into account the known average relationship between American urban and highway driving.

In addition, the US government passed a law requiring the sales-weighted average fuel consumption for each manufacturer's range of models to be progressively reduced from 1978 onwards to 33 mpg (27.5 miles per US gallon) by 1985. This is known as the Corporate Average Fuel Economy, or 'CAFE' law. In 1974 the sales-weighted average fuel consumption of all cars sold on the American market was 16.7 mpg (13.9 miles per US gallon). The term sales-weighted average means that a company such as General Motors will be allowed to sell certain numbers of Cadillacs, say, consuming fuel at the rate of 10 mpg, perhaps, provided these are balanced by certain numbers of Chevettes, say, consuming fuel at the rate of 40 mpg, maybe, to give the required average for the complete range of cars, taking into account the numbers sold of the various models.

Fines of $30 per mpg over the prescribed level (28.8 mpg or 24 miles per US gallon for 1982) may be imposed, but a special dispensation is granted to companies producing cars in small numbers – such as Rolls-Royce, which only has to pay large-car 'gas-guzzler' taxes.

Similar legislation is neither proposed nor needed in Europe. The typical European car is so much lighter, more compact and more efficient for a given carrying capacity than its American counterpart that its fuel consumption is already excellent. And further improvements are rapidly being forced into existence by the rising cost of fuel.

But European countries have also introduced government-sponsored mandatory fuel consumption tests – in Britain they came into force in 1978. In the long run, tests of this sort should be of immense benefit to the motorist, for no aspect of a car's behaviour is more widely misunderstood or more the subject of wild optimism, false claims and distorted comparisons than fuel consumption.

The basic problem is that fuel consumption is not easy to measure accurately. Technically, it is not difficult to fit a fuel flowmeter to a car and thus measure its consumption at a steady speed on level ground, but the figure thus obtained has very little to do with the consumption associated with normal driving on the road. To take an extreme example, imagine a car with a carburetter delivering a very lean mixture at steady speeds, but at the same time having a maladjusted accelerator pump (p. 109) which squirts in large doses of fuel every time the throttle is snapped open. The steady-speed consumption would then be very good, but the consumption in stop–go driving very bad.

But driving the car along a set route is not the answer, especially if economy modifications are being tested: it is too easy for the driver to be influenced by the results he expects. And if the route is realistic, changes in the pattern of traffic encountered prevent the average speed from being held within limits small enough for acceptable accuracy and repeatability.

A better approach is to put the car through a planned sequence of idling, acceleration, cruising and deceleration on a private test track, but even a test of this sort has its limitations. It is still subject to driver errors, while weather variations introduce further errors – and the test cannot be conducted at all in high winds and heavy rain.

By far the best method, therefore, is exactly the same driving cycle technique, using a roller dynamometer, as is employed for emissions testing. It reduces erors and is wholly objective, removing all driver bias. Hence for the British tests there is an urban fuel consumption figure derived from the standard ECE emissions driving cycle and (less satisfactorily) a highway figure derived from steady-speed cruising at 56 mph (90 kph). To conform with Continental practice, the consumption at a steady 75 mph (120 kph) is also quoted, even though this speed is above Britain's legal limit.

But there are critics of the test who feel that a special driving cycle is needed. They consider that the ECE cycle, while representing fairly the congested city-centre driving relevant to exhaust emissions, is not representative of average, more varied European town driving. So low is the 12 mph (19 kph) average speed, for example, that the results are heavily influenced by the consumption when idling. In addition, the test is kind to cars with automatic transmission systems, even though these normally carry a fuel consumption penalty of about 10 per cent (p. 187) compared to a manual gearbox. The reason for the flattery is that an automatic transmission system is free to select a high gear, whereas for a manual-transmission model the ratio in use at any point in the cycle is rigidly prescribed by the procedure. While objective fuel consumption tests are to be welcomed in general, therefore, it is to be hoped that a more realistic cycle will eventually be evolved for Britain.

Advanced emission control

Even after the fuel crisis the American motor industry remained under attack for failing to respond well to the need for cleaner air. Hence for 1975 the permitted Federal pollutant levels were greatly reduced from those of the previous year: from 3.0 g/mile for HC to 1.5 g/mile; from 28 g/mile to 15 g/mile for CO, the NO_x limit remaining at 3.1 g/mile. More sophisticated emission control equipment was needed and for most cars this took the form of a **catalytic converter** – already fitted to the majority of models sold in California.

A catalyst, as many of us will remember from our schooldays, is something which changes the speed of a chemical reaction – usually accelerating it – without itself changing. Very often it does so simply by having an absorbent surface of a very large area which brings the reacting chemicals more intimately in contact with one another than would otherwise be possible. For exhaust systems catalysts are generally used to complete the combustion of the HC and CO, thermal reaction with air injection forming the first stage of control and EGR being retained to keep NO_x production down.

Platinum was and is the material most often employed, sometimes with palladium. The amount needed for a single converter fitted to a typical American car is quite small – about 0.05 troy oz (1.5 g) because to obtain the very high surface area essential to the catalystic action, the platinum or palladium is deposited in a very thin layer on a **substrate**, an inert material usually made of ceramic. Sometimes pellets of substrate are used, sometimes the substrate is a **monolithic** or one-piece **honeycomb** (fig. 74) on to which the catalyst is deposited.

One important feature of the catalysts used is that they are quite rapidly poisoned by the lead added to petrol to raise its octane rating (p. 68), losing their effectiveness within a few thousand miles on a diet of leaded fuel. For this reason a special grade

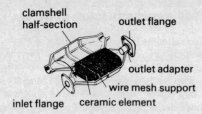

clamshell
half-section   outlet flange

outlet adapter

wire mesh support

inlet flange   ceramic element

fig. 74. A catalytic converter with a monolithic or one-piece honeycomb of inert material on to which the catalyst is deposited.

of 91-octane fuel with a very low lead content is sold in the States – from pumps with small-diameter nozzles designed to fit correspondingly small fuel filler necks to make it difficult for the leaded fuel to be used by mistake. Even on this low-lead fuel, the core of the catalytic converter generally needs replacing every 25,000 miles, violating the EPA's original requirement that nothing more than a tune-up should be needed at this interval and that an emission control system should last for 50,000 miles without major attention. Moreover the catalytic converter is nearly always located under the car, which means that the intense heat developed within it can create a fire hazard when parked on dry grass or the like.

Catalytic converters needed less 'seeding' with a rich mixture, so their adoption led to an improvement in fuel consumption. And under the pressure of high fuel costs as well as the EPA's consumption tests, the big American manufacturers began learning how to achieve the same emission results less wastefully, thus gaining further improvements.

After 1975, though, the Federal standards became even more severe, the limit for NO_x being reduced from 3.1 g/mile to 2.0 g/mile for 1977. This change brought into being a number of even more sophisticated and complex exhaust emission control systems.

Consider Chrysler, for example. In 1976, following their original Cleaner Air Package approach, Chrysler introduced their lean burn system, a commendable attempt to reduce

exhaust emissions by improving the basic efficiency of the engine rather than by surrounding it with clean-up devices. The basic principle was to make the engine run on a lean mixture with the 18:1 air/fuel ratio at which emissions of HC, CO and NO_x are all simultaneously low. This was achieved by using sensors to monitor a large number of variables, including engine speed, throttle position, rate of change of throttle movement, ambient air temperature, coolant temperature and manifold depression and by processing the signals thus produced in a microcomputer to determine the optimum ignition timing. As already mentioned (p. 80), such an array of controls is known generally as an electronic **engine management system** and has since become an important element in most packages developed to improve fuel consumption as well as to minimize exhaust emissions. Chrysler engines meeting the 1976 Federal regulations were able to dispense with catalytic converters, air injection and exhaust gas recirculation.

But Chrysler engines fitted with the lean burn system and meeting the 1977 Federal regulations additionally required catalytic converters and air injection. Only exhaust gas recirculation could be eliminated.

One of the most sophisticated emission control systems, introduced at that time and now used by almost all the manufacturers, owes its development partly to a major European component manufacturer – Robert Bosch GmbH. This system involves the use of a **three-way catalyst** which is capable of simultaneously cleaning up the HC, the CO and the NO_x emissions. The major difficulty is that the catalyst works fully only if the air/fuel ratio is maintained with extreme precision at the stoichiometric value. The accuracy required is far higher than can be achieved with conventional carburation – or even by the Bosch continuous flow K-Jetronic fuel injection equipment (p. 117) which forms part of the system. Accordingly, the Bosch engineers developed a control

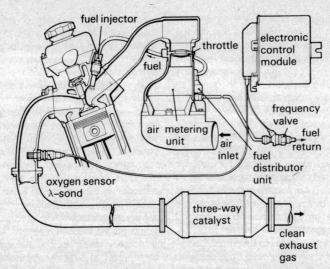

fig. 75. The Lambda-sensor system evolved by Bosch for use with a three-way catalyst uses an oxygen sensor in the exhaust system which gen- erates a feedback signal for an electronic control unit.

arrangement (fig. 75) using a probe sensitive to exhaust gas composition which feeds correcting signals back to the injection equipment as soon as the mixture strength deviates by a very small amount from the stoichiometric. This is a system of **closed loop control** employing negative feedback – negative because the sense of the control is such as to subtract from or cancel out the error signals generated by the probe.

With its help the catalyst works satisfactorily and the 1977 Californian regulations could be met without major loss of power or increase in fuel consumption. Adopted first by Volvo and Saab, the arrangement is called the Lambda-Sond system, the Greek letter Lambda being a symbol for another way of expressing air/fuel ratio, while sond is the Swedish word for sensor.

Three-way catalyst systems involving an exhaust gas sensor are now fitted to almost all the cars sold in the States, though in place of a full fuel injection system, the Lambda sensor may govern a 'feedback' carburetter or even a **throttle-body injection** system

using a single injector (p. 118). In some cases a second oxidizing catalyst is required, downstream of the first, with its own supply of injected air. But with all the current systems involving three-way catalysts, whether alone or with a second catalyst, the extremely severe Federal and Californian regulations in force since 1981 are easily met.

But whether these highly complex and very expensive systems confer a worthwhile benefit on mankind in the long term is much more questionable. Clearly the motorcar must not be allowed to foul its own nest, so restrictions of some sort on exhaust emissions are reasonable.

Unfortunately, though, the present American limits, now very close to those laid down by Senator Muskie, have no rational basis. Thus in the early 1980s the American National Academy of Science reported that *even in those places subject to photochemical smog such as Los Angeles*, atmospheric pollution due to car exhausts had improved so markedly as to establish beyond doubt the excessive severity of the regulations. In particular, it was suggested that the 3.4 g/mile CO limit be increased to 7.0 g/mile.

As to global rather than local levels of pollution due to car exhausts, it seems pretty clear, despite occasional alarmist scares to the contrary, that these represent little danger to the balance of the Earth's climate or to human life.

For it also became known that the amounts of HC, CO and NO_x emitted by man and his works including the motorcar are very small compared to those emitted by nature itself. Man's share is the highest for unburned hydrocarbons, estimates of his proportion of the total amount emitted annually ranging from 10 per cent to 30 per cent, but nature releases billions of tons of HC into the air every year from decaying vegetation in the form of CH_4, methane gas. Only about 10 per cent of all the CO released annually – some of it by fresh water and marine algae – is due to man; for NO_x the proportion is even lower.

More significant still was the discovery that nature and man together released far more pollution annually than is ever present in the atmosphere at any given time. Thus nature has its own ways of removing these pollutants – and pretty powerful ways, too. It is still not known exactly what these absorbing systems are – though the soil probably plays an important role in them – but their existence can be inferred with some certainty.

These discoveries mean that the earth's atmosphere behaves much more like a ventilated sieve than like a leakproof tank slowly filling with poison. They strongly suggest that exhaust emission controls of American stringency are pointlessly severe and not needed in Europe, though of course vigilant monitoring of atmospheric pollution should be continuously maintained to ensure that any changes do not pass unnoticed.

These matters are not merely academic. To begin with, a few European countries, notably West Germany and Switzerland, are

pressing for the adoption of much more severe exhaust emission limits, despite the absence of any rational basis for such proposals. Secondly, an elaborate exhaust emission control system of the three-way catalyst type is expensive and adds significantly to the cost of the car to which it is fitted – and it is ultimately the customer who pays for this extra cost. Moreover, a three-way catalyst requires a ratio of rhodium to platinum higher than exists in nature, and both are scarce and precious metals found mainly in countries widely regarded with disfavour in Europe: South Africa and the USSR. Thirdly, while the fuel consumption penalty associated with strict exhaust emission control is much less severe than it was in the early seventies, it is still appreciable, nonetheless. In particular, the stoichiometric (chemically correct) 15:1 air/fuel mixture required by the three-way catalyst of itself involves a fuel consumption penalty, since European engines tend to run on leaner part-throttle mixtures with air/fuel ratios around 17:1. And the next generation of lean-burn high-compression, high-turbulence engines with electronic management will certainly run on weaker mixtures still.

It is to be hoped, therefore, that in future the adoption of exhaust emission regulations will be governed by a more rational approach.

More about carburation

The compensation principle

The elementary carburetter (p. 55) with a single jet and a fixed choke (some carburetters have variable-size chokes, p. 111) is a highly ingenious device of classic simplicity. If air and petrol were basically similar fluids it would maintain a constant air/fuel ratio over the whole range of engine operation from the lowest speeds and loads to maximum power. But unfortunately air and petrol are not basically similar. Air, for instance, is compressible, while petrol, for all practical purposes, is not. Thus the mixture delivered by a simple, single-jet carburetter does not remain constant in strength: it becomes progressively richer as the engine speed and load rise.

To correct this deviation most modern fixed-choke carburetters incorporate a **compensation** system, often of the **air bleed** type. In such a system (fig. 76) petrol flows

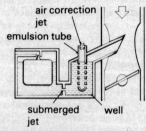

fig. 76. Air-bleed compensation: as the air flow increases, the level in the well falls, exposing the holes of the emulsion tube and introducing a gradually increasing air bleed to compensate for the enrichment tendency.

through a **submerged jet** to a well which communicates with the venturi and surrounds a **perforated emulsion tube**. The emulsion tube is open to the atmosphere through a calibrated **air correction jet**. At low speeds and loads the well remains filled with petrol, but as the air flow increases, the level in the well falls, successively exposing the holes in the emulsion tube and introducing a gradually increasing air bleed. This controlled air bleed progressively weakens the mixture, compensating for its enrichment tendency so that the air/fuel ratio can be maintained constant. And through the creation of an emulsion – a mixture of air bubbles suspended in the liquid fuel – atomization is considerably improved.

Economizers

Most fixed-choke carburetters are designed to deliver a specially weak mixture for econ-

omy during part throttle running. This is sometimes provided by a diaphragm-controlled air bleed valve which opens to admit additional air when the inlet manifold depression is high, thus weakening the mixture. Conversely, in other carburetters the mixture is enriched at large throttle openings and low values of inlet manifold depression – by shutting off an auxiliary air supply or opening an auxiliary jet – so that at small throttle openings and high values of inlet manifold depression the mixture becomes weaker.

The choke

The extra-rich mixture needed when starting from cold (p. 74) is often created by a **strangler** or **choke** – not to be confused with the choke tube or venturi. This is simply a flap, located upstream (fig. 77) of both the

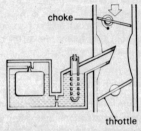

fig. 77. The choke or strangler flap enriches the mixture for cold starting.

throttle and the venturi, which can be swung across the inlet duct to close it almost entirely. In this position it greatly enriches the mixture both by severely restricting the flow of air and by increasing the partial vacuum available to suck fuel out of the jet. Usually a disc, not unlike a throttle valve, the choke is often pivoted about an offset spindle and allowed some freedom to turn through a small angle against the action of a light spring which holds it in the closed position. By offsetting the spindle in this way, it is partially opened by the pressure of the incoming air as soon as the engine fires, so that the initial enrichment is reduced.

Generally the choke is also mechanically linked to the throttle to raise the initial idling speed.

Weakening the mixture further as the engine warms up is a task which the driver is often called upon to perform. Some carburetters, however, have an automatic choke, generally controlled by a bimetallic thermostat spring. This is a strip of two metals, differing widely in their coefficients of thermal expansion yet bonded together. It can be designed to curl up tightly as the temperature rises and to unwind as it falls. For an automatic choke the bimetallic strip is usually warmed either by the exhaust system or by the cooling water so that the choke is fully open and ceases to have any action when the engine reaches its operating temperature.

In other installations the rich mixture required for starting is provided by a small auxiliary carburetter which is sometimes integral with the main unit but sometimes separate from it. As for the choke, the control is either manual or automatic.

Temperature and density

Combustion is highly wasteful and inefficient during the first few minutes after a cold start, so to speed the warm-up process and improve fuel consumption most engines have heated inlet manifolds. The heat is provided either by a water jacket or by the exhaust system via a **hot spot**. Heating the incoming mixture in this way reduces its density, thus decreasing the weight of air and fuel drawn in and theoretically leading to a reduction in power. But in practice the improved fuel consumption which results from the better vaporization of the fuel nearly always more than compensates for the loss.

Changes in the density of the incoming air not only affect the volumetric efficiency but also alter the mixture strength. For a carburetter only delivers fuel in the correct proportions for air of a certain density – the density for which it is designed, usually that corresponding to certain standard values of atmospheric pressure and temperature: 760 mm of mercury and 20°C. At higher air densities the mixture becomes weaker and at lower densities richer. Thus a conventional carburetter is sensitive to atmospheric pressure, to altitude and to ambient temperature.

Variations in atmospheric pressure – which seldom exceed ±3 per cent in Europe – are of little practical significance outside the test house, in which accuracy is important. Variations in altitude can have a much greater influence, though changes large enough to reduce power noticeably or cause rough running are encountered relatively rarely. The effect is of some concern, though, to those living at high altitudes. A carburetter calibrated to run correctly at sea level, for instance, will run 9 per cent rich at a place such as Denver, Colorado, USA, which lies at an altitude of 5280 ft (1610 m). Such a change is too large to be acceptable when emission laws are to be met, so the American Federal regulations have required from 1977 onwards that cars used at an altitude of 4000 ft (1220 m) or more must be fitted with altitude-compensated carburetters.

Changes in the temperature of the incoming air can also influence performance noticeably. The high underbonnet temperatures reached during very hot weather, for instance, reduce the density of the air much more than the density of the fuel. More significantly, the viscosity or resistance to flow of the fuel falls considerably. As a result of these changes, the mixture becomes excessively rich and the result is an unsatisfactory 'lumpy' idle – very similar to the idle you get if you leave the choke out too long.

Variations in the temperature of the incoming air, though difficult to avoid in a heatwave, are incompatible with the precise carburation now needed for efficient exhaust emission control, so in recent years many engines have been fitted with thermostatically controlled **inlet air temperature** systems.

In such a system a flap valve automatically mixes cold air at ambient temperature,

More About the Petrol Engine 109

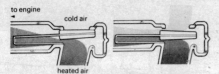

fig. 78. A British Leyland inlet air temperature control system. When the engine is cold (*left*) it is supplied only with air heated by the exhaust manifold, but when it is warm (*right*) the thermostatically controlled valve admits some cold air to maintain the intake air at a constant temperature.

usually drawn directly from the front of the car, with hot air which has been warmed by being passed over the exhaust manifold. A British Leyland control system of this sort (fig. 78) illustrates the principle well: it essentially consists of a mixing chamber and a flap valve which is directly attached to the end of a U-shaped bimetallic strip. When the engine is cold, the U remains open, the valve closes off the cold air inlet and all the air drawn in is heated by the exhaust manifold. As the induced air warms, differential expansion in the bimetallic U makes it close up, open the

valve and admit some cold air to maintain the temperature of the resultant mixture at a constant level. In very hot weather, though, such a system cannot maintain the supply of air to the carburetter at the preset temperature if the ambient air is at a higher temperature. Under most conditions, however, a constant temperature is maintained, and this allows the carburation to be more precise. Moreover, the temperature level chosen – typically about 50°C – is high enough to speed warm-up and improve fuel vaporization but not so high as to cause a significant power loss, though some systems incorporate a cold air by-pass which comes into operation at full throttle.

Accelerator pump

Fixed-choke carburetters are generally provided with **accelerator pumps** to provide the temporary richness needed (p. 75) when the throttle is suddenly opened. A typical accelerator pump consists (fig. 79) of a spring-loaded plunger or diaphragm located

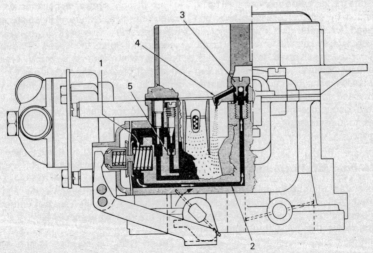

fig. 79. Acceleration enrichment: a sudden opening of the throttle causes the diaphragm, 1, to inject additional fuel via the duct, 2, the delivery valve, 3, and the jet, 4. When the throttle is opened slowly the fuel merely leaks back through the orifice, 5.

in a cylinder filled with fuel. When the throttle is suddenly opened, it forces the plunger or diaphragm along the cylinder, injecting an additional dose of fuel into the venturi, a non-return valve preventing a backward flow into the float chamber. A second non-return valve on the outlet side isolates the accelerator pump from the venturi and stops air from being drawn in during the intake stroke. A controlled leakage path prevents fuel from being injected when the throttle is opened slowly.

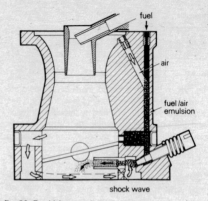

fig. 80. Ford Motorcraft IV carburetter – sonic idling system. The emulsified air/fuel mixture for idling is atomized by the sonic speed of the incoming air.

Carburetters

Carburetters are often classified by the direction imposed on the fuel and air passing through them. A **downdraught** carburetter, for instance, is one through which the fuel and air pass downwards before entering the engine. Most carburetters are either of this type or of the **sidedraught** kind with a horizontal choke tube, though **updraught** carburetters were also used many years ago.

Despite the increased sophistication being demanded by exhaust emission laws and the need for better fuel consumption, a relatively simple carburetter with a single, fixed choke is still used for many cars. Sometimes, however, the fuel is first drawn into a small auxiliary venturi which imposes a high speed on the incoming fuel and air to promote good mixing before the charge passes to the larger and concentric main venturi.

Ford Motorcraft IV carburetter

One example is the Motorcraft IV carburetter, fitted to a wide range of Ford models. It is a single-choke, single-venturi, downdraught device (fig. 80) with a single submerged main jet, an auxiliary venturi, an air bleed compensation system and an enrichment valve for full-throttle running operated by manifold depression. A simple choke flap, manually or automatically controlled, enriches the mixture for cold starts, the fuel being drawn from the main jet. A spring-loaded diaphragm pump provides acceleration enrichment. An overrun by-pass valve can be fitted if emission regulations require it.

But though simple in construction, the carburetter does feature an ingenious **sonic idling** system. This uses a stream of air accelerated up to the speed of sound or beyond which forms a highly effective means of breaking the droplets of fuel into a fine homogeneous **aerosol mist** which stays in suspension and has little tendency to stick to the manifold walls. As already mentioned (p. 73) the very large pressure drop across the small throttle opening associated with idling creates the necessary sonic flow in all conventional carburetters. But it can do little to improve mixture quality at the gap between the throttle and the choke tube, and in the Ford carburetter has been diverted to a special air/fuel mixing point.

Air for idling is supplied to the engine through a duct by-passing the throttle which is shut almost completely. Another duct supplies the fuel required, and this is emulsified with a small amount of air from a jet. The air and the lightly emulsified fuel are brought together at a nozzle in which the mixture is accelerated to sonic speed. The droplets of fuel are first drawn out into long strips as the mixture accelerates to the speed of sound and then compressed into flat discs in the shock waves formed as it decelerates back to subsonic speed on leaving the nozzle.

The homogeneity of the resultant mixture is such that the engine will idle with great stability and regularity on an air/fuel ratio as weak as 16:1 in place of the 9:1 usually required. Exhaust emissions during idling are greatly reduced and warm-up performance is also improved.

Maintaining a reasonably high gas speed through the venturi of a carburetter is a matter of considerable importance, as the sonic idling system of the Ford unit shows. The basic difficulty is that a venturi large enough to pass the air required at high engine outputs without excessive friction losses generally becomes too large for good carburation at low rates of air flow. Not only does the depression in the venturi then become too small to suck the fuel from the jet satisfactorily, but the subsequent speed of the petrol droplets is too low for efficient mixing with the air.

One solution to this problem is a twin-choke carburetter with a small-diameter primary venturi for idling and low-power running and, beside it, a larger secondary venturi with a secondary throttle which additionally comes into action towards full power. Perhaps the best-known twin-choke carburetters are those made by the Italian company, Eduardo Weber, now a wholly owned subsidiary of Fiat.

Following this approach to its logical conclusion leads to a carburetter in which separate stages are replaced by a single venturi, continuously variable in size, which automatically sets itself to a small aperture at low engine speeds and loads and to a large diameter at high ones.

SU constant depression carburetter

The possibility of such a 'constant depression' carburetter was understood more than seventy years ago and gave rise to the Skinner Union company's SU carburetter, using a leather bellows mechanism. This company, now part of the Austin-Rover Group, soon dropped the bellows in favour of a sliding piston, giving the unit the basic form which it retains to this day.

In place of a conventional venturi, an SU carburetter (fig. 81) contains a piston sliding up and down above a fixed bridge, forming an aperture which varies in size from very small for idling to very large at full power. A tapered brass needle attached to the piston, manufactured with precision to a carefully specified shape, engages with a fixed jet which is mounted in the bridge beneath it and is supplied with fuel from an adjacent

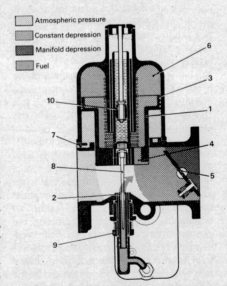

fig. 81. SU carburetter – general arrangement (engine on right). 1, piston; 2, jet; 3, piston guide; 4, depression duct; 5, throttle; 6, suction chamber; 7, vent to atmosphere; 8, needle; 9, jet holder; 10, piston damper.

float chamber. Thus needle and jet form a valve which meters the fuel.

The moving piston and bridge have a somewhat sharp-edged shape and therefore constitute more an orifice plate (p. 56) of variable size than a venturi. There is thus a low-pressure area immediately downstream of the two components which is connected to a suction chamber above the piston via a small duct in its trailing edge. It is this low pressure, acting on the upper surface of the piston (while atmospheric pressure acts on its lower surface) which lifts it up when the air flow increases.

Suppose, for example, the engine is idling and the throttle is then opened. The air flowing through the small gap beneath the piston is forced to speed up, so its pressure drops (p. 56), as does the pressure in the immediate downstream area. With less pressure above it than before, the piston is lifted until the upward force created by the new pressure level is exactly balanced by the downward force due to the weight of the piston. Because the piston's weight remains constant, it tends to take up a position such that the depressions in the jet beneath it, and in the suction chamber above it, are maintained at a roughly constant value and thus the speed of the incoming air is also constant. Hence a carburetter using this principle is generally described as being of the **constant depression** sort. In most SU carburetters nowadays, the piston is additionally forced downwards by a light spring, to tailor the depression to the particular engine, but this does not materially affect the principle. It is important to realize that the throttle plays no part in creating the depression which lifts the piston: a constant-depression carburetter will work satisfactorily even if the throttle is located several feet away from it. It is the piston and bridge themselves which create the depression – by constricting the passage through which the incoming air must flow. Similarly, the depression at the piston and bridge is only roughly the same as the manifold depression when the throttle is fully open.

Since the depression above the jet remains roughly constant, the metering of the fuel is controlled by the tapered needle which is given a profile carefully tailored to suit the particular engine. Acceleration enrichment is provided in a particularly simple way: by a fixed rod engaging with an oil-filled well in the piston guide rod to form a hydraulic damper, resisting rapid changes in piston motion. Thus if the throttle is suddenly snapped open, the piston lags in its response while the air flowing beneath it speeds up, its pressure drops and more fuel is momentarilly sucked out of the jet. In many versions of the carburetter, cold starting enrichment is equally simple – a lever and rod arrangement pulls the jet downwards away from the tapered needle, increasing the flow of fuel.

There is usually no special provision for economy at part load, but this is to some extent ensured by a certain inherent enrichment at high loads due to the associated strong gas pulsations which, for reasons too complex to give here, increase the supply of fuel. Such enrichment is common to most carburetters but particularly noticeable with the SU which may need no other form of economizer so long as the carburetter supplies only 2 to 4 cylinders. With more, the overlap between suction impulses makes the pulses too weak to be fully-effective.

SU HIF carburetter

The most advanced version of the SU carburetter is the HIF model which was evolved in response to exhaust emission requirements. It is similar in principle and layout to the basic unit just described, but differs from it in several details. The first of these is that the float chamber has been integrated into the body of the unit and encircles the jet, the plastic float having an arc shape.

The second springs from the sensitivity of the fuel flow rate, at any given piston position, to the exact alignment of the needle within the jet. In other versions of the SU carburetter the needle is designed to be exactly concentric with the jet, a satisfactory arrangement when fuel metering has to be only ordinarily precise. But in searching for greater precision it was found that the needle could not easily be maintained concentric with the jet to the accuracy required, and that small displacements from the central position significantly affect the fuel flow rate. In the **swinging needle** HIF carburetter, therefore, the needle is deliberately biased by a small spring to contact one side of the jet.

Another factor influencing mixture strength is the viscosity of the fuel or its resistance to flow, which varies with temperature, altering the amount able to pass in a given time through the sometimes tiny gap between the jet and the needle. To compensate for this, the jet of the HIF unit moves upwards or downwards by a small amount in response to temperature under the influence of a bimetallic strip or vane thermostat device.

A further refinement is a spring-loaded disc in the throttle plate which opens on the overrun when the manifold depression is high to admit extra fuel and air for more complete combustion. In addition, the HIF differs from other SU carburetters in having for some applications a special part-throttle system in the form of a by-pass duct which directs fuel and air towards a small cut-out in the throttle when it is almost closed. This takes advantage of the high-speed air flow at the edge of the throttle to give improved atomization. Enrichment for cold starting is provided by a separate cold-start valve which delivers an additional supply of fuel and air through a small duct downstream of the bridge.

Zenith CDSE carburetter

The other major constant-depression carburetter in use today is of more recent design than the SU, being known first as the Bendix-Stromberg unit, then the Stromberg and finally the Zenith after the company that has made it for many years. It is very similar in general principle to the SU (fig. 82), the major difference lying in the use of a flexible diaphragm to seal the sliding piston.

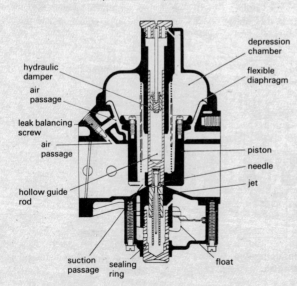

hydraulic damper
air passage
leak balancing screw
air passage
hollow guide rod
suction passage
sealing ring

depression chamber
flexible diaphragm
piston
needle
jet
float

fig. 82. Zenith CDSE carburetter. This is very similar to the SU, except that a flexible diaphragm seals the piston to the body. In this emission-control form of the carburetter, a thermostatically controlled air bleed compensates for changes in fuel viscosity with temperature. An overrun by-pass valve opens when the manifold depression is very high.

Like the SU HIF the CDSE version is designed for exhaust emission applications and incorporates similar refinements. It also has a swinging needle, for instance – indeed its makers were the first to adopt the concept. Compensation for fuel viscosity is not achieved through jet movement, however, but with a thermostatically controlled air bleed which alters the mixture strength to balance changes in the flow. Similarly, the overrun valve is not mounted in the throttle itself but in the carburetter body, opening a by-pass duct when the manifold depression is high. A separate valve supplies extra fuel for starting from cold.

Other constant depression carburetters

Until quite recently the use of SU and Zenith constant depression carburetters was confined almost entirely to British engines. But the ability of constant depression carburetters to improve fuel consumption and reduce exhaust emissions is becoming more widely appreciated so that both Ford and GM have introduced new designs of their own. Another example is the Solex 4A–1 carburetter (fig. 83) fitted to certain BMW and Mercedes models. It has a fixed choke first

stage for idling and low-power running and a constant depression second stage, but one which involves a hinged flap rather than a sliding piston.

Fuel injection

General

The carburetter is a relatively cheap and simple device – and a highly efficient one if used properly – but it does have its limitations. One of these is the reduced volumetric efficiency and increased pumping losses it creates through the obstruction presented to the incoming gases by its venturi – and by its throttle, even when this is fully open. Another is the uneven distribution which occurs when (as is commonly the case) one carburetter feeds several cylinders. For in-line engines it is then difficult to make the induction pipes equal in length; impossible to make them identical in shape and curvature. Hence it is also difficult to apply to them the tuned length technique which makes use of the gas pulsations in the system.

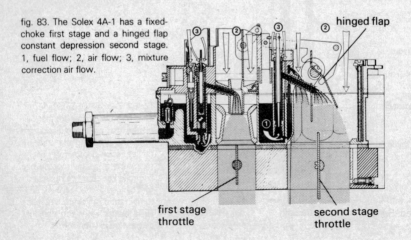

fig. 83. The Solex 4A-1 has a fixed-choke first stage and a hinged flap constant depression second stage. 1, fuel flow; 2, air flow; 3, mixture correction air flow.

hinged flap

first stage throttle

second stage throttle

Some of these disadvantages can be circumvented if each cylinder is provided with a separate carburetter – or, as is more usual, with separate venturis grouped in pairs which share common float chambers. Such arrangements have been used for high performance and racing engines but they are bulky, and the individual carburetters are difficult to synchronize. They remain, moreover, prone to another inherent defect: **surge** – the tendency for the fuel to be flung to one side in the float chamber when cornering hard, cutting off the supply to the jet. As with conventional carburetters, satisfactory vaporization of the fuel requires a good deal of heat to be applied to the inlet ducts, which lowers the density of the incoming charge, reducing volumetric efficiency.

An alternative solution, therefore, is to employ a fuel injection system in which petrol is sprayed under pressure into each cylinder from an individual injector. Almost all such arrangements employed for petrol engines have been **low-pressure injection** systems, injecting fuel at 20–120 lb/sq in (1.4–8 kg/sq cm) into the inlet ports, in contrast to the **high-pressure injection** systems fitted to diesel engines which run at around 2500 lb/sq in (175 kg/sq cm) because the fuel is injected directly into each cylinder at a pressure high enough to overcome the very considerable compression pressure (p. 120). All petrol injection systems used in Europe also feature a separate injector for each cylinder, thus ensuring excellent distribution. Moreover the type of injector employed usually incorporates (fig. 84) a spring-loaded needle designed to create a fine spray, so that atomization of the fuel is also good. But perhaps the biggest advantage of a fuel injection system is the way it allows, as already described (p. 86), each cylinder to be given a separate unobstructed induction pipe of a carefully chosen tuned length, and hence the power or torque to be boosted. Because of the extra cost involved, fuel injection systems are generally fitted to

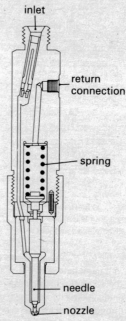

fig. 84. Petrol injection – a typical electrically controlled injector incorporates a spring-loaded needle and is designed to create a fine spray.

the more expensive, high-performance models in a manufacturer's range.

But there is nothing new about fuel injection: a crude system was a feature of an engine built in 1908 for the Wright brothers. But its application to petrol engines was given renewed impetus when the diesel was first fitted to a production car (a Mercedes in 1931) and the need to extract more power from aircraft piston engines stimulated a further wave of research during the last war.

To begin with, therefore, most petrol engine systems merely used existing diesel pumps adapted to low-pressure operation for injection into the inlet ports. The Bosch mechanical system, for instance, used by such companies as Mercedes and Porsche, incorporated a special version of an existing **jerk-type plunger** diesel pump. In appearance (more details p. 121) a pump of this

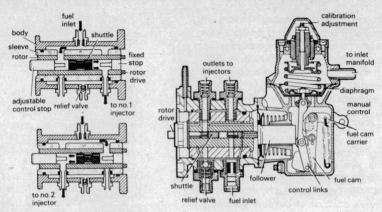

fig. 85. In the Lucas fuel injection system the petrol is injected by a shuttle displaced back and forth by the fuel itself between fixed and moving stops. A rotor distributes the doses of fuel to the various cylinders.

kind is not unlike a miniature in-line engine. But there is a camshaft in place of a crankshaft and the cams displace plungers – one for each cylinder – which force the fuel under pressure through pipes to the injectors in separate, timed doses for each combustion stroke. The needles of the injectors act as shut-off valves and their spring loadings determine the injection pressure. The amounts of fuel injected can be controlled by an ingenious arrangement which allows the effective stroke of each plunger to be varied as it moves up and down.

Lucas mechanical injection

A rather different principle is employed in the Lucas mechanical fuel injection system fitted to the Triumph TR5, TR6 and 2.5 PI models and widely used in racing.

Its novel feature (fig. 85) is a special metering unit in which the injection process is accomplished by a shuttle moved back and forth by the fuel itself, and a rotor sleeve surrounding it distributes the doses to the injectors. Fuel is supplied to the metering unit at a constant 100 lb/sq in (7 bar) by an external electric pump, and the amount injected is determined by the stroke of the shuttle. Rotation of the distributor sleeve first opens an inlet port at its left-hand end, and fuel enters, forcing the shuttle to the right and ejecting a dose of fuel on its far side through an outlet port to an injector. Further rotation of the sleeve opens a right-hand inlet port, the shuttle is forced to the left and another dose of fuel is passed to another injector.

But the development of a successful injection system involves solving a basic problem which highlights the simplicity and ingenuity of the carburetter. The problem is to measure the amount of air being drawn in, so that the fuel can be correctly apportioned to it. For many systems the amount of air induced is not so much measured as estimated, the most common basic parameter being the pressure within the inlet manifold. This is the only control factor used for the Lucas system: it is sensed by a barometric capsule controlling the position of the end-stop which governs the stroke of the shuttle.

But the inlet manifold pressure is not a very accurate measure of the weight of air being drawn into the cylinders; more sophisticated systems also take into account such factors as the temperature of the incoming air and the barometric pressure. The manipulation of several variables, however, calls for an expensive and complex computation system generally involving a **three-dimensional cam** or **space cam**. Such a cam might be displaced axially by one control factor and rotated by another, the 'output signal' generated by its heavily contoured surface being sensed by a roller follower.

Bosch D-Jetronic system

The cumbersome nature of such mechanical calculators led many to believe that their job would be much better done electronically, especially as the introduction of exhaust emission laws means that several further parameters may have to be added in any successful system, and this is quite easily accomplished when the control is electronic.

Most of the basic problems associated with an electronic fuel injection system were resolved in the Bendix Electrojector equipment designed in America. Some of the principles embodied in it are used in the Bosch Jetronic system, the first to be produced in substantial quantities.

In this system (fig. 86) the injectors, fed with fuel at a constant 28 lb/sq in (4 bar) from a ring main, are opened by electro-

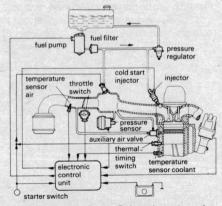

fig. 86. For the Bosch D-Jetronic system the injections are electrically controlled and timed.

magnets or **solenoids** and closed by spring pressure. The duration of injection is determined by an electronic control unit in response to various inputs, the most important again being inlet manifold pressure. In the latest D-Jetronic form of the system, however, barometric pressure, inlet air temperature, throttle position and throttle opening speed are also taken into account as well as (for starting) coolant temperature.

The injections are timed – up to a point – the injectors being triggered (by contacts mounted on the ignition distributor) in pairs for four- and eight-cylinder engines and in threes for six-cylinder engines. This means that some cylinders receive their dose of fuel when the inlet valve is shut, but this has little adverse effect on power, fuel consumption or exhaust cleanliness. Under licence from Bosch, Lucas in Britain make a variant of the system, with a digital rather than analogue electronic computer.

Bosch K-Jetronic system

A much more serious weakness of the D-Jetronic system – and others like it – is its 'guesstimation' of the mass of air flowing into the engine. A measurement system akin to that used by a carburetter is much to be preferred, for all its defects.

A mass air flow meter of this kind is therefore the essential feature of the latest Bosch K-Jetronic system (K for *Kontinuierlich* or continuous). It consists (fig. 87) of a horizontal circular plate a few inches in diameter, mounted on a lever and partially sealing the conical entrance to the plenum chamber. This plate is deflected upwards by the incoming air and works rather like the piston of a constant depression carburetter. If the downward control force on its lever is held constant, any rise in air flow causes the plate to be deflected through a distance just sufficient to increase the area of the annular passage surrounding it by the amount necessary to restore the velocity to its former value.

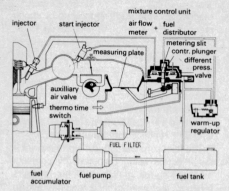

fig. 87. Air flow for the Bosch K-Jetronic system is measured by a swinging plate and conical orifice arrangement – similar in principle to a CD carburetter.

This plate governs a fuel metering and distribution valve which also exerts the downward control force. For any given condition the amount of fuel injected will be similar to that supplied by the D-Jetronic system, but it is spread over a continuous supply rather than being administered in separate timed doses. For the fuel – at a pressure of 48.5 lb/sq in (3.4 bar) passes continuously through the injectors, the needles of which are designed to chatter at 1500–2000 c/s (cycles per second) to improve atomization.

Bosch also make the hybrid L-Jetronic system which combines the timed injections of the D system with the air flow measurement of the K – though using a different mechanical arrangement involving a hinged flap. In another Bosch system, the cooling effect on a heated wire is used to measure the mass air flow.

Throttle body injection

The widespread adoption of the three-way catalyst system in the States has led to a search for devices which are simpler and cheaper than a complex fuel injection system yet capable of providing the exact stoichiometric air/fuel mixture required. Some American manufacturers have developed 'feedback' carburetters, which are basically conventional in construction but incorporate closed-loop control systems governed by an exhaust-gas sensor.

Other companies, however, have introduced simplified 'centrepoint' or throttle-body injection systems involving a single injector, locating in much the same place as a carburetter jet (though no venturi is needed) which sprays fuel under pressure towards the throttle valve. The fuel is injected in pulses, the durations of which are carefully controlled to provide the correct mixture. The main advantage of such systems is the ease with which they allow the fuel supply to be put under electronic control, and to be governed by a multiplicity of sensors if necessary.

four The Diesel and Other Engines

The Diesel

Although at present fitted to only a relatively small proportion of all cars sold, the diesel engine is fast becoming an important rival to the petrol engine under the pressure of rising fuel costs. Developed by Dr Rudolf Diesel at the turn of the century, a few years after the invention of the petrol engine, it is, of course, the power unit long used, in Europe at least, for the majority of large commercial and public service vehicles. Very similar to the petrol or spark-ignition engine in many ways, the diesel or compression-ignition power unit can work on either the four stroke or two stroke cycles, but has certain important characteristics of its own. In place of an air/fuel mixture it draws in air only, and heats this by a high degree of compression to ignite the fuel which is injected into the combustion chamber.

Diesel engines are inherently more efficient than petrol engines partly because they run at high compression ratios, ranging from 16:1 to 25:1. Since air alone is drawn in, and the fuel ignites immediately after injection, there is no combustible end-gas in the cylinder, so the diesel is not troubled by detonation. Two further reasons for high efficiency follow from the **stratified charge** principle upon which all diesels depend. In a stratified charge engine the fuel and air are persuaded to form a central kernel of mixture which is always rich enough to burn, no matter how small the dose of fuel or large the amount of excess air, a kernel which is surrounded by strata of progressively decreasing richness to which the flame spreads. Thanks to charge stratification, a diesel's power output can be controlled by varying the supply of fuel alone, not of fuel and air together. Hence the engine

can be allowed to induce air unchecked, so a throttle valve can be dispensed with and pumping losses reduced. In addition, very weak mixtures – with air/fuel ratios as large as 50:1 – can be used under part-load conditions, thus permitting significant fuel savings and contributing further to efficiency. And since there is no wetting of the manifold walls – or evaporation from them – acceleration enrichment is not needed. As a result of this efficient combustion, HC and CO emissions are very low, but a diesel cannot easily be made to meet very strict NO_x limits.

The diesel certainly has a number of other disadvantages. Its speed range is usually limited – to less than 5000 rpm – for example, and under certain conditions it is liable to emit smoke. But its most important disadvantage is its high price, much of which is associated with the cost of its fuel injection pump, a complex device made to a very high standard of precision. Against this can be set a long life – 100,000 miles is typical – low maintenance costs, and in many countries, low fuel costs also.

But a diesel engine must be stronger than a petrol engine of the same power output to withstand the higher cylinder pressures and more rapid combustion. This tends to make the diesel noisy, and leads to a 'spikey' torque characteristic calling for a stronger transmission system. Starting is more difficult, so a larger battery is another requirement. All these factors not only further increase the cost but also mean that the diesel with all its auxiliaries is in general considerably heavier than a petrol engine of the same power output. Most diesel cars, therefore, have until recently been powered by engines developing two-thirds of the power or less of their petrol-engined equivalents. Fuel consumption has certainly been improved, but at the expense of a drastic reduction in performance.

This situation is being changed by the introduction of lightweight high-speed diesels such as the engine developed by Volkswagen for the Golf. With a capacity of 1500 cc this develops the same power – 50 bhp – as the VW's 1100 cc petrol engine while weighing only 48 lb (22 kg) more. Except at idle it is little more noisy than a petrol engine and gives the Golf a lively performance for a small car yet exceptional fuel economy. The Golf diesel costs more than its petrol-engined equivalent, but seems likely to overcome most objections to the diesel car. A number of manufacturers, too, have introduced cars with turbocharged diesel engines which reduce the usual performance penalty to a more acceptable level while achieving exceptionally low fuel consumption by petrol-engine standards.

The diesel injection process

At the end of the compression stroke the air drawn into a diesel engine is raised in pressure to around 500 lb/sq in (35 bar) and in temperature to about 600°C – well above the ignition temperature of the fuel used. This has a higher boiling point (p. 66) and less volatility than petrol and is characterized by its readiness to ignite with the least delay – a readiness which is expressed by its **cetane number** after a reference fuel particularly strong in this quality. The greater the cetane number the more liable the fuel is to ignite rapidly and spontaneously – effectively the exact reverse of the quality expressed by octane number.

The diesel fuel is forced into the combustion chamber at 2000–3000 lb/sq in (140–200 bar) through tiny holes in the nozzle of an injector (fig. 88), forming a very fine spray, usually conical in shape. The injector is sealed by a needle or **pintle** which lifts under a pressure determined by its

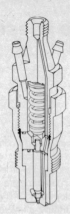

fig. 88. A typical diesel injector showing the spring-loaded needle and the return connection for leakage fuel.

spring loading. When the injection pump finishes its stroke and the pressure in the injector falls, the pintle shuts and the fuel passes back to the tank via a low-pressure return line. Any fuel leaking past the pintle guide is also diverted back to the tank along the same path.

To minimize this leakage, the pintle and injector are ground to fit each other in matched pairs to a very high standard of accuracy, tolerances of one ten-thousandth of an inch (two to three thousandths of a millimetre) being commonplace – another factor in the diesel engine's high cost. Such precision tolerances together with the tiny spray holes make the injector very vulnerable to dirt, but if the fuel and the incoming air are carefully filtered it nevertheless has a long service life. Lucas have introduced a new type of miniature injector, with an outward-opening pintle which needs no return line. Called the Microjector, it has been fitted in quantity to American diesel cars.

The injectors are fed with high-pressure fuel from an injection pump, a diesel engine's key component which in turn is supplied by a low-pressure feed pump. The oldest form of injection pump is the plunger type which

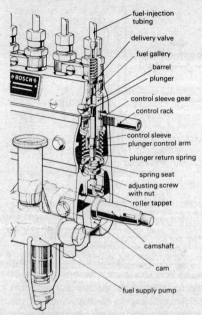

fig. 89. A jerk-type diesel injection pump has a plunger for each cylinder; it is fed by a low-pressure lift pump.

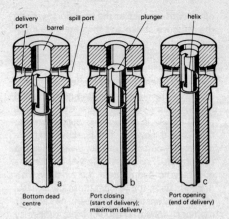

fig. 90. The diesel injection pump: how the fuel quantity is controlled. By rotating the plungers the length of the delivery stroke can be increased or decreased.

looks a little (fig. 89) like a miniature in-line engine. It has a camshaft in place of a crankshaft and the cams displace plungers – one for each cylinder – which force the fuel under pressure through pipes to the injectors in separate, timed doses for each combustion stroke. These doses of fuel are small – extremely small at idling – which once again means that very high standards of precision are needed, this time in the construction of the injection pump, if metering accuracy is to be maintained.

On its downward stroke (fig. 90a) the plunger uncovers a **delivery feed port** and a **spill port** and draws in fuel through both until it reaches bottom dead centre. Upward movement (fig. 90b) at first displaces fuel back through these ports to the low-pressure **feed gallery**. But as the plunger continues upwards it covers the feed port, the fuel can no longer escape and

is forced (fig. 90c) from the delivery chamber through a delivery valve along a fuel line and out of the injector. A vertical groove connects the delivery chamber to the annular space surrounding the central waisted portion of the plunger, but this offers no escape path to the fuel. Delivery continues, therefore, until with further upward movement a helical edge uncovers the spill port, providing an escape path for the fuel via the vertical groove, and collapsing the pressure in the delivery chamber, pipe and injector. Injection is stopped at once by the force which the pintle's return spring exerts and the delivery valve controls the pressure in the fuel line.

The effective injection stroke can be varied by rotating the plunger to change the point in its upward travel at which the helical shoulder meets the spill port. This is accomplished by a toothed control rack meshing with a pinion fixed to the sleeve which encloses the plunger. Lugs on the plunger engage with slots in the sleeve to which it is thus linked rotationally, while retaining freedom to slide axially. Hence movement of the control rack rotates sleeve and plunger, moving the helical shoulder to one side or the other with respect to the spill port, varying the effective stroke and thus the amount of fuel injected.

Coordinating the position of the injection pump rack with the speed and load presents certain problems, for the diesel power unit differs fundamentally from the petrol engine in its control requirements. Control of a petrol engine is generally relatively simple: the throttle governs the air flow and the carburetter automatically supplies fuel at the correct rate. For a diesel, however, there is generally no control over the air flow. This depends upon the temperature, the breathing characteristics of the engine and its rotational speed. The volumetric efficiency varies slightly with engine speed in the same way as for a petrol engine at full throttle, typically ranging from 80 per cent to 95 per cent, reaching a maximum at some mid-range speed and deteriorating at low and high rpm. While the air flow is substantially proportional to engine revs, the injection pump output for a given control rack position usually tends to increase as engine speed rises, leading to excess fuel delivery at high rpm.

These conflicting trends are generally reconciled by an **all-speed governor**, one function of which is simply to extend engine life by limiting speed and thus the high inertia loads imposed by a diesel's heavy moving parts. Its main purpose, however, is as part of a system (fig. 91) in which the accelerator pedal does not act directly upon the control rack but upon a spring controlling a centrifugal governor. The bob weights of the governor react against the other end of the control spring which is also linked to the injection pump rack.

Now suppose that the engine is idling when the accelerator is floored. Full depression of the accelerator displaces the control rack nearly to its maximum fuel position, since at idling speed the centrifugal governor exerts little restraining influence. But the engine develops more power, its speed rises and the bob-weights of the centrifugal gov-

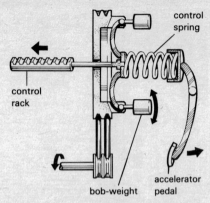

fig. 91. The all-speed governor – the accelerator pedal acts on one end of the control spring and the bob-weights of the centrifugal governor on the other.

ernor gradually compress the control spring, forcing the rack back towards the closed position. Eventually it reaches an equilibrium position determined by the speed of the engine, the position of the accelerator pedal and the stiffness of the control spring. If it is desired to maintain the same speed but the load increases – a hill is encountered, say – the accelerator pedal must be depressed further than before, compressing the control spring again. The control rack therefore moves away to a new position giving more fuel, relaxing the spring until the backward force on it – determined only by engine speed which has not altered – is the same as before. Thus the particular engine speed reached for a given accelerator position depends upon the prevailing road conditions, but the system is basically sensitive to speed rather than load.

The effect is often of a sharp power cut-off when the particular control speed is reached, making some older diesel cars jerky and unrefined to drive. A petrol engine, by contrast, tends to reach its 'equilibrium' speed more progressively, since its control system is more sensitive to load than to speed. But by careful tailoring of the governor spring characteristics, the objectionable 'cut-off' effect often associated with the diesel can be eliminated, as it has been for the Volkswagen Golf.

The diesel does not depend upon the evaporation of fuel from the manifold walls (which are not wetted) and the injector efficiently breaks up the fuel into a very fine mist. There is thus much less need for enrichment of the mixture when starting from cold than for a petrol engine: the mixture required is usually slightly richer than that used at full load.

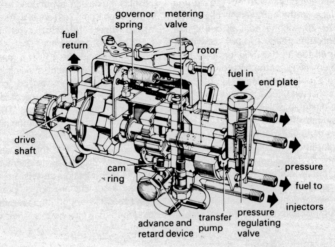

fig. 92a. The CAV DPA-type rotary injection pump. Fuel from the transfer pump – at a raised pressure determined by the regulating valve – is passed to the metering valve which admits a controlled quantity via the charging port to the central cavity of the rotor.

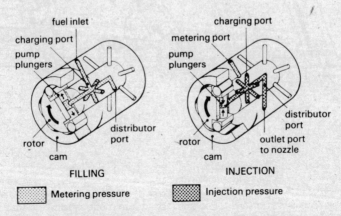

FILLING   INJECTION

Metering pressure   Injection pressure

fig. 92b. When the rotor distributor port registers with an outlet port connected to one of the injectors, the lobes of the cam ring squeeze the plungers together, injecting the fuel.

A much more important factor is the maximum compression temperature reached. When the ambient temperature is low, heat losses from the cylinders may prevent the induced air from reaching the fuel ignition temperature after compression at cranking speeds. Hence most diesels are fitted with electrically heated **glowplugs** which warm up the combustion chambers. After a 15–30 second heating period the engine becomes ready to start. However, accumulated fuel in the cylinders may lead to smoke emission for the first few minutes of running. Smoke emission is sometimes a problem at full load, too.

Since a diesel engine has no ignition system to switch off, it is not easy to stop. Nowadays the usual method is to cut off the fuel completely at the injection pump.

While the all-speed governor control principle is generally adhered to, many modern injection pumps are of a rotary type. To cut costs they effectively incorporate (fig. 92) a single plunger and sleeve, or equivalent metering chamber, working in conjunction with a distributor mechanism which passes the fuel to the cylinders in turn.

Types of diesel engine

Perhaps the most important feature of a diesel is the design layout used to create the stratified charge so essential to its operation. In the **direct injection** type of engine (fig. 93a) a tangential inlet port, sometimes working in conjunction with a masked inlet valve, imparts a violent swirling motion to the fresh charge of air which is accentuated by the upwards movement of a bowl-in-piston combustion chamber. The fuel is injected directly into this combustion chamber and the swirling action creates the required kernel of rich mixture surrounded by strata of progressively decreasing richness. Direct injection diesels are the most efficient kind, but are not at present well suited to cars, though improvements being developed may change this. Their very rapid

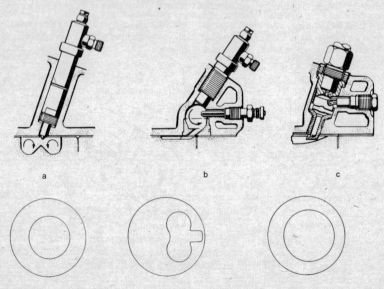

fig. 93. Basic types of diesel: (a) the direct injection type with a bowl-in-piston combustion chamber; (b) the Ricardo Comet indirect type with an auxiliary swirl chamber, and (c) the Mercedes indirect type with a pre-chamber.

combustion tends to make them rough and noisy and they are limited to modest rpm by the strangling effect of the energy-absorbing swirl action.

For an **indirect injection** diesel engine (fig. 93b) the initial kernel of rich mixture is formed within a small auxiliary combustion chamber communicating with the main one. Most modern indirect injection diesels now employ what is called a **swirl chamber**, and the best-known and most widely used of these forms part of the Ricardo Comet combustion system, named after Sir Harry Ricardo, a British pioneer of combustion research, whose company, Ricardo Engineering, remains at the forefront of internal combustion engine research.

The essential feature of the Comet system is an auxiliary swirl chamber having roughly 50 per cent of the total clearance volume and an entrance throat tangential to it, so that upward movement of the piston during the compression stroke imparts a violent swirling motion to the air inside. It is this swirling motion which atomizes the injected fuel and ensures smooth combustion. As an additional refinement there may be a pair of shallow recesses in the piston crown which induce two contra-rotating swirl movements in the burning gases during the combustion stroke. This system is widely and internationally respected as being one of, if not the most, efficient kinds of indirect diesel, and it is essentially the system used for the Volkswagen Golf's diesel engine.

Mercedes-Benz, however, are one of the few companies to adhere to a system involving a **pre-chamber** rather than a swirl chamber. The injector spray impinges on a cross-piece (fig. 93c) with a central bulge or 'pea' which gets very hot when the engine warms up and is relied upon to atomize and mix the fuel. The prechamber is connected to the main combustion chamber by a series of small holes and the action of the piston creates turbulence, not swirl. This arrangement is less efficient than the Ricardo system, but is claimed to give quieter, smoother combustion.

Stratified charge engines

The stratified charge principle for petrol or spark-ignition power units is as old as the internal combustion engine itself. It figures in Otto's original patent of 1876 covering the four-stroke cycle and was investigated by Ricardo as early as 1915. The basic purpose of such researches was originally to increase the efficiency of the spark-ignition engine by making it perform some or all of the diesel's tricks: the ability to run at very high compression ratios on very lean mixtures without a throttle. The difficult job is to accomplish all this without making the resultant engine as complex and expensive as the diesel itself.

Most stratified charge engines are still experimental – the main exception being the Honda CVCC unit announced in 1974. Naturally, all of them use the principle from which they get their name, so there is either no end-mixture to detonate at all as for the diesel, or this mixture is too weak to detonate readily. Thus in theory most of them are capable of running on higher compression ratios (though some do not) but these are not as high as in diesels, merely high in relation to the octane rating of the fuel used. Most stratified charge engines have to be throttled over the lower half of the load range.

In recent years engineers have turned to the stratified charge principle as a possible way of reducing exhaust emissions. With its ability to run without misfiring on mixtures with very lean overall air/fuel ratios a good stratified charge engine should be capable of combining exceptionally light fuel consumption with very low exhaust emission levels. Such engines – already in existence experimentally – can also run on compression ratios as high as 12:1 using very low octane, cheaply refined fuel of the 'wide cut' type (p. 67). But they require a complex ignition timing control, in addition to fuel injection or an elaborate carburation system, and tend to have modest power outputs.

Like diesels, stratified charge engines are

either of the direct, open chamber type, or have pre-chambers. Charge stratification is less easily obtained with the open chamber layout than the pre-chamber configuration, which is the one used for the Honda CVCC unit (the letters stand for Compound Vortex Controlled Combustion). In this engine a small prechamber (fig. 94) surrounds the sparking plug and is provided with its own very small valve which admits a tiny dose of rich mixture from an auxiliary carburetter. The jet of flame created when this burning mixture shoots out into the main combustion chamber ignites the much weaker mixture in the main combustion chamber obtained from the principal carburetter.

Strictly speaking the Honda power unit is not exactly a stratified charge engine but one which achieves 'torch' ignition of the weak mixture in the main chamber from the flame which spurts from the prechamber. Nor does it use particularly lean mixtures, while the power it develops is not very large. Its emission levels are inherently low for CO and NO_x but not for HC, so that it needs an oxidizing catalyst or a generously proportioned exhaust manifold to act as an after-burner. Moreover, it returns good – but not outstanding – fuel consumption.

Pre-chamber stratified charge engines are less efficient than the open chamber type for three reasons. They have to be throttled over a considerable part of the load range. The larger surface area of their two chambers plus the throat between them means greater heat losses, while further energy is wasted by fluid friction in the hot gases as they force their way from the pre-chamber to the main chamber. Much effort, therefore, has gone into the development of open-chamber designs. One example is the system which Texaco have been steadily developing since the forties and has been adopted for a forthcoming American military engine.

Called the Texaco Controlled Combustion System (**TCCS**) it involves fuel injection and a tangential inlet port (fig. 95) imparting a strong swirling action to the incoming air which is accentuated, as in most direct injection diesels, by the upward movement of a piston with a cavity in its crown. The fuel is injected late into the swirling air upstream of the sparking plug. When the mixture is ignited by the spark, the velocity of swirl is such that the flame cannot advance against it towards the injector, so that it remains stationary on that front and spreads downstream on the other.

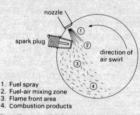

1. Fuel spray
2. Fuel-air mixing zone
3. Flame front area
4. Combustion products

fig. 95. The Texaco TCCS direct-injection stratified charge system in which swirl forces combustion to spread downstream of the sparking plug.

With engines of this type the major difficulty lies in maintaining stable charge stratification over a wide range of speeds and loads while the major disadvantage lies in the need for a fuel injection system (a high-pressure one for the TCCS unit) as well as complex ignition timing control. However Mitsubishi have put an open chamber strat-

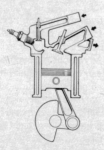

fig. 94. The Honda CVCC stratified charge engine. A tiny additional inlet valve admits a very small quantity of rich mixture, supplied by a special auxiliary carburetter, into the pre-chamber. The main combustion chamber is supplied with a weak mixture via an ordinary inlet valve.

ified charge engine into service for industrial use, while a similar engine developed by the West German MAN company seems promising.

But interest in the stratified charge principle is being weakened by the success now being achieved with relatively conventional high-turbulence, high-compression, lean burn engines, using combustion chambers of the May type (p. 79).

Lean-burn engines

Ordinary engines won't run without misfiring on mixtures with air/fuel ratios leaner than about 17:1, though Chrysler claimed to run slightly leaner still with the electronic engine management system of their Lean Burn engine (p. 104). But charge stratification is only one method of achieving very lean running, and because it involves deliberately making the mixture richer in one place than another, it might be classified as the **heterogeneous charge** approach.

Engines can also be made, however, to run on very lean mixtures by adopting exactly the opposite approach: making the incoming mixture as homogeneous or uniform as possible. A **homogeneous charge** is essentially one in which the fuel is either broken up into a very fine mist, or is fully vaporized, for it is the erratic behaviour of the heavy droplets of petrol normally present which causes uneven distribution and limits the leanness possible.

This homogenization of the mixture can be achieved by mixing the fuel with a stream of air travelling at the speed of sound or more, as is already done in the idling system of a current Ford carburetter (p. 108). The principle is extended to cover virtually the whole range of engine speeds and loads in an experimental carburetter called the **Dresserator** (fig. 96) developed by Dresser Industries Inc., an American company normally specializing in oil exploration and drilling equipment.

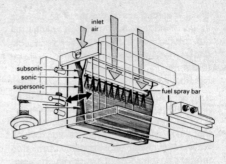

fig. 96. The Dresserator basically consists of a pair of jaws which can be moved further apart or closer together to form a convergent/divergent orifice of varying size. The fuel, sprayed from a bar, is finely atomized by the sonic air flow.

It depends upon the properties of convergent–divergent nozzles. In the convergent section of such a nozzle, the air will be accelerated to the speed of sound at its throat, providing the critical pressure ratio (p. 74) of a little less than 2:1 exists across it. In the divergent section, the air can, if the increase in area is gradual and moderate, be smoothly accelerated along the passage to progressively increasing supersonic speeds. But if the divergence is more sudden, a shock wave will be created (leading to a further improvement in mixture quality) the air will slow down to a subsonic speed and the pressure will rise towards the inlet value – atmospheric in this case. Because the Dresserator's nozzle is of this kind, and because it is also capable of being varied in size, it is able to maintain sonic flow conditions from idle up to about 1.5 lb/sq in (0.1 bar) below atmospheric pressure or nearly full throttle. During full throttle running there is relatively little that can be done to curb fuel demand anyway, and the condition is less important because it is little used during normal motoring; nevertheless the creators of the Dresserator say that at full throttle it performs at least as well as a conventional carburetter.

Fuel metering is easy since the choked nature of the flow (under almost all conditions) means that the weight of air passing at any given time is determined only by the size of the orifice throat. A simple needle and jet metering system, mechanically linked to the moving jaws which form the convergent–divergent orifice, accurately apportions the fuel supplied to the air drawn in. But so far no manufacturer has taken up a carburetter of this sort, and some engineers feel that the atomization effect of the sonic shock wave is relatively local so that the mixture tends to regain some of its uneven character by the the time it reaches the cylinders.

Another possibility is simply to vaporize the fuel fully with an advanced form of inlet manifold hot-spot such as the **Vapipe** (fig. 97) developed by Shell Research in con-

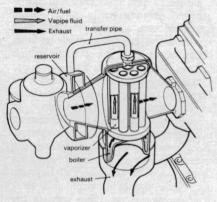

fig. 97. The Vapipe uses a a heat pipe to conduct warmth from the exhaust gases to the inlet manifold to evaporate the fuel completely. It is seen here in its ingenious variable charge form: if the heat input is larger than the heat required for vaporization, the contents of the boiler are evaporated away and pass through the transfer pipe to the reservoir, and the heat transfer rate is reduced.

junction with the National Engineering Laboratory. This uses a heat pipe to transfer energy from the exhaust gases to the incoming mixture. A heat pipe is merely a tube containing a liquid and its vapour. Heat supplied by the exhaust gases to the input end or boiler vaporizes this liquid which is driven to the condenser or output end, from which heat is extracted – in this case by the vaporization of the fuel. The liquid condensate is then returned to the boiler by gravity – though in other heat-pipe applications this may be done by the capillary action of a central wick which can be provided if required. By using a heat pipe in this way, the temperature at which the fuel is vaporized can be controlled, moderate and independent of the exhaust gas temperature. The energy needed can also be exactly matched to the vaporization requirements whatever the engine running conditions, though a heat control system is also necessary.

An engine will certainly run satisfactorily on very lean mixtures when fitted with a Vapipe, but only at the expense of a considerable loss in maximum power. This is probably partly due to the heating of the incoming air as well as the fuel, and to the obstruction presented by the heat exchanger in the inlet manifold. A successful device of this sort would represent a very cheap and simple way of obtaining significant improvements in fuel consumption and exhaust cleanliness. A number of companies, including Volkswagen, have introduced special inlet manifold heating devices, some of them electrical, to improve fuel vaporization, especially during the vital warm-up period.

Sleeve and rotary valve engines

There is another aspect of combustion which might be worth considering for an advanced engine of the future. This is the possibility that the red-hot exhaust valve which is a feature of every conventional engine might be partly responsible for detonation, for engines without this limiting component can run with high compression ratios on low octane fuels.

One such engine is the **single sleeve valve** type used for many years in aircraft. In place of two or more poppet valves it has (fig. 98) a sleeve perforated by apertures or

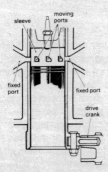

fig. 98. The sleeve valve – it lies between the cylinder and the piston and is given a combined rotary and vertical reciprocating motion by the small crank (at lower right) rotating at right angles to the cylinder axis. Ports in the sleeve move in and out of register with fixed ports in the sleeve housing.

ports, which fits between the cylinder and the piston. It is given a reciprocating motion both vertically and rotationally (by the crank drive) so that the ports in the sleeve move in and out of register with the ports in the cylinder. In some arrangements the sleeve has a central port shared between the stationary inlet and exhaust ports. Sleeve valve engines are capable of running at compression ratios as high as 10:1 on fuels having octane ratings as low as 88, probably because the sleeve does not run very hot.

Another alternative to the poppet valve is the Cross rotary valve, named after its inventor, the reliability of which was established by extensive trials in the 1940s. It essentially consists (fig. 99) of a tube, sealed by a diagonal partition, which rotates about an axis at right angles to the cylinder axis. In

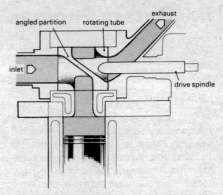

fig. 99. The Cross rotary valve is simply a rotating tube, driven by the spindle on the right, with an angled partition which deflects the fuel and air into the cylinder and the exhaust gases out again.

one position it deflects the incoming charge into the cylinder; after 180 degrees of rotation it deflects the exhaust gases out again. It is kept cool by this alternating contact with the incoming charge, but requires a complex loading system to ensure gas tightness and a complex drive arrangement, too, since a separate rotating tube is needed for each cylinder.

Such engines are almost certainly made pointless by diesel or stratified charge engines which also do not suffer from detonation, but for a different reason – the lack of any end-gas. Just conceivably, though, a sleeve or rotary valve engine running on a homogeneous mixture supplied by a Dresserator or Vapipe, could prove a viable alternative for the future.

It now seems almost certain, however, that the major motor manufacturers will soon be introducing lean burn engines which do not incorporate unusual devices or systems but depend rather on clever combustion chamber design and careful attention to detail.

five **Rotary Engines**

Almost as soon as the energy in heat was harnessed with the steam engine some 250 years ago, engineers developed a distaste for what they regarded as the clumsy back-and-forth movements of reciprocating pistons. Such movements need to be converted into rotation and, as we have seen, are certainly a major source of vibration. To a large extent the answer was the **steam turbine** introduced in 1884, but like the **gas turbine**, this differs fundamentally from a piston engine. To begin with, it is not a **positive displacement** machine: there is a gap between the blades of a turbine and its casing, the steam being constrained by the forces developed rather than by seals, valves or tightly fitting elements. In addition, a turbine utilizes the expansion of steam continuously, not cyclically or in batches as does a piston engine. Moreover, because the turbine works best at a very high and constant speed, it is not well suited to the road vehicle.

So the search went on for machines combining the positive displacement principle of a piston engine with purely rotary motion, and it continued with renewed enthusiasm when the four-stroke and two-stroke internal combustion engines were introduced at the end of the nineteenth century. But experience has shown that the creation of a successful positive displacement rotary engine is a task of quite extraordinary difficulty. Despite several hundred years of effort – some of the design proposals (fig. 100) even predate the steam engine – only one rotary has so far achieved any significant

fig. 100. For hundreds of years engineers have been devising different forms of purely rotary positive displacement engine. One or two have worked as steam engines, a handful as compressors, but only the Wankel (bottom right) has proved reasonably efficient.

success, though a few have been used as pumps or compressors. Yet by 1910 over 2000 rotary engine patents had been filed in Britain alone.

That one exception is the Wankel engine fitted to the NSU Ro80 introduced in 1967, and to a number of Mazda models, some of which remain in production today. This is the engine to which this chapter is devoted.

The Wankel engine

Layout and geometry

In its simplest form the Wankel engine (fig. 101) consists of a single rotor, roughly triangular in form, executing a planetary or orbital motion within a fixed casing which has a waisted, figure-of-eight shape. As the rotor turns, the three chambers between its flanks and the contoured housing alternately increase and decrease in volume in a way compatible with the four strokes of the Otto cycle. But before considering exactly how these chambers expand and contract to draw in fresh mixture, compress it, etc., it is best to look first at the motion of the rotor which is closely related both to its own shape and to the rather mysterious contours of the housing.

The rotor housing shape is defined by a curve called an **epitrochoid**, one of a family of curves known as **trochoids**, meaning 'wheel-like'. A trochoid is the path traced out by a point attached to a circle when it rolls without slip about another circle. When one circle, termed the **generating circle**, rolls outside a fixed **base circle**, the resultant curve is known as an *epi*trochoid (*epi* = on the surface of). An epitrochoid can be generated in more than one way, but the relevant method here is by (fig. 102) rolling the generating circle around the outside of a smaller fixed base circle enclosed within it (the result is sometimes alternatively called a peritrochoid). Imagine, for example, holding

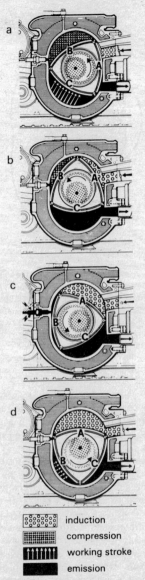

induction	
compression	
working stroke	
emission	

fig. 101. The Wankel. As the rotor turns, the three chambers between its flanks and the contoured housing alternately increase and decrease in volume to follow the sequence of the four-stroke cycle – see text.

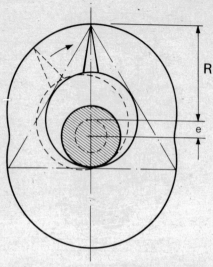

fig. 102. An epitrochoid can be generated by rolling a big circle around a small fixed circle located *inside* it. The radii of the two circles must be in the ratio of 3:2 if the epitrochoid is to have two lobes like the housing of a Wankel engine. The size of the epitrochoid is determined partly by the length of the generating radius, *R*, and partly by the eccentricity, *e* – the radius of the circle described by the centre of the generating circle as it rolls round the base circle.

a 10p piece in a fixed position on the surface of a table, and enclosing it with a small bracelet. The bracelet is then rolled round the coin.

The number of bulges or lobes in the figure traced out is solely determined by the ratio of the sizes of the two circles. If the generating circle is assigned a radius of three units, for instance, and the base circle a radius of two units (so that they are in the ratio of 3:2) the epitrochoid will have two lobes only, separated by a centre 'waist' or **minor axis**. (The maximum length of the epitrochoid in a direction at right angles to this axis is the **major axis**.) The size of the epitrochoid is determined partly by the length of the tracing arm or generating radius, *R*, and partly by the **eccentricity**, *e*,

which is the radius of the circle described by the *centre* of the generating circle as it rolls around the base circle. The ratio of *R* to *e* determines the proportions of the epitrochoid; the smaller the ratio the more waisted it becomes.

All these geometrical relationships are reproduced exactly in the mechanical layout of the Wankel engine. A fixed gear attached to the rotor end-housing (fig. 103) defines the base circle and an internally toothed annulus or ring gear attached to the rotor defines the generating circle, while a line from the centre of this circle to any of the rotor's three tips can be regarded as being the generating radius. Moreover the eccentricity, *e*, is also the crankthrow radius of the crankshaft which completes the rotor's location system and which allows the combustion forces exerted on it to be transmitted to the outside world. This crankshaft rotates about the centre of the base circle, or fixed guide gear, and its eccentric passes through the centre of the rotor.

How, then, does the rotor get its shape? In fact the tips of a straightforward equilateral triangle, centred on the crankpin and guided by the gear system, faithfully follow the contours of the epitrochoid, creating the three chambers required. But for an epitrochoid of Wankel-type proportions, such a

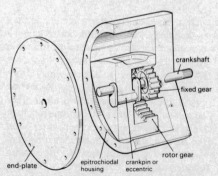

fig. 103. In a Wankel engine there is a fixed gear attached to the end-housing which defines the base circle, and an internally toothed annulus in the rotor which defines the generating circle.

purely triangular rotor would leave too large a space between itself and the housing, especially when one face lay across the minor axis. So the rotor flanks are bulged as much as is possible without fouling the housing. The shape required can be generated by an inversion of the former generating process in which (fig. 104) the base circle is

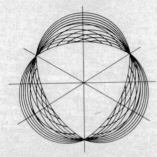

fig. 104. By rotating the base circle about the generating circle, the shape of the triangular rotor is traced out.

rotated bodily around the generating circle which becomes the fixed element. Another way of looking at the process is to imagine an over-sized rotor (fig. 105) traversing a rotary cutter conforming in shape with the

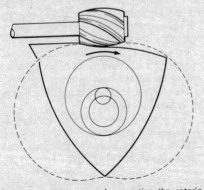

fig. 105. Another way of generating the rotor's shape would be to sweep an oversize rotor through a cutter shaped to conform with the minor axis area of the epitrochoid.

small part of the epitrochoid on either side of and including the minor axis.

A rotor contoured in this way and executing the motion described, combines with the housing shape to form a particularly simple and ingenious four-stroke engine. In fig. 101a, for example, unburnt mixture is being compressed in the chamber above face B of the rotor; expansion of the ignited fuel is taking place in the chamber below face C, a fresh charge is being drawn in adjacent to the upper part of face A and exhaust gases are being expelled by the lower part of face A. The process continues in fig. 101b, while in fig. 101c the fully-compressed mixture is ignited next to face B, induction is almost complete above face A and the exhaust stroke is half complete below face C. Fig. 101d shows a further stage with the engine at 'bottom dead centre' on the induction stroke.

But look now at the crankshaft. In each of the stages illustrated on figs. 106a–e, the rotor turns through 90° or a quarter of a revolution, but the crankshaft rotates through 270° or three-quarters of a revolution, hence completing three revolutions for each revolution of the rotor. Thus there is one combustion stroke for each revolution of the crankshaft. Two or more rotors can be coupled together to form multiple-rotor engines, and the housing can be watercooled (as shown) or aircooled.

Since the engine undoubtedly works on the four-stroke principle, in single-rotor form it is most nearly equivalent to a two-cylinder power unit of that type. Although some controversy about its capacity has been created, this is, by the same analogy, best regarded as being twice the swept volume of one working chamber (fig. 107) for a single-rotor engine – and as being this volume multiplied by the number of rotors for multiple-rotor engines. This is the definition accepted by most taxation and racing authorities.

There are other similarities between the Wankel and the reciprocating engine. Like a

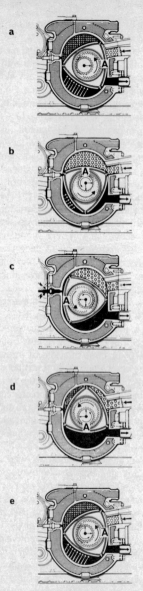

fig. 106. Rotor rotation versus crankshaft rotation in the Wankel engine. Each time the rotor turns through 90°, the crankshaft rotates 270°, completing three revolutions for each complete revolution of the rotor.

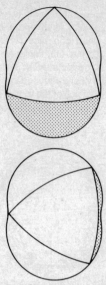

fig. 107. The swept volume of a working chamber: the large volume (top) minus the small volume (bottom).

reciprocating engine, for instance, it has a compression ratio, the maximum theoretical value of which is about 16:1 for typical geometry and a rotor with plain faces. But were an engine to be constructed in this way, its combustion space would not merely be very small, long and thin, but would also be very nearly divided into two separate halves by the inward bulge of the epitrochoid's waist. In practical engines, therefore, combustion recesses (fig. 108) are scooped out of the rotor flanks, reducing the maximum compression ratio possible, a typical value being about 9:1.

But whereas the conventional engine is easily sealed, essentially with two or three circular rings per piston, a Wankel of the same capacity has a sealing grid which is not only significantly longer − even when the ordinary power unit's valve seats are taken into account − but which also incorporates several joints and discontinuities. This sealing grid is in fact composed of two different

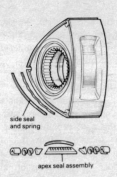

side seal
and spring

apex seal assembly

fig. 108. Combustion recesses are scooped out of a Wankel's rotor flanks to keep the compression ratio to an acceptable figure. Note the vital side and apex seals.

sets of seals joined together: the **side seals** and the **apex seals**.

Each side seal (fig. 108) is a long blade of metal (usually cast iron) located by a curved slot in the rotor flank which lies close to a face. It is held against the housing end plate by a corrugated strip which acts as a spring. But the force it exerts is needed only at cranking speeds, for when the engine runs, the side seal is forced against the end plate by the gas pressure which is itself made to do the work of sealing.

Largely because these side seals make an area contact with the end plates, they have proved efficient and trouble-free from an early stage in the development of the engine. The apex seals are quite a different matter, for they are subject to far more arduous working conditions. The motion of the rotor is such that the apex seal does not remain at right angles to the housing surface but meets it at a constantly varying angle. Hence it must have a radiused tip and makes only a line contact with the housing. In addition, the apex seal is subjected to violent and fluctuating forces, including a complete reversal of those due to inertia every time it passes the minor axis of the epitrochoid when they briefly act inward. Moreover, the apex seal's duties include preventing significant leakage of hot gases at peak combustion pressure from one chamber into the fresh mixture contained in the adjacent chamber.

The main apex seal element is a strip running across the tip of the rotor, which, like the side seals, is located by a slot and held against the rotor housing by a spring strip. The areas between the ends of the main element and the side plates are sealed by small triangular pieces, forced outwards by gas pressure, so that as they wear they move to fill the wedge-shaped spaces they occupy without leaving gaps. The cylindrical slotted corner pieces or 'bolts' into which they fit are in contact with the ends of the side seals and complete the sealing grids.

Advantages and disadvantages

All this adds up to an engine of remarkable simplicity and elegance. It is, to begin with, easily given perfect balance: dynamically speaking a single-rotor engine consists of a single out-of-balance rotating mass – that of the eccentric and the rotor. The rotor is symmetrical about its centre, so although its compound motion involves a rotation about this centre (as well as of that centre about the crankshaft centreline) no imbalance is created. Complete balance of single- or multiple-rotor engines is therefore easily achieved with some crankshaft counterweights.

It is partly from this perfect balance that the Wankel engine gets one of its principal virtues – smoothness. But a contributory influence is the duration of its combustion stroke which extends for 270° of crankshaft rotation compared to the 180° of a conventional engine. As a result of these two factors a single-rotor engine is much smoother than a conventional two-cylinder four-stroke, while a twin-rotor Wankel is at least as refined as a good six. Conventional V-8 or even V-12 engines, indeed, are little superior to the twin-rotor Wankel in this respect.

But perhaps a Wankel's most striking feature is its mechanical simplicity: a twin-rotor type has far fewer basic moving parts than a four-cylinder reciprocating power unit let alone the six-cylinder engine which it matches in smoothness. And because it is simple the Wankel engine is also compact. Even allowing for such auxiliaries as its carburetter, distributor, alternator and starter – which occupy much the same space on an engine of any type – conservative estimates put its total bulk at 30 per cent less than that of a conventional power unit.

But the advantage in lightness is not so great. The Mazda RX7 engine, for example, has an equivalent capacity of 2.3 litres and develops 130 bhp, but is not much lighter than an aluminium alloy reciprocating engine of similar size and power. The Mazda water-cooled twin-rotor units have aluminium alloy housings, but cast iron has to be used for the rotors due to the high thermal stress to which they are subjected. But the capacity of a twin-rotor Wankel could be as high as four litres while retaining good smoothness, when its superiority in weight as well as bulk would be marked. Another important advantage of the Wankel is its ability to run at high compression ratios on low octane fuel.

Despite these basic advantages, the Wankel power unit has passed through a number of crises during its short history. The first was premature failure – accentuated by short trip/cold-start 'doctor' patterns of motoring – of the NSU Ro80 engine's rotor tip seals. Partly because of this fault, never satisfactorily cured, partly because of the energy crisis, the engine went out of production in Europe and was discredited for a long period.

But the Mazda engines made by Toyo Kogyo in Japan never suffered from this weakness, and have grown ever more reliable since their introduction in 1967 – at least as reliable as equivalent piston engines.

Then it was widely believed that the rotary engine could never be made to meet the US exhaust emission regulations which were progressively being stiffened in the early seventies. Certainly the Wankel tends to suffer from high HC emission levels – though

correspondingly low NO_x levels. But the Toyo Kogyo engineers rose to the challenge, and using thermal reactors initially, catalytic reactors and other means later, soon introduced US-market rotaries which comfortably met the regulations.

But at this stage in the engine's development – during the middle and late seventies – came the next problem: poor fuel consumption. Some designers felt – and still feel – that both the high HC emission levels and the poor fuel consumption spring from the same fundamental defect, the peculiar elongated shape and high surface/volume ratio of the Wankel's combustion chambers. Once again, however, the Toyo Kogyo engineers in Japan rapidly introduced a series of modifications which led to significant improvements in fuel consumption, so that by the early eighties Wankel-powered Mazda cars were only slightly worse in this respect than their petrol-engined equivalents. Further improvements, including the adoption of the stratified charge principle, are likely.

The long-term future of the Wankel engine now depends almost entirely upon the energy with which Toyo Kogyo continue to develop, market and produce it. Any slackening of those efforts, any failure to match the conventional power unit in economy and reliability, will soon lead to the Wankel's extinction. But Koyo Kogyo's managing director, Kenichi Yamamoto, is a passionate advocate of the Wankel, and points out that it has benefited from a far shorter period of development than the conventional engine. A relatively small improvement in its fuel consumption would probably be enough to highlight its inherent advantages of lightness and compactness and lead to its adoption by other manufacturers. Only time will tell.

History

Felix Wankel, inventor of the rotary engine which bears his name, is a self-taught engineer born at the beginning of this century in south-west Germany. His interest in rotaries began in the ninteen-twenties when he set up his own research and development bureau specializing in the sealing problems of internal combustion engines, pumps and compressors. In 1951 he obtained a contract from the German company NSU, who were then only makers of mopeds and motorcycles, at first to develop a rotary valve engine, and a few years later he conceived the basic idea of his engine.

A prototype was completed by NSU in 1957, but it was rather different from the Wankel we know today: the epitrochoidal housing turned with the rotor (at 3:2 times the speed) giving both parts purely rotary motion, but making the design much more complex. The fresh mixture had to be drawn in along a fixed hollow shaft, the high-tension current was transmitted to the sparking plug via slip rings and an additional external housing was needed, increasing the engine's bulk. Even so, after some initial development, this 125 cc prototype developed 29 bhp at a speed – 17,000 rpm – high enough to prove the excellence of its balance.

But NSU's chief engineer, Dr Walter Froede, devised an inverted form of the engine with a stationary housing and orbiting rotor which ran for the first time during the following year. Although the motion of the rotor is less 'pure' in its rotation – which was why the transformation was bitterly opposed by Felix Wankel himself – the engine is much more practical in this form, which it has retained ever since.

Once the basic workability of the idea had been established, a joint company was set up to exploit it and licence agreements formed with many other firms including the American aircraft manufacturer Curtiss Wright in 1958, the Japanese makers of Mazda cars, Toyo Kogyo, in 1961 and General Motors in 1970. There are many other licensees including Rolls-Royce and Daimler Benz, though quite a few are now inactive. After NSU were taken over by Audi and the resultant group in turn absorbed by Volkswagen, the British international conglomerate Lonrho acquired a major interest in the Wankel licensing companies.

In 1963 NSU announced a two-seater sports car, the Spider, powered by a single-rotor Wankel engine, which was sold in modest numbers, essentially as a large-scale field trial. Following the success of this, the company introduced the Ro80 in 1967, a large front-wheel drive saloon fitted with a twin-rotor engine. Unfortunately the apex seals of the original engine suffered badly from premature wear under repeated cold start conditions, leading to many failures and a disastrous lack of confidence in the Wankel. The Ro80, though, has always been a magnificent motorcar, regardless of its power unit, and its production continued, albeit at a low rate, until 1977.

Paradoxically, Mazda's line of rotary engines, also introduced in 1967 – appearing first in the Cosmo 110S sports car – never suffered in this way. Instead they were attacked by critics for being incapable of meeting the American exhaust emission regulations, and when this proved untrue, acquired a bad reputation – this time largely justified – for poor fuel consumption. Confidence in the Wankel was given another blow by General Motors' failure to adopt it – they effectively relinquished their interest in 1977 having spent a good deal on research and development. Similarly, a second-generation European Wankel – for the Citroën Birotor introduced in 1973 and other models – was to have been produced by Comotor, a company specially set up for the purpose, but its activities soon stopped, largely killed by the fuel crisis.

Wankels are still made for outboards, lawnmowers and other applications, but the only automotive units now being produced are the Mazda range of engines.

More details

The Wankel engine has a 'hot lobe' around the sparking plug which is never swept by the cool unburnt gases – as is the combustion chamber of a piston engine – and which rises rapidly in temperature as the engine load increases. The consequent thermal stress is minimized by careful design of the rotor housing and its cooling system. When water is the coolant, this is pumped transversely across the engine in a series of parallel paths through passages in the rotor housings. Careful attention to the setting of the thermostat, its location in the cooling system and the type of by-pass flow (p. 62) also help to cut peak temperatures reached during acceleration.

An important part in the cooling of a Wankel engine is played by the lubricating oil which is pumped through the eccentric shaft to the interior of the rotor from which it conducts much heat as well as lubricating the fixed and moving guide gears. Circular seals on the sides of the rotor contain this oil so well that it is virtually uncontaminated by the products of combustion. For this reason NSU were eventually able to recommend the total abandonment of regular oil changes for the Ro80.

The apex seals are usually separately lubricated by a small metering pump injecting small doses of oil into the fuel which spreads it over the surface of the rotor housing. Despite the small total loss involved due to the eventual combustion of the lubricant, the oil consumption of a Wankel is similar to that of a conventional engine.

A Wankel engine may have either side or peripheral inlet ports, but the exhaust ports are nearly always peripheral. There are restrictions on the size and shape of a side inlet port, the first of which is that its outer 'opening' line, A (fig. 109), cannot be located too close either to the epitrochoidal housing or to its minor axis without causing the apex seal 'bolt' – which must have axial freedom for effective sealing – to fall through the aperture created, or at best to traverse a wear-inducing depression. This means that a side inlet port cannot open before top dead centre, so there can be little overlap between it and the exhaust port.

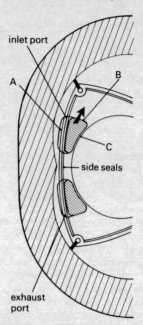

fig. 109. Side ports – there are restrictions on their size, shape and location. The annotations define the limitations on inlet port size.

There is no structural limitation on the location of the 'closing' line, B, but there is obviously little point in delaying port closure for very long after top dead centre. To obtain as large a port area as possible, therefore, the 'fully-open' line, C, needs to be as far inboard as it can be, but its location must also be limited, to avoid the path of the rotor oil sealing ring.

Side ports, therefore, cannot be very large in area, and also subject the incoming and outgoing gases to relatively long and tortuous paths. They are, moreover, inconvenient to introduce to the inner faces of twin-rotor engines. But the lack of overlap between them can be turned to advantage to improve low-speed torque as Mazda have done with their inlet system. The small primary stage of the carburetter fitted to their engine supplies mixture to one set of side ports for idling and low-speed running, and the larger secondary stage feeds another set of side ports for running at high speeds and loads. Peripheral exhaust ports are used.

Peripheral ports suffer from few of the disadvantages of side ports. Although their cross-sectional area may be restricted by the width of the rotor and its housing, they stay open for a long time and thus have ample capacity, while the gases that flow through them need not be turned through a right angle. Overlap is easily arranged – by moving the inlet and exhaust ports close to the minor axis of the epitrochoid. Such ports are theoretically opened and closed by the apex seals, but the intake chamber effectively becomes cut off from the exhaust port when the end of the combustion recess reaches the epitrochoid minor axis (fig. 110). Hence the true overlap is much shorter than the theoretical one.

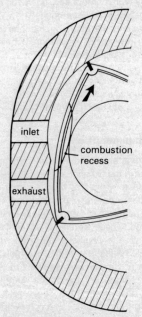

fig. 110. Peripheral ports give unimpeded gas flow, have a long opening time and can easily be arranged to give overlap.

Sealing

Before the Wankel went into commercial production in 1968, carbon was the material most generally used for its rotor apex seals. This material – impregnated with aluminium – was retained for several years by Toyo Kogyo who used it in conjunction with a chromium-on-steel surface for their aluminium alloy epitrochoidal bore. These seals gave little trouble, allowing the Mazda engine to be as reliable as an equivalent piston engine right from the start.

NSU, however, believed carbon seals to be vulnerable to damage by detonation, and so chose a completely different materials combination for the Ro80 unit. Its rotor housing, also made of aluminium alloy, was covered with a thin and exceptionally hard coating of a special nickel/silicon carbide material with a very high resistance to the formation of chatter marks by the seals passing over it. Initially, these were of a hard but conventional piston-ring iron. Unfortunately, although NSU investigated almost every possible wear condition, there was one they overlooked: a driving pattern of short runs and numerous cold starts – the type of usage imposed by a doctor. Under conditions of this kind, the apex seals wore with alarming rapidity.

To the glee of the 'establishment' manufacturers producing conventional engines, this problem attracted much publicity. With badly worn apex seals the engine would hardly run at all, and some Ro80s needed two or even three replacement engines in the first 20,000 miles, making the car something of a bad joke, especially in its home country, West Germany. The situation was not improved by dealers' general ignorance about the Wankel and by an over-generous warranty policy. By 1971 the wear rate had been greatly reduced with a new seal design, but not before the reputation of the Wankel had been dealt a tremendous blow.

Exhaust emissions

Research reports and engineering papers showed early Wankels to be characterized by rather poor bmep and specific fuel consumption values. Practical experience with the Mazda R100 and the NSU Ro80 soon confirmed these academic observations, both cars originally returning fuel consumption figures about 20 per cent worse than those of conventionally powered models. These faults were generally attributed to the undoubted peculiarities of the Wankel's combustion chamber: it is long and thin in shape, with a large surface-to-volume ratio, as well as being almost divided into two separate pockets by the waist of the epitrochoid at top dead centre. What is more, the flame is able to move little in the upstream direction against the bulk movement of the mixture which is swept round with the rotor.

The higher the compression ratio the less satisfactory the combustion chamber shape, so that a single-stage Wankel diesel hardly produces any useful power at all. This difficulty was neatly circumvented in a two-stage 'cottage loaf' diesel Wankel (fig. 111) developed by Rolls-Royce for a military contract. It featured a large-volume first stage providing initial compression for a smaller high-pressure second stage in which the combustion took place. Although highly promising, the project was eventually abandoned in the belief that better results could be obtained from conventional engines.

A (petrol) Wankel's combustion chamber peculiarities are also considered to be the cause of its exhaust emissions pattern. Its HC emission level is definitely worse than that of a conventional engine, though its CO level is about the same and its NO_x level is lower – thanks to the cool running which allows compression ratios of around 9.5:1 using two-star fuel. Critics were quick to suggest, though, that the HC level made the Wankel so inherently dirty that it was unlikely ever to be capable of meeting the American exhaust pollution regulations.

They were confounded, however, by Toyo Kogyo, who in 1973 introduced new Wankel-engined models, guaranteeing their ability to meet impending legislation. Their basic weapon was a thermal reactor which is particularly suited to the Wankel as it can be bolted very close to the ports and is more continuously swept by the exhaust gases than it would be on a conventional engine.

Fuel consumption

Unfortunately, to maintain and prolong combustion in the exhaust system, a rich mixture was used, while for the vital part-throttle conditions only one of the two sparking plugs was energized and the ignition timing was retarded. These settings had a disastrous effect on the Wankel's fuel consumption – and 1973 was the year in which fuel became scarce and expensive, so sales of Wankel-engined Mazdas in the States slumped.

But once again Toyo Kogyo rose to the occasion, promising – and achieving – a 40 per cent fuel consumption improvement within two years. The main factor in this improvement was a thermal reactor modified

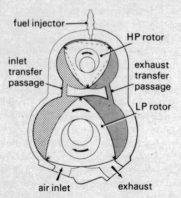

fig. 111. The Rolls-Royce experimental two-stage 'Cottage Loaf' Wankel diesel engine. The incoming air is given initial compression in the large low-pressure stage, before being further compressed in the second stage where combustion takes place. The expanding gases do work on both rotors.

to run on a considerably leaner mixture than before. To keep up its operating temperature, the additional air injected into it was preheated (fig. 112) while an exhaust port

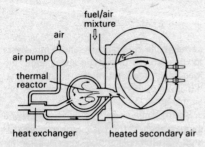

fig. 112. The Mazda lean burn engine and its thermal reactor. The reaction chamber is preheated by the exhaust gases – as is the injected air – and it is kept hot by an exhaust port insert.

insert or sleeve minimized heat losses to the rotor housing. Thus the clean-up reaction proceeded satisfactorily without either excessive retardation of the ignition or single-plug running.

Other modifications included improved apex seals, made of metal but still running on an aluminium housing lined first with steel then with chromium, though by a different process. Friction losses were also reduced, the port timing was altered to improve low-speed torque and the various

Wankel-engined models were given higher gearing.

All these changes improved the fuel consumption dramatically – from around 12 mpg for a US-market manual-transmission Mazda RX4 in the EPA urban driving cycle, to about 20 mpg. The Wankel-engined RX7 introduced in 1981 incorporated further improvements, but when tested by the weekly magazine *Motor* in European form achieved an overall fuel consumption of 20.9 mpg compared to the 25.4 mpg of an Alfa Romeo Alfetta GTV and the 25.2 mpg of a Porsche 924, both of which have similar performance to the RX7 but more accommodation. Further significant improvements in fuel consumption, however, have since been achieved.

Such is the importance of fuel consumption these days, though, that the continued existence of the Wankel nevertheless depends to a large extent on its maker's ability to match the petrol economy of conventional engines. It does, however, have considerable potential for still further improvement. The bulk movement of the incoming charge swept round by the rotor, for example, makes it ideally suited to the stratified charge principle. And with little need to use more than two rotors, a stratified charge Wankel would be significantly cheaper and simpler than a stratified charge conventional engine.

six

Alternative Sources of Power

Since about 1965 the motorcar has gone through a period of unprecedented change: its safety in collisions, its tendency to pollute the atmosphere and its thirst for scarce and valuable fossil fuels have all come under attack – and rightly so. In consequence, many careful investigations into alternative forms of propulsion have been conducted. We have already looked at stratified charge, sleeve valve and rotary valve versions of the conventional reciprocating petrol engine as well as at the diesel and the Wankel, but in this chapter we consider some of the more important fundamentally different alternatives: the steam engine, the gas turbine, the **Stirling engine** and electric propulsion.

Tens of millions of pounds have been spent since the mid sixties – most of it in the United States – merely on the development of steam engines for cars, while much more money has been poured into other projects such as the automotive gas turbine. All this effort might have been expected to lead to a completely different form of power unit – after all, in less than twenty years the aircraft industry changed over completely from piston engines to jets or turboprops for all but light aeroplanes. But the more the alternatives are examined, the better the conventional reciprocating or rotary petrol engine looks, even in its present state of refinement, let alone in some more advanced form.

The steam engine

The least promising alternative to the conventional petrol engine for cars is almost certainly the steam power unit. Enthusiasts for this form of propulsion speak about the 'beautiful simplicity' of the steam engine, but in any automotive application it is not simple at all.

Steam enthusiasts are right about one thing, however. The basic problems associated with the design of a boiler suitable for cars were solved fifty years ago by such engineers as Abner Doble. The steam generator evolved then, and used in virtually every steam car since, is called a **monotube** or **flash** boiler and consists of a continuous small-bore tube around 400 ft (120 m) long and coiled around the flame zone of the burner or furnace. The tube's large surface area means good heat exchange so that a working head of steam can be raised very quickly – in 20–30 seconds starting from cold – and its small diameter means that very little steam is contained in it at any given time so there is no significant explosion if it bursts.

But automotive steam engines have at least three other important requirements: they need a pump to force the fuel into the burner in a very fine spray, a blower to promote combustion by providing a forced draught, and, most important of all, a **feed-water pump** capable of controlling the supply of water to the boiler in answer to demand in a very precise and responsive way. In addition, any steam engine which is to be suitable for a car must have a **condenser** so that the water – or other working fluid used – can be recirculated. So much for the beautiful simplicity.

An experimental system (fig. 113), which was developed in a feasibility study by the Swedish motor manufacturer Saab, makes

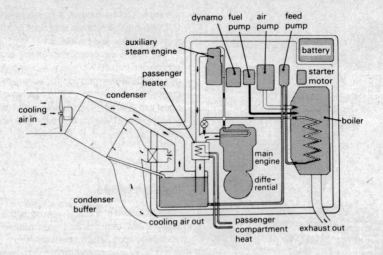

fig. 113. This experimental steam engine installation evaluated by Saab shows the likely complexity of a practical system.

the point. As you can see, it is not simple at all, and even incorporates a small auxiliary steam engine to drive the air blower and the fuel and feedwater pumps. It ought surely to be possible to do without this component, and the form of engine chosen, a nine-cylinder **swashplate** unit also seems rather complex. Even if such changes were made, the diagram shows that steam propulsion is not as straightforward as it seems, and it is clear that a complete system would occupy quite a lot of space.

Another myth of the steam engine is that it develops full torque at a standstill. So, under certain circumstances, it can, but only if steam is admitted to it under full boiler pressure throughout the power stroke. This is very wasteful because the steam gets no chance to expand and leaves the engine with much of its heat energy untapped. Both for this reason and because of the need to drive auxiliaries, a transmission system cannot easily be dispensed with, as was at first hoped. An automotive steam engine will almost certainly need some sort of clutch or

decoupling device so that it can idle when the car is standing still, and some sort of gearbox to multiply the torque developed.

A further problem is the condenser. Other things being equal, this needs to be roughly three times larger than the radiator of a petrol engine developing the same power. But here there is cause for hope, since Philips of Eindhoven have developed a new and much more efficient kind of heat exchanger in the course of their research on the Stirling engine. This (fig. 114) uses the usual tubes and fins but they are arranged in angled rows and make better contact with the cooling air.

Although the amounts of CO and HC emitted by steam-car combustion systems are low, it was until quite recently difficult to limit their generation of NO_x to below the levels specified by the American exhaust pollution regulations. But with redesigned burners promoting combustion in the presence of excess air, or incorporating exhaust gas recirculation systems to reduce the maximum temperatures reached, this problem now seems to have been solved. Next it was found that even though the proportions of pollutants emitted might be small, their total amounts on a grams per mile basis often

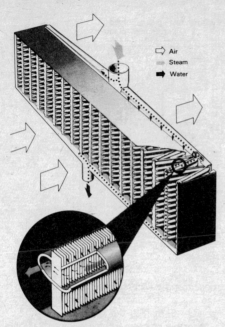

Air
Steam
Water

fig. 114. This advanced heat exchanger configuration greatly improves condenser efficiency.

exceeded the prescribed limits because the fuel consumption was so poor.

Again, this problem seems to have been solved, judging by a report describing the results obtained with a Chevrolet Vega converted to steam power with a turbine engine by the Aerojet Rocket Co. and a special car with a four-cylinder double-expansion engine built by Steam Power Systems, both American companies. But the fuel consumptions obtained highlight the basic problem of the steam car – its poor thermal efficiency. The more economical of the two cars, for instance, the Aerojet conversion, achieved a Federal Highway driving cycle consumption of less than half what can be obtained from the standard Vega. A good stationary steam engine can have a very high thermal efficiency indeed, but only by using steam at very high temperatures and pressures, expanding it through many stages to a low

pressure and running at a constant speed. But high-pressure steam is fiendishly difficult stuff to contain and handle, and it is doubtful if even a triple expansion reciprocating engine or a turbine with several stages would allow sufficient expansion for adequate efficiency, while the modest size of a typical car does not permit much more complication. This thermal efficiency limitation seems fundamental.

Gas turbines

Next in order of merit is perhaps the gas turbine. Jet engines and gas turbines are immensely powerful for their size and weight and supremely suited to aircraft because their efficiency increases with rising airspeed, unlike the propeller which reaches a limit at about 450 mph. They are also essentially simple in construction, and they are reliable. But compared to other heat engines they are not particularly efficient. At full power a modern jet may attain the thermal efficiency of a good petrol engine, maybe a mediocre diesel, but is rather less efficient at its cruising regime.

The kind of gas turbine appropriate to cars is less efficient still, especially during the part-throttle running which forms so large a proportion of modern motoring, but it will run happily on a cheap fuel such as paraffin (kerosene). It generally consists (fig. 115) of a centrifugal compressor forcing air into a series of combustion chambers where fuel is burned, creating a large volume of expanding hot gases which drive the compressor turbine and a power turbine. By mounting this on a separate shaft, torque can be developed at a standstill and a gearbox eliminated.

To return an acceptable fuel consumption, any automotive gas turbine must be fitted with heat exchangers which extract some of the waste heat in the exhaust gases to preheat the incoming air. Usually these take

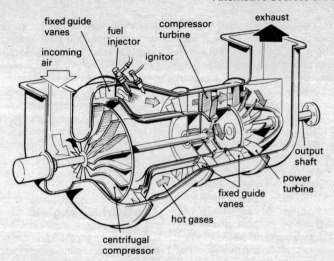

fig. 115. The gas turbine principle.

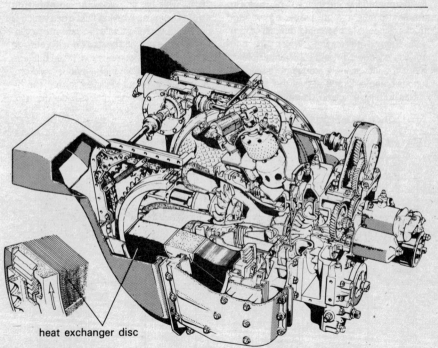

heat exchanger disc

fig. 116. The gas turbine. It is basically simple, but automotive versions require slowly rotating glass-ceramic heat exchanger discs to extract some of the waste heat in the exhaust gases. Swivelling power turbine guide vanes would probably be required too.

the form of a pair of slowly rotating glass-ceramic discs (fig. 116). One sector of each disc lies in the path of the exhaust gases which pass through its honeycomb passages to leave the engine. By rotation (at about 15 rpm) this warmed sector moves into the path of the incoming air which is thus pre-heated.

Unfortunately a gas turbine is essentially a constant speed device which works inefficiently under varying load conditions and responds sluggishly to changes in demands for power. A practical automotive gas turbine would therefore almost certainly need variable geometry guide vanes for the power turbine governed by an electronic control system. Thus with these complications a gas turbine loses its basic simplicity. Even without them, many of its components, such as the output turbine, are far too expensive. But the gas turbine is more promising for large trucks, since it is becoming difficult to provide them with engines which are both adequately powerful and sufficiently quiet to meet the increasingly stringent noise regulations being enforced all over the world.

Gas turbine efficiency is critically depen-dant on the maximum temperatures at which the very highly stressed rotating components can safely be run, and relatively small increases produce large increments of efficiency. Thus the development of ceramic turbines, if these can be made sufficiently accurately to maintain aerodynamic efficiency, would constitute a technological breakthrough. So far, however, ceramic components of this sort have only been produced experimentally.

The Stirling engine

A slightly more promising form of power unit is the Stirling engine, patented by Robert Stirling, a Scottish presbyterian minister, in 1816. This is an **external combustion engine** using as working fluid a gas which is permanently sealed into a system of cylinders and pistons and heated from the outside by some form of combustion. It can thus run on any combustible fuel – even a solid one such as coal. In its idealized form it can be imagined as consisting of a cylinder (fig. 117)

fig. 117. The principle of the Stirling engine: (a) gas in cold space; (b) gas compressed; (c) gas transferred to hot space; (d) gas expands.

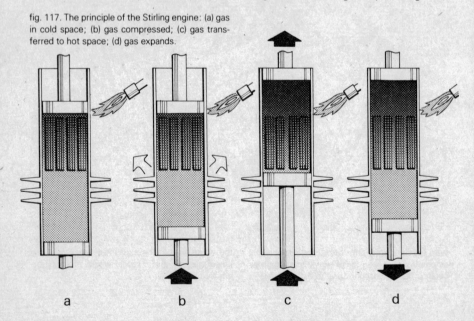

a b c d

filled with an inert gas under pressure and sealed at its ends by a pair of pistons. Towards one end of the cylinder is a zone heated from the outside called the **hot space**, while towards the other is a cooled zone called the **cold space**. Between them is a heat exchanger called a **regenerator** which can consist of an array of metal tubes or wires of high thermal capacity through which the gas can pass freely. The function of the regenerator is to take up and restore heat in the working gas as it is transferred from the cold space to the hot space and back.

At the first stage in an idealized Stirling cycle, almost all the gas is in the cold space (fig. 117a). Then the bottom piston is pushed upwards (fig. 117b) to compress the working gas, just as the mixture in an internal combustion engine is compressed before combustion. Next, both pistons are moved upwards (fig. 117c) so that the working gas is displaced to the hot space through the generator without any change in volume. As it is transferred, it picks up heat imparted to the regenerator during the previous cycle. While the gas remains in the hot space, heat is poured into it from the external source, so it expands to do useful work on the lower piston (fig. 117d). Finally, both the upper, displacer piston and the lower, power piston are moved downwards again to displace the gas back to the cold space so that the cycle can begin again and the working gas be re-used.

One of the major attractions of this form of engine is its very high theoretical efficiency. It need generate no electrical interference, is very quiet because the pressure fluctuations inside it are smooth and gentle and it can be a multi-fuelled power unit. These features make it very attractive from a military point of view, which is why Philips of Eindhoven revived interest in it with a research programme that began before the war. Continuing in the fifties, they were able to reduce pumping losses and improve efficiency by 50 per cent by using hydrogen

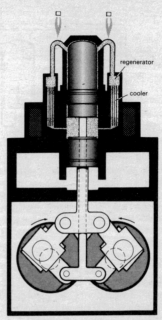

fig. 118. The Philips rhombic drive mechanism involving two contra-rotating cranks gives the displacer and power pistons the correct sequence of movements.

instead of air as the working gas. They also invented a compact and elegant mechanism called a **rhombic drive** (fig. 118) involving a pair of contra-rotating crankshafts to phase the motion of the two pistons involved, the **power piston** and the **displacer piston**.

In recent years work has also been done by the United Stirling company of Sweden who built a four-cylinder engine on these lines. But they considered the rhombic drive, though simpler than earlier mechanisms, too complex and expensive for a commercially acceptable engine. Accordingly, they devised a system of cylinder interconnection (fig. 119) which allows each piston to combine the functions of displacer and power generator and the phases of a Stirling cycle to be established in the correct sequence by a single crankshaft which is basically of the ordinary automotive sort.

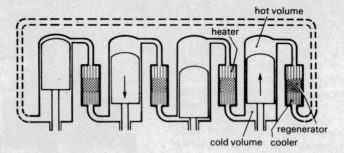

fig. 119. As a simpler and cheaper alternative to the rhombic drive mechanism, the Swedish United Stirling company adapted the in-line cylinder layout to the engine's principle using a crankshaft which is essentially conventional in form.

A series of double-acting V-4 prototype engines working on this principle have been constructed with some success: high efficiencies have been obtained experimentally. But Stirling engines need a complex power output control system (which varies the weight of the working gas) and, as for steam engines and gas turbines, the liquid fuel burners they normally use need careful design to keep down NO_x emissions. They also need expensive high-temperature alloys for the generator, and are not likely to be seen in cars for some years.

The electric car

Although it is the clear favourite of motoring's most vociferous critics, the electric car is unlikely to have much impact on road transport for many years; it will neither save energy nor reduce the overall level of atmospheric pollution, though it should certainly help to transfer pollution from urban areas to the source of electric power.

The biggest disadvantage of any electric car using current technology is not – as has sometimes been suggested – its modest performance, but its very limited range due to the high bulk and weight of lead–acid batteries (p. 161). The Enfield electric car, for instance, briefly produced in the mid seventies, carried no less than 680 lb of batteries (fig. 120), had about half the carrying capacity of a Mini and a claimed range of only forty miles. This is barely adequate, even for a commuting journey. It is roughly fifteen miles from the centre of London to its edge, for example, so a round trip of thirty miles plus some additional shopping mileage could leave one stranded on the way home. Even with a fifty-mile range, the electric vehicle would remain a very specialized limited-use second car, yet would almost certainly have the same initial cost as a conventional car of similar size. Its immediate running costs might be lower, but its batteries would need to be replaced every two years or so. But a car with a hundred-mile range would require batteries weighing around 2000 lb – more than the total weight of a smallish conventional car – and would thus be quite impractical.

Of course the picture would change completely if some markedly superior form of electric storage were to be developed. Several such systems are being investigated, but there is space here to consider only two. The first is the **sodium–sulphur** battery invented a few years ago by some engineers working for the Ford Motor Co. It runs at

fig. 120. The Enfield electric car had little accommodation and a range of only 40 miles, yet carried 680 lb of batteries.

350°C and involves (fig. 121) an electrode of liquid sodium metal reacting electrochemically with another of molten sulphur through a solid electrolyte, a ceramic material called beta alumina. Each cell has an electrical potential of over 2 V and stores more than seven times more energy per pound than a lead–acid battery.

But liquid sodium and sulphur are amongst the most highly reactive substances known and thus constitute a considerable safety hazard. Stainless steel is needed to contain the sulphur electrode which lines the cell, and further enclosure of groups of cells in containers filled with an inert gas would probably be essential for safety. The cost of this type of battery would therefore be many times greater than that of a lead–acid battery. And even with very good heat insulation, the maintenance of the high operating temperatures makes it mainly suitable for daily (e.g. commercial) use rather than intermittent (e.g. private car) operation.

Another interesting possibility is the **zinc–air cell**. Until quite recently, research on this kind of battery seemed to have reached a dead end because of the difficulty of developing a satisfactory zinc electrode. It was found difficult to prevent it from forming spongy protrusions or **dendrites** which tended to short out each cell. But a French company may have succeeded in circumventing this problem with a new form of the battery in which the zinc 'electrode' is a slurry or powder which is pumped round the cell along with the electrolyte.

A zinc–air cell should store five to six times more energy per pound than a lead–acid battery, so the successful development of such a system would be a big breakthrough. But without such an advance the electric car is sure to remain impractical.

Some long-term hope is offered by the **fuel cell** – a sort of battery in which the two 'electrodes' are air or oxygen with a fuel such as hydrogen or methanol. It is potentially efficient, but heavy, complex and expensive. The General Motors Electrovan (fig. 122) illustrates these disadvantages well.

It was introduced as long ago as 1966, but later systems developed by other companies do not seem to have become much lighter or simpler. The hydrogen–oxygen fuel cell of the GM van was said to give it a top speed of 70 mph and a range of 150 miles, but it weighed nearly 4000 lb. A methanol–air fuel cell would be more practical for a car, but

fig. 121. Molten sodium and sulphur form the electrodes of the sodium-sulphur battery, the electrolyte being the special ceramic material which separates them.

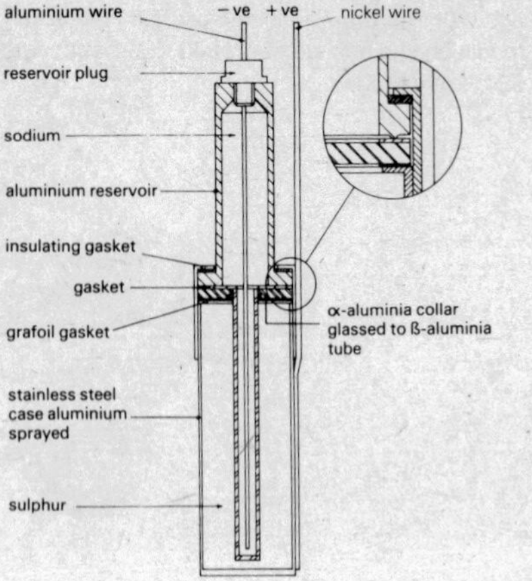

the catalysts required are expensive and the output per unit weight is poor.

Another possibility is the hybrid car in which a small engine charges batteries which in turn drive the wheels. The aim is to improve efficiency and reduce exhaust pollution by running the engine at a well-chosen constant speed, using the battery to store energy needed for sudden power demands. But current thinking is that the inefficiencies of the generator, battery and electric motors involved would render any advantage marginal.

aluminium wire

−ve +ve nickel wire

reservoir plug

sodium

aluminium reservoir

insulating gasket

gasket

grafoil gasket

α-aluminia collar glassed to ß-aluminia tube

stainless steel case aluminium sprayed

sulphur

fig. 122. The fuel cell, seen here in the General Motors experimental Electrovan, remains bulky and expensive.

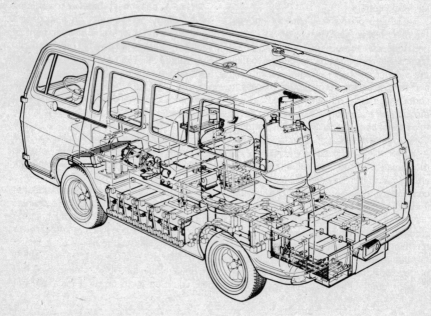

seven The Electrical System

We have already learned (p. 59) that a car's electrical system consists of several components: a generator which is the main source of electrical power; its associated control system; a battery which supplies current when the engine is not running and is charged by the generator, an ignition system which generally consists of a coil, a contact-breaker and a distributor, and finally a starter motor. The lights and windscreen wipers are further important users of electricity, which is also consumed by such devices as the heater fan, rear window demister and radio, if fitted. To understand these components and how they interact, let us first learn a little about electricity itself.

Basic principles

Between the terminals of a source of electrical energy such as a battery or dynamo, there exists (fig. 123) an **electro-motive force (emf)** or **potential** which is measured in **volts**. This **voltage** can be thought of as the force which pushes an electric current

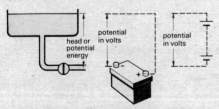

fig. 123. Voltage is like the head of water in a hydraulic system.

through a conductor. In a hydraulic system, the 'head' of water – or the height of one level above another – represents the potential or stored-up energy which is available to do work but does none unless released to do so – say by opening a tap and allowing the water to turn a paddle-wheel. Similarly, the potential difference of so many volts between the terminals of a battery or dynamo represents the potential energy stored-up or being generated, and this energy does no work unless the terminals are connected together by a conductor of electricity. Most metals are good conductors of electricity, but other substances such as rubber are insulators and conduct hardly at all.

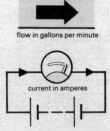

flow in gallons per minute

current in amperes

fig. 124. The flow of electric current is measured in amperes – it is like the flow of water in gallons or litres per minute.

The electric current which flows through a conductor (fig. 124) when a source of potential is connected across its ends is measured in **amperes**, usually shortened to **amps**. It is analogous to the flow of water in, for example, gallons or litres per minute.

Just as a large-diameter pipe offers little **resistance** (fig. 125) to the flow of water, and a small-diameter pipe a large resistance, so a thick wire has a low resistance to the passage of current, while a thin wire has a high resistance. Resistance is measured in **ohms**.

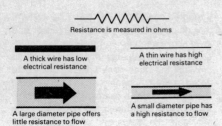

Resistance is measured in ohms

A thick wire has low electrical resistance

A thin wire has high electrical resistance

A large diameter pipe offers little resistance to flow

A small diameter pipe has a high resistance to flow

fig. 125. Resistance is measured in ohms – thin wires are more resistive than thick ones.

The potential (fig. 126) in volts, V, the current in amps, A, and the resistance in ohms, R, are all interrelated (by the equation $V = AR$). A large voltage is needed to force a given current through a high resistance, but the same current can be forced through a low resistance by a low voltage.

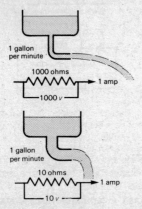

1 gallon per minute

1000 ohms — 1 amp
1000 v

1 gallon per minute

10 ohms — 1 amp
10 v

fig. 126. The current is proportional to the voltage and inversely proportional to the resistance, or $V = AR$.

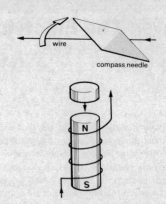

fig. 127. An electric current creates a magnetic field.

Associated with the flow of electric current is a **magnetic effect**. When a current is passed through a coil of wire, it becomes a magnet (fig. 127) and will attract pieces of iron or steel. The magnetic field is strengthened if the coil of wire is wound round a soft iron core.

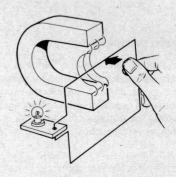

fig. 128. A voltage is induced in a conductor when it cuts lines of magnetic force.

The magnetic effect is to some extent reversible. If a conductor is moved about in a magnetic field (fig. 128) so as to cut or pass through the lines of force, an emf is **induced** in it (but no current flows unless the ends of the conductor are connected to an external circuit). The important point is that the emf is only generated when the conductor is actually moving, and that the movement must cut the lines of force and not be parallel to them. A further point is that the quicker the conductor is moved the higher the voltage – the induced emf is proportional to the rate at which the lines of force are cut. An emf will also be induced if the conductor is held still while the magnetic field is altered in strength. But however it is generated, its polarity or sense is always such as to set up a current which opposes the cause producing it.

oppose the cause producing it, a resistive torque appears as soon as any power is drawn from the dynamo.

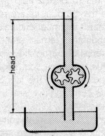

Charging the battery

The dc dynamo

A loop of wire rotating between the poles of a horseshoe magnet (fig. 129) continuously cuts the lines of magnetic force and forms a simple generator. The direction and rate of cutting the lines alters as the loop rotates, but by connecting its ends to a **commutator** the changes in the sense of the induced emf can be compensated for, so that the current which flows from the fixed contacts or **brushes** bearing on it, is uni-directional or **direct current** (dc). The fixed magnet need not be a permanent one: it can be an electromagnet energized by the rotating loop or **armature** – there is always enough residual magnetism in the core of this electromagnet or **field coil** to cause an emf to be generated in the first place, and after that the output builds up rapidly. In a practical dynamo the loop is replaced by a coil of many turns, and by winding several of these coils on the armature the fluctuation in the output voltage is minimized.

Because the induced current tends to

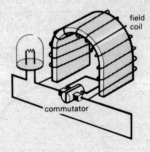

fig. 129. A loop of wire rotating between the poles of a magnet forms a simple generator. By connecting the ends of the loop to a commutator, direct current can be produced.

The alternator

Some years ago batteries were generally charged by dc dynamos, but nowadays nearly all cars are fitted with alternators which generate more power at low engine speeds and are more compact. Whereas in a dynamo the magnetic field remains stationary and the conductors are rotated in it, for an alternator the magnetic field is rotated and the conductors remain stationary. Continuous reversal of current flow is the result.

In fig. 130a, when the South pole is up and the North pole is down the induced voltage polarity and current flow are in a certain direction as shown. When the poles are reversed as in fig. 130b, both voltage polarity and current flow are also reversed.

Current which changes direction like this in a regular and repeated fashion is known as ac or **alternating current** – fig. 131 shows the **waveform** of one complete cycle. The number of cycles occurring in one second

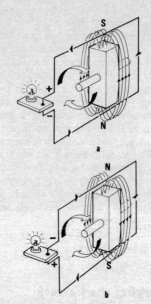

fig. 130. In an alternator the conducting coils are held still and the magnetic field is rotated. The resultant output voltage alternates or continually reverses its polarity.

fig. 131. The waveform of an alternator's output.

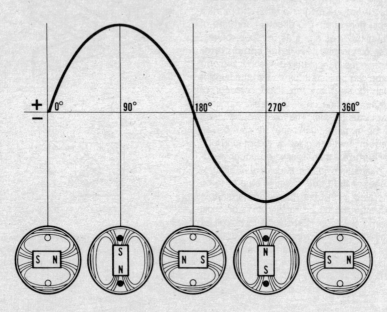

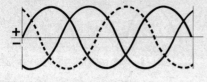

fig. 132. Practical automotive alternators are usually of the three-phase kind, generating three separate waveforms simultaneously.

is called the **frequency**. The frequency depends on two factors: (i) the number of pairs of magnetic poles carried by the armature; (ii) its speed of rotation. Thus if the single two-pole magnet of fig. 131 were rotated at 50 revolutions per second, the frequency would be 50 cycles a second.

The **amplitude** or maximum voltage of the output depends on three factors: (i) the number of turns of wire on the stationary coil; (ii) the strength of the magnetic field;

(iii) the speed at which the armature rotates.

In a practical alternator it is usual to employ three separate coils of wire (**phase windings**) so that the rotating magnet causes three separate waveforms to be generated simultaneously (fig. 132).

Thus a practical alternator (fig. 133) is composed of the following basic parts:

1. A stationary winding assembly, the **stator**.
2. A rotating electromagnet, the **rotor**, carrying a field coil.
3. A **slip-ring** and brush assembly.
4. A **rectifier** assembly – not yet described.
5. Two end-frames.
6. A cooling fan.

Rectification

Since one of the main purposes of the alternator is to keep the battery charged, it is necessary to convert its output from ac to dc. This process is called **rectification** and involves the use of a device which will pass current in one direction only. The **rectifier** can be compared to a non-return valve in a hydraulic system.

fig. 133. Alternator construction. The rectifiers are built into the assembly.

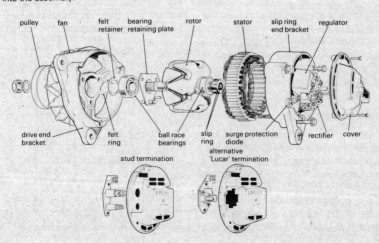

pulley   fan   felt retainer   bearing retaining plate   rotor   stator   slip ring end bracket   regulator

drive end bracket   felt ring   ball race bearings   slip ring   surge protection diode   rectifier   cover
stud termination   alternative 'Lucar' termination

fig. 134. A single diode gives half-wave rectification.

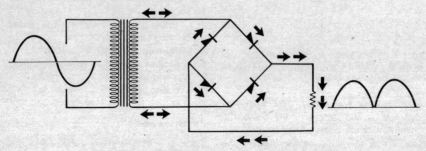

fig. 135. Full wave rectification fills in the gaps between the pulses.

The simplest form of rectifier circuit (fig. 134) is the **half wave** type. When an alternating current is applied to the rectifier, it conducts for only one half of the alternating cycle and the output is pulsating dc. **Full wave** rectification is a better system – the arrows (fig. 135) show that the current always flows in the same direction through the load connected across the output of the circuit. This is a **single phase** circuit. **Three-phase** rectification – generally required for car alternators – is a little more complicated (fig. 136) but the principle is the same.

Voltage and polarity

The nominal (more details later) emf of a motor car alternator when rectified, and of a dc dynamo, has almost always been 12 V, though some cars – notably older versions of the Volkswagen Beetle – have been fitted with 6 V systems. Similarly, the negative terminal of the battery is nearly always **earthed** to the steel chassis or bodyshell of the car (if it has one) which forms a convenient common return path for many of the circuits. Some British cars, however, built between 1935 and 1965, had positively earthed electrical systems, an arrangement which helped to reduce erosion of the sparking plug electrodes and corrosion of the battery terminals under the conditions of that period. It is no longer considered necessary.

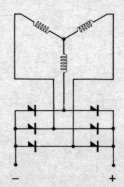

fig. 136. A three-phase rectification circuit.

Output control – the dynamo

When a dc dynamo is fitted, an isolating device must be placed in the circuit by which the battery is charged. If the dynamo were permanently connected to the battery, all would be well so long as the dynamo voltage remained higher than the battery voltage; but if the dynamo were at rest or turning slowly the battery voltage would be higher than the dynamo voltage and the battery would try to drive the dynamo as if it were a motor.

A non-return valve (fig. 137) or **cut-out** prevents this from happening. It consists (fig. 138) of a pair of contacts controlled by a

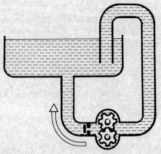

fig. 137. A cut-out is the equivalent of a non-return valve in a hydraulic circuit.

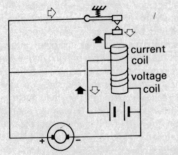

current
coil

voltage
coil

+   –

fig. 138. The principle of the cut-out. The voltage coil closes the contacts and the current coil holds them in contact. (Current flow and contact movement shown by open arrows.) When the battery voltage exceeds the dynamo voltage the current flow is reversed and the contacts open (solid arrows).

solenoid wound with a voltage coil which is connected **in parallel** with the dynamo or across it, and a current coil which is connected **in series** with the dynamo and thus carries its total current output. When the dynamo voltage reaches a certain level, the magnetic field exerted by the voltage coil pulls the contacts together against the tension of a spring and connects the dynamo to the battery, and the charging current which consequently flows through the current coil holds the contacts together more firmly. (Current flow and contact movement indicated by open arrows.) But as soon as the battery voltage exceeds the dynamo voltage, the direction of the current flow in the current coil is reversed (solid arrows) and the magnetic field created by it opposes that due to the voltage coil and thus causes the contacts to fly apart and the dynamo to be disconnected from the battery.

Regulation

The voltage output of a dynamo rises with its speed of rotation. Without regulation the lights would become brighter and dimmer as the engine was revved and allowed to idle, and all the electrical components would be overloaded at high rpm.

To eliminate this variation the generator circuits of cars may be fitted with a **voltage regulator** which essentially consists (fig. 139) of an electromagnet connected across the output terminals of the dynamo. When the engine is revved up, the dynamo voltage increases and the electromagnet attracts towards it against the tension of a spring a moving contact which is mounted on a soft iron armature. Connection to a fixed contact is broken so that the current to the dynamo field coil has to flow through a **resistor** and is reduced. The fixed magnet of the dynamo is weakened, there are fewer lines of force from it and the output of the dynamo falls. At low engine speeds, on the other hand, the voltage output is correspondingly low, and the electromagnet or solenoid

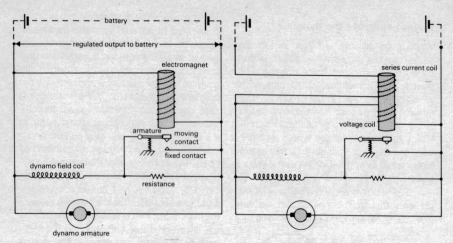

fig. 139. The principle of the voltage regulator: when the output voltage rises too high, the contacts are broken, inserting a resistor in series with the dynamo field coil and reducing the output.

fig. 140. The compensated voltage regulator – the voltage regulating action is inhibited when heavy currents are drawn from the dynamo.

cannot hold the fixed and moving contacts apart. The current then flows directly to the field coil and the output of the dynamo is increased.

The moving contact vibrates rapidly back and forth, achieving regulation by the proportion of time spent in the open and the closed positions. If the dynamo output voltage is low, for example, the vibrating contact may spend 75 per cent of the time in the closed position, whereas if the output is high, the contact may spend 75 per cent of the time in the open position. In this way the voltage is maintained at a constant level – around 16 V for a 12 V system – regardless of dynamo speed.

The compensated voltage regulator

A voltage regulator of the kind already described can only cope with one type of change – the change in output voltage with speed. Changes in the amount of current demanded of the dynamo, however, must also be taken into account. In particular, the dynamo must not be overloaded when the battery is flat.

To prevent this from happening, the voltage regulating action is inhibited (fig. 140) when heavy currents are drawn from the dynamo. An additional coil is wound on the regulator solenoid in the same sense as the voltage coil and connected in series with the supply to the battery. The magnetic field created by this coil is proportional to the *current* flowing in the charging circuit and *not* the voltage output of the dynamo. When the current demanded is high, therefore, the magnetic field in the regulator solenoid is increased in strength, so that the moving contact spends more time in the open position, the output voltage falls, and the current supplied is kept within a safe limit. Thus the current coil gives a 'drooping' characteristic to the regulated output so that the voltage falls as the current increases.

The current–voltage regulator

In the most advanced form of control unit now generally used with a dynamo, control of the current is separated from control of the voltage, allowing the dynamo to deliver a greater output without fear of overloading, and thus to give more rapid charging of the battery. Hence the **current–voltage regulator** (fig. 141) has a current coil and a voltage

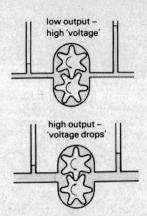

fig. 142. A dynamo's output voltage tends to drop when a large current is drawn from it.

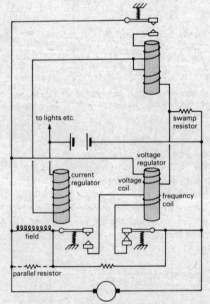

fig. 141. Current control is separated from voltage control in the current–voltage regulator.

coil each with its own pair of contacts. These contacts are connected in series with each other and with the field coil, while the controlling resistor is connected across them. The voltage regulator is set to begin vibrating when the maximum rated voltage is exceeded, and similarly, the current regulator is set to begin operation when the maximum safe current is reached.

Since the dynamo voltage tends to drop (fig. 142) when the current drawn from it is large, the voltage regulator is at rest when the dynamo is connected to a discharged battery, but the current regulator is vibrating to limit the current to the safe maximum. Conversely, when the battery is fully charged the current regulator will be at rest but the voltage regulator will be vibrating to maintain the output voltage constant.

Several refinements are usually incorporated in a current–voltage regulator unit. To give smoother control a 'bucking' or frequency coil is wound on the voltage regulator core through which the field current passes when the contacts are closed to assist the voltage coil and increase the frequency of vibration of its contact. The effect of the change in resistance with temperature of the two voltage coils is minimized by connecting a **swamp resistor** in series with them. The swamp resistor has a very much higher value of resistance than the two voltage coils, and is made of a special type of wire which shows little change of resistance with changes in temperature. Thus although the resistance of the voltage coils might change considerably, the total resistance in the voltage coil remains nearly the same, so the current flowing through it remains the same as do the magnetic fields created by the voltage coils. Hence the settings do not alter

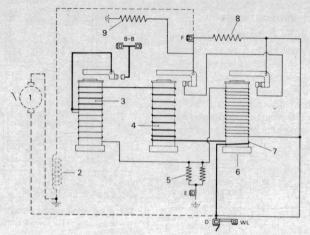

fig. 143. A current–voltage regulator/cut-out unit: 1, dynamo armature; 2, dynamo field coil; 3, cut-out relay; 4, current regulator; 5, swamp resistor; 6, voltage regulator; 7, additional series turn for certain applications; 8, field resistor; 9, field parallel resistor.

significantly with changes in temperature.

The cut-out usually forms part of the complete unit (fig. 143).

Output control – the alternator

An alternator is more easily controlled than a dynamo: it does not need a cut-out, for instance, since its rectifiers block reverse current flow, though sometimes a relay controlled by the ignition switch is fitted to isolate the field coil from the battery. A second relay controls the warning lamp. Similarly, current regulation is not needed, since this is taken care of by the behaviour of the field coil.

For when a coil or a winding is energized by an alternating current, a **back emf** is continually being induced in it which increases its effective resistance – or its **reactance**. Unlike pure resistance, reactance increases with the frequency of the alternating current, and as this rises with speed, the output current is always limited to a safe value.

A voltage regulator is needed however, and it works (fig. 144) on the same basic principle as the voltage regulator of a dynamo, a control resistance in series with the field coil being brought in and out of circuit by a vibrating contact. Nowadays, though, the switching action is usually performed by transistors and the voltage control unit is mounted inside the body of the alternator itself.

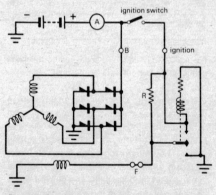

fig. 144. An alternator voltage regulator works in the same way as a dynamo voltage regulator, though transistors are generally used to do the switching, not vibrating contacts.

The battery

The galvanic cell

By various physical and chemical means it is possible to create positively or negatively charged particles called **ions**. Many chemical compounds, for instance, ionize freely when dissolved in water. Thus although pure water is almost a non-conductor of electricity, the presence of charged particles in an aqueous solution means that if two electrodes are immersed in it and connected to an external source of electrical potential, the positive ions will be attracted to the negatively charged electrode and the negative ions to the positive electrode. Chemical decomposition of the dissolved substance will ensue, and a current will flow through the solution and the external circuit. Any solution or liquid which conducts electricity in this way is called an **electrolyte**; solids sometimes behave as electrolytes also.

Certain metals and solid chemical compounds also tend to ionize when placed in an electrolyte, in much the same way as molecules evaporate from the surface of a liquid. Different materials have different tendencies to ionize, so when two dissimilar materials are immersed in an electrolyte compatible with them both, a potential difference builds up between them and they may form a *galvanic cell*, which is a source of electricity.

Types of galvanic cell

Although many substances other than metals have differing ionization potentials and might be used as electrode materials, a lot of possible combinations are eliminated by the difficulty of finding an electrolyte which is compatible with the two electrode substances in question; that is, which does not react in some unwanted way with either. Many theoretically useful voltaic cells work perfectly until a significant current is drawn from them, when the resultant chemical action within the cell causes polarization –

bubbles of gas or deposits of an inert compound build up at one or both of the plates, effectively insulating them from the electrolyte and stopping all further action.

A further group of galvanic cells, which includes the expendable dry battery, deliver useful current but undergo irreversible chemical changes during discharge and must eventually be thrown away. Hence if a reversible galvanic cell is required, which can be recharged by passing an electric current through it, the number of possible arrangements known is quite small.

The car battery

One of the best known of these is used for the car battery which in the charged state essentially consists (fig. 145) of a plate of lead and a plate of lead peroxide immersed in a solution of sulphuric acid. When the battery is being discharged lead sulphate is deposited on both plates and water is formed, diluting the sulphuric acid electrolyte and reducing its specific gravity.

The battery can then be recharged by passing through it in the reverse direction a current from an external source. The water in the solution then re-combines with the

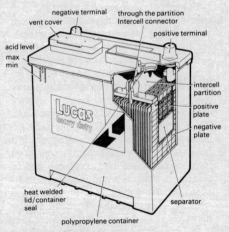

fig. 145. The lead-acid battery.

lead sulphate deposited on both plates to form sulphuric acid (the specific gravity of which therefore rises) and to form lead which is deposited on the lead plate and lead peroxide which is deposited on the lead peroxide plate. If the current from the external source continues to be applied after the battery has been fully recharged, the water present will be electrolytically decomposed into gaseous oxygen and hydrogen. This can create an explosion hazard, so good ventilation is essential.

Construction

The basic lead–acid cell described develops just over 2 V when fully charged so the standard 12 V car battery contains six such cells connected in series and separated from each other by partitions in the battery case. It is vital that there should be no leakage of acid from one cell to another.

Each plate embodies a central grid made of lead alloyed with antimony to increase mechanical strength and corrosion resistance. By complex manufacturing processes coatings of, in one case spongy lead and in the other porous lead peroxide, are deposited on these grids to form the negative and positive plates respectively.

To increase the area of active material in contact with the electrolyte and, in addition, to reduce the internal resistance by increasing the cross-sectional area of the circuit path in the electrolyte, each cell contains not simply one negative plate and one positive plate, but sets of interleaved plates, generally numbering five, seven, nine or eleven, according to the capacity in ampere-hours required. For a number of reasons there are usually more negative plates than positive ones – a typical five-plate battery containing three negative and two positive – and to balance out the quantity of material contained in the two groups of plates, the negative plates are usually made slightly thinner.

The internal resistance is further reduced

and the battery made more compact by mounting the two sets of plates as close together as possible. These conditions necessitate the introduction of an additional component – the **separator** – the design of which is critical to the proper functioning of the battery.

The separator is a sheet of material interposed between each pair of plates and must not only be electrically insulating (otherwise the plates would be shorted together) but also microporous to allow the free passage of ions. In addition, it must be mechanically strong to withstand vibration and to resist the pressure created by the build-up of lead sulphate deposits during the discharge process. Similarly, the separators must overlap the plates on either side of them to prevent possible short circuits due to sludging or the formation of growths.

The separator material used varies from manufacturer to manufacturer, that used by Lucas being a micro-porous thermo-setting material.

The construction of the battery is finally completed by a system of lead bars which link the sets of plates and the cells together, and by the lid and filler cap or caps incorporating vents to allow excess hydrogen and oxygen to escape freely during overcharging.

Storage capacity

The required storage capacity of a battery (measured in ampere-hours, the product of current and the time for which it is available) is determined more by the starting current needed than by the total load which could be imposed by all the electrical apparatus fitted to the car. The criteria used by Lucas, for example, are that in general under winter cold-start conditions the battery should turn the engine at 75-100 rpm and its output should not fall below 9 V (for a 12 V battery). Batteries designed to meet these requirements are easily able to cope with any normal load imposed upon them and have a capacity of around 30 Ah for a small car, about 38 Ah for a medium-sized car and of roughly 60 Ah for a large car.

During a cold start the initial current may be as high as 450 A (the stalled current drawn by a typical starter motor) but if all is reasonably in order, remains at this magnitude for a fraction of a second and tails off rapidly thereafter. Contrary to popular belief, therefore, relatively little charge is taken out of a battery in good condition during a normal cold start.

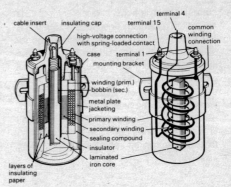

fig. 146. The ignition coil: its primary coil is a few turns of thin wire, its secondary many turns of fine wire and both are wound on a core of soft iron laminations. The windings are often immersed in oil.

The ignition system

The coil

The basic component of all modern ignition systems is a coil – essentially a transformer, or to be more precise, an induction coil of the sort found in school laboratories. Like the dynamo and alternator it depends upon the principle of **electromagnetic induction**. Just as an emf is induced in a coil which is moved through lines of magnetic force – or held still in a magnetic field which is varying in strength – so a back emf is induced in a coil by changes in its own magnetic field. This back emf opposes the applied emf. If such a coil is connected to a dc supply, its magnetic field grows relatively slowly, so the induced back emf is relatively small. But when it is *dis*connected by a switch or contact-breaker, the resistance in the circuit becomes almost infinite virtually instantaneously, causing the magnetic field to collapse very rapidly and a large back emf to be induced. This can easily be demonstrated by connecting a neon lamp – which will not flash at less than 300 V – across a coil of a few hundred turns, just like the primary of an ignition coil. When the coil is disconnected from its 12 V supply, the lamp flashes, showing that an emf of at least 300 V has been induced. A voltage of about this value is therefore the effective primary emf of an ignition coil and it is multiplied at least fifty-

fold by magnetically coupling it to a secondary winding having many thousands of turns.

Thus an ignition coil (fig. 146) consists of two windings, wrapped around a former, enclosing a core of soft iron laminations. Next to the core is placed the secondary winding which has several thousand turns of fine enamelled wire, while above it lies the primary winding composed of a few hundred turns of much thicker wire. The two coils are connected together at one end and brought out to a common terminal which is earthed. The 'live' end of the primary is connected to the positive terminal of the battery via the contact breaker – while the live end of the secondary coil is connected, via the distributor, to the centre electrodes of the sparking plugs. The side electrode is earthed, completing the secondary circuit. In practice the secondary is generally wound so that the centre electrode is made negative with respect to the earth electrode, as this improves the formation of the spark.

The contact breaker

The ignition coil would not work at all without the contact-breaker which supplies the current interruptions necessary to its operation. As already described (p. 59) this is operated (fig. 147) by a cam with a lobe for each cylinder which is driven at half engine speed. One contact, made of a material which resists spark erosion such as tungsten, is mounted on a spring-loaded rocker arm with a plastic heel bearing on the camshaft. The other, made of the same material, is essentially fixed, but it can be adjusted so that the gap can be set (at around 0.015 in, usually).

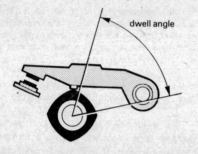

fig. 147. The contact breaker – it is operated by a cam with a lobe for each cylinder and runs at half engine speed. The dwell angle is the angle through which the contact-breaker cam rotates between the instant at which the points close and that at which they reopen. It must be as large as possible to allow the primary current to build up to its maximum.

When the contact-breaker **points** close, the magnetic field in the primary takes an appreciable time to become re-established, so it is important for the period of closure to be as long as possible. This period is partly determined by the **dwell angle**, the angle (fig. 147) through which the cam rotates between the instant of closing and the instant of opening again. The dwell angle should remain substantially constant with rising speed, but of course the time interval it represents is smaller at high revs than at low revs. For this reason the voltage output of the coil tends to deteriorate at high rpm, especially in engines with many cylinders

which require a large number of sparks per minute at any given engine speed.

The back emf in the primary tries to force a current across the points when they open, tending to create an arc and to burn them, and also to reduce the speed with which the magnetic field collapses. This effect is greatly reduced by connecting across the points a **condenser** or **capacitor** which essentially consists of two sets of conducting plates separated by an insulator. A capacitor acts like a spring which responds to *changes* in voltage. When the voltage across it remains steady, it does not conduct at all, but current flows into it when the voltage varies. When the points open, therefore, the capacitor stores the energy which would otherwise be dissipated as an arc, then discharges it through the primary coil.

The distributor

The high tension supply is fed to the sparking plugs by a distributor (fig. 148) which gen-

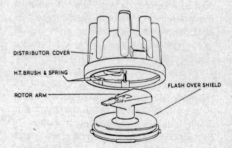

fig. 148. The high-tension voltage is fed to the sparking plugs by a distributor which lies above the sparking plugs.

erally lies immediately above the contact breaker. A carbon brush connects the main high tension lead to a **rotor arm** which passes in turn close to fixed contacts in the **distributor cap**, each of which is connected to a sparking plug. There is no actual connection between the rotor arm and the fixed contacts: the spark jumps the small gap between them.

Advance and retard

To advance the timing of the spark (p. 72) with rising engine speed the contact-breaker cam is provided with a special centrifugal mechanism. A circular baseplate mounted on the distributor and contact-breaker drive shaft (fig. 149) has two pins, A and B, projecting

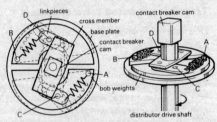

fig. 149. Centrifugal advance and retard. As the speed of the contact-breaker shaft rises, the bob-weights twist the cam round with respect to its shaft as engine speed rises, advancing the spark.

from it upon which are pivoted two approximately semicircular bob-weights. Link-pieces pivoted in the bob-weights at C and D are coupled to a crossmember which is in turn attached to the shaft carrying the contact-breaker cam; this shaft is free to rotate in a bush in the centre of the circular baseplate. The ends of the link-pieces are connected to the fixed pivot pins by tension springs.

As the drive shaft rotates, centrifugal force pulls the bob-weights outwards against the restraining force of the springs and twists the contact-breaker cam round in relation to the drive shaft, advancing the ignition timing. By a suitable choice of the geometry of the linkage and the strength of the springs, the amount of advance with increasing engine speed can be made to fit different curves. A more recent type of centrifugal advance mechanism uses bob-weights pivoted against fixed contoured cams (fig. 150) thus enabling the designer to fit the amount of advance required to a wider range of requirements.

Additional advance for part-throttle running (p. 73) is provided by a vacuum-

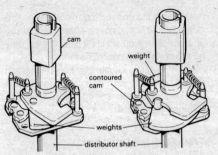

fig. 150. By pivoting the bob-weights on contoured cams, the advance curve can be tailored to a wide range of requirements.

operated mechanism. This essentially consists of a chamber divided into two parts by a spring-loaded flexible diaphragm (fig. 151) one side of which is at atmospheric pressure and the other connected to the induction tract at the carburetter. The centre of the diaphragm is joined through a linkage to the contact-breaker plate which is free to turn about the contact-breaker cam.

As the pressure in the inlet manifold falls, the diaphragm flexes and turns the contact-breaker plate around the cam, advancing the ignition timing. By placing the connection to the induction tract just outside the carburetter butterfly, the pressure remains at atmospheric with the ignition fully retarded when the engine is idling. But when the throttle is partly open the connection is covered by the butterfly and is thus subjected to the full manifold depression.

When the throttle is fully open, on the

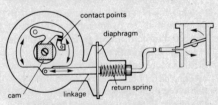

fig. 151. Vacuum advance. A diaphragm acted on by inlet manifold depression gives the additional advance needed for weak-mixture running. At idle and full throttle the manifold connection is clear of the carburetter butterfly.

other hand, the connection to the diaphragm is virtually at atmospheric pressure, and the amount of ignition advance is controlled only by the centrifugal mechanism.

In a few cars, notably certain Volkswagen Beetle models, inlet manifold depression has been used to control both forms of advance and retard.

Transistorized systems

The weak link in any conventional ignition system is the contact-breaker. Even when it is in perfect condition, its reducing dwell-time leads to a decreasing voltage as engine speed rises. One obvious solution would be to increase the dwell angle, but mechanical limitations prevent this from being much more than about twice the contacts-open angle. Similar limitations may cause the points to bounce or float at very high revs – just like valves – to the further detriment of the high tension voltage.

When starting in cold weather, on the other hand, the cranking speed and battery voltage may fall so low that the contacts do not open with sufficient rapidity to generate an adequate spark. Under such conditions the difficulties may be increased by the presence of conducting combustion deposits on the sparking plug, partially short-circuiting the electrodes, and reducing the high tension voltage still further. If the time the high tension voltage takes to reach its maximum – its **rise time** – is also long, the high tension current tends to leak away through these deposits before a spark can be generated. To overcome the effects of fouling, therefore, the high tension voltage must be high and its rise time short.

But a much more important defect of the mechanical contact-breaker is its deterioration in performance with time due to wear of the plastic heel and erosion of the points; a change in the carefully chosen preset gap between its points influences the ignition timing as well as the spark characteristics. There is a significant deterioration in spark voltage and timing after a few thousand miles of operation. One consequence is a noticeable worsening of fuel consumption, another is a measurable increase in exhaust pollution levels – both unacceptable in these days of high fuel costs and emission regulations.

Transistor-assisted contact system

One way of minimizing the disadvantages of a conventional ignition system is by reducing the current which the contact-breaker has to handle. This can be done (fig. 152) by a **TAC** (transistor-assisted contact) system in which the contact-breaker, instead of switching the primary winding of the coil on and off, switches a transistor on and off, a transistor which in turn controls the primary current. In such an application the transistor acts as both a switch and an amplifier: it can be made to conduct or insulate as required and it does so in response to a signal current which is many times smaller than the current being switched. Thus the contact-breaker points no longer have to carry the full primary current, only a much smaller signal current, and suffer far less from pitting, from corrosion and from fouling. Although with suitable circuitry it is possible to reduce this current to a tiny value, in practice a current of about 0.25 A has been found to have a beneficial cleaning action on the contacts. By comparison the full primary current is usually in the 3–5 A range.

Another advantage is that the switching action depends largely on the transistor circuit which flips extremely rapidly from the on state to the off state even when the points open slowly. The effective dwell angle is therefore larger than for a mechanical system, and the performance during marginal cold-start conditions far better.

Breakerless ignition systems

But in a TAC system the mechanical deficiencies of the contact-breaker remain: a

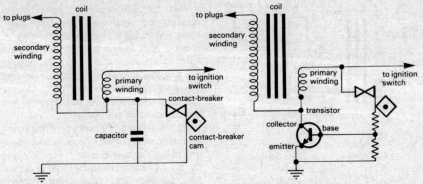

fig. 152. Conventional ignition system (*left*) the contact-breaker carries a current of several amps, but in a transistor-assisted ignition system (*right*) the contact-breaker carries a small current only, switching a transistor circuit which controls the primary current.

much more satisfactory approach is to eliminate it altogether. The most popular substitute (fig. 153) is a magnetic pick-up consisting of a rotating element which alters the magnetic flux in a sensing coil or which alters the magnetic coupling between two or more coils. It thus generates a signal which can be used to trigger a transistor switching circuit. Systems of this **breakerless** sort – which eliminate a major servicing requirement and contribute to the maintenance of good fuel consumption – are being increasingly adopted as original equipment and are likely to become near-universal in a few years' time. Another form of trigger uses a light source, a simple revolving shutter and a light-sensitive transistor.

Capacitor discharge systems

There is a further and rather more complex **capacitor discharge** form of electronic ignition characterized by a very rapid rise time which is effective in combating fouled sparking plugs. It may either be breakerless

fig. 153. Breakerless ignition systems, such as this one here triggered by a magnetic pickup, are gradually replacing mechanical contact-breaker systems.

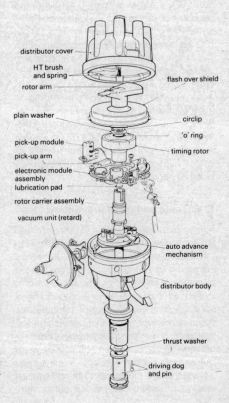

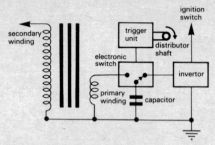

fig. 154. A capacitative discharge ignition system – it is characterized by a very fast voltage rise.

or triggered by transistor-assisted mechanical contacts. The interrupted dc (fig. 154) triggered in either of these ways and generated by a special electronic unit called an inverter is used to charge a capacitor to about 300 V. When a spark is required, the capacitor is discharged into another transformer not unlike an ordinary ignition coil but with a smaller secondary: primary turns ratio. The overall effect is to produce a high tension voltage 'spike' with a very high maximum value and a very short rise time indeed – just what is needed to overcome plug fouling.

Unfortunately, such a short, sharp spark does not always ignite weak mixtures satisfactorily. What is needed is a hybrid system with a very short rise time but a spark of longer duration. Such systems are currently being developed.

Electronic engine management

The widespread adoption of transistorized ignition systems by the major motor manufacturers is only one example of the rapidly increasing use of electronics to control the operation of engines. For when an electronic system is being developed, an additional sensor – to measure coolant temperature, say – is relatively easy to fit and the information it provides is relatively cheap to process. (This is not so, of course, with mechanical control devices such as an advance/retard mechanism.) In addition, an electronic system can provide much more

precise control. Moreover, the advent of the versatile microchip solid-state digital computer has made it comparatively easy to process data inexpensively. The resultant ability to take numerous factors into account has proved a godsend to engineers required to reconcile the often conflicting requirements of improved fuel consumption and reduced exhaust emissions.

For these reasons a number of integrated electronic management systems have come into being, the best-known in Europe being the Bosch Motronic system fitted to certain BMW models. This digital system controls the spark, the spark advance and the fuel injection through a central computer monitoring a number of inputs (fig. 155). These

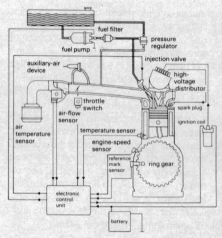

fig. 155. The Bosch Motronic engine management system.

include signals from a flywheel-mounted 'reference mark sensor', which provides basic timing information, engine speed signals from another flywheel-triggered sensor and air-flow signals from a meter which measures the amount of air being drawn into the engine at any given time so that the amount of fuel injected can be correctly apportioned to it. (The air-flow meter is of the hinged flap type and forms part of the

Bosch L-Jetronic fuel injection system (p. 117), which has been integrated into the overall system.) The central computer also takes account of additional signals from a throttle-position switch, a coolant-temperature sensor and an air-temperature sensor. US-market versions of the Motronic system further incorporate a 'Lambda' sensor in the exhaust system. This generates yet another feedback signal, which is used to maintain the air/fuel ratio at the stoichiometric or chemically correct value required by the three-way catalytic converter fitted to meet the stringent American exhaust pollution regulations. Engines with high compression ratios or turbochargers may have control systems additionally fitted with 'knock' sensors which detect the onset of detonation and generate signals which can be processed by the central computer so that the ignition can be retarded just enough to avoid it.

The next generation of electronic control units are likely to manage the transmission system as well as the engine itself. It is a logical step, since the same basic signals, such as engine speed and throttle position are needed in each case. And through electronic control of a sophisticated automatic transmission system – perhaps of the continuously variable (p. 205) type – the engine could be maintained at all times in the most economical mode of operation relative to the demands being made on it, and thus be made to give a significant improvement in fuel consumption.

Sparking plugs

A modern sparking plug (fig. 156) essentially consists of an outer steel shell to which the earth electrode is attached, a centre electrode and terminal and an insulator capable of withstanding high temperatures, severe thermal shocks and large thermal gradients without cracking. Nickel alloys are generally used for the two electrodes, while a form of ceramic, usually aluminium oxide, is usually

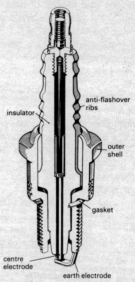

fig. 156. The sparking plug.

employed for the insulator, the exposed top of which incorporates **anti-flash-over ribs** to discourage arcing between the terminal and any nearby earthed object. A special material seals the centre electrode to the insulator and the insulator to the shell. Nowadays plugs generally have a 14 mm thread diameter and a thread reach of 0.50 in or 0.75 in with a captive sealing gasket.

The most important requirement of a sparking plug is that its insulator be maintained at a **'self-cleaning' temperature** in the 500–600°C region, well above the temperature at which excessive fouling by carbon deposits occurs – around 350°C – yet well below the pre-ignition temperature, which is about 950°C. To satisfy this requirement, the rate of loss of heat from insulator to body must be chosen to suit the amount of heat imparted to the plug during each combustion cycle. In a low-output engine the amount of heat imparted to the plug is small and the combustion chamber remains relatively cool, yet at the same time the plug insulator must run hot enough to prevent fouling. The rate of loss of heat from the insulator to the plug body and the cylinder head must therefore be small.

In a high-output engine a great deal of heat is given up to the sparking plug, which must run cool to avoid pre-ignition. Hence the rate at which heat is conducted away from the insulator – the thermal conductance – must be large. As the output of a spark-ignition engine can vary from the 20 bhp/litre or less of a cement-mixer paraffin engine, to the 200 bhp/litre or more of a Grand Prix racing engine, a wide range of plugs is manufactured, each type having a different thermal conductance.

This range of thermal conductance is achieved by varying two features of plug construction. First is the **gas capacity** (fig. 157) which is the volume of the space

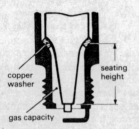

fig. 157. The insulator is kept at the required self-cleaning temperature by a suitable choice of gas capacity and seating height.

between insulator and body accessible to the flame of combustion. By varying the gas capacity the amount of heat reaching the plug insulator can be controlled. Second is the **seating height** which determines the length of the heat-flow path from the tip of the insulator to the copper washer which allows the heat to be conducted away into the plug body.

A plug intended for a low-output engine – to run hot in cool conditions – is called a hot plug and has a large gas capacity and a large seating height (fig. 158). Conversely, a cold plug designed for a high-output engine must

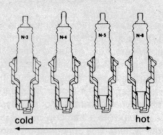

fig. 158. The heat range: on the right a hot plug for use in a low-performance engine, and on the left a cold plug for use in a high-performance engine.

run cool in hot conditions and has a small gas capacity and a small seating height.

Starters

A starter motor pinion is often coupled to its flywheel gear ring by a **Bendix** or **inertia** drive. Effectively, pinion and armature shaft are threaded (fig. 159) so that when the starter motor is energized while the engine is at rest, the pinion is screwed into engagement with the starter ring. The torque of the motor then holds the pinion against a shoulder on the armature shaft and in engagement with the starter ring which is driven round to start the engine. When the engine fires and the motor is switched off, the torque is reversed, the starter ring speeds up and the pinion is screwed out of engagement with it.

But in a typical modern starter of the type made by Lucas (fig. 160) the thread on which the pinion runs is not machined on the armature shaft itself but on a sleeve which is splined to the shaft and able to move axially along it against a heavy spring. This arrangement is designed to cushion the very considerable shock of engagement. When the pinion slams against its shoulder a part of the reaction force created by motor torque and inertia is taken by the lands of the threaded sleeve, which promptly screws itself along the shaft inside the pinion, compressing the spring and absorbing some of

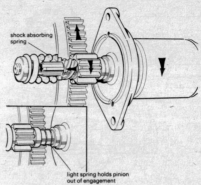

shock absorbing spring

armature

light spring holds pinion out of engagement

fig. 160. In a practical application of the Bendix drive the starter pinion is generally mounted on a threaded sleeve, not directly on the starter motor shaft.

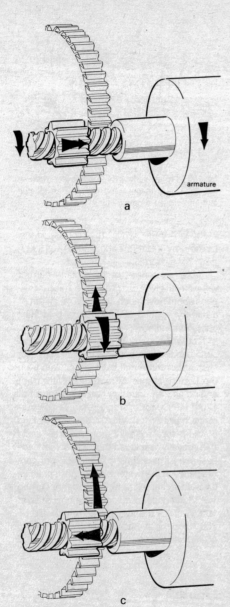

fig. 159. The Bendix drive: the starter motor screws the pinion into engagement (a) with the starter gear (b); when the engine starts the pinion is screwed out of engagement (c).

the reaction force. This reaction force is stored until the engine starts and the motor torque is released when the sleeve is pushed back to its initial position.

The rotary part of the screwing action arises through the ability of the sleeve to turn within the pinion on its threads; the axial part is allowed by the splines on sleeve and shaft. It is a neat little exercise in relative movement, difficult to work out from theory, but easy to understand when you have the mechanism in your own hands to play with. A further complication is a light restraining compression spring that holds the pinion out of engagement with the flywheel gear when the starter motor is not energized.

A failing of inertia drives is the tendency for the pinion to be thrown sharply out of engagement by isolated firing strokes when starting in cold weather, which is why many cars nowadays are fitted with **pre-engaged starters**.

The pinion of a pre-engaged starter is forced (fig. 161) into engagement by a solenoid which is energized when the starter key is twisted: contacts attached to the solenoid plunger close when the pinion is in mesh to energize the motor. The pinion is given a twisting movement by the shaft helix so that the driving torque holds it in engagement.

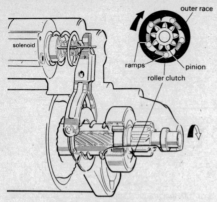

fig. 161. The pinion of a pre-engaged starter is held against the flywheel gear by a solenoid; a free-wheel clutch prevents the starter from being driven when the engine fires. The arrangement gives better starting in very cold weather than the Bendix system.

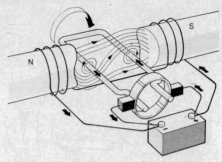

fig. 162. A rotatable loop of wire, placed between the poles of a magnet and fed with an electric current, forms a simple motor.

On tooth-to-tooth abutment, an engaging spring is compressed, allowing the solenoid contacts to close so that the motor torque can index the pinion and provide entry. The shaft helix also supplies added engaging thrust. A one-way **roller clutch** or **free wheel** prevents the engine from driving the motor after start-up.

But the key component of a starter is a dc electric motor which is similar in basic construction to a dc dynamo, except that current is applied (fig. 162) to the rotating loop of wire, not drawn from it, creating a magnetic field which reacts against the magnetic field of the permanent magnet or field coil. The commutator cyclically changes the direction of the current flow in the loop or armature windings, maintaining undirectional rotational motion.

Electric motors in which the field coils are connected in series with the armature windings have the useful characteristic of being able to develop full torque when completely stalled and so are the type used for starters, the maximum torque developed varying from around 7.5 lb ft (1 kg m) for small engines up to about 22 lb ft (3 kg m) for the biggest

European V-8s, while the corresponding maximum currents are about 380 A and 500 A (for 12 V systems).

Public awareness of these high current values has given rise to some misconceptions about how much charge is taken out of a battery in good condition by a cold start operation and how long it takes to replace it. In fact with a quick-starting engine in good condition the high currents involved pass for such a short time that the charge taken from the battery is quickly replaced. With a hot engine and an underbonnet temperature of 120°F (49°C), for example, the average current is typically 100 A for 0.5 seconds making 50 amp-sec, so a 22-amp dynamo could theoretically replace this in 5 seconds assuming a pessimistic overall 50 per cent efficiency in the system, although in practice it would recharge in a tapering manner taking 10–15 seconds to do so. For a cold start at 10°F (−12°C) the average current would be 150 A and the average time 1.5 sec requiring 40–60 seconds for a recharge.

Lights

Almost all headlamp reflectors are wholly or partially paraboloid in shape – even when the lens is rectangular – because light striking

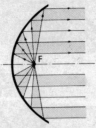

fig. 163. Light from a paraboloid's focal point is reflected parallel to its axis.

fig. 165. The Continental dip system uses an axial filament ahead of the focal point and shielded by a reflector beneath it.

the surface of a paraboloid from a point source at a focal point on its axis of symmetry (fig. 163) is reflected outwards parallel to that axis. A real lamp filament, of course, does not constitute an ideal point source of light and will allow some spreading of the beam if given, say, an axial orientation (fig. 164)

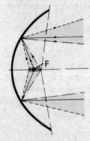

fig. 164. With real filaments, which are not point sources, there is some spreading of the beam.

when centred on the focal point. Such a beam, though weakened, will be composed of a bright central circular patch from the parts of the filament on or very near to the focal point, and an outer ring of lower intensity from more distant parts of the filament: not a bad pattern for a main beam with plenty of light shining down the centre of the road yet sufficient spread to illuminate its sides.

All light shining upwards from points in front of the focus is reflected downwards. This phenomenon is used to create the sharply cut-off asymmetrical Continental

dipped beam from an axial filament ahead of the focal point (fig. 165) with a metal shield mounted in the bulb beneath it to prevent light from getting to the lower half of the reflector. Usually the corresponding main beam filament of such a standard Continental bulb is the shape of a horizontally aligned V with its tip at the focal point. The transverse rather than axial dispersion of the filament from the focal point gives the required spread of light in a horizontal plane to illuminate each side of the road.

British and American headlamps use the same idea for main beam, generally having transverse horizontal filaments. They also take advantage of the effect of lateral rather than axial deviation from the focal point for the dipped beam, which is produced by a filament mounted above the focal point so that most of the light from it is reflected downwards. Although a small auxiliary reflector is incorporated in the bulb to catch stray light shining straight outwards without reflection, there is no shield under the dipped beam filament as there is in the Continental type of headlamp. The effectiveness of the system therefore depends considerably on the design of the glass lens at the front of the unit. For Continental lamps, however, the function of the lens is more to clean up the beam pattern, and a good dipped beam depends largely on the accurate juxtaposition of reflector, filament and shield.

It was to achieve the required precision for the British/American optical arrangement –

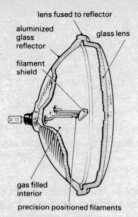

lens fused to reflector
aluminized glass reflector
glass lens
filament shield
gas filled interior
precision positioned filaments

fig. 166. The sealed beam unit, now obsolete in Britain, effectively consists of a large light bulb with a built-in reflector.

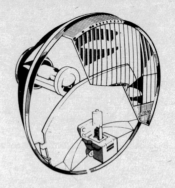

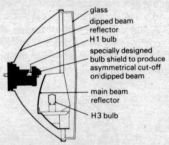

glass
dipped beam reflector
H1 bulb
specially designed bulb shield to produce asymmetrical cut-off on dipped beam
main beam reflector
H3 bulb

fig. 167. Prefocus metal/glass headlamp units use a small replaceable bulb inserted from the rear. The illustration shows a more advanced form of headlamp with separate halogen H3 and H1 bulb for the main and dipped beams.

and to avoid dulling of the reflector by corrosion – that the **sealed beam** type of headlamp unit was evolved. Effectively (fig. 166) this is one large light bulb which encloses the filaments, is filled with an inert gas and has a built-in reflector. With circular lenses, such lamps generally have a diameter of 7 in – or 5¾ in for a four-headlamp system. In such a system one pair of lamps has 50 W single main filaments for long range illumination and the other has twin filaments of 50 W each for the dipped beam and of 37½ W each to augment the main beam with a spread of light.

Any breakage or failure, though, entails a relatively high replacement cost, and in practice the illumination provided by sealed beam lamps – even four of them together – has proved rather disappointing. Thus, although they remain the standard type in the USA, they have been largely superseded in Britain by the alternative **prefocus** or **metal/glass** headlamps (fig. 167) using a small detachable bulb inserted from the rear. Continental headlamps have always been of this kind, and have been developed to a very high level

of efficiency, in France particularly. For this reason the sharply cut-off Continental dipped beam is gaining favour in Britain.

This efficiency has been partly achieved through the use of very large reflectors, often with rectangular or trapezoidal lenses – which effectively make the filament smaller and more concentrated at the focal point. An alternative approach is to worry less about reflector size and to concentrate on designing a smaller and more intense source of light. Such a source is the **halogen bulb**, the filament of which runs at a higher temperature than in a conventional bulb, greatly increasing the light output – by at least 50 per cent for a given wattage. The associated increase in the tendency of the bulb to become blackened is curbed by a cycle of chemical composition and decomposition involving a halogen gas such as chlorine, bromine or iodine. High performance bulbs of this kind are available in both single and twin filament forms.

Sundries

Apart from the side, tail and numberplate lamps, a modern car carries many more electrical components, but there is not space to mention more than a few, such as the windscreen wipers, the flasher unit (fig. 168) and the rear window demister – the fuel pump is sometimes electrically operated, too. The elaborate nature of the electrical system makes a typical wiring diagram a complex affair.

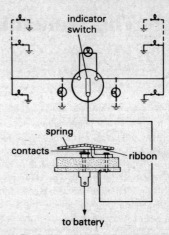

fig. 168. The flasher unit. When the indicator switch is turned to the left or right, current at first flows to the indicator lights through the contacts, a metal ribbon and a bow-shaped spring, which are normally closed. But the current flowing through the ribbon causes it to expand, allowing the bow-shaped spring to relax and open the contacts. The ribbon then cools, contact is made again, and so on.

eight **The Transmission System**

The internal combustion engine has two important deficiencies as far as the motorcar is concerned: it will not run at all below about 500 rpm and the power it develops is not well matched to the power required for propulsion. The first deficiency calls for an isolating or decoupling device, the second for a set of gears or some other means of both multiplying and varying the torque developed. The part of the car which meets these two requirements is called the transmission system and it also includes the differential and drive shafts through which the engine's power is conveyed to the wheels.

The clutch

In a manual-transmission car the decoupling device is the clutch which nowadays is generally of the **diaphragm spring** type (fig. 169). Its pressure plate is forced against

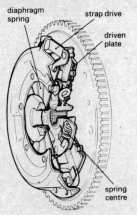

diaphragm spring · strap drive · driven plate · spring centre

its driven plate by a single, slotted and conical diaphragm spring rather than by a set of small springs as in the simple clutch described in Chapter 1 (p. 9). In its relaxed state this spring assumes a conical shape, but is forced flat against the pressure plate during assembly. When the clutch pedal is depressed, the thrust bearing forces the spring to form an oppositely orientated cone, relieving the pressure plate of axial force. A set of pins fixed to the clutch housing act as reaction points.

In a coil-sprung clutch the pressure plate is generally coupled, rotationally speaking, to the housing by pins or lugs which slide to give it the axial freedom it needs. In a diaphragm spring clutch, however, this function is usually performed by a **strap drive** of strips which flex to give axial freedom but are arranged tangentially to transmit the engine's torque in tension or compression. In addition, modern clutches are often additionally provided with a **spring centre** incorporating several coil springs arranged tangentially to absorb torsional or twisting shocks.

Rolling resistance and drag

To understand the need for a gearing system between the engine and the driven wheels, we must first consider the various resistances to the motion of a car at steady speeds

fig. 169. In modern clutches the force on the pressure plate is generally exerted by a diaphragm spring – a single, very large, conical slotted spring washer, sometimes called a Belleville washer.

on a level road when there is no wind. The friction in the wheelbearings, drive-shaft universal joints, etc., creates the smallest of these resistances – as is to a large extent apparent from the relative ease with which a car may be pushed along a level, surfaced road, once its inertia has been overcome. A much more important resistance to motion (at higher speeds) is that due to the tyres. Since the bottom of the tyre flattens where it meets the road, rotation constantly distorts it, and this distortion absorbs energy – significantly more for the obsolescent type of cross-ply tyre than for the modern radial-ply tyre. The power absorbed by the tyres is proportional to the load they carry, and increases with speed, though very slowly below about 100 mph. The sum of the frictional resistance and the tyre's resistance is known as the **rolling resistance**.

But at speeds above 30–40 mph the largest resistance to motion is wind resistance or aerodynamic drag. As explained in Chapter 11 this is proportional to a car's **frontal area** and to its **drag coefficient** and the power required to overcome it increases with the *cube* of the speed. As the speed rises, therefore, the power required increases with a rapidity which is not always appreciated (fig. 170). Suppose, for example, it is required to increase the maximum speed of a car from 90 mph to 120 mph, and that 60 bhp is absorbed by aerodynamic drag at the lower speed. The power required to overcome wind resistance at 120 mph will then be:

$$60 \times (120/90)^3 = 60 \times 1.33^3 = 142 \text{ bhp}$$

– or more than twice as much power as before. This factor alone often makes nonsense of the improved performance claimed by engine tuners.

Transmission losses

All this assumes that the power reaching the driven wheels is essentially the same as that available at the flywheel of the engine. In practice, though, around 10 per cent of the engine's power may be absorbed by friction and oil-churning losses in the transmission system, about 5 per cent being dissipated by the final drive gears alone. If an automatic gearbox is fitted, the transmission losses will be greater still.

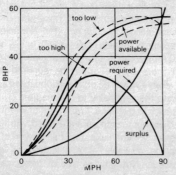

fig. 170. The power required to propel a car, mostly due to aerodynamic drag, rises very steeply with speed. The graph also shows the effect of different final drive ratios. Ideal gearing allows the car to achieve the highest top speed possible with the engine fitted; lower gearing improves acceleration at low speeds but reduces the maximum speed and makes high-speed cruising noisy and fussy; high gearing gives relaxed high-speed cruising but reduces both the maximum speed and acceleration at low speeds. The surplus power curve reaches its peak around 45 mph which is when top gear acceleration is at its best.

Gearing in top

Now let us see how the power available at high speeds (taking these transmission losses into account) can be related to the power required for propulsion on the flat. This relationship is basically defined by the final drive ratio – which is the same as the overall gearing ratio in top when this is direct and has a 1:1 ratio. When top is not direct, its ratio multiplied by the final drive ratio gives the overall gearing ratio. (The road-speed equivalent to 1000 rpm is influenced by the size of the driven wheels as well as the final drive and gearbox ratios, being given by the formula:

$$\text{mph}/1000 \text{ rpm} = \frac{60{,}000}{\text{tyre revs/mile} \times \text{gearbox ratio} \times \text{final drive ratio}}$$

The gearbox and final drive ratios are usually quoted in road tests or brochures, but tyre revs/mile values are only available from the tyre manufacturers.)

One possibility is to fix the final drive by trial and error so that the engine reaches its maximum power exactly at the maximum speed of the car (fig. 170). This is sometimes described as perfect or ideal gearing, for the maximum speed achieved is then the highest possible with the engine fitted. Many cars are geared in exactly this way.

Some designers feel, however, that such gearing leaves insufficient surplus power in top for acceleration or climbing gradients. Accordingly, they choose a final drive which is described as 'lower', giving rise to lower gearing – because lower road speeds are associated with a given engine speed – though the actual ratio is numerically higher (e.g. 3.9:1, say, instead of 3.7:1). Such a lower final drive shifts the power available curve to the left with respect to the power required curve, increasing the gap between them at low and medium speeds for which more surplus power is thus made available. But high-speed cruising becomes more noisy and fussy, and the maximum speed achieved is lower because the engine 'runs out of revs' before the car can go any faster.

In these days of motorways and high fuel costs, therefore, it is more usual for the gearing to be a little higher than the ideal (e.g. for the final drive ratio to be numerically lower: 3.5:1, say, instead of 3.7:1). Again the car doesn't achieve the highest possible top speed, because the power available curve is below its maximum where it intersects the power required curve – or in other words because the engine 'won't pull maximum

revs in top'. The engine runs more economically since a larger throttle opening is required at any given speed (p. 94) and less fussily also, but at the expense of top-gear acceleration.

These two conflicting requirements – for low engine rpm yet good acceleration at high speeds – can to a considerable extent be reconciled for a manual-transmission car by fitting a five-speed gearbox in place of a four-speed unit, or by retaining a four-speed gearbox and adding an overdrive unit which provides the additional ratio required in a different way. Fourth gear can then be chosen to give good acceleration for overtaking at high speed, and fifth or overdrive for relaxed and economical cruising.

Gearing – the lower ratios

A car provided merely with a clutch and a pair of final drive gears would not perform satisfactorily, no matter how well-chosen their ratio. It would not, for example, be capable of running at all at much below about 20 mph without stalling the engine. And even at more than 20 mph the surplus power available would be quite inadequate to accelerate the car briskly to the required cruising speed, to overtake, or to climb gradients.

For this reason cars are fitted with gearboxes which make the full power of the engine available at a selection of lower speeds. Note that a set of gears cannot multiply the power developed by an engine running at a given speed, only its torque. Suppose, for example, an engine developing 50 lb ft at 4000 rpm drives an input pinion meshing with an output gear three times larger as in fig. 2. The power being applied to the input shaft is (p. 28) $2\pi \times 50 \times 4000/33{,}000 = 38$ bhp.

The torque acting on the output shaft, on the other hand, is three times greater. But its rotational speed is also three times lower, giving the same power output as before.

Now imagine the engine to be directly connected to this output shaft which is turning at only 4000/3 = 1330 rpm. The torque developed would be very much lower than before – say 12 lb ft – giving a power output of $2\pi \times 12 \times 1330/33,000 = 3$ bhp. Hence by gearing the engine in the sense described its speed is raised for a given output shaft speed, making more power *available* than before.

Thus in a typical modern car maximum engine power is developed at around 30 mph in bottom gear (fig. 171) giving ample avail-

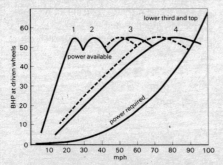

fig. 171. The vertical distance between the curve giving the power available at the driven wheels in the gears and the 'power required' curve at any point gives the surplus power available for acceleration. The dotted curves show the effect of lower third and top gears – which improve acceleration in some conditions but reduce maximum speed.

able power for brisk acceleration away from rest. In fact the ratio of bottom is usually determined by the need to be able to move away from a standstill up a steep slope. Each motor manufacturer lays down slightly different requirements, but a modern car should be able to restart up a one-in-three gradient – rare though this is – the severity of the requirement ensuring an ample margin for ordinary motoring and for other conditions such as the towing of a caravan. In sports and high-performance cars, however, bottom is generally higher (numerically lower) because the ability to attain a highish speed in this gear when starting off is held to be more important. The gap between bottom

and top is then smaller, so the intermediate ratios can be nearer to each other, forming a **close-ratio gearbox**. This in turn means that the engine speed drops relatively little at each upward change and the available power is maintained at a maximum.

The most logical way to choose the intermediate ratios, of which there are usually two – second and third – is to make the steps between them equal so the drop in engine revs is the same at each upward change. This occurs when there is a constant **difference ratio** or constant ratio between the ratios, or when:

$$\frac{\text{second gear ratio}}{\text{first gear ratio}} = \frac{\text{third gear ratio}}{\text{second gear ratio}} =$$

$$\frac{\text{top gear ratio}}{\text{third gear ratio}} = \text{constant}$$

This arrangement, incidentally, puts the ratios in a geometrical progression.

Practical problems often prevent this scheme from being adhered to. And in any case most designers prefer a system in which the upper ratios are closer together. This can be arranged so as to give constant differences between the maximum speeds in each gear (e.g. 30, 50, 70, 90 mph).

The constant-mesh gearbox

General layout

In early gearboxes the ratio-changing process involved sliding a gearwheel along a splined shaft into or out of engagement with another gearwheel. But successful engagement called for considerable skill from the driver (and the practice of a technique known as double-declutching) while to allow sliding engagement the teeth had to be of the noisy **straight cut** type, that is, had to lie parallel to the axis of the shaft carrying them. The teeth were also particularly prone to damage. Modern gearboxes, therefore, are always of the **constant mesh** type in which all the gears remain constantly in mesh with one another and the sliding elements for the selection of a particular ratio are dog clutches. The gears used are of the **helical** kind, with angled teeth which run more quietly because more than one of them is in contact at any given time. To lubricate these teeth the gearbox is generally partly filled with oil, but some modern units have their own pump.

For a rear-wheel drive car a typical gearbox (fig. 172) has three main shafts, though one of them is very short. This is the input shaft driven via the clutch by the engine, and it is known as the **primary** or **first-motion shaft**. On its end is a pinion meshing with a gearwheel driving the offset **layshaft** or **second-motion shaft** to which (in a typical four-speed unit) four further gears are permanently fixed. Three of these gears mesh with associated output gears which are mounted on an **output shaft** but spin freely on it. The output shaft in turn drives the smaller of the two final drive gears. The fourth gear on the layshaft forms part of the train which provides reverse. The output shaft usually carries a bearing which supports the free end of the stubby input shaft, making the two shafts look as if they were one at a casual glance, when in fact they are completely independent.

From one side of each output gear pro-

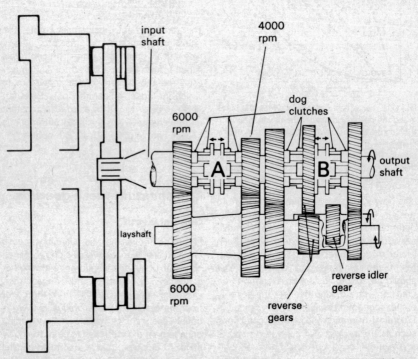

input shaft

4000 rpm

dog clutches

6000 rpm

[A]   [B]

output shaft

layshaft

6000 rpm

reverse gears

reverse idler gear

fig. 172. A typical constant-mesh gearbox for a rear-wheel drive car has a short input shaft, an offset layshaft and an output shaft carrying two sliding dog-clutch units, A and B. The drawing also illus-trates the need for synchronization: during an upward change the clutch driven plate, input shaft and layshaft will need to be slowed down (from 6000 rpm to 4000 rpm in the example shown).

trude the coarse square teeth, or dogs, which form one half of a dog-clutch. The other halves are formed in two sliding units splined to the output shaft, the left-hand unit (A) for third and top, the right-hand unit (B) for first and second. Fixed to this second dog-clutch unit, and moving with it, is the second gear of the reverse gear train.

By sliding one of these units into position, a particular output gear can be coupled to the output shaft and the desired ratio selected.

By moving unit B to the right, for example, first gear is selected, and second gear is selected by sliding it to the left. Third gear is obtained when unit A is displaced to the right, and by moving it to the left the output shaft is coupled directly to the input shaft to give top, leaving all the other gears to idle without transmitting power.

Reverse is provided in a variety of ways. For the gearbox illustrated, an additional reverse idler gear is moved into mesh with the reverse gear carried on dog-clutch unit B, which is left in its central, neutral, position. Thus the reverse gears on the layshaft and output shaft are linked by an additional gear which gives the required reversal of direction.

In five-speed gearboxes, one or more of the pairs of gears often lie at one end of the layshaft and output shaft, on the far side of a supporting partition.

Synchromesh

Unfortunately, before any forward gear can be selected by the engagement of a dog-clutch, the speed of one half of it must be made the same, or nearly the same, as the other half – otherwise they cannot be made to lock together. By its very nature, though, a gearchange means that these speeds will not be the same.

Consider, for example, an upward change from third to top at maximum revs – say 6000 rpm – with a gearbox in which the layshaft runs at the same speed as the input shaft and the ratio of third is 1.5:1. (In fact

the layshaft usually turns more slowly than the input shaft, but this does not affect the reasoning.) Both input shaft and layshaft (fig. 172) will then be revolving at 6000 rpm, but the output shaft at only $6000/1.5 = 4000$ rpm. Since this is determined by the road speed, which changes little during a gearchange, the engine, the input shaft and the layshaft must all be slowed to this speed.

As it is established practice to release the accelerator briefly during an upward gearchange, the engine should slow down without further intervention. And because the clutch is released at the same time, the input shaft, freed of any drive torque, should also slow down. But any reduction in speed is opposed by the rotational inertia not just of the input shaft alone, but also of the layshaft and clutch driven plate. The combined rotational inertia of all these parts generally prevents the gearbox input shaft from decelerating sufficiently for its speed to become synchronized with that of the output shaft in the fraction of a second available. During a downward change the input shaft, clutch driven plate and layshaft must be speeded rather than slowed, but again this is resisted by their rotational inertia.

These problems are largely resolved by incorporating a synchromesh device in each dog-clutch unit. This requires the provision (fig. 173) of cone friction surfaces on the faces of the two gears to be engaged, A and B (in constant mesh with layshaft gears C

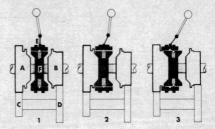

fig. 173. A simple synchromesh device involves a cone friction clutch which helps to synchronize the speeds.

and D). The synchromesh unit has a central hub, F, incorporating two mating friction surfaces to create a cone clutch when pressed against gears A or B, synchronizing the two moving parts before the dogs are brought into engagement.

Usually these dogs form part of a separate piece: a sleeve, E, splined to the inner hub, F, and therefore able to slide over it – but linked to it by a set of tiny balls spring-loaded into **detents** or depressions. Initial movement of the gearlever forces the two halves of the cone clutch together, synchronizing

their speeds, and with further movement the spring-loaded balls are over-ridden, bringing the sleeve dogs into engagement with the gearwheel dogs. Slightly curved or **chamfered** ends to the dogs guide them into their mating spaces when there is tooth-to-tooth abutment.

The weakness of this device is that during a fast change, or when excessive force is used, the two sets of dogs can be pushed together before their speeds have become synchronized, subjecting them to unnecessary wear and creating an unpleasant grating

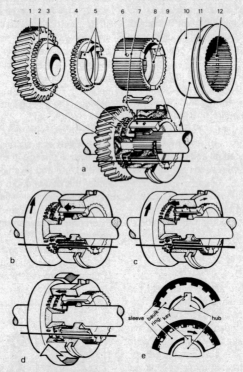

fig. 174. Baulk ring synchromesh devices incorporate an auxiliary ring carrying dog-teeth, which must be correctly aligned before engagement becomes possible: 1, gear; 2, gearwheel dog-teeth; 3, gearwheel cone surface; 4, baulk ring dog-teeth; 5, baulk ring slots; 6, spring-loaded detents; 7, keys which locate in baulk ring slots; 8, central hub carrying female half of cone clutch; 9, spring ring retaining keys; 10, outer sleeve carrying dog-teeth; 11, selector fork groove; 12, splines. Drawings b, c and d show the sequence of engagement, while drawing e shows how synchronization is blocked until the synchronizing torque disappears.

noise. For this reason nearly all modern synchromesh units are of the **baulk ring** type originally invented by the famous Dr Ferdinand Porsche, founder of the company making sports cars of the same name. In a system of this kind (fig. 174) the outer face of the cone clutch forms part of an additional and separate baulk ring carrying auxiliary dogs on its outer circumference which during engagement lie just in front of the gearwheel dogs. Thus the selector sleeve dogs must first be passed over the baulk ring dogs before engagement with the gearwheel dogs becomes possible. But the synchronizing torque is used to move the baulk ring dogs slightly out of alignment with the sleeve dogs, blocking engagement until proper synchronization has been achieved. The synchronizing torque then disappears, the baulk dogs move into alignment with the gearwheel dogs and full engagement follows. If the system is well designed, all this takes place within a fraction of a second and little obstruction is felt by the driver.

The details of such systems vary considerably, but as fig. 174 shows, one way of constraining the baulk ring yet giving it freedom to twist slightly, is by providing it with slots which mate with narrower keys protruding from the inner hub – which also carries the spring-loaded balls. The synchro-

nizing torque holds one side of each slot against its corresponding key, holding the baulk ring dogs out of alignment with the sleeve dogs until the speeds have been equalized.

The selector mechanism

Each synchromesh unit is moved into position by a **selector fork** operated by the gearlever and mounted on a **selector rail**. These days the gearlever is nearly always floor mounted, the complexity and doubtful virtues of steering-column gearchanges having made them unfashionable. The number of selector rails used varies, but the simplest arrangement – pioneered by Ford – involves only one.

The two main selector forks are supported by this single selector rail (fig. 175) yet are free to slide along it. A pin or lever protruding from the rail engages with a slot in a tongue forming part of the first–second selector fork, when the gearlever is tilted to the left of its central neutral position. Similarly, the selector lever engages the third–fourth fork when the gearlever is tilted to the right, a separate fork being used for reverse.

Since the selection of two gears at once

fig. 175. A single-rail selector system. A pawl on the selector rail engages one of the forks while an interlock plate keeps the other out of engagement.

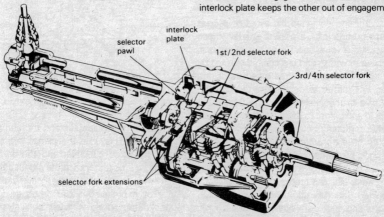

selector pawl

interlock plate

1st/2nd selector fork

3rd/4th selector fork

selector fork extensions

constitutes something of a mechanical disaster, it is prevented from happening by an **interlock mechanism**. For the Ford gearbox this is a plate pivoting on the gearbox casing which engages with the actuation slot of the selector fork not being used (or with both forks when neutral is selected).

Generally the gearlever has to be lifted or depressed against a spring before reverse can be obtained to prevent its accidental selection.

Epicyclic gears

Nowadays manual gearboxes always use simpler spur gears meshing together in different combinations, but a different and more complex type of gearing is used for overdrive units and automatic transmission systems. This is the **epicyclic** arrangement (fig. 176) in which there is a **sun gear** mesh-

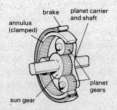

fig. 176. An epicyclic gear system with a clamped annulus.

ing with, and encircled by, a set of **planet gears** mounted on a **planet carrier** which may itself revolve bodily. The planet gears in turn mesh with – and are again encircled by – a large internally toothed **annulus** or ring gear. For torque to be transmitted through any two of these elements, the third must be held still to form a fixed reaction member.

The usefulness of an epicyclic gear train lies in the ease with which its ratio may be changed by clamping or releasing one of its elements with a brake or clutch – no synchromesh is required. The actual ratio obtained depends upon the particular conditions and is seldom obvious. Take a look,

for instance, at the epicyclic gear of fig. 176 in which the input turns the sun gear, the output is taken from the planet carrier and the annulus is clamped. As the planet gears are turned by the sun gear they are forced to roll round the fixed annulus, taking the planet carrier with them. Clearly the large-diameter planet carrier revolves more slowly than the small-diameter sun gear, but in what ratio? The calculation methods needed to answer such questions are not so much difficult as lengthy – too lengthy to quote here. In fact the sun gear speed/planet carrier speed ratio for such a configuration is given by $2(P+S)/S$ where S and P are the numbers of teeth on the sun and planet gears respectively. In a typical case S might be 19, P might be 20, giving a ratio of $2(19+20)/19 = 4.1:1$.

Used in this way such an epicyclic system acts – like all the gear systems so far discussed – as a **reduction** or **step-down** gear in which the output shaft turns more slowly than the input shaft but develops more torque. But an epicyclic system can also act as a **step-up** gear in which the output shaft torque is lower, but its speed is higher than that of the input shaft.

Suppose, for example, that the input (fig. 177) turns the planet carrier, the output

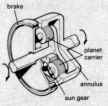

fig. 177. An epicyclic gear train with the sun gear clamped.

is taken from the annulus and the sun gear is clamped. This time the planet gears roll round the fixed sun gear and the annulus revolves a little faster than the planet carrier. Keeping to the convention we have used so far – of expressing a gear ratio as input speed/output speed – this particular arrange-

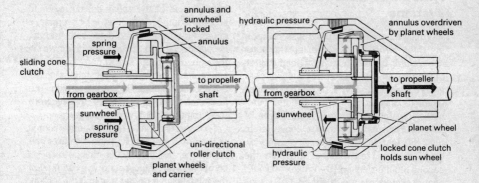

fig. 178. The Laycock overdrive unit: (a) in the disengaged mode, the clutch clamps the sun to the annulus, making the complete gear train rotate bodily; (b) the overdrive is brought into engagement by a cone clutch which locks the sun gear to the fixed casing of the unit.

ment has a ratio of $S+2P/2(S+P)$ or 0.756 using the same values as before.

Overdrive units

An epicyclic gear train of this sort forms the basis of most overdrive systems such as the Laycock unit (fig. 178). It is brought into operation by sliding the central member of a cone clutch so as to clamp the sun gear to the casing of the unit. It is disengaged by sliding this member in the opposite direction: the clutch then couples the sun gear to the annulus, making the complete epicyclic unit rotate bodily and giving the normal direct top 1:1 gearing. A refinement is a one-way clutch, linking input and output shafts, the two halves of which are jammed together when rollers ride up ramps. It transmits torque when the output shaft turns at the same speed as the input shaft but releases when the output shaft turns faster than the input (and also in reverse when the drive is maintained by the cone clutch). It maintains the drive during the initial stages of engage-

ment and allows the engine to speed up during a disengagement (which is equivalent to a downward gear change).

The cone clutch is actuated by hydraulic pressure from a small pump which forms an integral part of the unit. This pressure is controlled by a solenoid, so that overdrive can be selected merely by flicking a switch. Interlock switches usually prevent overdrive from being obtained in first or second gears – the torque transmitted is too high – but it can generally be engaged in third. Often there is little point in doing so, however, as frequently the ratio of overdrive third is virtually identical to that of direct top.

Overdrive units allow motor manufacturers to add an extra ratio to luxury or high-performance cars sharing a four-speed gearbox with cheaper models while avoiding the heavy investment associated with the introduction of a proper five-speed gearbox. They often fit very conveniently into the space otherwise occupied by the gearbox **tailshaft housing**, an assembly found on some cars which accommodates the front splines of the propeller shaft and reduces its tendency to vibrate by keeping down its length. But they add cost, complexity and weight (about 50 lb) to a car, and must introduce small additional transmission losses. A well-designed five-speed gearbox is therefore a better way of providing an additional ratio if one is required.

Automatic transmission systems

Any fully automatic gearbox must incorporate three basic parts: some form of automatic clutch or fluid coupling; a gearbox with ratios that are easy to select mechanically and a control system which correctly decides when to change gear. Conventional automatic transmission systems use a type of fluid coupling called a torque converter to fulfil the first function, a train of epicyclic gears compounded together to satisfy the second requirement and a complex hydraulic control system to meet the third. Let us look at the first of these basic components, the torque converter.

The torque converter

The torque converter has its origins in the simple fluid coupling or fluid flywheel mentioned in Chapter 1 which was made famous by Daimler. A fluid coupling (fig. 179) incor-

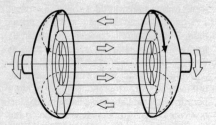

fig. 179. Hydraulic fluid thrown by centrifugal force from one half of a fluid coupling to the other is a very effective way of transmitting torque.

porates a bowl of hydraulic fluid attached to the engine output shaft and rotated by it. Dividers or vanes in the bowl or impeller impose the circular motion on the fluid which is therefore flung outwards to the rim by centrifugal force and across a small gap into a turbine upon which it thus exerts a torque. The turbine, identical in construction to the impeller, is attached to the gearbox input shaft to which the drive is therefore imparted. In side view the impeller and

turbine are not simple bowls, since the central parts of the vanes are cut away to accommodate guide rings which create a doughnut-shaped or toroidal path for the circulation of the fluid. This is drawn in through the impeller's inner ring of apertures and ejected from its outer ring into the corresponding outer ring of the turbine. The fluid then passes back to the impeller from the turbine's inner ring of passages.

Thus the fluid has a high tangential speed at the rim of the coupling and a smaller one near its centre, and it is this change in speed combined with the circulatory, mass flow of the fluid which together transmit the torque. When starting off, the turbine is held at a standstill while the impeller can rotate at up to several hundred rpm, generating a large centrifugal 'head' which creates a substantial mass flow into the turbine. As the car moves off and the turbine begins to rotate, it generates an opposing centrifugal head which gradually cuts down the flow. But the impeller always wins, and eventually the turbine speed stabilizes at 95–98 per cent of the impeller speed, the slip between them being enough to create a mass flow of fluid large enough to support the full torque of the engine.

The basic limitation of the fluid coupling, however, is that it transmits the engine's torque but does not multiply it. This deficiency is overcome in the torque converter by introducing a fixed reaction member called a stator between the impeller and the turbine. Its presence allows the turbine blades to be so shaped as to create a far larger change in the tangential speed of the fluid and hence in its angular momentum, and in this way to transmit a far larger torque to the output shaft. Under stall conditions, in fact, when the turbine is held at a standstill, this change in angular momentum is so large as to involve a reversal of fluid velocity, though the flow is difficult both to visualize and to illustrate because it involves axial as well as tangential changes in direction. The fluid (fig. 180) enters the turbine with a tangential velocity A, in the direction of impeller

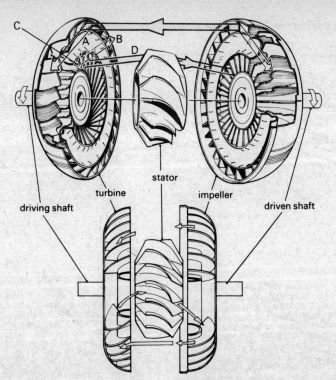

fig. 180. In a torque converter the heavy curvature of the turbine blades actually reverses the direction of the fluid flow and the fixed stator or reactor turns it back into the direction of rotation again.

rotation, but the heavy curvature of the blades reverses it, so that the fluid emerges with a tangential velocity, B, in the opposite direction, creating a change in momentum which multiplies the torque transmitted; the arrow C shows the tangential velocity which would exist if the turbine blades were not curved. The stator receives fluid at D and reverses its tangential velocity, turning it back into the rotational direction of the impeller at F. In this way the torque transmitted can be multiplied several times, though only when the impeller is turning significantly faster than the turbine.

To reduce frictional losses in the hydraulic fluid, the stator is mounted on a freewheel or one-way clutch. As the turbine speeds up when the car moves off, the movement of

its blades alters the direction of flow which gradually moves round until eventually the fluid strikes the vanes of the stator from behind, making it freewheel with the impeller and turbine and letting the converter operate as a straightforward and much more efficient fluid coupling. But the free-wheeling stator does introduce some fluid friction losses, while the maximum efficiency both falls and occurs at a lower design speed the higher is the **stall torque ratio**. For this reason, although stall torque ratios of 4:1 can be achieved, few modern torque converters develop more than 2.5:1. But this is enough to increase greatly an automatic transmission's overall gearing during the critical period when the car moves away from rest, corresponding to the clutch-slip phase of a manual system. The churning losses involved, however, contribute to the fuel consumption penalty of around 10 per cent associated with all but the latest and most advanced automatic transmission systems by comparison with a manual gearbox.

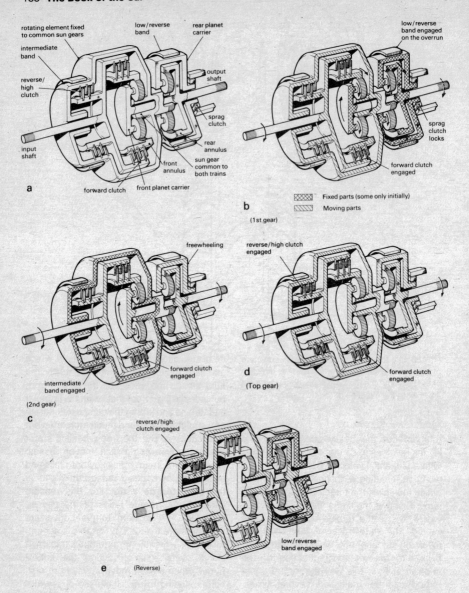

rotating element fixed to common sun gears

intermediate band

reverse/ high clutch

input shaft

forward clutch   front planet carrier

front annulus

a

low/reverse band

forward clutch

rear planet carrier

output shaft

sprag clutch

rear annulus

sun gear common to both trains

low/reverse band engaged on the overrun

sprag clutch locks

forward clutch engaged

b

(1st gear)

⬚ Fixed parts (some only initially)
⬚ Moving parts

freewheeling

forward clutch engaged

intermediate band engaged

(2nd gear)

c

reverse/high clutch engaged

forward clutch engaged

d

(Top gear)

reverse/high clutch engaged

low/reverse band engaged

e   (Reverse)

fig. 181. The Simpson gearset consists of two epicyclic trains coupled together with a common sun gear and gives three forward ratios and reverse: (a) bottom gear is selected simply by engaging the forward clutch; (b) the selection of second gear requires the engagement of both the forward clutch and the intermediate brake band; (c) to select top gear, the forward and reverse-high clutches are engaged; (d) reverse is obtained by releasing the forward clutch, engaging the reverse-high clutch and applying the low-reverse band brake.

The epicyclic gearbox

In a conventional automatic gearbox the torque converter drives a train of two or more epicyclic gears (p. 184) which can be coupled together in various ways to produce the ratios required. One arrangement known as the Simpson gearset gives three forward ratios and reverse and is composed (fig. 181a) of two epicyclic gears having a common sun wheel with planet and ring gears of a common size. Some of the elements are carried on drums and can be braked to a standstill by externally contracting **band brakes**. Others can be coupled together with **multiplate** clutches. In place of a single friction plate these incorporate several such plates which increase the torque capacity for a given overall diameter – a dimension important to an automatic transmission, which must be kept as small as possible. The greater thickness of a multiplate clutch is less significant.

Bottom gear is selected merely by engaging the forward clutch (fig. 181b) allowing the input shaft to drive the annulus of the front epicyclic gear and turn its planet gears clockwise. But the front planet carrier is fixed to the output shaft and hence is constrained by the driven wheels, at first to stand still and then to turn only at low speed. Thus the common sun gear rotates anticlockwise, making the rear planet gears rotate clockwise and exert an anticlockwise torque on the carrier which is held still by a one-way **sprag clutch**. The rear planet gears in turn drive the rear annulus and hence the output shaft in the forward direction, giving a compound reduction. When slowing down in this gear, the reversed sense of the torque transmitted frees the one-way clutch, so to give engine braking the low-reverse brake is applied.

To obtain the intermediate or second gear, the forward clutch is again engaged (fig. 181c) and also the intermediate brake band which clamps the common sun gear to the casing of the unit. The input shaft again drives the front annulus which drives the front planet gears and thus the front planet carrier to which the output shaft is attached, giving a smaller gearing reduction. The rear annulus, planet gears and planet carrier merely freewheel round the fixed sun gear, taking no part in the transmission of torque.

Top gear (fig. 183d) is selected by again engaging the forward clutch, but also the reverse-high clutch which couples the sun gear to the front annulus, making the complete gear train revolve as one unit at the same speed as the input shaft. Reverse is obtained (fig. 181e) by releasing the forward clutch, engaging the reverse-high clutch and applying the low-reverse band brake. The input shaft then drives the sun gear which drives the rear planet gears. Since their carrier is fixed by the low-reverse band brake, the rear annulus rotates in the opposite direction to the sun gear, giving the required reversal of direction to the output shaft.

Most conventional automatic transmission units use epicyclic systems of a similar kind, though the details may vary and more gears will be required if there are four forward ratios. But the same basic principle is common to them all: changes in ratio are effected either by coupling elements together or by holding them at a standstill.

One system which does differ in some respects, however, is made by the British Automotive Products company for transverse-engined front-wheel drive cars such as the Mini and is designed to share the engine's lubricating oil. Its basic feature is the use of bevel gears in place of straightforward epicyclic gears, to reduce the size of the unit. But similar principles again apply, for a bevel gearset is like an epicyclic system in which (fig. 182) the planet gears run at right angles to the main axis of the system and the sun gear has been moved to one side. The 'sun gear' and the 'annulus' are of the same size, but by using two bevel gear clusters – one inside the other – four forward ratios and reverse can be obtained from a very compact arrangement.

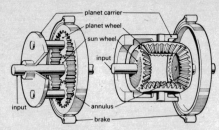

fig. 182. A bevel system is simply an epicyclic train folded into a ring.

Control and hydraulic system

An automatic gearbox is completed by a control system that decides which ratio is needed under any given set of conditions and selects it. Generally this decision is determined by two control signals, one representing road speed and the other the load on the engine. Often the road-speed signal is generated by a centrifugal governor driven by the gearbox output shaft and hence at a speed proportional to road speed. The centrifugal governor has bob-weights (fig. 183)

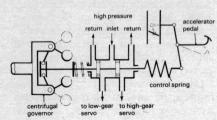

fig. 183. The principle of automatic gearbox control: a centrifugal governor running at road speed acts on one end of a control spring and the accelerator pedal on the other.

restrained by springs which move outwards as the road speed rises, displacing a control lever or plunger. Inlet manifold depression may be used to represent load, though it is more usually represented by throttle opening which can be communicated to the control unit by a simple mechanical linkage.

Selection of the correct gear depends upon balancing the road speed demands against the engine load demands, and this

can be done by interposing a spring between the governor plunger and the throttle position linkage. As the road speed rises, the governor plunger is forced to the right tending to cause a high gear to be selected, but this movement is opposed by the throttle linkage spring, so the more power the driver needs for acceleration or the climbing of a gradient the longer a low gear is held. This principle is extended by the kickdown mechanism by which second gear (or third for a four-speed unit) is selected when the throttle is floored, so long as the road speed allows it.

All conventional automatic transmission systems rely on hydraulic pressure to actuate the clutches and brake bands which make the gearchanges (though Renault make a unit in which the control signals are generated electrically and processed electronically). This pressure is usually generated by an engine-driven pump, sometimes augmented by a second pump driven by the gearbox output shaft which takes over when the road speed is high enough. Since lubrication of the gears is also a function of these pumps, the presence of one driven by the gearbox makes it possible to tow the car involved without causing damage. Because churning losses would be very high if the automatic gearbox were filled to the brim with fluid, a further function of the pump or pumps is to keep the torque converter filled. Apart from the Automotive Products unit, most automatic gearboxes use a special hydraulic fluid which lubricates the various moving parts while being compatible with the friction material of the clutches and brakes. A very complex system of passages and valves is needed to translate the signal from the control unit into demand for a particular gear.

A good modern epicyclic-plus-torque-converter automatic transmission can undeniably provide an impressive combination of almost imperceptible gearchanges combined with the ability to cope with virtually every traffic condition. But in return for the convenience of two-pedal control, it exacts a fuel consumption penalty, especially in town, of around 10 per cent by comparison with a manual gearbox. This is partly due to the power consumed by the small hydraulic pump which actuates the band brakes and clutches, but mostly to losses in the torque converter. When the car has reached its cruising speed and the torque converter is acting merely as a fluid coupling, these are small – a few per cent only – but during the torque multiplication mode they are generally very much greater.

Under the pressure of rising fuel costs, designers have in recent years begun to take steps to combat these losses and bring the efficiency of the automatic transmission closer to that of its manual counterpart. One common fuel-saving measure has been to add an overdrive fourth gear to a typical three-speed unit, just as overdrive fifth gears are being added to four-speed manual gearboxes (or even overdrive fourth gears to four-speed gearboxes). The addition of a lockup clutch, used to clamp the two halves of the torque converter together except when torque multiplication is essential, is another popular modification – and reduces the hydraulic churning losses significantly.

Slightly different is the torque-split system adopted for certain automatic gearboxes, notably the Ford ATX unit fitted to the US Escort range. In this arrangement the transmission's torque converter drives the annulus of an additional epicyclic train, while the turbine is coupled to its sun gear, the planet carrier being coupled to an auxiliary output shaft.

In bottom gear the torque converter is allowed to work in the normal way, the drive to the main epicyclic trains being taken from its turbine. But in second gear, when considerable torque multiplication is needed, it is the planet carrier shaft that drives the gearbox. This is pushed round mainly by the directly driven annulus, but partly by the more slowly rotating sun gear, coupled to the turbine. The net result is that the converter retains its ability to multiply the torque but transmits some 60 per cent of it only, the remainder being transmitted mechanically,

so that the churning losses are proportionately reduced. In top gear, when impeller and turbine revolve at virtually the same speed, the additional epicyclic gear is effectively locked up, making the driver over 90 per cent mechanical and again reducing the frictional losses.

Semi-automatic gearboxes

Since the last war a number of motor manufacturers sought to provide for their cars some of the conveniences of a fully automatic transmission system without using an expensive bought-out component or incurring the high cost of developing a unit of their own. These endeavours led to a breed of **semi-automatic** gearboxes, most of which have now gone out of production, two survivors until relatively recently being the Porsche Sportomatic and the Citroen Convetrisseur systems. They require the driver to change gear for himself – or herself – but eliminate the clutch pedal.

Such systems usually consist of a torque converter coupled to a conventional clutch and an ordinary synchromesh gearbox. Pressure on the gearlever knob closes a switch controlling a clutch release mechanism energized by a vacuum servo or any other convenient source of power. The absence of a clutch pedal makes driving in heavy traffic much more comfortable, and the presence of a torque converter means that the car will move away from rest in any gear – though rather sluggishly in top. But smooth downward changes require if anything rather more precise co-ordination than is needed for a manual gearbox, and there is a tendency for users to remain too long in a high gear to the detriment of the fuel consumption.

Daf/Volvo automatic transmission

One novel automatic transmission relies on a system of belts connecting pulleys which are made to expand and contract to alter the ratio between them. Designed and built for the Daf range of small cars, it was originally

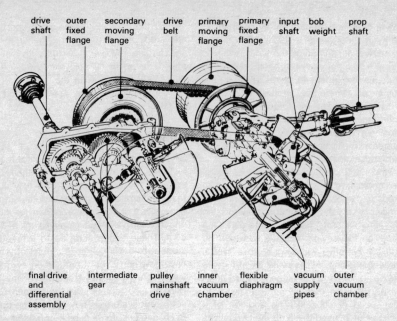

drive shaft | outer fixed flange | secondary moving flange | drive belt | primary moving flange | primary fixed flange | input shaft | bob weight | prop shaft

final drive and differential assembly | intermediate gear | pulley mainshaft drive | inner vacuum chamber | flexible diaphragm | vacuum supply pipes | outer vacuum chamber

fig. 184. The Daf transmission system involves an ingenious arrangement of expanding and contracting pulleys.

called the Variomatic system, but when Volvo took over Daf manufacturers it was rechristened the CVT (Continuously Variable Transmission) system (fig. 184).

It uses a **centrifugal clutch** in which pivoted bob-weights, gradually pulled outwards by centrifugal force, clamp the pressure plate against the driven plate as engine speed rises. The driven member of this clutch is connected to a short propeller shaft terminating in a small bevel gear meshing with two further bevel gears which have dogged faces. These are carried on a cross-shaft, but are free to rotate on it. The two bevel gears can be coupled singly to the cross-shaft by a dog clutch sliding on splines between them which gives forward, neutral or reverse.

At each end of this cross-shaft is a primary pulley the effective diameter of which can be varied. It has a V-shaped working groove defined by a fixed flange and by a sliding flange governed by a control system. When the sliding flange moves close to the fixed flange the drive belt encircling it – also V-shaped in cross-section – is forced outwards to run at a large diameter. The rearmost pair of secondary pulleys are similar in construction but controlled by powerful springs so that they automatically set themselves to a small diameter when the primary pulleys are large and vice versa, since the drive belts are fixed in length and do not stretch appreciably.

On the Daf 33, 44 and 55 models each secondary pulley forms part of a swing-axle assembly (p. 241) and drives a back wheel through a reduction gear so that there is no differential. On the Daf 66 model, however, with its de Dion rear suspension (p. 252), the two secondary pulleys drive a single central reduction gear connected to a conventional differential which is coupled to the drive shafts. The system is essentially the same for the Volvo 66 and 343 models except for a different selector lever arrangement.

As for other systems, the ratio selected depends upon engine speed and load: centrifugal bob-weights sensitive to engine speed force the primary pulley control flanges inwards to seek a high ratio, and they are forced outwards to seek a low ratio by inlet manifold depression in response to engine load. The centrifugal clutch often tends to be a little jerky in its action, but once away from rest the completely continuous nature of the ratio changes makes the system very smooth and rather pleasing in character. But its performance when moving away from rest up very steep slopes is rather poor, and in pre-Volvo versions the car can inadvertently jump forward when starting from cold if a set procedure is not carefully followed. So far as it is possible to tell (no exact comparisons can be made), it incurs about the same fuel consumption penalty as other automatic transmission systems: around 10 per cent.

Transmission layouts

Hotchkiss drive and live axle

In all cars having a front-mounted engine and rear-wheel drive the drive from the gearbox – or from the back of the engine for a car with a rear-mounted gearbox (p. 18) – to the back wheels is conveyed rearwards by a propeller shaft. The simplest layout, sometimes known as the **Hotchkiss drive**, involves an **open propeller shaft** driving a live rear axle mounted on leaf springs as shown in fig. 3.

In such an arrangement the front end of the propeller shaft is more or less fixed relative to the frame of the car – the engine/gearbox unit to which it is attached has little freedom to move – but its rear end must be free to move with the axle as it is deflected on its springs by bumps and dips in the road. To accommodate these movements, a universal joint is fitted to each end of the propeller shaft. Such joints are often of the simple Hooke type (fig. 185) in which two U-shaped yokes lying at right angles to

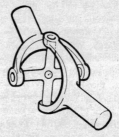

fig. 185. The simple Hooke universal joint allows the rotational drive to be turned through an angle.

one another pivot on the ends of a cross-shaped linking piece.

The leaf springs pivot directly on the chassis at their forward ends, but are attached to it through small swinging **shackles** at their rearward ends to accommodate their lengthening as they are flattened by upward movement of the axle. This same lengthening forces the axle to move backwards as well as upwards, so the propeller shaft also needs to be in two splined halves to allow it to shorten and lengthen by the required amount.

An open propeller shaft must additionally be carefully balanced; if it is not, it tends to execute a whirling motion at high speeds which creates an unpleasant and characteristic **prop-shaft rumble**, felt throughout the structure of the car. To attain the rigidity combined with lightness which helps to combat this condition, it is generally tubular in construction.

As described in Chapter 1 the propeller shaft is coupled to a pair of gears in the axle's central casing which turn the drive through 90° and provide the final speed reduction ranging from around 3:1 for a large, powerful car to just under 5:1 for a small, slow one. For a live axle these final drive gears (p. 13) consist of a large bevel crown wheel driven by a small bevel pinion. The crown wheel carries the differential (p. 201) which allows one driven wheel to rotate faster than the other when negotiating a corner.

The differential drives the two half-shafts

which are connected to the rear wheels and – when part of a live axle – encased in tubes. In early arrangements the wheels were supported in ways which placed various bending, compression and tension loads on the half-shafts, but for modern **fully floating** live axles the half-shafts transmit torque only. Vertical, bending and axial loads are all taken by a pair of taper roller bearings which support the wheel on the axle tube.

When a live axle is deflected upwards at one end only, it is pushed backwards by the flattening of the spring on that side, while the spring on the other side either remains unchanged in effective length or (as in a corner) becomes more bowed and hence shorter. The resultant misalignment of the axle when viewed in plan creates an unpleasant, even dangerous, deviation in the path of the car. But this is only one of several unwanted forms of movement to which a live axle mounted on leaf springs is prone. The leaf springs, for example, must also resist the tendency for the axle to be twisted about its own axis (p. 200) by drive torque, and in doing so are bent into an S-shape. Thus the basic defect of the Hotchkiss drive is that the leaf springs are not merely required to absorb road shocks, but must also locate the axle, permitting some forms of movement but preventing or limiting others.

Torque tube drive

More details of live rear axle location problems and an account of how they may be solved are given in Chapter 9. For modern cars a common solution is to mount the axle on coil springs and to locate it with a system of links. But some improvement in location can be obtained through the use of a tube (fig. 186) which is rigidly fixed to the rear axle casing and encloses the propeller shaft. The rear axle is thus prevented from twisting about its own axis under the influence of engine torque. In the original form of this arrangement, the forward end of the torque

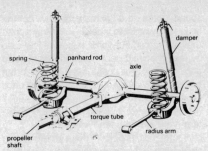

fig. 186. A torque tube prevents a live axle from being twisted about its own axis by engine torque. In this arrangement the torque tube does not extend all the way to the gearbox but only to a cross-member where it is connected to a short open propeller shaft. The torque tube and radius arms locate the axle.

tube was connected to the gearbox by a large ball joint, while the propeller shaft inside it had a universal joint at the same point. In such an arrangement no other universal joints are required for the prop-shaft, which is relatively small in diameter, often supported by one or more **steady bearings** and usually solid rather then tubular in construction. When leaf springs are fitted, they are shackled at both ends and pivoted at their points of attachment to the axle to eliminate the conflict of arcs that would otherwise exist, allowing the axle to swing in a large-radius arc about the torque-tube ball joint.

Front engine/ independent rear

When a front-mounted engine drives two independently-sprung rear wheels the arrangement is often similar in certain respects to the Hotchkiss drive, involving an open propeller shaft with a universal joint at each end linking the gearbox to the final drive unit, though this is fixed to the chassis of the car and is not subject to suspension movements. Generally the propeller shaft is enclosed by a rigid tube when the gearbox as well as the final drive unit is mounted at the rear of the car.

Swing-axle system

In the simplest and crudest form of independent rear suspension a pair of swinging drive shafts link the wheels to the final drive unit (the term is used to embrace the differential as well as the final drive gears). These drive shafts have universal joints at their inboard ends only, the plane of the wheel always remaining at right angles to the drive shaft at its outer end where there is no universal joint. Usually the drive shafts are protected by swinging axle tubes and the arrangement must be completed by an additional link or links which locate the wheel in the fore-and-aft direction. This **swing-axle** system gives such poor handling and roadholding that it has now been virtually abandoned.

De Dion and other systems

For de Dion systems, however, and all other forms of independent rear suspension (Chapter 9) the arc of movement of the (usually exposed) drive shaft does not correspond with the arc of movement of the suspension linkage. The drive shafts (fig. 187) therefore require universal joints at each end and must be made in two splined halves or incorporate some other means of

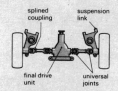

fig. 187. When driven rear wheels are located by a modern independent suspension system (this one is known as the semi-trailing type) each drive shaft generally requires two universal joints and some means of accommodating plunge such as a telescoping splined coupling.

accommodating **plunge**, the small in-and-out movement created by the conflict in geometry.

But conventional splines tend to lock up when transmitting torque, interfering with the free movement of the suspension linkage. Some expensive cars are therefore fitted with **roller splines** in which the axial friction is much reduced, but sophisticated universal joints designed to accept plunge without locking up are now readily available.

Combined engine/ transmission units

So far we have considered only the transmission systems of front-engined/rear-wheel drive cars in which the final drive unit, or a combined gearbox and final drive unit, is remote from the engine. But in a very high proportion of modern cars, engine, gearbox and final drive unit are grouped together to form a single integrated assembly. If the engine is mounted longitudinally, most arrangements of this sort – from a rear engine driving the rear wheels to a front

fig. 188. A typical longitudinally orientated combined engine/transmission unit. This arrangement can be used in four different ways: as part of a front-wheel drive system with the engine either ahead of the gearbox or behind it; as part of a rear-wheel drive system with the engine right at the rear of the car, or with the engine mounted towards the rear but ahead of the gearbox – the so-called mid-engine system.

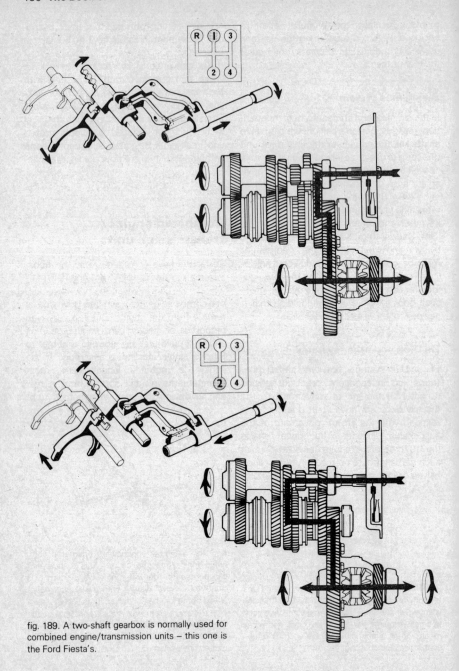

fig. 189. A two-shaft gearbox is normally used for combined engine/transmission units – this one is the Ford Fiesta's.

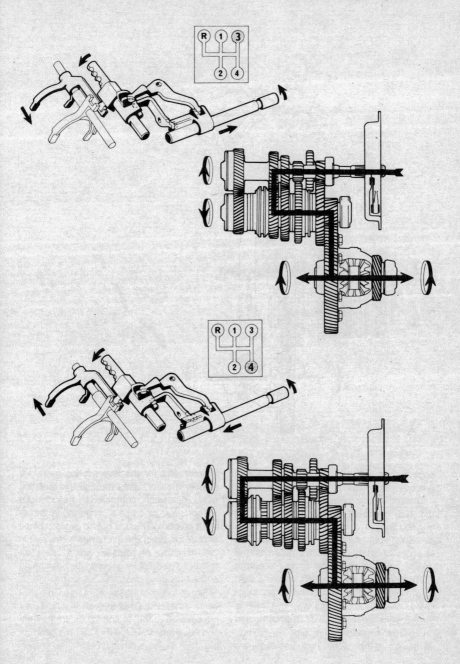

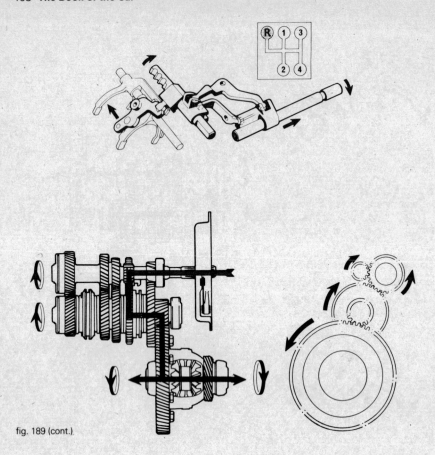

fig. 189 (cont.)

engine driving the front wheels – use a gearbox which is basically the same in layout.

This is of the two-shaft type in which (fig. 188) the drive is taken away from the engine along a combined input/layshaft, a separate input shaft being dispensed with. The power then flows back towards the engine and final drive unit along the output shaft. Sometimes each shaft carries a synchromesh unit, sometimes the output shaft carries them both. In this way the drive is turned back on itself to fit the combined engine/transmission unit type of layout. All the ratios (fig. 189) – including top – are

indirect. But for the lower ratios there are smaller friction losses through the meshing of two gears only, compared to the four used in the lower ratios of a conventional three-shaft gearbox. The use of two gears in place of four (or direct drive) creates a reversal in the direction of rotation which must be compensated for by appropriate positioning of the final drive gear.

Similar gearboxes are often used in transverse installations, but the way in which they are coupled to the engine varies. In the Mini and Peugeots 104, 204 and 304 the gearbox (fig. 190) lies beneath and behind the engine

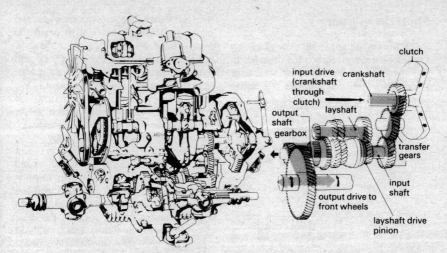

clutch

input drive
(crankshaft
through
clutch)

crankshaft

output
shaft
gearbox

layshaft

transfer
gears

input
shaft

output drive to
front wheels

layshaft drive
pinion

fig. 190. Transfer gears are needed to couple the engine to the gearbox when this lies behind the engine in a transverse installation as in several Peugeot and B-L models. The illustration shows a typical B-L arrangement involving a short input shaft separate from the output shaft. An indirect gear is shown engaged, but in top the input shaft is coupled directly to the output shaft by a sliding synchromesh unit.

(sharing the engine oil) and is driven from the clutch by two or three transfer gears. (The Mini, however, has a three-shaft gearbox.)

But such an arrangement is noisy and wasteful of power as well as excessively complex. A neater system, used for the Fiat 127, VW Polo and many other front-wheel drive cars, is simply to mount (fig. 191) the gearbox directly on the end of the engine as in a conventionally laid out car. By using a two-shaft type, the drive can be brought back to a final drive unit lying just behind the gearbox but integrated with it. As this is offset from the centreline of the car, one drive shaft may be longer than the other. Sometimes the longer drive shaft is tubular rather than solid to attain the same torsional stiffness as the shorter one and so equalize the initial tractive force applied by the front wheels. But the arrangement is thought to have adverse effects on handling, so in some installations the drive shaft lengths are equalized using a fixed **jackshaft** running from the final drive unit to a steady bearing on the far side of the engine.

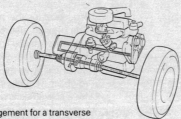

fig. 191. The simplest arrangement for a transverse installation is to mount the gearbox directly on the end of the engine.

Final drive gears

When the engine is mounted longitudinally rather than transversely and the drive has to be turned through 90°, the most basic form of crown wheel and pinion is the **spiral bevel** type (fig. 192) in which the pinion

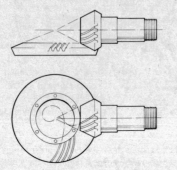

fig. 192. The pinion axis in a spiral bevel final drive intersects the crown wheel centre.

centreline intersects the crown wheel centre. The teeth have a spiral form as the name suggests and more than one of them are in mesh at any given time for smooth and quiet engagement.

Most cars with longitudinally aligned engines, however, have **hypoid** final drive gears (fig. 193) in which the pinion centreline

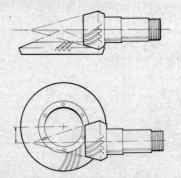

fig. 193. Most final drives are of the hypoid type which allows the pinion to be offset below the crown wheel centre.

is offset below the crown wheel centre, allowing a lower propeller shaft when the drive is from the front to the rear wheels. But the spiral is more acute and the teeth slide as well as roll, which is why a special lubricant is used. Hypoid gears are also employed in combined engine/transmission units, sometimes with the pinion offset above the centre of the crown wheel which then rotates in the opposite direction.

An alternative form of final drive, in recent years used only by Peugeot, is the worm and wheel system in which the crown wheel is not a bevel gear but a spur gear and the worm is a screw thread which engages with it. In transverse engine systems the drive does not need to be turned through 90° and a pair of ordinary spur gears can be used.

Torque reaction

When the final drive gears form part of a live rear axle, the torque applied to the pinion by the engine creates two reaction effects. The first **torque reaction** (fig. 194) is due to the

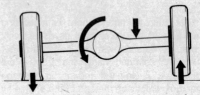

fig. 194. Torque reaction – lateral. The pinion tries to twist the axle casing round with it, lifting one wheel (usually the offside one) and pressing the other more firmly to the ground.

tendency for the pinion to turn the whole axle casing round with it, pressing the nearside wheel more firmly on to the ground and trying to lift the offside wheel away from it (for a car with the usual clockwise engine rotation). This effect can be quite significant for a powerful car accelerating hard in a low gear, relieving the offside of a considerable load and making it spin much more easily than would otherwise be the case, if the differential is not of the **limited slip** type (p. 202). The same effect can reduce cornering power in right-hand bends when it reinforces lateral weight transfer (p. 239). This torque reaction may be cancelled with a special linkage but it is rarely used.

The second torque reaction is much bigger, being equal to the first multiplied by the final drive ratio. It is the tendency of the axle to turn in the opposite sense to the wheels – which must have something to exert leverage against (fig. 195). It can be resisted by a torque tube or by upper and lower radius arms.

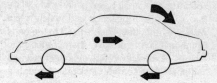

fig. 196. Under acceleration the front of the car tends to lift and the rear to sink, whichever wheels are driven.

of gravity. During acceleration, though, some of the torque reaction will be due to the torque absorbed in giving rotational acceleration to the transmission shafts and gears and to the driven wheels. This means that some lifting effect exists when the car spins its wheels, even if it stands still.

Differentials

When a car goes round a corner the outside wheels have to travel farther and faster than the inside ones. This is no problem when the wheels are not being driven, since they are free to find the correct speed, but if the driven wheels are directly connected by an axle they will skid every time a corner is traversed, leading to diminished roadholding and increased tyre wear.

This problem is resolved by a device called a differential which is nearly always of the type shown in fig. 197. The crown wheel

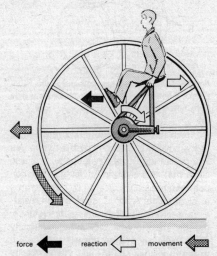

force ◀ reaction ⇦ movement ⬅

fig. 195. Torque reaction – axial. The axle tends to twist about its own axis in the opposition direction to the torque it exerts on the driving wheels.

In cars with combined engine/final drive units, this second reaction torque is resisted by the flexible mountings of the assembly and there are no residual reaction torques which affect the lateral weight distribution. There is, however, in all cars, whether rear-wheel, front-wheel or four-wheel drive, a tendency for the front to lift under acceleration. This is partly due to torque reaction, and partly to the backward reaction moment (fig. 196) due to inertia acting on the centre

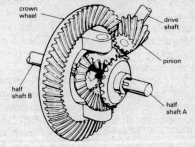

crown wheel — drive shaft — pinion — half shaft B — half shaft A

fig. 197. The bevel gear differential. It can be used to add or take the difference between the speeds of the shafts A and B.

supports two small bevel pinions which are free to rotate in bearings and which mesh with two other bevel gears fixed to the ends of the half-shafts or drive shafts turning the wheels. If the crown wheel is held still and half-shaft A is turned clockwise through a certain angle, the movement will be transmitted through the bevel pinion to half-shaft B which will turn anticlockwise by the same amount. Similarly, if half-shaft A revolves in one direction at a certain speed, half-shaft B will revolve at the same speed but in the opposite direction. Since these movements are relative to the differential cage, exactly the same thing will happen if, at the same time, the complete differential cage revolves bodily. Thus if the differential cage is revolving at 300 rpm and half-shaft A is turning 3 rpm faster, half-shaft B will be revolving 3 rpm backwards or slower, and the speeds of the two half-shafts will be 303 and 297 rpm. In this way a pair of wheels can be driven while retaining the freedom to rotate at the correct speed.

A differential will also work in the reverse way – hence the curious things which happen if you play with the driving wheels when they are jacked up. If the two half-shafts are driven in the same direction at 303 and 297 rpm, the gearbox output shaft will rotate at 300 rpm which is ½(303+297) rpm, while if they are driven at these speeds in opposite directions it will rotate at a speed given by ½(303−297) or 3 rpm. Thus the ability to find the sum or *difference* between two speeds gives the differential its name and makes it invaluable in a wide variety of machines. Differentials can also be constructed with spur gears, but nearly all are of the bevel type described.

But a differential also divides up the torque being transmitted. Since the small bevel pinions of a differential are forced round with the differential cage to which they are attached, it is helpful to think of them as pushing against the two bevel gears fixed to the half-shafts (fig. 198). It is then clear that a differential constitutes a system of levers

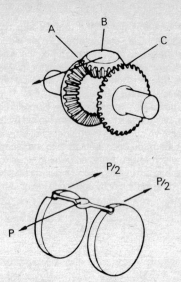

fig. 198. The differential also acts as a lever system so that if one wheel spins freely, no torque will be transmitted to the other.

in which the force P exerted by the engine at the point B is balanced by the two forces $P/2$ transmitted to the half-shafts. It is also clear that this system of levers depends upon the resistance offered by the fulcrums or pivot points A and C, so that if no resistance is offered by fulcrum A, for instance, the half-shaft to which it is attached simply spins uselessly and no drive is transmitted to the other half-shaft – and this is exactly what happens when one driving wheel loses adhesion on a slippery surface.

One defect of the conventional differential, therefore, is that it tends to do its job when it is least wanted. This defect is reduced in a **limited slip differential** (fig. 199) sometimes fitted to powerful cars. The tendency of the differential cage bevel gears to force the half-shaft bevel gears outwards is used to engage clutches locking them to the differential cage – the greater the applied torque the greater the locking tendency. Usually the clutches are lightly spring-loaded to ensure that some drive will be applied to

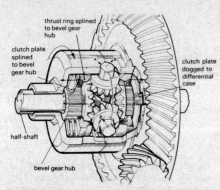

fig. 199. In the most common form of limited slip differential the differential cage bevel gears force the half-shaft bevel gears against friction clutches, locking them to the differential cage.

the wheel which is not spinning when adhesion is very low.

Another kind of limited slip differential working on another principle is made by the German ZF company. It involves a pair of fluted surfaces bridged by sliding plungers which lock up under the friction induced by torque.

Universal joints

There are several different kinds of universal joint in addition to the Hooke joint already described (p. 193). One of these is the **de Dion** or **pot** type of joint (fig. 200) designed

to accept plunge or axial movement as well as to allow angular deflection. When the angular misalignment to be accommodated is small, **flexible couplings** which incorporate a rubber bridge piece are also used to join two shafts.

Most simple types of universal joint suffer from an important fundamental drawback. When the two shafts they link are inclined to one another, the rotational speed or angular velocity of the driven shaft varies cyclically even when the driving shaft is turning at an absolutely steady angular velocity. The greater the angle between the two shafts the more pronounced are these cyclic variations which can set up damaging torsional vibrations and objectionable jerks if generated by the outer joints of front-wheel drive cars, especially when the steering is on full lock.

The cause of these velocity variations becomes clear if we examine a Hooke joint linking two shafts which are inclined to one another. When shaft A (fig. 201) is turned

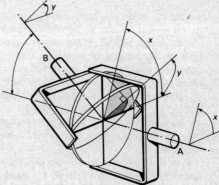

fig. 201. Because the angle *x* for shaft A is larger than the angle *y* for shaft B, ordinary universal joints transmit cyclic velocity variations.

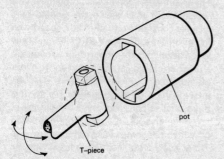

fig. 200. The de Dion or pot type of universal joint accepts plunge as well as allowing angular deflection.

through an angle x, for example, the ends of the yoke attached to it are turned through the same angle in a vertical plane, but when this angle is projected on to the plane perpendicular to the other shaft B, it becomes the smaller angle y. Thus if shaft A is turned through angle x in a given time, shaft B turns through the smaller angle y in the same time and so moves more slowly. Hence although both sides of the universal joint complete any given revolution in the same total time, the speed of one side varies cyclically with respect to the other.

The easiest way of creating a **constant velocity** joint which does not transmit these cyclic variations in rotational speed is to connect two Hooke joints together (fig. 202)

fig. 202. Two Hooke joints connected together constitute a constant velocity joint, but a clumsy and bulky one.

so that the oscillations generated by one are cancelled out by the equal and opposite oscillations generated by the other. A propeller shaft consists of two Hooke joints connected together in this way, which is one reason why it does not suffer much from velocity variations, another being the small deflections involved which are from 10° to 15° compared to the 40° to which the outer joint of a front-wheel drive car may be subjected.

But even when the two Hooke joints are connected together back to back, the resultant combination is bulky and clumsy, so more sophisticated constant velocity joints are used nowadays. One of the best-known is the Birfield-Rzeppa type (fig. 203) fitted to such cars as the Mini in which the drive is transmitted through a set of ball bearings rolling in grooves between the two halves of a ball and socket joint. The grooves are shaped to maintain the balls in the plane

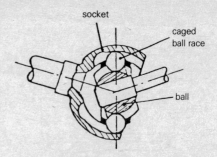

fig. 203. The Rzeppa-type constant velocity joint as used for the Mini and other cars transmits the drive through ball bearings in the grooved surfaces of a ball and socket joint.

bisecting the angle between the two shafts – this is the condition for constant velocity transmission. Special plunge-accepting versions of these joints are available. Another kind of plunge-accepting constant velocity joint, the tri-axe type, is a three-pronged form of pot joint and is widely used in French front-wheel drive cars.

The future

The transmission system has so far been treated as something of a necessary evil, needed mainly to match as far as possible the demands of the driver with the ability of the engine to meet them. In the future, however, it may well be required to perform an additional function – that of achieving the minimum fuel consumption compatible with any given set of conditions. In practice, this would mean maintaining the engine at a roughly constant and rather low speed with its throttle nearly open all the time. Only when accelerating – from rest or to overtake – or when cruising at any speed above about 50 mph, say, would high rpm ever be attained. The concept applies mainly to a petrol engine controlled by a throttle valve, for when this is only partly open, such a power unit becomes very inefficient (p. 94). There would be less advantage with an unthrottled diesel or stratified charge engine.

For a transmission system of the kind proposed – which would, of course, be automatic – the first requirement would be an electronic microprocessor to control it. It would need next a gearbox unit with a wide range of ratio variation and low frictional losses. This last condition rules out the conventional automatic transmission with the churning losses in its torque converter, and some other forms of continuously variable transmission.

One possible experimental alternative is the Perbury-Hayes toroidal roller transmission system fitted to cars in the thirties for a short time but improved fundamentally since then and now used in a constant-speed drive for aircraft alternators. It involves (fig. 204) two outer discs A, driven, say, by

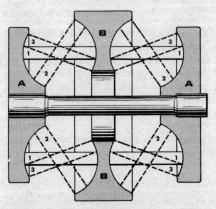

fig. 204. Tilting rollers between the driving outer discs A and the driven inner disc B allow the effective gearing ratio between them to be continuously varied: 1, ratio of 1:1; 2, low gear; 3, high gear.

the engine; inner disc B attached to the output shaft and a set of tilting rollers between them. When the rollers are in position 1 the ratio between the outer discs and the inner one is 1:1, but when tilted to position 2, the contact path diameter on discs A is much smaller than on disc B, so

that disc A will rotate faster than disc B. In position 3 the reverse state of affairs obtains and the inner disc rotates faster than the outer ones. Such a system is highly efficient and capable of a ratio range, from low to high, of nearly 4:1. By coupling it to an epicyclic gear train (fig. 205) it can be made

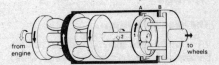

fig. 205. A Perbury gear combined with a single epicyclic train gives two forward speed ranges, a geared neutral and reverse. The two input discs are coupled to the sun wheel of an epicyclic gear, the central output disc is connected to the annulus and the output of the combined transmission (clutch A engaged and clutch B released) is taken from the planet carrier. If the epicyclic gear has a 2:1 reduction ratio from sun to annulus, and the disc and roller drive is set to a 2:1 ratio, the sun shaft will be completing two revolutions for every one of the annulus in the other direction, and the planet carrier will stand still, giving a geared neutral. Altering the engine speed will in fact have no effect on the planet carrier output because the proportions remain unchanged, but lowering the 2:1 ratio of the disc and roller drive, say to 3:1, will make the vehicle travel backwards, while raising it above 2:1 will make it go forwards, though the highest attainable gear in this regime will be rather low. But by releasing clutch A and engaging clutch B the output shaft can be coupled directly to the output of the drive in the normal way and higher ratios up to a considerable overdrive can then be obtained.

into a very wide ratio transmission, extending continuously from overdrive through 'geared neutral' to reverse.

This particular form of continuously variable transmission system is not likely to appear in production, but all the large motor manufacturers are experimenting with advanced forms of the belt and pulley type which will be introduced shortly by Fiat, Ford and others.

nine **Springs, Dampers and Steering**

Springs

The need for springs

Why do cars need springs? The question can be answered by considering what would happen to a car with no springs at all as it passed over a sharp vertical step in the road (fig. 206). Neglecting, for a moment, the elasticity of the tyres, it would be subjected to an almost infinite vertical acceleration, subjecting the occupants to very severe discomfort, if not injury.

It is the **springs** that absorb the shocks – not the so-called 'shock absorbers' – the tyres constituting auxiliary springs, much stiffer than the others above them. Vertical forces from the road can only be transmitted to the body of a sprung car through the compression of its springs. When a sprung car meets a vertical step in the road (fig. 207), therefore, its front springs compress by an amount equal to the depth of the step

fig. 206. A car with no springs and solid tyres would be subjected to an almost infinite vertical acceleration.

(perhaps a little more if it is traversed at high speed) transmitting a very moderate upward force to the body. The snag is that afterwards the body tends to wag up and down on the springs with which it forms an oscillatory system. It is to limit the duration of these oscillations – hopefully to one cycle at the most – that the dampers or incorrectly named 'shock absorbers' are needed.

fig. 207. When springs are fitted, the shocks due to road irregularities are absorbed in exchange for a tendency for the body to oscillate up and down.

Types of spring

Most springs are made of steel and the steel used is a special alloy which, after heat treatment, can withstand very high stresses without permanent deformation. The oldest form of steel spring is the leaf spring, already described in Chapter 1 (p. 14 and fig. 3) and further discussed in Chapter 8 (p. 193). Leaf springs tend to be large, expensive and heavy in relation to the load they support and are not very efficient locating elements. They are fitted mainly in conjunction with live axles, but not exclusively so. Transverse leaf springs, for example, form part of the swing-axle rear suspension of the Triumph Spitfire and of the MacPherson strut rear suspension of the Fiat 128.

By far the most widely used form of spring today is the coil spring (fig. 208). It consists of a rod of spring steel which is bent into a helix or coil and which acts wholly in torsion or twisting. In fact the steel rod need not be twisted into a coil: a straight and rather

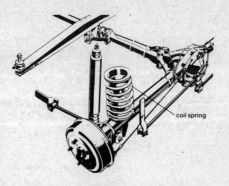

fig. 208. The most common form of spring is the coil type, seen here at the rear of the Rover 3500. Note the rubber bump stop within the spring at the top.

thicker rod forms another type of spring called a torsion bar (fig. 209). Torsion bars are also common, and as their inboard ends can readily be fixed to adjustable anchorages, they make it easy for the ride height of the car to be trimmed if necessary. Their disadvantage is their length which takes up space across or along the car.

But steel is not the only springing material employed, one well-known alternative being rubber. The springs of the Mini, for example, consist (fig. 210) of hollow cones of rubber working in compression and **shear** which is a parallel, tearing type of deflection.

fig. 209. Torsion bar springs, running longitudinally, are used for the wishbone front suspension of the Renault 5. A lever attached to the fixed end of each bar abuts against an adjustable cam plate allowing the ride height to be trimmed. Torsion bars are also used for the trailing arm rear suspension of the Renault 5, but they run transversely across the car.

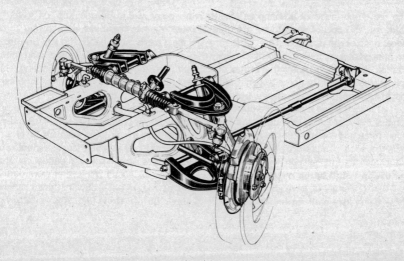

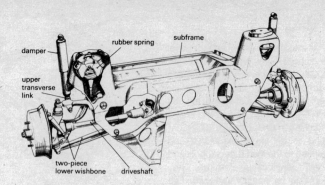

damper

upper
transverse
link

rubber spring

subframe

two-piece
lower wishbone

driveshaft

Another type of springing medium is a gas – and if you do not think a gas is springy, try depressing the plunger of a bicycle pump when your thumb is over the outlet. A **gas spring** usually consists of a small spherical steel container sealed by a flexible diaphragm (fig. 211) and containing nitrogen at 400–800 lb/sq in (28–56 kg/sq cm).

Both gas and rubber springs need to exert large forces through small displacements if they are to be efficient and compact, so they are usually deliberately made to act at a large mechanical disadvantage. The Mini's rubber springs, for example, work at a mechanical disadvantage of about 4:1.

Softness and travel

The real importance of a spring lies in its softness. You do not need to be a professional engineer to realize that the softer are the springs of a car the more comfortable its ride is likely to become: the softer the springs the smaller the force transmitted to the body by a given disturbance from the road. But by the same token, the softer the springs the more they are deflected by a given force and the greater the suspension travel needed. Thus for a softly sprung French car the total suspension travel, from **full droop** to **full bump** might be as much as 10 in (25 cm) but perhaps only 3–4 in (7.5–10 cm) for a stiffly sprung model.

fig. 210. The Mini's springs are hollow cones of rubber working in compression and shear. This is the 'dry' system, used for various versions of the Mini, with separate external dampers and no front/rear interconnection.

Coping with loads – variable rate springs

There is, however, a major limitation on the softness possible. Make the springs too soft and the car will scrape its underside along the ground when fully – or even partially – laden with passengers and luggage.

One way of coping with this problem is to fit **variable rate springs** which get progressively stiffer with each successive unit of displacement from the static position. If a coil spring is to be given this characteristic, the rod or wire from which the coil is wound must taper in thickness. The thinner turns deflect easily, soon becoming **coil bound** or pressed together, shortening and thus stiffening the remainder of the spring. Gas and rubber springs are generally of the variable rate sort.

Even when variable rate springs are not fitted, the geometry of many independent suspension systems is such as to give a spring stiffness at the wheel or **wheel rate** which rises somewhat with deflection. This is usually increased still further towards the end of the wheel's upward travel by the rubber **bump stops** (fig. 208) or auxiliary

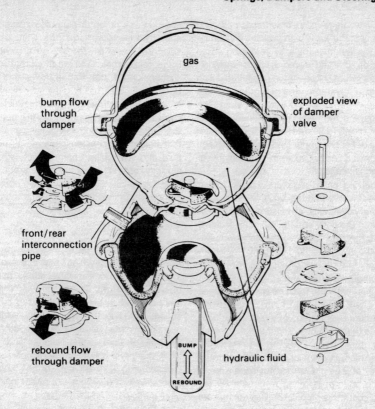

gas

bump flow
through
damper

exploded view
of damper
valve

front/rear
interconnection
pipe

rebound flow
through damper

BUMP

REBOUND

hydraulic fluid

fig. 211. A typical gas spring: a small hemispherical steel container sealed by a flexible diaphragm and containing nitrogen under pressure. In this case the spring forms part of the Austin-Morris Hydragas system (p. 212) and is actuated hydraulically.

springs fitted to nearly all cars to prevent violent contact between the suspension and the chassis. These bump stops are sometimes very large and come into play after no more than an inch or two of suspension movement when they begin to increase the overall spring rate considerably. To reduce road noise, suspension links these days nearly always pivot on rubber bushes which can also add significantly to the overall spring rate.

Self-levelling springing

But heavy loads will still use up all the suspension travel if the springs are given the exceptional softness needed for ultimate comfort. One solution is to adopt a self-levelling springing system of the sort pioneered by Citroën and used by Rolls-Royce, and by Mercedes for their most luxurious models. In such a system the springs are not directly connected to the suspension links, but instead are operated through tubes of hydraulic liquid. Liquids are to all intents and purposes incompressible, and so form admirable low-friction pushrods for tasks of this sort – hence their use in braking systems. But for this application the basic advantage of such hydraulic pushrods or rams is the ease with which they can be varied in length simply by removing some liquid or squirting in more under pressure. This is what happens in a self-levelling springing system: the lengths of the hydraulic rams interposed between the springs and the body are continuously and automatically adjusted to compensate for spring deflection under load (not bumps) and thus maintain a constant ride height or ground clearance.

Achieving all this generally calls for an engine-driven pump (fig. 212), some height-sensing valves which measure the distance between the body and the suspension links, and some fairly complex plumbing to distribute the hydraulic fluid. Usually, there are two separate circuits, one for the front of the car and another for the rear, but in all cases the adjustment rate must be slow, otherwise the system would fight normal suspension movement over bumps in the road surface; there is therefore no compensation for **dive** under braking (p. 269) or **squat** under acceleration. For similar reasons there must be only one height sensor for each axle so that no attempt is made to counteract roll (more about this on p. 213). Gas springs are generally but not invariably used for self-levelling purposes.

A springing system can be made to maintain a constant ride height without the complication of a pump or plumbing, using self-energized, self-levelling struts. Units of this sort are made by the German company Boge, for example, and are fitted to the rear suspension of the Range-Rover and the Rover 3500. Each has two telescoping parts, is partially filled with hydraulic fluid and contains an auxiliary gas spring. An ingenious system of pistons and valves is so arranged that normal suspension movements pump fluid into a working chamber beneath the auxiliary gas spring until the correct ride height is reached – the process is normally complete within 200 metres of starting from rest.

Unsprung weight

Another limitation which may threaten the attainment of a comfortable ride is that of **unsprung weight**. This is the weight of all the parts which are not supported by the spring, including the wheels, the axles or hub carriers, the brakes if mounted outboard, the bulk of any locating linkages and generally the lower halves of the dampers, plus perhaps also a small part of the springs themselves. The weight – or rather inertia – of all these parts limits the force available to keep the wheel on the road.

When, for example, the unsprung mass is accelerated violently upwards by a bump, it may acquire sufficient velocity for the wheel to leave the road altogether. Similarly, it may not be able to move downwards with sufficient rapidity to follow the contours of a pothole. In both cases this is because the spring force is not large enough to give the

fig. 212. A self-levelling suspension system: when the car is loaded more hydraulic fluid is pumped between the spring and the suspension link to restore the ride height to its former value.

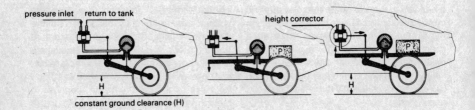

pressure inlet   return to tank   height corrector

H
constant ground clearance (H)

unsprung mass sufficient acceleration. In the static position the spring force is simply the sprung weight at that corner of the car, and it can easily be shown that the acceleration initially attainable by the sprung mass is given by the sprung/unsprung weight ratio.

Thus the unsprung weight must be kept as low as possible if good roadholding is to be combined with a comfortable ride. In addition, dampers which have been correctly set to control the sprung weight (the body) will be unable to control the much more violent movements of the unsprung weight if this is large. Stiffening the dampers may give some measure of control but the ride will suffer.

Bounce and pitch

The basic disadvantage of a car's springing system is its inherent tendency to make the body move rhythmically up and down, or to oscillate in response to disturbances from the road surface. In fact the frequency of these oscillations is often used as a measure of the springing system's excellence. It is usual – and useful – for this purpose to treat the front and rear of the car as being independent with separately calculable frequencies. Very soft, comfortable springing is equivalent to around 60 cycles per minute, while at the other end of the scale, 90 cycles per minute represents hard, stiff springing.

But the way these oscillations combine has an important influence on the ride comfort. If the front of the car on the front springs, for example, oscillates in phase with, and at the same frequency as, the rear of the car on the rear springs, the result is a vertical motion called **bounce** (fig. 213a). If the bounce frequency is low – around 60 cycles per minute or 1 cycle per second, say – the motion is sometimes described as **float**, and it can be very uncomfortable indeed, making many people feel car-sick.

Stiffer damping is generally the cure, but another kind of motion called **pitch** is not so easily dealt with. This occurs when the front

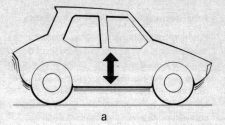

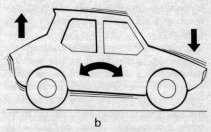

fig. 213. Bounce and pitch: a, bounce; b, pitch.

and rear oscillations are out of phase with one another, so that as the front of the car moves upwards the rear moves downwards – and as the rear moves upwards the front moves downwards. In fact the car rotates (fig. 213b) back and forth about a transverse pitch axis located somewhere within the wheelbase. Some designers regard this as the most uncomfortable ride movement of all, as it can impose quite large backward and forward movements on the car passengers' heads.

If the frequency at the front, however, is about 10 per cent lower than that at the rear, the phase relationship is altered and the tendency is reduced. Another possibility is to give the car large overhangs at front and rear like those typical of a full-sized American saloon. These increase the car's rotational inertia or 'flywheelness' about the pitch axis and hence its resistance to oscillation about that axis. Unhappily, though, a car which is ponderous and sluggish in pitch, tends to be equally ponderous and sluggish in **yaw** or in a steering and cornering sense.

Interconnected springing systems

Pitching oscillations develop because as soon as one end of the car is pushed down or pulled up the springs exert a restoring force to resist the movement. But this restoring force or pitch resistance can be eliminated by mechanically or hydraulically connecting the front springs on each side of the car to the rear springs on the same sides. The principle is used in the British Leyland **Hydrolastic** and **Hydragas** springing systems, and also in the suspension of the Citroën 2CV.

In all cases the basic idea is to arrange the suspension so that the front and rear suspension links on each side of the car effectively act at opposite ends of a single central spring (fig. 214). As the force at one end of the spring must be the same as that at the other, the reactions on the body at the two suspension mounting points to an upward force on *one* wheel are the same. And if – as in the simple case illustrated – these reactions are equidistant from a centrally located centre of gravity, their moments about it will be equal and opposite. (When the centre of gravity is not central the same condition can be attained by suitable adjustment of the wheel/spring leverages at front and rear.) Thus the deflection of a single wheel creates no tendency to pitch at all, and since no restoring force can exist to resist angular deflection about (in this case) the centre of gravity, the pitch frequency is zero. But an interconnected system's absence of response to pitch-inducing forces applied by the wheels, is matched by a complete lack

of any resistance at all to changes in pitch attitude produced by forces acting directly on the body, created either inertially – during acceleration and braking, for example – or by variations in load distribution. Hence the tendency for interconnected cars to stand on their noses under braking and to point themselves skywards when the boot is heavily loaded. All practical systems, therefore, are a compromise, in which the front/rear interconnection is partial rather than complete.

For the Hydrolastic and Hydragas systems (fig. 215) the technique is to provide full

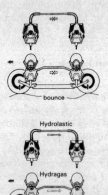
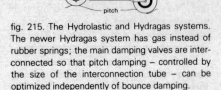

fig. 215. The Hydrolastic and Hydragas systems. The newer Hydragas system has gas instead of rubber springs; the main damping valves are interconnected so that pitch damping – controlled by the size of the interconnection tube – can be optimized independently of bounce damping.

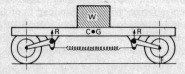

fig. 214. The front/rear interconnection principle: the two upward reactions due to a single-wheel disturbance can be equalized so as to eliminate any pitch oscillation tendency.

front/rear interconnection but then to add some independent auxiliary rear springs to increase the pitch resistance. The front and rear main springs are separate but are made to share fully any single-wheel input by a hydraulic connection between them – and this is the important effect, not the front/rear 'levelling' mechanism sometimes referred to. On their own such systems would provide a very low pitch resistance, but for the Hydrolastic arrangement this is augmented by special anti-pitch rear torsion bar springs. For the very similar Hydragas system, the pitch resistance is provided by the rubber torsion bushes of the rear trailing arms.

These systems have in any case a certain inherent pitch resistance due to the variable-rate nature of their springing: when the body is displaced in pitch, the compressed spring exerts a greater force than the relaxed spring, creating a restoring force. The Hydrolastic and Hydragas systems get their rising rate partly from the non-linear nature of their springs themselves, and partly because increasing volumes of hydraulic fluid are displaced at each successive increment of piston stroke.

Such interconnected systems have the additional advantage of providing softer springing for a single-wheel bump than in roll. None of the systems gives an exceptional ride, however, which suggests that the best compromise between all the variables has not yet been found.

Other effects – wheel hop and roll

Not only does the body tend to oscillate on its springs, but also the wheels on the much stiffer springs which the tyres constitute. The movements are much smaller and the frequencies higher – 10–15 cycles per second compared to 1–1½ cycles per second for the body. These **wheel hop** oscillations tend to be filtered out by the spring and they are also diminished by the dampers. They are seldom sensed by the occupants of the car except when caused or accentuated by out-of-balance in the wheels.

One further and major drawback of any springing system which has so far been ignored is the freedom it gives the body of a car to lean outwards in a corner, or to **roll**. For roll is not merely an uncomfortable form of motion in itself, it is also the enemy of good handling and roadholding in any car with independent suspension at one or both ends. With independent suspension linkages of every sort the wheels tend to lean out-

wards on corners to a greater or lesser extent, robbing the tyres of some of their cornering power (p. 235).

This is why many cars today are fitted with **anti-roll bars** at the front or rear – or both – which give increased **roll stiffness** and also affect handling profoundly (p. 239). An anti-roll bar (fig. 216) is a torsion spring which

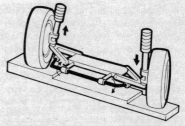

fig. 216. An anti-roll bar – it increases the roll stiffness more than it increases single-bump stiffness and does not increase the bounce or pitch stiffness.

couples the suspension on one side of the car to that on the other. It has cranked ends and passes through mountings fixed to the chassis. When both wheels are simultaneously deflected upwards as when the car bounces or pitches, it merely rotates bodily in its mountings, adding nothing to the spring rates. When one wheel alone is deflected upwards it is twisted a little, increasing the spring stiffness somewhat, but when one wheel is deflected upwards and the other downwards – effectively what happens in roll – it is twisted much more, thus giving a preferential increase to the overall spring stiffness in roll.

But there is a limit to the maximum acceptable stiffness which an anti-roll bar can be given. If very stiff it will increase the normal spring rates too much and perhaps lead to an unpleasant side-to-side swaying motion, particularly noticeable at low speeds on bad surfaces called 'roll-rock' or 'anti-roll-bar-waddle'.

Thus for the designer of high-performance luxury cars there is at present no easy way of reconciling the very soft springs needed for comfort with their accompanying very high roll angles which reduce cornering power. Complex linkages which permit suspension movement but prevent roll have been devised, but these are unlikely to be seen on road cars. A more interesting proposition for the future is a hydraulic no-roll suspension system of the sort developed experimentally by Automotive Products. It is essentially a self-levelling system of the Citroën sort, but one with a set of very ingenious pendulum valves which permit normal suspension movement but keep the car upright in corners. With the help of such a system the springs could be made extremely soft for great comfort at no sacrifice in handling qualities at all. Another possible approach, which has been tried experimentally by Lotus, is to devise an 'active' system of high-response servo mechanisms which force the wheels up and down to conform with the irregularities in the road surface.

Dampers

Mechanical systems liable to oscillation are damped most effectively if opposed by a resistance which is proportional to – or at least increases with – the relative velocity involved. This type of resistance is in turn most easily generated by forcing a liquid through an orifice – which is the principle of the automotive hydraulic damper. These days such dampers are nearly always telescopic in construction, though the lever type is still occasionally used.

In essence a telescopic damper is merely (fig. 217a) a piston pierced by small orifices and immersed in a cylinder of hydraulic fluid. As the piston is forced back and forth, oil flows through the orifices, generating a resistance which is roughly proportional to the square of the piston's velocity. The first problem arises when the piston is connected

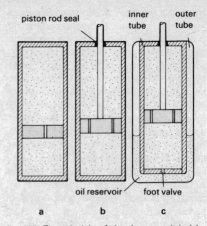

fig. 217. The principle of the damper – it is (a) a piston pierced with orifices forced back and forth in a cylinder of oil. When the piston is attached (b) to a piston rod, a reservoir must be provided (c) to accommodate the oil displaced.

to the rod necessary to drive it (fig. 217b). Compression of the damper introduces into it an increasing volume of rod which must somehow be accommodated. In the conventional **two-tube** type of damper, oil displaced by the piston rod is forced (fig. 217c) through a further orifice at the foot of the cylinder and into a reservoir formed by a concentric outer tube.

It would seem logical to use the flow through the piston orifices to provide damping during both the compression and the extension stroke. However, a sudden compression of the damper can increase the volume above the piston faster than it can be filled by the oil passing through the piston orifices. The resultant drop in the pressure of the oil above the piston is to be avoided. It can lead, for example, to **cavitation** – suddenly collapsing bubbles which can wear away metal parts in the course of time. By using the foot orifice to provide damping on the compression stroke, the space above the piston is maintained at a pressure higher than atmospheric, and this possibility is avoided. But both the piston orifices and the

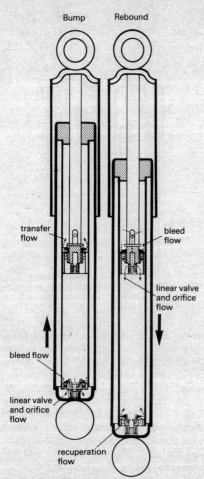

Bump   Rebound

transfer flow

bleed flow

linear valve and orifice flow

bleed flow

linear valve and orifice flow

recuperation flow

fig. 218. Both the piston and the foot of a practical damper are equipped with valves.

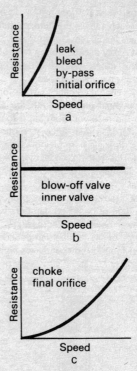

Resistance

leak
bleed
by-pass
initial orifice

Speed
a

Resistance

blow-off valve
inner valve

Speed
b

Resistance

choke
final orifice

Speed
c

fig. 219. The characteristics of the three basic orifices: (a) the bleed or leak orifice; (b) the blow-off or linear valve; (c) the larger final orifice.

foot orifice need valves to ensure that they offer little resistance on their inactive strokes.

In practice, both the piston and the foot of the damper are equipped with relative complex systems of valves and openings (fig. 218) so that the damping characteristics can be tailored to the needs of the suspension system. Generally (fig. 219a) there is a small **bleed** or **leak** orifice, open all the time, which provides the damping when the piston moves slowly, offering a resistance roughly proportional to speed. Next a **blow-off** or **linear** valve (fig. 219b) opens progressively to maintain a roughly constant resistance for a middle range of speeds. At higher speeds still, the blow-off valve opens fully a larger **final orifice** (fig. 219c) which then governs the damping, offering a resistance roughly proportional to the square of the piston speed. Typical damping curves do not conform exactly to these theoretical characteristics. And to minimize interference with the shock absorbing function of the spring, most of the damping is done on the rebound rather than the bump stroke.

The very considerable amounts of energy

absorbed by a damper are all dissipated as heat which raises the temperature of the hydraulic fluid used. Unfortunately, this heat cannot easily escape from a twin-tube damper, the outer tube of which effectively encloses an insulating space.

Under severe conditions, therefore, the oil may overheat and mix with the air or gas above the reservoir, forming a foam which offers far less resistance to motion than a liquid, drastically reducing damping efficiency. This frothing tendency increases with the inclination of the damper away from the vertical.

This disadvantage is less pronounced in single-tube or gas-filled dampers which are therefore becoming increasingly popular. One type of single-tube damper such as the Girling Monitube unit contains a tightly fitting

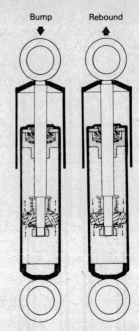

fig. 221. The gas required to accommodate piston rod displacement is dispersed in bubbles throughout the oil in the Woodhead Monotube damper.

additional free piston (fig. 220) separating the oil from an expansion space containing a gas under pressure which compresses to accommodate the piston rod. In another type, notably the Woodhead Monotube damper, the gas is interspersed – in bubbles – throughout the oil in a high-pressure emulsion (fig. 221). This is not unlike the foam which is to be avoided in conventional dampers, but it is carefully formulated for consistent behaviour with changes in temperature and the damper is especially designed to use it. In both types of single-tube damper the gas acts as an auxiliary spring, though generally one of relatively small stiffness.

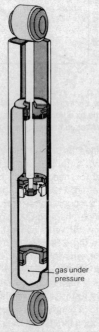

gas under pressure

fig. 220. In the Girling Monitube single-tube damper an additional free piston separates the oil from the gas in the expansion chamber.

Steering

The Ackermann system

The two front wheels of horse-drawn vehicles were often steered by a centre-pivoted axle (fig. 222) which seriously reduced lateral stability as it neared full lock – when it converted the dray or coach of which it formed a part into something approaching a three-wheeler. It was to eliminate this source of instability that the system of steering patented – but not invented – by Rudolph Ackermann in 1818 was developed.

In an Ackermann steering system (fig. 223) each wheel pivots separately and is connected by a **track rod arm** to a central **track rod**. The track rod arms are angled so that when the front wheels are in the straight-ahead position their axes intersect at the

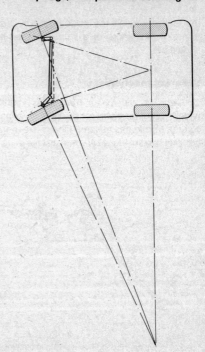

fig. 223. The Ackermann steering system – the two wheels roughly follow the correct geometrical paths if the track rod arm axes meet at the rear axle's centre when the wheels are in the straight-ahead position.

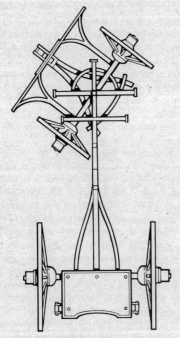

fig. 222. A centre-pivoted steering system – on full lock it supplies little support.

centre of the line passing through the centres of the rear wheels. Whatever the radius of the corner, the front wheels then remain roughly tangential to the circular paths they theoretically follow.

Though all modern cars use this basic form of linkage, in many of them the Ackermann geometry is not precisely obeyed, for its relevance is mainly confined to turns taken very slowly. At any speeds much above a walking pace, the slip angles in the tyres (p. 231) change the behaviour of the car completely. When cornering hard, moreover, the outside front wheel does most of the work and this will automatically be set by the driver at the angle required to follow a given path. Under such conditions it does not matter very much if the inside front wheel is turned a little more or a little less than it should be.

Steering mechanisms

On vehicles with beam front axles – still widely used for light vans – the steering column terminates in some kind of steering box mechanism (fig. 224). This can take many

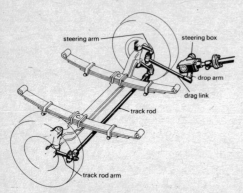

fig. 224. A typical steering box working in conjunction with a beam front axle.

forms but in principle always involves a worm attached to the steering column and meshing with a gear-wheel or some substitute for it such as a peg or nut. The gearing ratio is generally around 20:1, so the steering wheel has to be turned through 20° for every 1° of front-wheel movement. Such a mechanism is highly **irreversible**: there is more frictional resistance to movement of the steering wheel by the front wheels – quite apart from the mechanical disadvantage conferred by the gearing – than to movement of the front wheels by the steering wheel. This reduces **kickback**, or shock torques sometimes generated on a bumpy surface, but by the same token it also reduces feedback or feel – the transmission of forces to the driver's hands which help to warn him when the front wheels are beginning to lose adhesion.

The gearwheel, peg or nut of the steering

box turns a **drop arm** coupled, via a ball joint, to a **drag link** which is similarly linked to a **steering arm**. A track rod linking the two front wheels through track rod arms completes the system.

When a system of this sort is applied to a car with independent front suspension it becomes a good deal more complicated. A single track rod cannot be used, since it would conflict with the separate arcs of movement of the front wheels on their suspension linkages, so instead a **three-piece track rod** must be fitted. The steering box (fig. 225) actuates an operating lever which is directly connected to the wheel on the same side by a short track rod. It is also connected to a long track rod running across the car to an **idler** or **relay lever** on the far side of the car, linked to the other wheel by a second short track rod.

Compare this arrangement with the far simpler and more elegant rack-and-pinion system briefly described in Chapter 1 (fig. 3) and now fitted to most cars – it requires four ball joints instead of six, for example. A rack and pinion is generally highly reversible and thus is sometimes provided with a hydraulic **steering damper** which reduces kickback without affecting normal steering movements.

The rack can be made less reversible by skewing the pinion across it. To understand why, imagine the pinion to be so highly skewed that it becomes a worm wheel rotating about the longitudinal axis of the rack itself; if the thread of the worm wheel were given a fine pitch it would become almost impossible to turn the steering wheel by pushing on the rack – though still possible to steer the front wheels by turning the steering wheel. A modest skew angle is often used nowadays, partly because the resultant jointed steering column tends to fold during a collision and cannot easily be pushed back into the driver.

It is essential that the arcs of movement of a rack-and-pinion system's track rods, and of the two outer track rods of a steering box

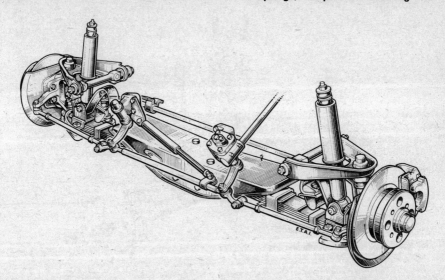

fig. 225. A three-piece track rod is required when a steering box is used with independent front suspension. In this particular system shock forces are controlled by a hydraulic steering damper, which is linked at one end to the centre track rod near the steering box, and is fixed to the chassis at the other via the relay lever casing.

linkage, correspond as exactly as possible to the arcs of movement of the front wheels on their suspension linkages. If they do not, the resultant conflict will create bump steer, making the car wander on a poor surface. This is why long track rods linked to the centre of a steering rack are sometimes necessary in place of short ones linked to its ends.

While one rack-and-pinion mechanism is much the same as the next, there are several variations in the mechanism of the steering

box, all directed towards reducing friction in the basic worm-and-wheel-system. In the **cam and roller** type, for example, the cam is in fact a worm (fig. 226) and it meshes with a roller which is free to rotate about its own axis but is mounted on the drop arm or operating lever shaft. But the most popular system today, fitted to many Japanese cars, is the **recirculating ball type**. In this the worm is enclosed by a nut (fig. 227) 'lubricated' by ball bearings which are rolled out of its threads by rotation of the worm, but are recirculated back again.

Another important characteristic of a

fig. 226. A cam and roller steering box: the cam or worm is fixed to the end of the steering column and the roller to the cross-shaft on which the operating lever is mounted.

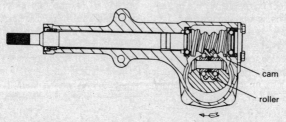

cam

roller

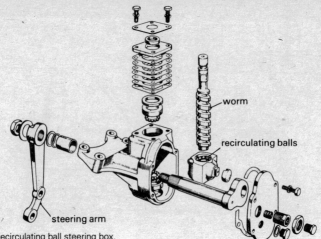

worm

recirculating balls

steering arm

fig. 227. A recirculating ball steering box.

steering system is its directness. Thus in some cars 2.5 turns only of the steering wheel suffice to displace the front wheels through their complete range of movement, whereas in others as many as six turns may be required. But since the range of movement or **steering lock** varies widely from one car to another, this is not a good indication of directness. A better measure, used by magazines such as *Motor*, is the number of steering wheel turns required to follow a circle of a certain size, say 50 ft (15 m). If 0.8–1.0 turns are required, the steering is pleasantly direct; for large saloons the range is generally 1.0–1.3 turns, though for a few cars the values are as large as 1.4–1.6 turns.

Large steering movements of this sort make a car very tedious to drive, especially in town, but they follow from the adoption of a low-geared steering mechanism to reduce effort when the car is heavy at the front. This effort, incidentally, is several times greater at parking speeds than when on the move. One way of reducing the exertion associated with parking without increasing too much the wheel movements required for ordinary driving, is to fit a steering system the gearing

ratio of which increases on either side of the straight-ahead position. Such a characteristic is not easily given to a rack and pinion system, but is readily built into a steering box mechanism by making the threads of its worm fine at each end and coarse in the middle. Its effect is to require a gradual increase in steering wheel rotation for each successive step in front wheel deflection from the straight-ahead position. This leads to a gradual reduction in the torque needed at the extremes of steering lock associated with parking manoeuvres.

But such a **variable ratio steering** system can give the car an inconsistent feel when cornering and in any case can only achieve a limited reduction in the effort required. Thus if the car is heavy at the front and has large tyres which are difficult to turn at low speeds it may be necessary to fit **power assisted steering**. Power assistance can be incorporated in any form of steering mechanism, the most critical component in all cases being the control valve.

In a typical rack-and-pinion application (fig. 228) this consists of three basic elements of which the first is a fixed external

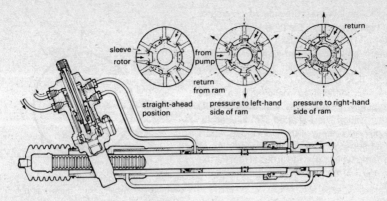

fig. 228. A power-assisted steering rack. The tor-sion-bar control rotor and its sleeve allow high-pressure hydraulic fluid to be directed to one side of the hydraulic ram or the other.

body. Inside this valve body turns a cylindrical sleeve attached to the steering pinion and incorporating longitudinal slots cut into its inner surface. One of these slots lies to the left, one to the right of each of two or three (depending upon the particular design) inlet ports through which hydraulic fluid is admitted from the engine-driven pump. Inside the sleeve in turn fits a rotor embodying similar slots. It is also attached to the steering pinion but via a torsion bar, and so can turn through a small angle within the sleeve. A small relative rotation to the left causes high-pressure fluid to be directed to one side of the hydraulic actuating ram so as to force the steering to the left; similarly, a small angular displacement of the rotor relative to the sleeve to the right causes the steering to be forced in the opposite direction.

For such a system the resistance at the steering wheel is determined only by the stiffness of the torsion bar. Unfortunately this is often far too light, robbing the driver of all feel, or sense of communication with the front wheels. The tell-tale lightening which warns of a greasy or icy patch on the road is either absent or too small to be detected. With a stiffer torsion bar the system becomes much more comfortable to use, but the provision of true feel involves careful attention to other factors.

An inherently superior system is one of the **reactive** type employed by Mercedes. A spring is still used, but it is very light and the feel is provided by feeding a small proportion of the high-pressure fluid force directly back to the steering wheel, either by giving the control valve a small-area reactive surface, or through some additional system of pistons with the same purpose. The result, exactly as in a brake servo (p. 265) is to make the force exerted by the driver some fixed proportion – a tenth, say – of the force exerted by the hydraulic system.

Virtually all power steering systems are **hydrokinetic** in action, using vane-type pumps displacing relatively large volumes of fluid at relatively high velocities and relatively low pressures up to a maximum of about 900 lb /sq in (90 bar). They are called **open-centre** systems since the valve never shuts completely and it is the restriction of the flow to the low-pressure side which creates the high pressure in the other side.

Citroën, however, use a high-pressure system requiring a closed-centre valve which does not act to restrict flow but simply admits fluid to one side of a ram or the other. It is very difficult to make such a valve acceptably progressive, which is why a spring-loaded heart-shaped cam is used for the power steering of the DS models, and a speed-sensitive hydraulically-loaded cam of the same type to provide artificial feel for the SM and CX models.

Steering geometry

There are several important details to be considered in the alignment of the front wheels and their steering axes. One of the simplest of these is **toe-in**, a small inward inclination of the wheels in plan (fig. 229)

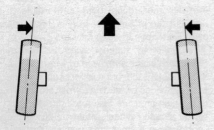

fig. 229. Toe-in – an inward inclination of the wheels in plan to compensate for play in the steering linkage.

when the car is at rest which ensures that they run parallel at speed, not splayed out. It compensates for the effect of the drag of the road on the wheels which tends to extend the steering linkage slightly by taking up play in its ball joints. Independently suspended rear wheels are often given some toe-in for the same reason. The forces on the front wheels of front-wheel drive cars are such that **toe-out** is generally specified.

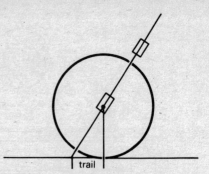

fig. 230. Castor gives the front wheels a self-centring action by making them trail behind the pivot axis.

To make the wheels inherently self-centring, the steering pivot axes are nearly always given a **castor angle** – a backward inclination when viewed from the side (fig. 230). Each steering axis then meets the ground ahead of the point at which the wheel contacts it, creating **castor trail**. This means that the front wheels trail behind their effective pivot axes like furniture castors, and so tend to return to the straight-ahead position when left to themselves – inherently safe and stable behaviour.

But castor angle has a side effect because it gives the wheel a component of rotation about a horizontal axis. This is easily perceived by imagining the steering axis to be laid completely flat (when it would no longer

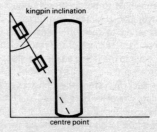

fig. 231. Kingpin inclination makes it easier to arrange the steering axis so that it meets the ground at the centre of the tyre.

allow the wheels to be steered, of course). This horizontal component of rotation raises the wheels – and hence lowers the car – as the steering is turned from the straight-ahead position.

The steering axes are in addition nearly always inclined outwards when viewed from the front (fig. 231). The purpose of this **king-pin inclination** is to make the steering axis meet the ground at or near the centre of the **contact patch** of the tyre which is thus made to turn about that centre rather than being dragged round in a small circle.

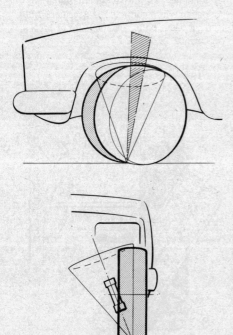

fig. 232. Kingpin inclination gives the wheel a camber angle when the steering is turned from the straight-ahead position. The movement can be visualized by imagining the wheel to be moved round the surface of a cone, centred on the kingpin axis.

This is not easily done by using a vertical steering axis, since there is seldom space within the wheel to fit two swivel pins or ball joints. When the steering axis meets the ground exactly at the centre of the contact patch, the car is said to have **centrepoint steering**.

Kingpin inclination also has a side effect: as the steering is turned from the straight-ahead position it gives the wheel itself an inclination with respect to the vertical called a **camber angle** (fig. 232). This is very notice-able when the kingpin inclination is large, as on dragsters or cars of old-fashioned design such as the Citroën 2CV: each wheel flops over to one side as the steering is turned from the straight-ahead. This is because of the conical motion involved, as you can verify for yourself with the help of a piece of paper twisted into a cone.

As the steering is turned from the straight-ahead position and the wheel acquires a camber angle, the inner part of the tyre tread is tilted away from the ground, but the outer part is tilted into it, raising the car. The effect is exaggerated when, as for most cars, the steering axis meets the ground inside the centre of the contact patch, creating a small amount of **positive offset**. Thus if the steer-ing were turned through 180° (not possible of course) then points A on the tyres (fig. 233) would be pushed down to points B.

Until fairly recently the majority of cars had varying degrees of positive offset. But the arrangement does have a disadvantage if diagonally divided brakes are fitted (p. 268) when a failure of one circuit will lead to unbalanced braking. With a large decelera-tive force on one wheel and a small force on the diagonally opposite rear wheel, the car is liable to slew sideways or even to spin round.

Now consider a front wheel (fig. 234) with positive offset when it is transmitting a large unbalanced braking force to the car, the other front brake exerting no force at all. The rearward braking force creates a moment or turning effort about the steering axis tending

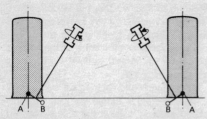

fig. 233. Lifting effect: camber change with lock due to kingpin inclination raises the car slightly and the effect is exaggerated by positive offset.

to steer the car in a direction which exaggerates the slewing effect of the braking imbalance. The movement will be small if the driver's hands are clamped firmly on the wheel, but the likelihood is that they are not and the course deviation will be greater than that due to braking imbalance alone.

It was to counteract this effect that Volkswagen introduced a new form of steering geometry with their Audi 80 model: they made the steering axis meet the ground at a point *outside* the centre of the contact patch. This **negative offset** reverses the sense of the turning moment due to an unbalanced braking force (fig. 235) creating a tendency for the wheel to steer in a direction which corrects the deviations from the chosen path resulting from braking imbalance.

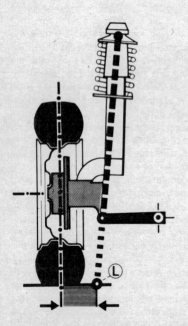

fig. 234. Positive offset increases the slewing effect due to unbalanced braking.

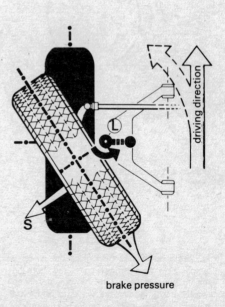

brake pressure

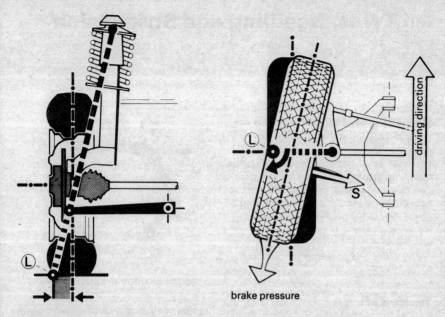

brake pressure

fig. 235. Negative offset reduces the slewing effect
due to unbalanced braking.

ten **Tyres, Handling and Suspension**

Handling and Roadholding – The Pneumatic Tyre

It is hardly an exaggeration to say that a car's most important components are its tyres. Certainly, without its pneumatic tyres the modern car would be largely lacking in the speed, comfort and safety which characterize it today. And it is the tyres, above all, which ultimately govern its roadholding, cornering ability and **handling** or road behaviour.

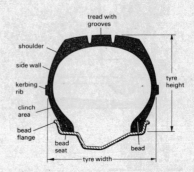

fig. 236. The basic parts of a pneumatic tyre.

The parts of a tyre

Undoubtedly one of the most important parts of a tyre is the air inside it which is maintained at a pressure ranging from around 15 lb/sq in (1 bar) to about 35 lb/sq in (2.2 bar). Nowadays it is generally retained by the **carcass** or body of the tyre itself with the help of an airtight rim. Some tyres, though, still require the separate rubber **inner tubes** almost universally fitted many years ago. Wire-spoked wheels, which are not airtight, also need inner tubes, but they constitute a largely unnecessary and easily damaged additional component, and a tyre with a tube tends to deflate more rapidly when punctured than a tubeless tyre.

The foundations of a tyre are its **beads**, strong, inextensible and fairly stiff hoops of wire which are held firmly against the **bead flanges** of the wheel rim (fig. 236) by the air pressure. Because the beads do not stretch, the wheel rim has a **well** into which they can be worked, one after the other, so that the tyre can be fitted to the wheel.

From the beads extend the **sidewalls** which are sometimes equipped with **kerb-**ing ribs or strips to protect against damage from side impact. The part of the tyre which rolls on the ground is provided with a pattern of grooves to drain away water and is called the **tread**; it is thicker at the **shoulders** where it joins the sidewalls.

Construction

From the beginning the rubber carcass of a pneumatic tyre has been reinforced by cords or plies, originally always of textile, though nowadays often of steel or various manmade fibres. Until the early fifties, the **cross-ply** form of reinforcement was almost universal. As its name implies, a cross-ply tyre is reinforced by unidirectional plies or cords of rayon or nylon which cross each other (fig. 237) at an included angle of about 45° in alternate layers, the plies of each layer lying at an angle of about 38° to the centreline of the tread. Although one set of plies is separated from the next by a layer of rubber, in combination they form a grid which is 'lozenged' by the flexing of the tyre, and this lozenging action generates heat.

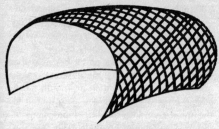

fig. 237. The reinforcing cords of a cross-ply tyre pass over each other at an angle.

Why, then, do the plies have to cross at all? It must first be understood that tyres have to withstand several sets of stresses: radial – inwards due to bumps on the road surface, outwards due to centrifugal force and air pressure – tangential, due to driving and braking forces and lateral due to steering and cornering.

Unfortunately there is a conflict between the requirements of comfort and those of stability. If the plies are set wholly radially, for example, the carcass becomes very supple but the tread squirms on the road far too much for acceptable roadholding. If, on the other hand, the plies are circumferential, or nearly so, the tyre becomes very rigid and stable but harsh and unyielding.

But happily there is an alternative form of tyre construction which allows the requirements of comfort to be reconciled with those of stability. This is the **radial ply** arrangement in which the plies of the carcass are indeed set radially (fig. 238) but work in conjunction with additional layers of cords running circumferentially, or nearly so, to form a flexible but inextensible belt which braces the tread – hence the alternative term, **braced-tread** construction. The radial plies give the sidewalls freedom to flex and thus provide good comfort, while the inextensible belt improves stability in several ways. It is strongly resistant to centrifugal growth, distributes strains around the circumference of the tyre much more than in a cross-ply, keeps the tread flat on the ground and prevents it from squirming, giv-

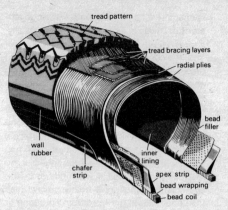

fig. 238. In a radial-ply tyre the carcass plies run radially but the tread is braced by a belt of cords which run nearly circumferentially.

ing a significant improvement in roadholding in both wet and dry conditions. The greater stiffness of this form of construction makes the tyre much better able to withstand high speeds without overheating, reduces its rolling resistance and gives it a life markedly longer than that of a cross-ply tyre.

As always there are snags, one of the most important being increased cost. In addition, a radial-ply tyre differs fundamentally from a cross-ply in the sort of road noise it generates, requiring specially designed suspension systems with **compliance** or fore-and-aft flexibility to reduce the **bump-thump** produced. But these are relatively minor disadvantages, and the majority of tyres sold today are radials.

A third kind of tyre, the **bias-belted** type, combines some features of cross-ply construction with those of the radial ply, but it is produced mainly in America and is not widely used.

Tyre/road friction

When one object slides over another the frictional force which opposes their relative motion (p. 39) is equal to the load pressing them together multiplied by a constant which is characteristic of them both – their **coefficient of friction**. Expressed mathematically, $F = \mu R$ where F is the frictional force, μ or 'mu' the coefficient of friction and R the load pressing the two objects together. Looking at it another way, the coefficient of friction is equal to the load divided by the resistive force, or $\mu = R/F$.

For ordinary objects such as smooth wood or metal blocks sliding on smooth surfaces, the frictional force almost never becomes equal to the load pressing them together, no matter how large this is. In other words, the coefficient of friction is nearly always less than one. Indeed the maximum cornering or side force coefficient sustainable by an ordinary road car on ordinary road tyres seldom exceeds 0.75. But note that if the coefficient of friction were to be equal to one, the frictional force on the sliding body would become the same as its weight, so its resultant deceleration would be the same in magnitude as that due to gravity. In such a case the body would be subjected to a deceleration of 1 g, which is 32.18 ft/sec² (feet per second per second) or 9.81 m/sec² (metres per second per second). Hence when $\mu = 0.75$ in a corner the maximum **lateral acceleration** is 0.75g, and if $\mu = 1.0$ the maximum lateral acceleration would be 1 g.

In a corner this lateral acceleration is created by the outward-acting **centrifugal force** – and indeed represents a way of defining it. (To be more precise, lateral acceleration is the consequence of **centripetal force**, for when a car follows a curved path it is continually being made to accelerate *inwards*, towards the centre of the curve, and away from the straight line its inertia would otherwise make it follow.)

For rubber tyres, however, the coefficient of friction with a dry road surface is not limited to a maximum value of one. Under braking at low speeds in the dry, for example, almost all modern road-car tyres provide enough grip for a deceleration of around 1 g. And an American dragster reaching around 200 mph in under 6 seconds from a standstill, sustains a *mean* acceleration of around 1.5g with a much higher initial acceleration, while modern racing cars routinely corner at still higher g levels. This is partly because the surface of a tyre acts more like a pinion engaging with a rack than a smooth block sliding on a smooth surface. The rubber in the tread cogs into the tiny depressions in the road surface and moulds itself over the small projections, creating exceptionally tenacious adhesion. But it is also because the rubber forms momentary but definite chemical bonds with the road surface over which it rolls.

Tread pattern and drainage

For good grip in the dry a tyre does not need a tread pattern – indeed it may perform better if completely bald, by putting a greater area of rubber in contact with the road. This is why **slick** or dry-weather racing tyres have no tread at all.

In the wet it is a different story. From an early stage in the development of the tyre it was realized that better wet grip was obtained with a pattern cut in the surface of the tyre, incorporating channels to allow the water to drain away and knife cuts or **sipes** to mop up the remaining water and to bite into the surface of the road.

Later experiments showed that the adhesion available falls off rapidly as speed rises, and a deeper understanding of the deterioration in grip with rising speed was arrived at in the early sixties as the result of a research programme conducted by Dunlop. Dunlop identified the problem of **aquaplaning** which can occur in heavy rain particularly when the road surface is covered by a continuous film of water, even though it may be no more than 1/10 in or 2.5 mm thick. The problem is that at 60 mph, for example, a tyre has to disperse roughly one gallon of water every second if it is to grip the road, although each element of its tread remains in contact with the road surface for only 1/150 second. If the tyre has a worn or badly designed tread with a poor drainage capacity, it will in such conditions simply plane along the surface of the water, losing virtually all adhesion. The coefficient of friction available is then so low that the wheels may not rotate again after being locked even when the brakes are released.

This research programme had two effects. It highlighted the dangers of bald tyres – which provide very little adhesion in the wet above 30 mph – and led to the legal requirement for a minimum tread depth. It also led to improved tread patterns incorporating generous circumferential drainage channels to remove the water from the front of the contact patch, transverse channels or tunnels – as in Dunlop's own Aquajet tyre – to disperse it sideways and a multiplicity of sipes to complete the process. Hence for a well-designed tyre the unbroken film of water exists only in the front path of the contact patch. Behind this zone (fig. 239) lies a second in which the bulk water has mostly been cleared away, and at the rear of the contact patch is a third zone in which the sipes mop up the remaining water leaving almost dry tread in contact with almost dry road.

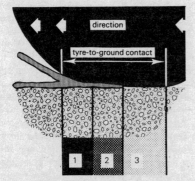

fig. 239. The tread of a well-designed tyre running on a wet road wipes the road almost dry: 1, unbroken water film area; 2, water partly removed along circumferential and transverse tread grooves; 3, road wiped nearly dry by sipes or slots in tread blocks.

Tread compound

When the tread does not have to contend with a film of water but merely a wet surface, its grip is significantly influenced by the type of rubber compound employed – some blends containing a high proportion of synthetic rubber do markedly better than others.

The distinguishing characteristic of such compounds is the association of the extra grip they afford with high **hysteresis** losses – i.e. they absorb energy when deflected, bouncing back with less force than a low hysteresis rubber which behaves more like a low-friction spring. This leads to a 'cling' effect which is partly responsible for the high grip, though other factors are involved.

High energy losses mean heat, though, the enemy of every tyre designer, which is why the high hysteresis rubber is used only for the tread of a tyre. And its adoption was only made possible because high-quality rayon or nylon reinforcing cords had already been developed which were capable of withstanding the temperatures reached. High energy losses also mean an increase in rolling resistance – another characteristic to be avoided – especially these days when fuel consumption is so important, but the penalty is very small.

Tyre sizes and ratings

The size of a modern tyre is generally defined by two numbers, which for a cross-ply will be in a form such as 6.50–14. This means a tyre with a section width of 6.5 in which fits on a wheel 14 in in diameter. But a tyre has another important characteristic, the proportion of its section height to its section width – its **profile** or **aspect ratio** (fig. 240). The standard aspect ratio of a cross-ply tyre is 88 per cent, but for a radial-ply tyre it is 82 per cent.

The section width of a radial is usually given in millimetres, leading to a dimension such as 165–14. But many radial-ply tyres now have a 70 per cent aspect ratio, and are

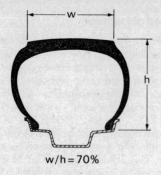

w/h = 70%

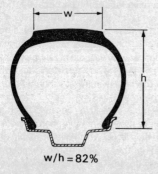

w/h = 82%

fig. 240. The ratio of a tyre's height to its width is called its aspect ratio. Below, a tyre with the 82 per cent aspect ratio of a standard radial; above, a tyre with the increasingly popular 70 per cent profile.

generally designated as such: 165/70–14, say. A new generation of tyres with even lower profiles – down to 40 per cent – has now been introduced.

Tyres are also classified by three speed ratings: SR, HR and VR. An SR is safe up to 113 mph (180 kph), an HR to 130 mph (210 kph) and a VR at over 130 mph.

The wheel

In general, the wider a tyre the wider the wheel rim it needs, though this is no longer always the case for very advanced tyres of exceptionally low profile such as the Michelin TRX which are designed to bulge outwards from relatively narrow rims. Various types of

rim are made (designated J, K, etc.) but the differences between them are small.

The main requirements of a wheel – apart from adequate strength – is that its well and bead flanges should be correctly and carefully designed. And as already mentioned, the rim must be airtight, unless the wheel is of the wire type when this is not possible. In addition a wheel must be accurately concentric and properly balanced, both statically and dynamically (p. 213).

For most cars these requirements are met by wheels which are simple in construction and fabricated from steel sheet. But unsprung weight can be reduced by using more expensive wheels which may be cast in alloys of either aluminium or magnesium.

Trends

With the help of computers it has been possible to design wider and wider tyres giving more and more grip under all conditions – the provision of adequate drainage for wide tyres in wet weather is no longer a problem. At the same time designers have found it possible to use very low profiles for greater rigidity of construction and tread stability at little sacrifice in harshness or road noise generation. By the standards of a few years ago the tyres of high performance cars in particular have thus become very wide and low in profile. Further increases in width and reductions in aspect ratio are likely to occur slowly now, but low, wide tyres are being adopted for a much wider range of cars, benefiting the roadholding and safety of the ordinary family saloon.

Additional improvements in cornering and braking ability are likely to follow from research into the interaction between the tyre and the road surface. Such investigations have not yet led to improvements in tyre design, but they have led to the development of special road surfaces such as Shellgrip and Dunlop Delugrip which give significantly improved grip in the wet.

A third trend which is developing derives

from the need to minimize both the danger and the inconvenience of a flat tyre. The danger is usually created when a side force pushes a deflated or partially deflated tyre right off the wheel rim which then digs into the ground, often making the car overturn. This danger can be reduced by filling the well of the rim in some way – hence the various 'safety' wheels which have been evolved. A better solution is a **run-flat** tyre which also enables the spare wheel to be dispensed with entirely.

So far only one such wheel and tyre combination has ever been put on sale, the Dunlop Denovo (although it is no longer produced). This involves (fig. 241) a wide tyre on a special wheel with a narrow rim and carefully shaped bead flanges which do not cut into the sidewalls after a deflation. These sidewalls are designed to fold outwards without damage when the pressure in the

tyre falls. In its original form the Denovo wheel incorporated a series of canisters designed to rupture during a deflation, releasing a fluid to lubricate the sidewalls, seal the puncture, and by vaporizing to reinflate the tyre a little. But the canisters were later dispensed with, the inside of the tyre merely being smeared with a jelly which lubricates and seals, the heating of the residual air being relied upon for partial reinflation.

A further, more recent trend has been the development of a new generation of tyres with especially low rolling resistance to help reduce fuel consumption.

Slip angles

Think of a tyre being subjected to a side force – as it is in every steering or cornering manoeuvre at any speed above a walking pace. The beads of the tyre are forced (fig. 242) in one direction by the side force acting on the body and wheel, yet the tread is retained in the other direction by the grip of its contact patch on the road. The tyre is

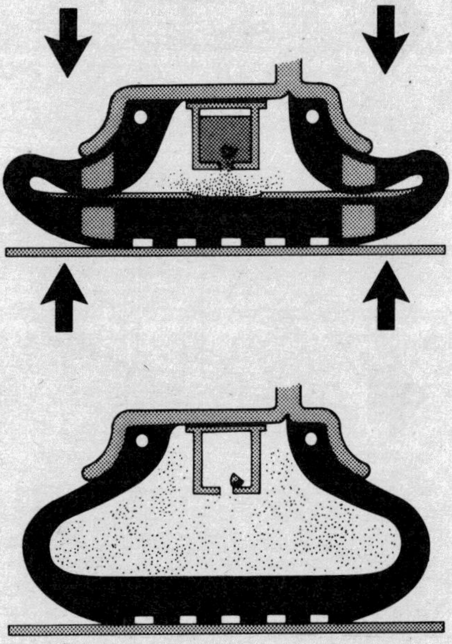

fig. 241. The Dunlop Denovo tyre can run flat with its sidewalls flexed; a lubricant reduces friction and restores some pressure by vaporization.

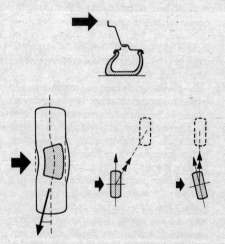

fig. 242. A side force sets up a slip angle which allows the tyre to move sideways as well as forwards without sliding on the road.

therefore forced to bulge in the direction opposite to that of the side force. Thus an element of rubber in the tread straddling the centreline will be pulled progressively farther from the wheel centre plane as it passes to the rear of the contact patch before springing back towards the centre plane as it leaves the ground. In this way it is possible for the tyre simultaneously to move sideways as well as forwards while remaining in rolling, not sliding contact with the ground. If the wheel is subjected to a side force, due to a side wind or camber, while running in the straight-ahead position, for example, the tyre will respond by developing a lateral velocity and a **slip angle** between its plane of rotation and its actual direction of travel. This will cause it to drift away from the side force. But by turning the wheel towards the side force, the resultant velocity can be aligned with the straight-ahead position, cancelling the drift; the lateral velocity is then developed with respect to the angled wheel, not the car.

As the side force rises from a low value, so the slip angle at first begins to increase. Small changes in slip angle can have a marked – indeed profound – influence on the behaviour of the car, especially in a corner. Because of the steering gear ratio, an increase in the front slip angles of only 1° may call for a corrective steering wheel movement of 15°–20°.

Eventually, however, a maximum slip angle is reached – of about 12° for road tyres – at which the ultimate sustainable side force for a given load is attained. The tyre then reaches its breakaway point, and with any further increase in side force begins to slide sideways, losing all rolling contact with the road. It then becomes nothing more than a friction pad, lacking any ability to steer or guide, merely exerting a force which opposes the sliding motion – and which is appreciably lower than the maximum sustainable side force just before the breakaway point. This behaviour is governed by numerous influences: increasing the size of

a tyre, changing from one of cross-ply to one of radial-ply construction and raising the inflation pressure all tend to postpone the breakaway point to a higher cornering speed and to reduce the slip angle created by a given side force – though many other factors are equally important.

For any given tyre and set of conditions there is a maximum sustainable force which can be shared between a cornering force and a braking or an acceleration force. If the sum (fig. 243) of the cornering force and either the braking force or the acceleration force, taking into account their differing directions, exceeds the maximum force sustainable, then the tyre loses its grip and

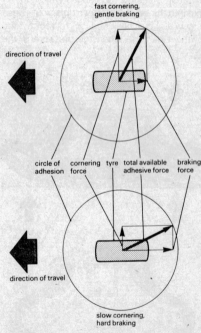

fig. 243. There is a limit to the amount of grip a tyre can provide before sliding, and if more is taken for cornering (*top*) less will be left for braking and vice versa (*bottom*). A 'circle of adhesion' defines the total adhesion available under combined braking and cornering.

starts to slide. One practical consequence is that if you brake gently while cornering hard (or brake hard while cornering gently) you diminish the available cornering force and risk provoking a slide. The same applies to excessive acceleration, though gentle acceleration helps to stabilize a car in a corner.

The side force exerted by the tyre (in opposition to the side force on the car) acts at a point behind the vertical line through the centre of the wheel creating what is called **pneumatic trail**. This adds to the castor trail due to the castor angle, and creates a **self-aligning torque** which the driver must resist through the steering. It is because the self-aligning torque tends to fall off as the tyre loses its grip that the driver may receive advance warning of an impending loss of front-end adhesion if the steering system is well designed.

Now let us consider the effect of the vertical load sustained by a tyre on its cornering behaviour – as defined by graphs relating side force and slip angle at different values of load (fig. 244). This family of curves

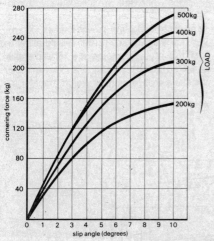

fig. 244. Side force, load and slip angle. The downward-drooping shape of the curves means that an increase in load does not proportionately increase the maximum available side force.

can readily be made to yield useful and interesting information.

The first thing to notice is that none of the lines are straight and all have a downward-drooping shape. This means that if the load on a tyre is raised, the maximum side-force it can sustain before sliding increases, too – but not in proportion. If, for example, the load is increased from 200 kg to 300 kg, then for the tyre to which fig. 244 refers the maximum available side force with a slip angle of 10° would rise from about 154 kg to 208 kg. Hence multiplying the load by 1.5 has raised the maximum sustainable side force by only 1.35.

For the first loading the maximum side force value represents a lateral acceleration of 0.77g, equivalent to a speed of 33.9 mph round a circle of 100 ft radius, and for the second the lateral acceleration is 0.69g, equivalent to a speed of 32.1 mph before sliding, round the same circle. In effect, therefore, the **cornering power** of the tyre has been reduced by the increase in load.

These figures highlight an important aspect of cornering. Increasing speed by only 5.6 per cent from 32.1 mph to 33.9 mph raised the lateral acceleration by 11.5 per cent from 0.69g to 0.77g. This is because the centrifugal or side force increases with the *square* of the speed through a corner. Relatively small increases in speed therefore mean relatively large increases in lateral g. So beware of anyone claiming that a slight modification makes his car 10 or 20 mph faster through a given corner – it is most unlikely.

Another significant fact emerges from this worked example. If increasing the load decreases the cornering power of a tyre, reducing the load *increases* its cornering power. Putting it another way, fitting larger, more lightly loaded tyres to a car will generally improve its cornering power. However, the space within a car's wheel arches limits the size of wheel and tyre that can be fitted to it, and various undesirable effects such as excessive kickback in the steering may soon outweigh any advantages.

These arguments are applicable to the cornering speeds usual in ordinary motoring. Suppose, for example, that with a 200 kg load we are not cornering at the limit of adhesion but at a sober 0.5g, equivalent to a slip angle of a mere 4.2° for our tyre of fig. 244. If we now double the load upon it to 400 kg, the slip angle will rise to around 6.3° to sustain the same 0.5g lateral acceleration. We will thus have to turn the steering wheel a good deal more to follow a chosen path and will also have to resist a larger self-aligning torque. The lightly loaded car will therefore be more responsive and require less wheel-twirling when driven on a twisty road.

The response of a tyre to varying loads has a further and very important influence on the cornering behaviour of a car, due to **lateral weight transfer**. Whenever a car corners, centrifugal force (fig. 245) acting on its centre of gravity tends to reduce the load on the inside wheel and to increase it on the outside wheel – it is as if a weight had been transferred from one side of the car to the other. The effect is large: even at moderate cornering speeds the outside wheel can easily be carrying twice the load of the inside wheel, and many modern cars can be cornered hard enough to lift one inside wheel – usually the front one – off the ground

entirely so that it supports no load at all, leaving the outside front wheel to do all the work at that end of the car. The centre of gravity of most modern cars, incidentally, is generally low enough to ensure that it will nearly always slide before it turns over, though it will certainly do this if it hits an obstacle such as a kerb, or if it acquires overturning momentum by sliding from a low friction to a high friction surface.

The total weight transferred depends only upon the height of the centre of gravity (which determines the overturning moment or tilting effect), the width of the **track** or lateral distance between the wheels (which determines the self-righting moment) and the magnitude of the side force. But the weight transfer at the front relative to the rear depends partly on the roll stiffness of the front springs relative to that of the rear springs. In general, if the front springs are very stiff and the rear springs very soft, most of the weight will be transferred at the front – and if the rear springs are stiffer than the front ones, the reverse will be true, of course.

This is where the tyre's sensitivity to load comes in. Consider, for example, a pair of tyres each supporting a static load of 300 kg; without weight transfer this would allow a total maximum side force at a 10° slip angle of 416 kg for the tyre of fig. 244. Now imagine the loads changing under weight transfer to

fig. 245. Lateral weight transfer increases the load on the outside wheels in a corner and reduces the load on the inside wheels.

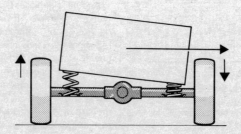

400 kg on the outside wheel and 200 kg on the inside wheel. (Since the car does not get any lighter or heavier when cornering, the sum of the two loads must remain unchanged.) Using the values of fig. 244 again, the unequal loads would allow a maximum side force (at the same slip angle) on the outer wheel of 248 kg and on the inner wheel of 154 kg — total 402 kg. Thus the effect of weight transfer is to reduce the overall cornering power; this is much more marked at still higher slip angles, towards the limit of adhesion.

Because of the downward droop of the curves, *the increase in side force obtained by raising the load on the outside wheel does not compensate for the reduction in available side force which results from reducing the load on the inside wheel.* Other things being equal, therefore, fitting or stiffening an anti-roll bar at one end of a car (or increasing the roll stiffness there directly) reduces the cornering power of the tyres at that end with respect to the other. And the effect is a double one: not only will the cornering power be reduced at the end with the increased roll stiffness, but also the lower weight transfer on the tyres at the other end of the car will increase their cornering power. But notice that the rule was prefaced with the qualification 'other things being equal' — this is very important indeed. For suspension design is such a complex business, involving so many factors, that increasing the roll stiffness may not always have the effect described.

One of these many factors is the effect of camber, or a wheel's inclination to the vertical. If the wheels splay outwards at the top (fig. 246) or lean in the direction of the applied side force they are said to have **positive camber** — which reduces cornering power considerably. If they lean inwards at the top or away from the applied side force, they are said to have **negative camber** — which increases cornering power considerably. The maximum cornering power is usually generated at a few degrees of negative camber.

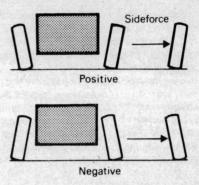

fig. 246. Camber: wheels that splay outwards at the top or lean in the direction of the side force are said to be positively cambered, while those which lean inwards at the top or away from the side force are said to have negative camber.

It is for this reason that the wheels of many modern cars, particularly the front ones, are given some static negative camber. As all independent suspension systems tend to make the heavily loaded outside wheel lean outwards in a corner — or give it positive camber — the usual aim is to use enough static negative camber to keep it nearly upright when cornering hard.

fig. 247. (a) A tyre with a camber angle forms part of a cone and has a tendency to rotate about its apex; (b) Too much negative camber at the front may create steering wander.

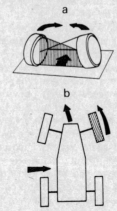

But cambering a wheel also makes it steer. This is because the tyre effectively forms part of a cone (fig. 247) and tries to rotate about its apex. Another way of looking at it is that the tyre exerts a residual side thrust – inwards when the wheels are negatively cambered – even when it is in the straight-ahead position and no slip angle is being generated. This steering effect can lead to straight-line twitchiness with negative camber, but can be corrected by toeing the wheels outwards slightly.

Oversteer and understeer

Whether a car handles well or ill depends largely upon the relative sizes of the front and rear slip angles and their relative rates of change with respect to side force or cornering speed. To understand why, imagine two men carrying a large sheet of glass in a steady side-wind (fig. 248a). As each man lifts a foot from the ground he is forced slightly sideways and returns it to one side of the place on which he trod before. Thus although neither man turns either to the right or the left, the wind pressure makes them drift sideways, just as a side force makes a tyre develop a slip angle and gives it a lateral as well as a forward velocity.

Now consider what happens when the two men are of equal strength and they enter a curve with their sheet of glass. Let us make the convenient, if rather fanciful, assumption that the wind blows steadily from the centre of the curve (fig. 248b). The pressure this creates gives the man at the rear a tendency to drift outwards which steers the glass sheet towards the centre of the curve. This tendency, however, is matched by the exactly equal outward component of lateral velocity imposed by the wind on the man at the front. He is heading or 'steering' to the left to follow the curve, but not by any more than he would if there were no wind trying to push him sideways.

The net result is that the glass sheet follows the curved path precisely, but acquires a small **attitude angle** to its actual direction of motion.

This situation corresponds to the **neutral steer** condition for a car. The rear slip angles steer the car into the corner but this tendency is balanced by the exactly equal front slip angles, so the path followed corresponds fairly closely to the one predicted by Ackermann. Thus the driver has to turn the steering wheel neither more nor less than seems appropriate to the geometry of the turn. Some cars are almost neutral steering at low levels of cornering force, but hardly any maintain the characteristic at high levels.

Whatever the handling characteristic of the car, incidentally, it always maintains a nose-in tail-out attitude angle to its actual direction of travel. For the wheels must always be angled inwards slightly to oppose centrifugal force, and the rear wheels of a car always lie more or less parallel to its longitudinal axis. This attitude angle can rise to 10° or 12° at the limit of adhesion, but is rarely noticeable unless some datum line makes it apparent. It is sometimes detectable in photographs of cars cornering hard in steeply banked turns, when their front wheels are usually perceptibly further away from the top railings than the rear wheels. Only when the rear tyres have been forced to exceed the normal limit of adhesion and are sliding across the road do more marked attitude angles occur – such as are assumed by rally cars on loose surfaces.

Let us now consider what happens if the man holding the front of our sheet of glass is weaker than the man at the rear. The man at the front develops a larger lateral velocity than the man at the rear, causing the glass sheet to deviate outwards from the chosen path (fig. 248c) following a gentler curve with a larger radius. This corresponds to the condition called **understeer** in a car where the front slip angles are larger than the rear ones, and means that to keep on course the driver has to turn the steering

fig. 248. (a) A car experiencing a side force acts rather like a glass sheet being carried in a high wind; like the sheet it drifts sideways even if the wheels point straight ahead because the tyres develop slip angles and a lateral as well as a forward velocity. Oversteer and understeer: the situation in which both men have the same tendency to drift outwards (b) is equivalent to neutral steer in a car. The car can follow a circular path without any additional steering wheel movement, but does acquire an inward-pointing attitude angle; (c) if the front man is weaker than the rear one the sheet tends to drift outwards, away from the chosen path, and this is equivalent to understeer in a car; (d) if the rear man is weaker than the front one, the tail of the glass sheet swings out and it tends to describe an ever-tightening circle – this is equivalent to oversteer.

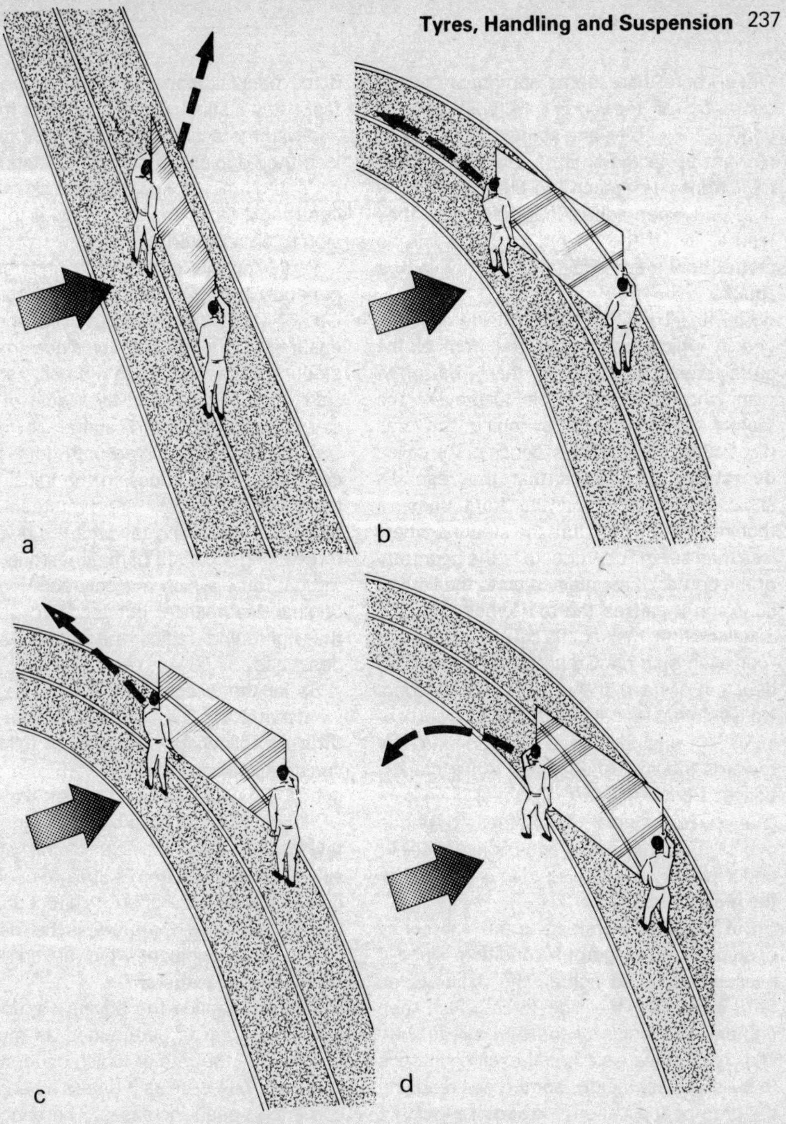

wheel more than seems appropriate to the geometry of the corner. Almost all cars understeer initially, and some continue to do so right up to the limit of adhesion so that their front tyres reach the breakaway point first, and when adhesion is finally lost they tend to fly off the road in a straight line no matter how much additional steering lock is applied.

The final condition to be considered is the one in which the man at the front of the glass sheet is stronger than the other man who becomes unable to prevent the rear of the sheet from swinging outwards (fig. 248d). In a car this condition is called **oversteer** and means that the rear slip angles are larger than the front ones; it requires the driver to turn the steering wheel less than seems appropriate to the geometry of the corner. If maintained up to the limit of adhesion it causes the rear wheels to lose adhesion first, making the car slew sideways – or even spin right round to face its initial direction of travel if the oversteer is strong. No cars oversteer initially but a few, particularly rear-engined ones, do so strongly towards the limit of adhesion. A fair proportion of front-engined/rear-wheel drive cars change from initial understeer to gentle oversteer at the limit of adhesion, especially under power, since this reduces the grip of the rear wheels.

But strong oversteer is an inherently unstable and dangerous condition, since it causes the car to tighten the radius of its turn, increasing the side force which then tightens the radius of the turn still further, and so on. Because it is self-exciting it tends to build up very rapidly, sometimes requiring the prompt application of **opposite lock** – a rotation of the steering wheel in a sense opposite to the normal – if the car is to stay on course. Very few drivers are capable of applying opposite lock effectively – especially in an emergency situation on the public roads.

On the other hand most drivers find understeer relatively easy to cope with. Generally,

if the bend tightens up or they take it too fast, they instinctively do the right thing by applying more lock. And if the front tyres do lose their grip on the road, an understeering car's tendency to go straight on reduces centrifugal force, making it easier for adhesion to be regained.

Partly for this reason mild understeer is generally held to be an essential characteristic of a safe road car. But it also helps to ensure straight-line stability, since an understeering car responds to a small disturbing side force – generated by a gust of wind, say, or a change in road camber – by moving away from it in a curved path generating a centrifugal force opposing the initial disturbance. In contrast, an oversteering car responds by moving towards the disturbing force along a curved path generating a centrifugal force which not only augments the original disturbance, but tends to grow by the tightening radius mechanism already described.

So far the discussion has been based on what mathematicians call **steady-state conditions**: following – or trying to follow – a constant radius or circular path at a steady speed. Real-life motoring is not like this at all, for quite apart from variations in speed, few corners are exactly circular in shape and all are approached from a straight or another corner turning in the opposite direction. What matters above all, therefore, is the response of the car to conditions which are continually changing – or **transient**.

Thus in practice the driving comfort and safety of a car is determined as much as anything by the rate at which understeer or oversteer builds up as it enters a bend or its cornering speed increases. The dangers of sudden oversteer and the difficulty with which it is corrected have already been mentioned, but a car with sudden understeer which requires an unexpectedly large amount of steering wheel rotation for a moderate increase in side force is equally unpleasant to drive and also potentially dangerous.

Such behaviour changes may be influenced – though in complex ways not fully understood – by a car's polar moment of inertia, its 'flywheelness' about a vertical axis through its centre of gravity. This depends not upon a car's weight, nor even upon its front/rear distribution, but upon the inboard/outboard nature of its weight distribution. If its major assemblies – such as its engine and gearbox – lie close to its centre of gravity and well within its wheelbase, the polar moment of inertia tends to be low and in general the car is responsive in turning manoeuvres. But if the heavy parts are spread out, as in a typical full-sized American car with large overhangs at front and rear, the polar moment of inertia will tend to be large, making the car sluggish and ponderous in turning manoeuvres.

We already know enough to be able to understand several basic causes of understeer and oversteer. *Other things being equal*:

A car tends to understeer if the inflation pressure of its front tyres is lower than that of its rear tyres, and to oversteer if the inflation pressure of its rear tyres is lower than that of its front tyres.

A car tends to understeer if there is more weight on the front tyres than on the rear ones, and to oversteer if there is more weight on the rear tyres than the front ones. The reason lies in the downward droop of the tyre behaviour curves (fig. 244). The cornering power of the tyres carrying the most weight is not proportionately raised by their increased load, leaving the set at the other end of the car with greater cornering power.

A front-wheel drive car tends to understeer, since a driving torque tends to reduce a tyre's cornering power (as does a braking torque). The corollary – that a rear-wheel drive car tends to oversteer – is not so true, since the tendency to oversteer created by the driving thrust which the rear tyres transmit is often balanced by an understeer tendency due to a forward weight bias. Rear-engined, rear-wheel drive cars, though, do tend to oversteer.

A car tends to understeer if there is more lateral weight transfer in corners on the front tyres than on the rear ones, and to oversteer if there is more lateral weight transfer on the rear tyres than the front ones. Increasing the roll stiffness by fitting or stiffening an anti-roll bar often increases the lateral weight transfer, but this is also influenced by other factors such as the roll centre height (p. 242) in ways too complex to describe in this book.

A car tends to understeer if the front wheels assume larger positive camber angles then the rear ones in corners, and to oversteer if the rear wheels assume larger positive camber angles than the front ones.

But in considering these tendencies it is most important to remember the qualification stated at the outset: that any one of them only has the effect stated if *other things remain equal*. In practice they sometimes do not, so that design changes do not always have the expected effect, vehicle handling being a very complex business involving many interacting factors. Fitting a front anti-roll bar, for example, might reduce understeer, not increase it, if it increased the front cornering power by reducing roll and camber angles more than it reduced front cornering power by increasing lateral weight transfer.

Moreover, few of the tendencies are so dominant that they cannot be balanced by other tendencies. Hence front-wheel drive cars can be made to corner and handle extremely well, without excessive understeer. It is more difficult to cope with a marked rearward weight bias, but later versions of both the Hillman Imp and the Porsche 911 handle very well, though the latter car does become difficult to control at the (admittedly very high) limit of its adhesion.

A major factor in modern suspension design is the compliance or flexibility given to the wishbone bushes, sub-frame mountings, etc., to reduce road noise. It is the designer's job to compensate the errors in wheel geometry which compliance introduces with other errors such as those inherent in the linkage system used, so that the car's handling is always safe, predictable and progressive. This can now be done with such success that top-class handling need no longer mean a harsh, crashy suspension system with inflexible joints.

Suspension requirements

Several alternative forms of independent suspension are in use today, each having different influences on roadholding and handling. A helpful way of exploring these systems and their influences is to begin by considering why independent suspension

fig. 249. The effect of gyroscopic torque: if the wheel is tilted from the vertical – as it may be when passing over a bump – or in other words is twisted about a horizontal axis, H, it develops a gyroscopic torque about the steering axis, S. This can lead to a violent steering oscillation called shimmy, especially if the two front wheels are coupled together by a beam axle.

has entirely superseded the beam front axle, which superficially seems a simple and sensible arrangement. One of its virtues, for example, is that unlike independent suspension systems it keeps the wheels vertical and the treads of the tyres flat on the road when the body rolls, maintaining cornering power – except at very high levels of side force when the inside wheel may lift.

The basic weakness of the beam front axle, however, is its susceptibility to **gyroscopic torque**. This is the torque exerted by any revolving object while its plane of rotation is being displaced. When the wheel at one end of a beam axle is deflected upwards by a bump in the road, for example, it is tilted from the vertical about the other wheel (fig. 249) and responds by developing a gyroscopic torque which tends to make it **precess** or steer about a vertical axis. This is a rather mysterious physical effect, but one which is easily verified with a toy gyroscope or the wheel of an upturned bicycle.

Independently suspended wheels may also be subject to gyroscopic torque when deflected by bumps; the difference is that a beam axle couples the two wheels together. Thus with a beam axle the other wheel is also tilted and also develops a steering impulse which acts in the same direction. If

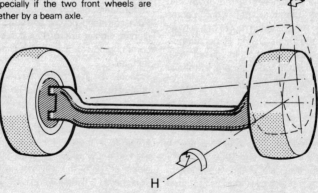

there is any play in the steering linkage at all, these impulses make the front of the car snake from side to side. They tend to build up, moreover, setting the front axle into a violent conical motion called **shimmy**.

The front axle, particularly when located only by leaf springs, can also be excited under heavy braking into a similar form of motion called **tramp**. This is triggered if the spring on one side is wound up by braking torque and is then sharply released when the wheel momentarily loses adhesion.

There is a modern school of thought – though a small one – which suggests that these problems are largely eliminated if the axle is well-designed and properly constrained by a system of locating links. Certainly beam front axles are widely used for vans and commercial vehicles, while the successful – and admirable – Range Rover has a live (i.e. power-transmitting) beam front axle. But even when such axles are properly located, constant small steering corrections are nearly always required on a bumpy surface which are not needed when a good independent front suspension system is fitted.

But the beam front axle has the further disadvantage that in most cases it wastes space in a front-engined car. Unless the centre of gravity is to be rather high, the engine must be mounted behind it rather than above it. With independent front suspension, on the other hand, the engine can easily be mounted between the front wheels, leaving more space for the passengers behind it.

There are few objections to a light, dead axle at the rear of a car – it is a feature of several excellent front-wheel drive models – or to a de Dion axle, but there are many objections to a live rear axle which can tramp under acceleration as well as braking. A live rear axle, moreover, has a considerably higher unsprung weight than a good de Dion or independent system.

Accepting, therefore, the value of independent suspension, what are the charac-teristics expected of a satisfactory system? There are several, and all can be illuminated by reference to the least satisfactory independent suspension system, the swing-axle type which has already been briefly mentioned (p. 195).

The first requirement, perhaps, of a good independent suspension system is that the wheel should not be steered by the upward and downward movement of the suspension links, though small steering effects do exist in many arrangements, and for a swing axle are created when fore-and-aft location is provided by a **radius arm** or locating strut parallel to the longitudinal axis of the car and close to the wheel (fig. 250a). In the case of the Volkswagen Beetle this radius arm is a flat blade which actuates the torsion bar spring and is flexible enough to accommodate the inward swing of the axle. As the radius arm moves upwards, its arc of movement pulls the wheel forward, creating toe-in on bump. To be fair to the swing-axle, though, the amount of bump-steer created is not enough to cause significant straight-line wander, and is, as we shall see, beneficial when cornering. Moreover the defect is not inherent and can be eliminated by straddling the swing-axle with a wishbone (fig. 250b).

Next, each wheel should move up and down over road surface irregularities with the minimum amount of **scrub** or sideways movement (fig. 250c) across the road – mainly because this increases tyre wear. Scrub is partly determined by the height of the pivot points – if very high, for example, the wheel would swing across the road like a pendulum.

In addition, normal suspension movement should not be accompanied by too large a change in camber angle (fig. 250d). But both scrub and camber change increase as the **swing arm length** decreases. When the pivot points lie on either side of a differential, as for a typical rear swing-axle system, the swing arm length is at its shortest – less than half the **track** or transverse distance

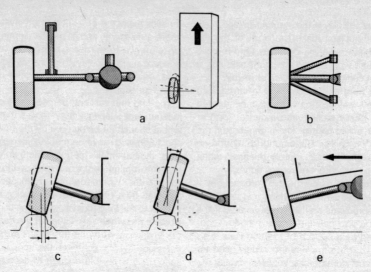

fig. 250. The swing-axle: a, the common radius arm form of fore-and-aft location pulls the wheel forwards and inwards as it rises, creating roll understeer if the swing-axle is at the rear; (b) this roll-steer effect can be eliminated by locating the swing-axle with a wishbone; c, scrub, or sideways movement with wheel deflection; d, camber change with wheel deflection; e, the jacking effect which greatly reduces cornering power.

between the centreline of the two tyre treads.

A much more important factor is the amount of camber change in a corner when the car is being acted upon by a side-force and the body rolls. All independent suspension systems allow the outside loaded wheel – the one that does most of the work in a corner – to assume a greater or lesser positive camber angle which reduces the cornering power of the tyre. All, that is, allow the wheels to lean in the same direction, though by varying amounts, as the body. But the swing-axle system is the worst of all, allowing the outside wheel to assume a larger positive camber angle than the roll angle of the body, greatly reducing the cornering power of its tyre at quite moderate levels of side force. The toe-in of the same wheel as the car rolls creates a steering effect which counteracts this reduction very slightly.

This large positive camber angle is a result of the **jacking effect**, the tendency of centrifugal force to lever the body upwards about the outside wheel (fig. 250e) instead of making it roll. The effect exists because the swing-axle system has high pivot points which also mean a high **roll centre** – the centre about which that end of the body rolls. The lower the roll centre in relation to the centre of gravity the more the body rolls and the less it tends to jack up, and when the roll centre is at ground level as it is for some suspension systems, there is no jacking effect at all.

Front suspension systems

Two kinds of suspension have already been discussed at some length, the beam axle and swing-axles. Both can be used at the front of a car. The Range-Rover is the only modern vehicle which can reasonably be called a passenger car and has a rigid axle at the front as well as the rear – but for good reasons. Beam axles allow large wheel movements for good ride comfort to be combined with the generous ground clearance essential to cross-country motoring – which would be lost with independent suspension. These requirements plus the need to drive the front as well as the rear wheels took precedence over other factors such as a low centre of gravity (the engine is mounted above the front axle, not behind it).

In any case the car handles and rides surprisingly well on normal surfaced roads, perhaps helped by the secure location of both axles. At the front this is accomplished by two **torque arms** (fig. 251) which resist brake and drive torques and also provide fore-and-aft location. They pivot only on the chassis, being clamped to the axle at their forward ends via rubber bushes with sufficient flexibility to prevent the axle from being twisted in roll or single-wheel deflection as if it were a giant anti-roll bar. Lateral location is provided by a **Panhard rod**, a long strut running across the car, pivoting on the chassis at one end and on the axle at the other.

Swing-axle suspension is as rare at the *front* of a modern car as the beam axle; in recent years only the rear-engined Hillman Imp has been equipped with it. Again, there were good reasons, the main one being to reduce the cornering power of the front tyres (in conjunction with a low inflation pressure) and hence to introduce some understeer to compensate for the oversteer inherent in the rearward weight bias. Moreover, the massive wide-based wishbone construction (fig. 252) of the Imp's swing-axles ensures proper fore-and-aft location, while with pivots very close to the centreline of the car

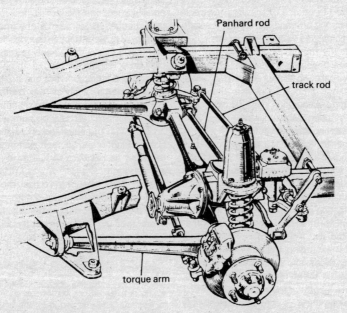

fig. 251. The Range-Rover front axle is located by a pair of torque arms and a Panhard rod.

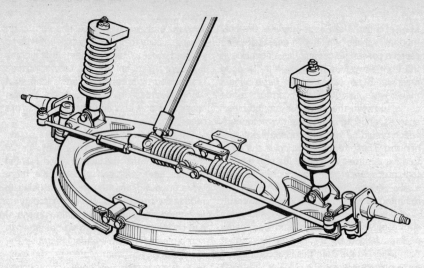

fig. 252. The front swing axles of the Hillman Imp.

they are given the maximum possible length. These pivot points were too high in early models, but when these were lowered the Imp proved to be one of the very few rear-engined cars with handling which was safe and predictable as well as enjoyable.

As already mentioned, the faults of the swing-axle depend partly on its high pivot points and partly on its short length (fig. 253a) but it is not difficult to devise alternative independent suspension systems which lack both these undesirable characteristics. Consider the swing arm length first.

Imagine, for example, a wheel located by a pair of equal-length links (fig. 253b) pivoting at each end and converging towards each other. Although the two links are much shorter than an ordinary swing axle, they act in combination as a much longer one, pivoting about an imaginary point on the other side of the car. This point is easily found merely by extending the axes of the links until they meet, and its distance from the centreline of the tyre defines the 'virtual swing arm length' of the system.

By making the links converge less sharply towards each other, the virtual swing arm length can be increased (fig. 253c) until it becomes infinitely long when the two links are parallel (fig. 253d). Such an equal-length parallel wishbone system is now relatively rare, though it is still used at the front of the Citroën CX. Its attraction springs from the fact that it forces the wheels to move vertically on bumps in the road, with no camber change and little sideways scrub. There are other systems, such as the **trailing arm** type (fig. 254), which also constrain the wheel to move vertically on bumps, and by analogy with the equal-length parallel wishbone arrangement, all such systems can be regarded as having a virtual swing arm of infinite length.

Apart from ensuring vertical movement on bumps, these infinite-length systems have another important virtue which can be understood by looking back at fig. 253c. This illustration shows you how to find the roll

fig. 253. Swing arm length. By replacing the simple swing-axle (a) with two links as in (b), the virtual swing arm length can be increased. In (c) it is increased still further and in (d) the equal-length parallel links give an infinitely long swing arm.

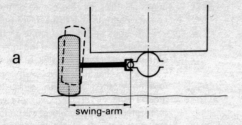

a

swing-arm

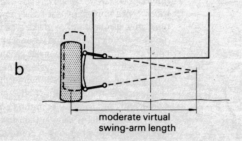

b

moderate virtual
swing-arm length

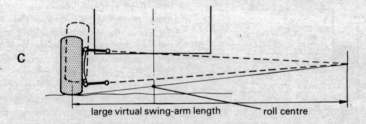

c

large virtual swing-arm length   roll centre

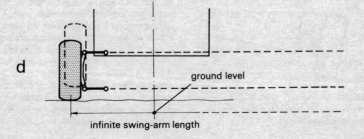

d

ground level

infinite swing-arm length

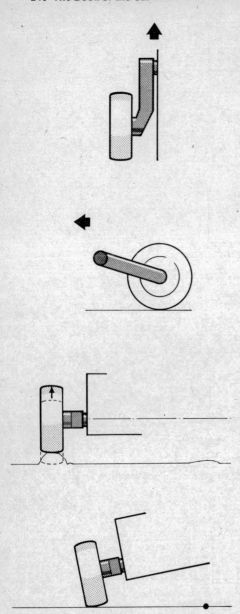

fig. 254. The trailing-arm system gives vertical wheel movement on bumps and thus has a virtual swing arm of infinite length.

centre: simply join the centre of the tyre's contact patch to the virtual pivot point, and – for reasons beyond the scope of this book – the roll centre is located at the intersection of this line and the centreline of the car. It is easy to see that as the pivot point moves off to infinity, the roll centre sinks towards ground level. All vertical movement systems, therefore, have ground-level roll centres and hence do not suffer from any jacking effect. Advantage number two.

Unfortunately, these disadvantages are outweighed by a disadvantage which is much more important, especially to a modern softly sprung car. For unlike a beam axle (fig. 255a) which keeps the wheels upright in corners, equal-length parallel wishbones, trailing arms and similar systems make the wheels lean outwards in corners (fig. 255b) at the same angle as the body, and this significantly reduces the cornering power of the tyres. A system allowing some camber change on bumps but less in corners is very much preferable.

A far superior arrangement, therefore, is the very widely used **unequal-length** system of converging wishbones, the uppermost of which is always the shorter (fig. 255c). By varying the angles at which the two wishbones are set and their degree of convergence, both the roll centre height and the virtual swing arm length can be varied. It should not be too long, otherwise the system approaches the equal-length parallel layout and there is too much positive camber in corners; about 1½ times the track is a typical value (fig. 256). The camber

fig. 255. Camber change in bump and roll: a, the beam axle prevents any camber change in roll (except under extremely hard cornering) but allows a little on bumps; b, equal-length /parallel wishbones (and trailing arms) impose vertical movements of the wheels over bumps but allow them to lean at the same angle as the body in corners; unequal length wishbones c, and MacPherson struts d, allow some camber change on bumps but can be designed to keep the heavily loaded outside wheel nearly upright during hard cornering.

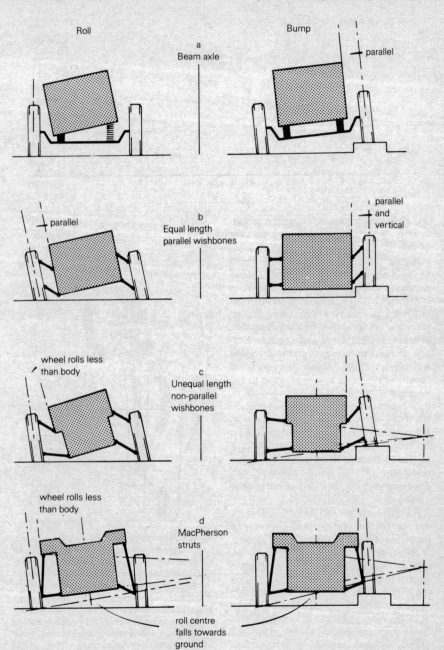

Roll

Bump

a
Beam axle

parallel

parallel

b
Equal length
parallel wishbones

parallel
and
vertical

wheel rolls less
than body

c
Unequal length
non-parallel
wishbones

wheel rolls less
than body

d
MacPherson
struts

roll centre
falls towards
ground

fig. 256. Typical double-wishbone geometry.

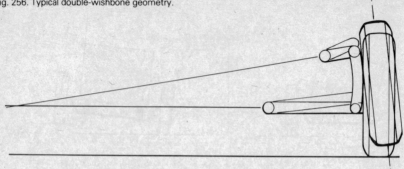

change, however, depends upon the relative lengths of the two links as well as their degree of convergence, and in a well-designed system these geometrical effects can be used to maintain the heavily loaded outside wheel not far from the upright when cornering hard. The wishbones can be rigid one-piece structures, when viewed in plan, but are often composed of transverse links or **track control arms** and separate fore-and-aft **reaction arms** which resist braking and driving forces. These reaction arms sometimes lie at quite a large angle to the longitudinal axis of the car and often terminate in large, soft rubber bushes to cushion the fore-and-aft impact of the tyre with bumps in the road which are responsible for the form of low-frequency road noise known as **bump-thump**. Suppressing the other basic type of road noise, high-frequency **road-roar** calls for more general attention to insulation.

Another popular and effective system, with similar but not identical geometry of movement to that of the wishbone system, is the MacPherson strut (fig. 255d), named after its inventor, a former chief engineer of Ford of Britain. In this arrangement (fig. 257) the bottom of the hub carrier is located by a wishbone as before, but the top is clamped to a telescopic damper strut which also forms the upper steering swivel – a ball joint forms the lower one. In its simplest and

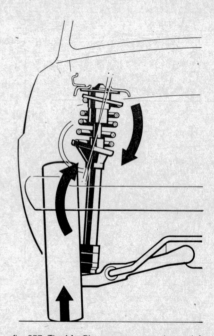

fig. 257. The MacPherson strut – another satisfactory suspension system with geometry similar but not identical to that of unequal-length wishbones. The upward reaction on the wheel (lowest arrow) due to the downward force exerted by the weight of the car creates a bending effect (lower curved arrow) in a MacPherson strut which tends to make it stick. Angling and /or offsetting the spring creates an opposite bending effect (upper curved arrow) which helps to keep the strut free.

original form, the system incorporated an anti-roll bar the ends of which formed the fore-and-aft reaction arms locating the bottoms of the hub carriers in conjunction with transverse links. Coil springs are usually employed, but torsion bars, actuated by the wishbones, may also be used.

One advantage of the MacPherson strut system is that it feeds the suspension loads into widely spaced and hence easily resisted points in the structure of the car. The spring and damper loads at the tops of the struts themselves, for example, can be fed into the bodyshell close to the very stiff scuttle area. Another advantage is that it frees the space in the engine compartment which would otherwise be occupied by the upper wishbones, and because very little obstruction is presented to drive shafts it is ideally suited to front-wheel drive. One disadvantage is that the bending loads applied to the strut may cause friction opposing suspension (i.e. telescopic) movements, though this can be reduced by using a coil spring which is both angled with respect to the strut and offset from its centreline as in fig. 257. Also the considerable offset between the wheel

centre and steering axis makes the system sensitive to unbalanced wheels.

Rear suspension systems

Some cars still retain live rear axles driven via open propeller shafts and located only by leaf springs, despite the roll-steer (fig. 258) inherent in such systems. Mounting the dampers inboard or at an angle to the vertical makes them act at a mechanical disadvantage with respect to disturbing forces which act directly on the wheels themselves. Thus the dampers should be mounted as upright and as outboard as possible, while they can help to control spring wind-up and hence tramp if one is mounted behind the axle and the other in front.

Further improvements in the location of

fig. 258. A live axle located only by leaf springs is susceptible to roll steer. Normally the outer spring flattens, pushing that end of the axle back, while the other spring becomes more curved, pulling the other end of the axle forwards. The resultant skewing movement creates the steering action.

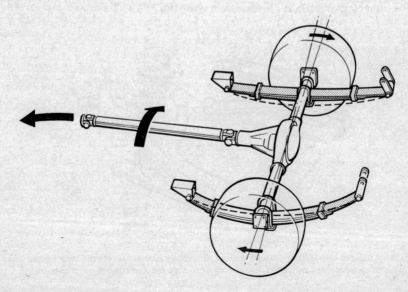

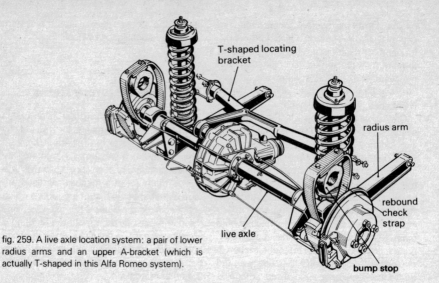

T-shaped locating bracket

radius arm

rebound check strap

live axle

bump stop

fig. 259. A live axle location system: a pair of lower radius arms and an upper A-bracket (which is actually T-shaped in this Alfa Romeo system).

the axle and control of its unwanted movements can be achieved by adding a pair of radius arms, but on most European cars with a rigid rear axle, coil springs are fitted which play no part in its location. This is provided with greater precision by a system of links. One of the simplest of these involves lower radius arms and an upper, central, wide-based **A-bracket** (Alfa Romeo use a bracket (fig. 259) which is T-shaped) which stops the axle from moving sideways as well as preventing it from twisting under driving or braking torques. Nowadays a **four link** system (fig. 260) is more popular: in place of the

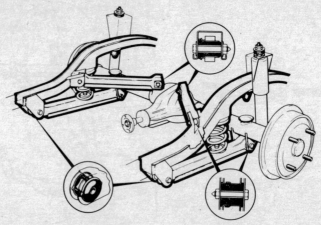

fig. 260. A four-link system: the two upper links are splayed to provide lateral as well as fore-and-aft location. Also shown are the rubber bushes used to suppress road noise as much as possible.

fig. 261. A five-link system for a live axle using a
Panhard rod to provide lateral location.

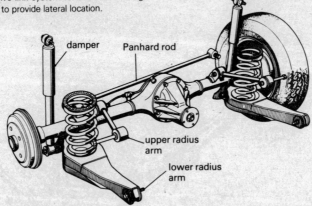

A-bracket are two upper links which are
angled outwards to give the required lateral
location.

But there is some fight between the
various arcs of movement, so a slightly
better system is one involving upper and
lower radius arms and some separate means
of lateral location such as a Panhard rod
(fig. 261). Alternatively, lateral location can
be provided by a **Watt linkage** (fig. 262)

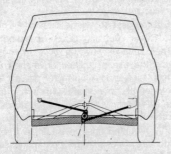

fig. 262. A Watt linkage allows vertical movement
while preventing horizontal displacement. Here it
is being used to give lateral location to the (shaded)
beam axle.

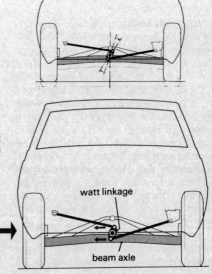

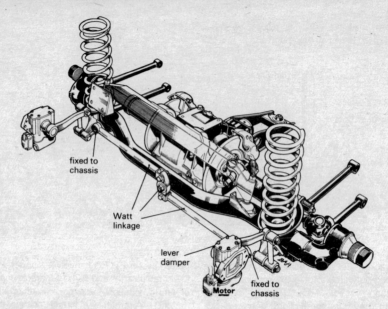

fixed to
chassis

Watt
linkage

lever
damper

Motor

fixed to
chassis

fig. 263. A de Dion axle keeps the wheels upright and has a low unsprung weight. This is the system fitted to the Aston Martin DBS in an early form with remote-controlled adjustable dampers. Radius arms locate the de Dion tube longitudinally; a Watt linkage does so laterally.

which allows vertical movement while preventing sideways displacement. Watt linkages can also be used longitudinally to provide fore-and-aft location.

A very much better form of rigid rear axle is the de Dion type, basically a cranked tube (fig. 263) connecting the two wheels which are linked to the final drive unit by a pair of swinging drive shafts which are designed to accept plunge (p. 195) and have universal joints at each end. Because the wheels are kept upright, very good cornering power and traction is possible, while the ride can be improved through the reduced unsprung weight, the inner halves of the drive shafts as well as the final drive unit becoming part of the sprung weight, and the brakes, too, if they are mounted inboard as they usually are in this arrangement. The axle tube can be

located in just the same way as a live axle – with upper and lower radius arms and a Panhard rod, say.

But the best-known de Dion axle – of the Mk I Rover 2000 and 3500 – is laid out in a rather unusual way (fig. 264). In order to avoid the use of splined drive-shaft joints which tend to lock up under power, it has fixed-length drive shafts which also locate the axle laterally. (A Panhard rod forms part of the system, but only to locate the very softly mounted final drive unit.) To accommodate the arcs of movement of these drive shafts, the axle tube is jointed, its two halves moving in and out with suspension deflection. Fore-and-aft location is provided by two Watt linkages, the forward arms of which also form the spring pans.

With even less unsprung weight the dead rear axle is a perfectly satisfactory suspension system if properly located and is widely used for front-wheel drive cars. It can be located by the same methods as are used for live and de Dion axles.

The simplest form of suspension giving complete independence to the driven

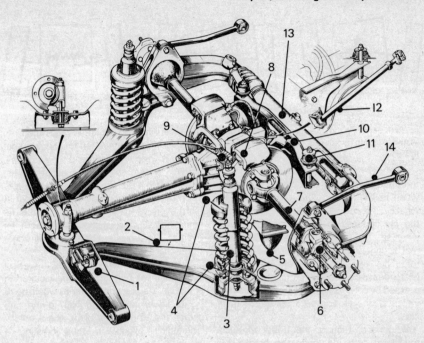

fig. 264. The Rover de Dion axle (the one illustrated here is the 3500 model's) has a telescoping joint and works in conjunction with fixed-length drive shafts, which provide lateral location. Fore-and-aft location is supplied by a Watt linkage at each end of the axle tube. 1, insulated forward subframe; 2, box section of lower links; 3, damper/spring assembly; 4, rubber spring cushion; 5, bump stop; 6, roller-bearing wheel hub; 7, fixed-length drive shaft; 8, brake caliper; 9, handbrake linkage; 10, rear subframe; 11, rear subframe rubber mounting; 12, insulated rear subframe from behind showing Panhard rod which locates it, limiting movement on mountings; 13, de Dion tube the two halves of which telescope within the rubber bellows gaiter. Just above this gaiter can be seen the far end of the subframe Panhard rod which is fixed to the car's frame.

wheels is the swing-axle type already discussed – which is highly unsatisfactory at the rear of a car. It is at its most dangerous when fitted to a rear-engined car and when

the driver suddenly slows down in a corner. A rear-mounted engine tends to make the rear wheels take most of the lateral weight transfer in corners; suddenly slowing down throws some weight on the front wheels, but lifts the tail, encouraging the jacking effect (fig. 265a).

One way of improving the cornering power of a swing-axle system, therefore, is by lowering its pivot points and hence the roll centre height with respect to the centre of gravity (fig. 265b). This not only reduces the jacking effect but also gives the wheels some negative camber, helping to keep the outside wheel more upright when cornering hard.

Another trick is to soften the rear springs, making the front springs take a larger share of the roll stiffness, reducing the cornering power of the front tyres to match the poor cornering power of the rear tyres and thus cutting down oversteer. But with soft springs the rear suspension may bottom, or reach

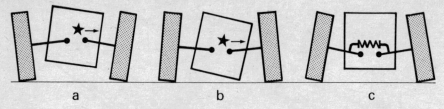

    a   b   c

fig. 265. Lowering the pivot point of a swing axle system helps to improve its cornering power – up to a point.

the limit of its travel too easily, especially when heavily loaded. One answer is to fit what can only be described as an **anti-bump bar** (as opposed to an anti-roll bar) which increases the vertical stiffness of the two rear springs (fig. 265c) but has no effect on roll. This was the approach adopted by Mercedes who used a central spring compressed by calipers linked to the swing-axles which at one time were a feature of their cars.

In general, though, the effect of such measures is to postpone the breakaway point to higher cornering speeds at which it becomes all the more sudden, making the car treacherous in its handling. Only in the (front-engined) Triumph Spitfire – and in post-1973 versions of it – is a swing axle system fairly well tamed by allowing all but one of the leaves of the transverse leaf spring – which is a feature of the arrangement – to tilt about a central pivot in corners and thus reduce roll stiffness.

Trailing arms are hardly ever used for driven wheels, but **semi-trailing link** systems are very common. In these the trail axis (fig. 266) lies at an angle to a transverse axis through the car, creating a system partway between pure trailing arms swinging longitudinally, and swing-axles swinging laterally. In this way the virtual swing arm length can be increased and the roll centre lowered, reducing camber change and jacking effect.

The system's big advantage is that it requires only two pivots lying slightly below

hub level which do not intrude too much into the valuable space needed for the rear seat and boot. Properly developed the semi-trailing link system can give excellent results, but although it is characterized by some toe-in on bump, it tends to create oversteer at high levels of cornering force and has its limitations – its virtual swing-arm length, for example, is typically no more than about three-quarters of the track.

Since a vertical or near vertical spring/damper unit is generally required in any case, a logical improvement would be to fix its lower telescoping half to the hub carrier and to give the pivot axis a wholly longitudinal alignment, thus creating a

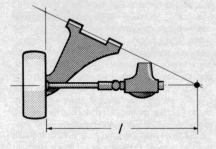

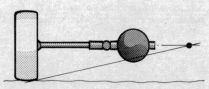

fig. 266. The semi-trailing link system, part swing-axle, part trailing arm; its virtual swing-arm length, 1, is usually about three-quarters of the track.

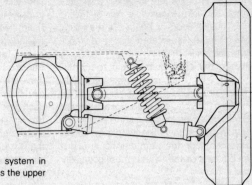

fig. 267. The Jaguar rear suspension system in which the fixed-length drive shaft forms the upper wishbone.

MacPherson strut. The geometry would be far superior and the wishbone introduced in this way could be even lower than the angled arm of a semi-trailing system, freeing more space. Rear MacPherson struts have been used with success by Lotus, Fiat and Lancia.

Another approach to good handling is through the use of a straightforward double wishbone system at the rear, and this is indeed a feature of many sports and high-performance cars in which space is not at a premium. An intelligent alternative is the **Jaguar** rear suspension (fig. 267) in which a fixed-length drive shaft effectively forms the upper wishbone.

In recent years a new form of independent suspension, related to the semi-trailing type and called the **torsion beam axle**, has been introduced for the undriven rear wheels of front-wheel drive cars. This configuration was developed by Audi from the rear suspension arrangement used by them for a long time in which a dead rear axle effectively forms its own anti-roll bar, being twisted by the radius arms fixed rigidly to each end. (A similar system is used by Alfa Romeo for the Alfasud.) The new system is an intermediate between this and the other extreme, so to

fig. 268. A typical torsion beam axle – this one is from the Vauxhall Astra. The important point to note is that the linking cross-beam is not co-axial with the pivot points but lies part-way between them and the wheels.

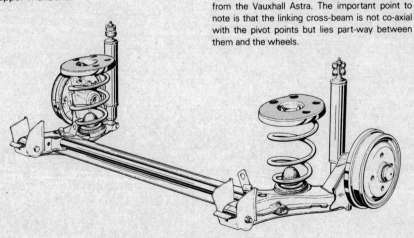

speak: an arrangement in which a straight anti-roll bar links together a pair of trailing arms. Thus for a torsion beam axle the linking cross-member is located some distance down the trailing arms, roughly half-way between the pivot bushes and the wheel hubs (fig. 268). The cross-member is usually an open-section channel, often U-shaped, so as to be relatively low in torsional stiffness and relatively high in lateral stiffness.

This system retains the simple mounting requirements of the semi-trailing arrangement but locates the wheels more positively and has better geometry in corners. The improved location comes from the cross-beam, which reduces the tendency of the trailing arms to bend when subjected to side-forces, thus minimizing 'toe-steer'. In roll the transverse torsion beam twists in a complex way, but to a first approximation its centre can be regarded as being fixed, allowing each half of the axle to behave as a semi-trailing arm, keeping the wheels more upright and giving better cornering power than would be possible with a pure trailing arm system.

eleven **The Brakes**

The safety of a car depends to a large extent upon the efficiency of the system used to slow and stop it – its braking system. This is basically a system of clamps through which the driver can impede the rotation of the wheels by pressing a pedal with his foot or pulling on a lever. To obtain the clamping effect, pads or shoes faced with a special friction material are forced against steel surfaces rotating with the wheels. The energy absorbed – which is very large even when stopping from moderate speeds – is dissipated as heat.

While the main or foot braking system is pedal operated, it must always be supplemented by a **handbrake** or **parking brake** which may be operated by a lever. The forces required are generally very much higher than those a driver is capable of exerting unaided, so the system which links the pedal or handbrake lever to the brakes themselves must incorporate considerable leverage.

Until the middle thirties the linkage

fig. 269. The pressure in a liquid acts equally in all directions.

systems used were almost always composed of rods or cables. But such systems all too easily gave unbalanced braking, a highly dangerous condition in which the brakes on one side pull more than those on the other side of the car, causing it to slew or skid. The varying friction in the numerous pivots involved, the difficulty of equalizing the effective lengths of the rods used or the tensions in the cables, made exact balance difficult to attain. And once attained it was soon lost, for these purely mechanical systems quickly went out of adjustment. They were also subject to considerable wear.

Hydraulic actuation

All modern braking systems, therefore, are hydraulic: in place of actuating rods they have columns of incompressible liquid in high-pressure tubing. These columns of liquid suffer little from friction and are inherently self-balancing because the pressure in an incompressible liquid acts equally in all directions (fig. 269). Consider, for example,

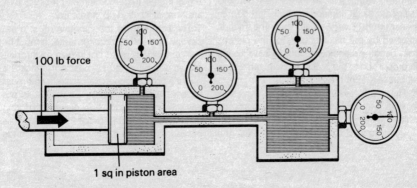

100 lb force

1 sq in piston area

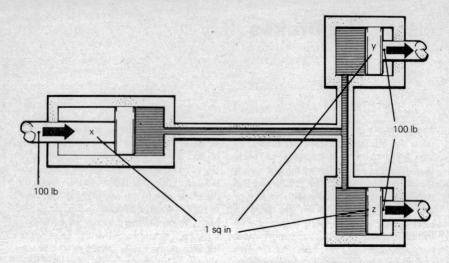

100 lb

100 lb

1 sq in

a system of tubes connected in a T-configuration and sealed by three pistons each 1 square inch in area (fig. 270). Now imagine a force of 100 lb to be applied to piston x. This creates a pressure in the hydraulic fluid of $100/1 = 100$ lb /sq in (pressure = force /area). But since the pressure acts equally in all directions it is also exerted without any change or reduction on pistons y and z. The force on each of these pistons, therefore, will also be 100 lb/sq in × 1sq in = 100 lb (pressure × area = force). Thus the force exerted by piston y (on the left-hand front brake, say) will be the same as that exerted by piston z (on the right-hand front brake, perhaps) so long as their areas are made the same to within a close tolerance – and this is not a difficult engineering task. If the force transmitted is very small, then the friction exerted by the flexible seals of the pistons may become significant, but this is negligible in proportion to the pressures exerted during all but very light braking.

The ready availability of hose which is flexible but does not expand significantly under the highest pressures reached – about 2400 lb/sq in (170 bar), neatly solves the

fig. 270. The force by *both* the two output pistons is equal to the force on the input piston when all have the same area.

problem of actuating the brakes of the steered front wheels. With purely mechanical systems, it is difficult to do this without steering movement affecting brake actuation, and without brake actuation tending to steer the wheels. Moreover the rigid pipes used to distribute the brake fluid about the chassis can follow the most tortuous paths without in any way diminishing the pressure transmitted. These pipes are made of high-quality steel, and, like the flexible hoses, have a burst pressure which is five to six times higher than the highest pressure they are normally called upon to carry.

The **brake fluid** they contain must meet several demanding requirements: it must be self-lubricating, must not freeze at temperatures down to −40°C, must not attack the metal pipes or rubber piston seals and must have a high boiling point so that it is not easily vaporized by the heat dissipated during braking. Conventional brake fluid is a mixture of vegetable-based polyglycol compounds

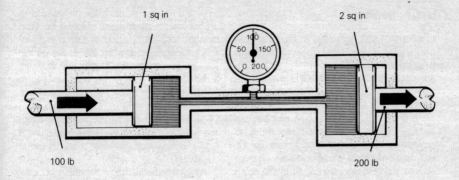

fig. 274. A hydraulic system can be given a mechanical advantage by making the area of the output piston greater than that of the input piston.

formulated to a rigidly controlled international specification. Its main disadvantage lies in the ease with which it absorbs water from the atmosphere and its sensitivity to this contaminant: the addition of no more than a small proportion of water is enough to reduce its boiling point greatly. Regular replacement is therefore recommended.

Another virtue of a hydraulic actuation system is the ease with which it can be made to give a leverage or mechanical advantage. Look again at the system of fig. 270 and you can already see that it gives some multiplication of the effort put in, for 100 lb is being transmitted yet two separate forces of 100 lb – a total of 200 lb – are being received. This is because the total area of the two receiving pistons is twice that of the transmitting piston.

But very large forces are required at each brake, so still greater multiplication is needed. This is partly obtained by making the area of the **master cylinder** – which contains the piston operated by the pedal – smaller than the areas of the **slave** or **wheel cylinders** which actuate the brakes (fig. 271). Suppose, for instance, that a force of 100 lb is exerted on a master cylinder with

an area of 1 sq in, and that the wheel cylinder has an area of 2 sq in. The pressure in the system will be 100/1 = 100 lb/sq in, but the force on the wheel cylinder will be 100×2 = 200 lb – double the size of the force on the master cylinder piston.

As for ordinary lever systems, of course, the snag is that the master cylinder piston has to be moved further than the wheel cylinder pistons. For the volume of fluid displaced by a given linear movement in the master cylinder is smaller than that in the slave cylinder. If there were only one wheel piston, the movement would simply be greater in proportion to the slave cylinder: master cylinder area ratio, but in a practical system this must be multiplied by the number of slave pistons, each of which increases the total volume of fluid to be displaced. Thus if the slave cylinder: master cylinder ratio is 3:2, there are eight slave pistons and each moves 1/20 inch, the total movement of the master cylinder piston will be 8×3/2×1/20 = 0.6 in. This will generally be multiplied roughly five times by the mechanical leverage in the pedal linkage, giving a total pedal travel of 3 in (7.5 cm).

Drum brakes

Until the 1950s, hydraulic systems of this sort were always used to actuate **drum brakes**. In their simplest form (fig. 272) these consist of a cylindrical **brake drum** encircling two semi-circular **brake shoes** carrying **brake linings** of friction material. The shoes pivot on the **backplate** at one end but can be forced outwards against the drum to provide the required braking torque by the two pistons of a slave cylinder. Return springs hold the shoes away from the drum when the brakes are not required.

When the brakes are not in operation it is important that each shoe be as close as possible to the drum without actually touching it, so some form of adjustment mechanism to compensate for the gradual wear of the linings is always provided. As fig. 273 shows, one type involves a wedge which can be moved away from the backplate by a screw, forcing the tips of the shoes further apart.

Rear drum brakes are often provided with an automatic adjustment mechanism. The system adopted by Lockheed for a brake of the type illustrated in fig. 273 involves the handbrake mechanism. This in turn involves a handbrake lever, and displacement of the handbrake lever away from the backplate forces the cross-strut A against the left-hand shoe, the tip of the handbrake lever using the right-hand shoe as a fulcrum at point B – and hence simultaneously forcing it against the drum.

When a self-adjusting mechanism is incorporated, however, the cross-strut is differently shaped (fig. 272) having an abutment C, against which the right-hand shoe is spring-loaded. The cross-strut also abuts at D against an adjuster plate pivoting on the left-hand shoe. It further terminates in a lug which protrudes through a hole in the adjuster plate. When the shoe movement is large due to lining wear, there is no longer any

fig. 272. A typical leading–trailing shoe drum brake.

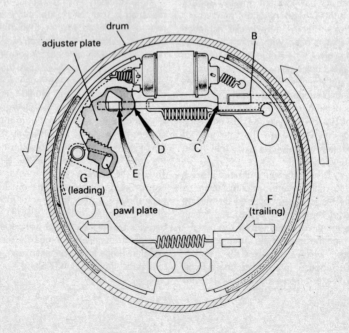

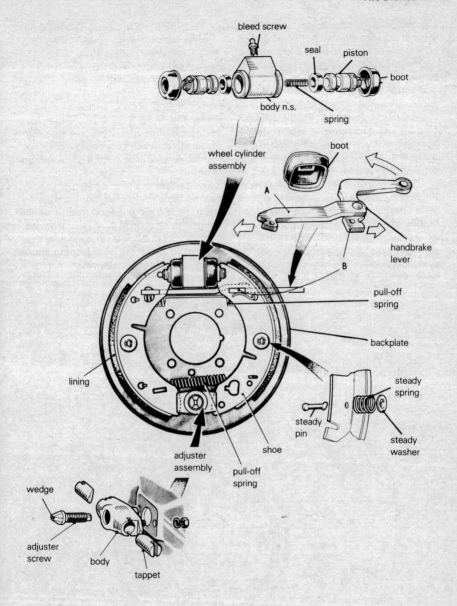

fig. 273. A drum brake with both manual and automatic adjustment mechanisms. The two shoes are operated by the double-ended cylinder at the top; the leading shoe benefits from a self-servo action, but the trailing shoe does not.

clearance between this lug and the adjuster plate at E. The adjuster plate is therefore pulled inward as the brakes are applied, slipping one tooth with respect to the spring-loaded pawl plate, moving closer to the cross-strut at D and thus eliminating the excess clearance.

It is also important that all air be excluded from the hydraulic system. If it is not, deflection of the brake pedal will compress air bubbles in the hydraulic fluid rather than actuating the brakes. At best this will give the brakes a spongy feel, at worst prevent them from working at all. Accordingly, each slave cylinder is provided with a small **bleed nipple** with which air can be purged from

fig. 274. A two-leading shoe brake with separate hydraulic cylinders at top and bottom. Both shoes benefit from a self-servo effect.

the system if a simple procedure is followed.

In the simple braking system of fig. 272, shoe F, called the **trailing shoe**, tends to be pushed away from the drum by the action of the drum's rotation and so gives a lower braking torque in relation to the applied force at the shoe tip. Shoe G, on the other hand, the **leading shoe**, tends to be pulled against the drum by its own rotation, creating a **self-servo** effect which considerably increases the decelerative torque for a given applied force.

This self-servo effect is generally used to improve the performance of the drum brakes fitted to the front wheels of a car – where they are called upon to do most of the work. Both shoes can be made to lead rather than trail by adopting the **two-leading shoe** arrangement (fig. 274) in which they are actuated at opposite ends. The braking

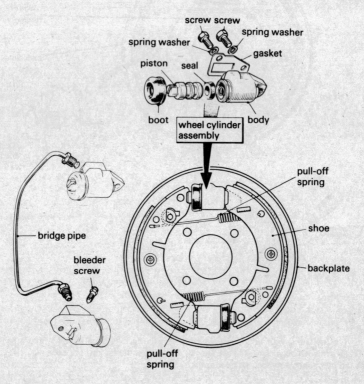

torque for a given applied force is then roughly double that of a leading–trailing shoe brake. The principle is carried a stage further in the **duo-servo** brake in which one shoe floats around the drum to act on the other. Once common at the front of American models, this system is now very rare. It is usual to retain the leading–trailing system for the rear brakes of a car, since both the two-leading shoe and duo-servo types are less efficient when stopping a reversing car.

The big disadvantage of the two-leading shoe type of drum brake is that its self-servo effect depends upon the coefficient of friction of its lining, and this in turn diminishes with rising temperature. The dependence is critical, moreover, a small reduction in coefficient of friction leading to a large reduction in the self-servo effect, greatly increasing the pedal force required to maintain a given deceleration. This is very important because the energy to be absorbed during braking can be very large – and is entirely dissipated as heat.

Fade

The resultant high temperatures common in braking affect both the drum and the lining, leading to the alarming reduction in efficiency known as **fade**. When this occurs the driver finds himself obtaining a progressively decreasing deceleration in return for a given pedal force – until in an extreme case the brakes become virtually inoperative.

The direct cause of fade is mostly the fall in coefficient of friction with rising temperature which is characteristic of the friction material. This is generally compounded of a special resin binder with a filler largely of asbestos (though alternative materials are increasingly being used nowadays), but sometimes additionally containing chopped metal wire to reduce wear and improve thermal conductivity. At high temperatures the resin melts in the outer layers of the lining, forming a temporary lubricant which reduces its coefficient of friction. This reduces the braking torque for a given applied force, even when it is directly proportional to the coefficient of friction, but the loss is much greater in a brake depending upon self-servo effect such as the two-leading shoe type.

But the indirect cause of fade is the inability of the brake to keep cool. Drum brakes are especially prone to fade, because the heat is generated within them and must pass to their outer surfaces before it can be dissipated to the ambient air. To make matters worse, moreover, the drum tends to expand away from the shoes – and remember that a very small increase in shoe displacement leads to a large increase in pedal travel. In extreme cases, too, so much heat may be generated that the hydraulic fluid in the actuating pipe boils (especially if it needs replacing and its water content has become too high) in which case the brakes will temporarily stop working altogether.

Disc brakes

For these reasons the front wheels of all but the cheapest, slowest or lightest cars are nowadays fitted with **disc brakes** (fig. 275) in which an exposed disc of steel or cast iron is clamped between two **pads** of friction material by a **caliper** mechanism. Disc brakes also suffer from fade, but to a much lesser extent. This is mostly because the heated surface of the disc is in direct contact with the surrounding air to which it can readily – and rapidly – dissipate its thermal energy. In addition, there is generally no self-servo effect in a disc brake so it does not have an accentuated sensitivity to changes in the coefficient of friction of its pads as their temperature rises. Finally, the only expansion which is significant occurs across the thickness of the disc; this is tiny and takes place towards the pads rather than away from them.

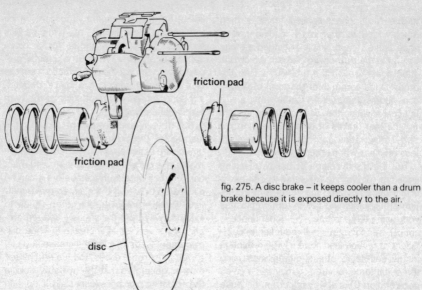

friction pad

friction pad

disc

fig. 275. A disc brake – it keeps cooler than a drum brake because it is exposed directly to the air.

The disc brake shown in fig. 275 is a common type, having a pair of hydraulic cylinders and pistons forcing pads on to opposite sides of the disc. In an alternative **floating caliper** type (fig. 276) there is a

simpler hydraulic system involving one piston only which forces a moving pad against the disc – and a fixed reaction pad against the other side through the sideways displacement of the caliper in grooves.

The front brakes of powerful cars are often provided with **ventilated discs**. A ventilated disc (fig. 277) runs at a lower temperature for

fig. 276. A floating caliper disc brake needs a single operating cylinder only.

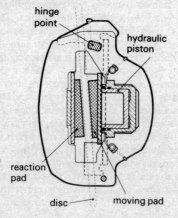

hinge point

hydraulic piston

reaction pad

disc

moving pad

fig. 277. Ventilated discs, used on high-performance cars, run cooler than solid discs.

a given heat input than a solid disc of the same diameter, having a larger thermal capacity as well as internal passages and vanes which draw in cooling air at its hub and centrifuge it out at its rim. Powerful cars, incidentally, may also have plain or ventilated disc brakes for the rear wheels as well as the front ones.

The vacuum servo

Reducing the pedal effort required to an acceptable level has never been an easy problem to solve. Even when drum brakes with their self-servo characteristics are fitted all round, it may be difficult to keep the pedal force within reasonable bounds – 50–75 lb (23–34 kg) for a 1g stop is a typical range these days – especially if the car is fast and heavy. And if disc brakes are fitted at the front (let alone at the rear as well) the

maximum force required may well be beyond the strength of most drivers.

Most modern braking systems are therefore fitted with a **vacuum servo** to augment the pedal force exerted by the driver. A typical vacuum servo consists (fig. 278a) of a large-diameter cylinder containing a piston sealed by a flexible diaphragm. Displacement of the brake pedal actuates a control valve so that atmospheric pressure acts on one side of this piston and inlet manifold vacuum on the other, the difference generating a force which adds to that exerted by the driver's foot.

When the brakes are off, inlet manifold vacuum is applied (fig. 278b) to the right-hand side of the piston as well as the left-hand side, through the air passage, the annular space around the control valve and the vacuum passage. But the control valve can move axially within the sleeve attached to the piston and is displaced to the left by initial pressure on the brake pedal. This displacement (fig. 278c) shuts off the inlet

fig. 278. A vacuum servo: a, construction; b, brakes off; c, brakes being applied; d, force stabilized.

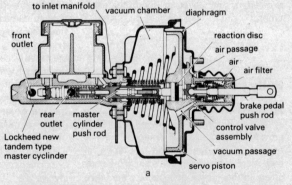

to inlet manifold · vacuum chamber · diaphragm

front outlet

reaction disc
air passage
air
air filter

brake pedal push rod

rear outlet · master cylinder push rod

control valve assembly

Lockheed new tandem type master cyclinder

vacuum passage

servo piston

a

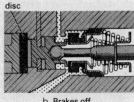

b Brakes off

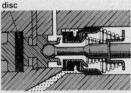

c Brakes fully applied

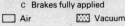

☐ Air   ▒ Vacuum

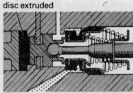

d Brakes held

manifold vacuum from the right-hand side of the piston and admits air to it via a filter surrounding the brake pedal pushrod. The resultant difference in pressure on the large-area piston creates a substantial force on the master cylinder pushrod which augments that exerted by the driver.

But the raised pressure in the master cylinder creates a backward reaction force causing a special rubber reaction disc to extrude into the space between it and the control valve. The movement of this disc (fig. 278d) starts to shut the control valve again, regulating the partial vacuum on the right-hand side of the piston, and it becomes fully closed when the backward reaction force exactly balances the forward force being exerted by the driver. Since this reaction force is always a fixed (but small) proportion of the force acting on the master cylinder piston, proper braking 'feel' is ensured, the driver receiving an accurate sensation of the braking effort exerted. The amount of assistance provided by the servo ranges from around 1½ times the force exerted by the driver to approximately 5 times.

Fully powered brakes

An alternative approach is to fit a braking system in which *all* the power required is provided by an external source. This has been the technique adopted by Citroën for their more expensive models since the early fifties. In these cars, deflection of the brake pedal – notable for its very short travel and rather sensitive action – merely compresses a spring, opening a control valve which admits high pressure hydraulic fluid to the brakes. The high-pressure fluid is provided by an engine-driven pump which does all the work (and also that associated with the self-levelling suspension system). A hydraulic accumulator – effectively a spring-loaded reservoir – maintains the pressure at a constant level and also provides a reserve of stored energy large enough for several stops if the pump should fail. A similar braking system has been used by Rolls-Royce since the introduction of the Silver Shadow in 1966.

The reduction in pedal travel possible with fully powered brakes allows the effective legroom available to the driver to be increased quite noticeably. As a result the BMW 7-Series cars have been given fully powered brakes, though in a system using the low-pressure hydraulic pump which also energizes the power steering. The reserve of stored energy available if the engine stops or the pump fails is considerably greater than that available from a vacuum servo system.

Circuit division

There is one sense in which a hydraulic braking system may be much more vulnerable to damage than a mechanical one: a fracture or significant leak *anywhere in the system* can – unless preventative measures are taken – lead to complete loss of braking *on all four wheels*. Pressing the pedal will not actuate the slave cylinders, but merely pump fluid out of the system through the fracture or leak. Accordingly, the hydraulic circuits of modern braking systems are very often divided into two separate parts so that a failure in one leaves the other still operative.

Isolation systems of this kind generally involve a **tandem master cylinder** (fig. 279a) which contains a free piston in addition to the one linked to the brake pedal. During normal braking this free piston is merely pushed to and fro by the hydraulic fluid, but if system A should fail (fig. 279b) it bottoms against the end of the cylinder, sealing the line which supplies it and allowing system B to work almost as normal. If

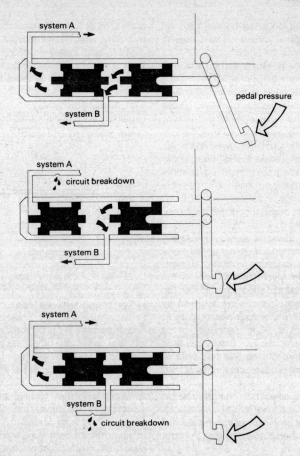

fig. 279. The tandem master cylinder: a, normal operation; b, system A fails; c, system B fails.

system B should fail, on the other hand, increased pedal travel (fig. 279c) brings the main piston into contact with the free piston, which then operates system A.

In the simplest form of division used, the rear brakes are actuated by system A and the front brakes by system B. If it is the rear brakes that fail, this system works well since the front brakes provide most of the braking effort in any case and so can usually manage a 0.75 g stop in the dry on their own without difficulty.

But if it is the front brakes that fail the situation is rather different. There is often a greater increase in pedal travel, and the rear brakes on their own are seldom capable of providing a deceleration of more than about 0.3 g. These two changes in combination may cause the driver to believe that the brakes have failed completely and thus to abandon pressing the pedal.

But even if he does not, there is a limit to the braking torque that can be applied before the rear wheels begin to lock and a car with locked rear wheels is directionally unstable (p. 270). This limit is determined by the load, and for a front-engined car the static load on the rear wheels is generally relatively small. Moreover it is reduced still more under braking when weight is transferred forwards (p. 269). The maximum deceleration possible by braking the rear wheels alone is therefore modest in most cases, though slightly higher for rear-engined cars.

For these reasons a straightforward front/rear circuit division is not a very satisfactory safety measure. A better arrangement is one in which the efficiency of the front brakes is little affected whatever the mode of failure. This can be achieved by fitting **four-piston** or **four-pot** calipers to the front brakes. One hydraulic circuit (fig. 280) operates the rear brakes and both front brakes through the first two pairs of pistons, while the other actuates both front brakes only through the second set of pistons which are larger than the other set to increase the mechanical advantage available. The first circuit gives normal braking with full efficiency and the second, acting on the front

brakes, gives reduced efficiency, but a level of braking which is still acceptable. An alternative 'L-split' system involving two circuits each actuating both front brakes and one rear brake is sometimes used, but has little advantage.

A cheaper alternative to this complex and expensive arrangement is the common diagonally split system (fig. 281) in which one

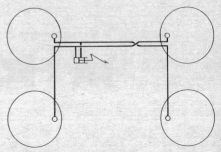

fig. 281. Diagonally divided brakes.

circuit operates the right front brake and the left rear, while the other operates the left front brake and the right rear. Braking with one circuit failed does create a tendency to slew the car sideways, but this can be corrected with the steering, and it is considered that the driver still has a better chance of retaining control and avoiding an accident than if both front brakes fail completely as might happen with a front/rear circuit division. The slewing tendency can be diminished by the negative offset steering system described in Chapter 9 (p. 224).

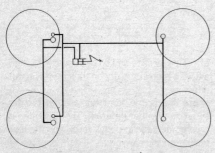

fig. 280. Twin-circuit using four-pot calipers; one circuit actuates all four brakes, the other actuates the front brakes only.

The handbrake

All modern cars must by law be fitted with a parking brake, and this is generally operated by a lever or pullout handle. In American cars, however, the parking brake is usually operated by an additional pedal with a ratchet mechanism which automatically locks it and is released by pulling a knob under the facia.

The hand or parking brake is nearly always cable operated and nearly always works on the rear wheels. It is not difficult to devise a system of levers for drum brakes which will give a high mechanical advantage and a satisfactory parking or emergency deceleration in conjunction with the self-servo effect available. With disc brakes the problem is much less easily solved, which is one reason why drum rear brakes are generally retained for all but the fastest and heaviest of cars. In some cases the handbrake acts directly on the main set of pads, but often there is an auxiliary caliper which forces a small additional pair of pads against the disc. Sometimes a small auxiliary drum brake is incorporated into the centre of the disc.

Whether the handbrake acts on discs or drums, it is far more effective on the front wheels than on the rear ones, but unhappily front-wheel handbrakes are rare.

fig. 282. The forward reaction on the body under braking creates dive.

Weight transfer

Under braking the tyres are subjected to the backward force which imparts the deceleration, but there is also a forward reaction force on the car (fig. 282) due to its own inertia which tries to keep it moving. Exactly the same kind of inertia force acts on the occupants of the car, throwing them forward when it slows down. Since the inertia or mass of the car acts at its centre of gravity, and since this lies above ground level, the forward reaction force creates a moment or leverage which tries to lift the rear wheels from the ground and to press the front wheels into it. Effectively, a weight is removed from the rear wheels and added to the front ones. For any value of deceleration this **weight transfer** is larger in cars with high centres of gravity than those with low ones, and larger in cars with short wheelbases than those with long ones. The centre of gravity height determines the length of the lever available to the inertia force, while the wheelbase or horizontal distance separating the two pairs of wheels determines the opposing leverage they can exert.

But for a vehicle of given dimensions, the harder the braking the greater the weight transfer. The maximum possible deceleration, however, in turn depends upon the coefficient of friction. On a polished wet surface, for example, the coefficient of friction could be no more than 0.2, allowing a

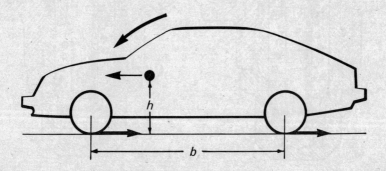

maximum deceleration of only 0.2 g. Under such conditions the front/rear 55/45 static weight distribution of a car with a centre of gravity say, 22.5 in above the ground (fig. 282 again) becomes a dynamic weight distribution of 61/39. This is not a large change, but for the same car braking hard at 0.8 g on a dry surface the dynamic front/rear weight distribution becomes 79/21.

These changes have an important influence on braking because the maximum frictional force sustainable by a tyre before sliding is determined by the load on it. There is a danger, therefore, that too much braking effort may be applied to the lightly loaded pair of wheels which will then lock and slide. And when a wheel is locked it loses all ability to steer and provides significantly less deceleration on wet or slippery surfaces, though there is not much change in the dry. If the front wheels lock, their lost capacity to steer makes the car slide forward in a straight line. But if the rear wheels lock the car becomes directionally unstable, tends to slew to one side and may

easily spin round – a considerably more dangerous condition. Thus it is important that the front wheels always lock before the rear ones.

For a front-engined car the easy solution would be to make the front/rear division of braking effort equal to the dynamic front/rear weight distribution under the heaviest braking possible – usually taken to be at 1 g for a road car – which would be about 80/20 for a car with 55 per cent of its weight on its front wheels statically. This would mean that at any deceleration up to the maximum possible there would never be too much braking effort on the rear wheels which

fig. 283. A spring-loaded pressure-reducing valve: under moderate braking pressure (*left*) the fluid entering at A has free access to the rear brakes via band C, the ball valve being held off its seat by the taper plunger. Higher pressures, acting on the head of the plunger, force it downwards (*right*) trapping the pressure in the rear lines. Heavier braking opens the valve again, but a new rear pressure limit is re-established.

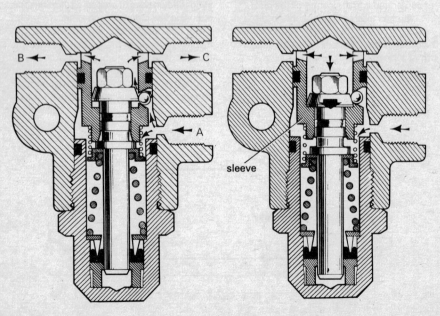

sleeve

would therefore never lock prematurely – that is, before the front wheels.

Unfortunately, with such a division the rear brakes would hardly do any work at all, leading to overloading and excessive wear of the front brakes. For most front-engined/rear-wheel drive cars, therefore, the division of braking effort is fixed at some compromise ratio – such as 70/30 which distributes more of the work to the rear brakes without much increasing the risk of rear-wheel lock-up under heavy braking.

This may not be enough, however, for a front-wheel drive car with a 60/40 front/rear static weight distribution which can change to 90/10 under heavy braking. Many front-wheel drive cars, therefore, are fitted with a spring-loaded **pressure-limiting valve** (fig. 283) which limits the pressure in the rear brake circuit to a predetermined level. In a more sophisticated form of pressure-limiting valve, the limitation is controlled by the deceleration itself through a ball-and-ramp mechanism.

Another factor to be taken into account, though, is the variation in load with the presence or absence of passengers and luggage. Nose-heavy front-wheel drive cars are again very sensitive to this: the proportion of the total weight carried by the rear wheels changes a great deal more than that carried by the front wheels as the car is loaded up, especially with rear-seat passengers and luggage. Hence the development of the **load-sensitive pressure-relief valve** (fig. 284) controlled by a spring-loaded link between the chassis and the rear suspension which limits the pressure to the back brakes in proportion to the load upon them as measured by the deflection of the rear springs.

A rear-engined car, with a 40/60 front/rear static weight distribution is a different matter. Under light braking the rearward weight bias remains, but under heavy braking there is a forward weight bias as before, and it is with this that the apportionment of front/rear braking effort must conform. The danger then is of premature *front-wheel* lock-up on slippery surfaces, and no pressure-relief valve can be fitted to avoid this without seriously prejudicing the car's ultimate stopping power in the dry.

It would be a mistake to conclude from all

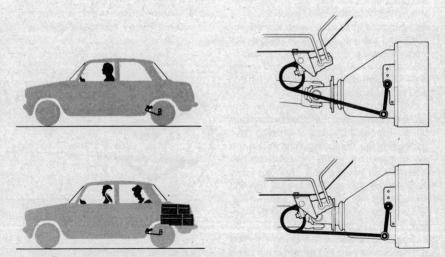

fig. 284. A load-sensitive pressure-reducing valve: (*top*), unladen; (*bottom*), laden.

this – as many do – that the braking of a nose-heavy front-wheel drive car is inherently inferior to that of a car with more weight on its rear wheels. For tyres do not behave in the same way under braking as they do when cornering. Under braking, the maximum frictional force available is near enough exactly proportional to load, so the increase in maximum friction from the front wheels under weight transfer compensates almost entirely for that lost by the rear wheels. Thus the braking efficiency of a car with a 90/10 dynamic weight distribution will be little different from that of a car with a 50/50 dynamic weight distribution – so long as the rear wheels are prevented from locking prematurely.

Anti-dive

When weight is transferred under braking, the front springs are compressed and the rear springs extended, allowing the tail of the car to rise and the nose to dip or dive. This is not only uncomfortable for the driver and passengers but may also have adverse affects on handling and roadholding by deflecting the front suspension towards full bump and the rear suspension towards full droop. Accordingly, many modern cars – especially luxurious models with soft springing – have **anti-dive** characteristics built into their front suspension systems.

One method by which dive can be cancelled is most easily understood by considering the Citroën 2 CV, the only car to have leading arm front suspension and trailing arm rear suspension (fig. 285). For such a car two effects come into play under braking: firstly the inertia of the car acts forwards, levering the body upwards about the front wheel. Secondly, this action is augmented by brake torque which at the front tends to twist the leading arm anticlockwise and upwards and at the rear twists the trailing arm in the same

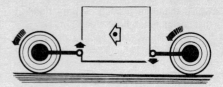

fig. 285. The basic anti-dive principle – the front of the body tries to rise rather than fall under heavy braking.

direction but downwards. The overall result is to make the front of the car rise and the rear fall – the reverse of what normally happens.

In modern cars with double wishbone front suspension these effects can be harnessed by inclining the pivot axes of the two wishbones towards each other in side view to create a virtual leading arm (fig. 286). MacPherson struts can be given the same geometry and so can live axles through a suitable arrangement of torque arms. It is possible to cancel dive completely in this way but to avoid the large changes in castor angle inherent in such an arrangement, it is usual to limit the cancellation to 50–60 per cent. If the rear wishbones or links are similarly inclined to form a virtual trailing arm, this will not merely contribute to the anti-

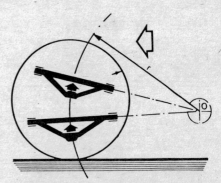

fig. 286. By making the wishbone axes converge in side view, a virtual leading arm is created with which dive may be partially or wholly cancelled.

dive action but also creates an **anti-squat** effect or a resistance to the fall of the rear of the car under acceleration.

Dive cancellation can also be achieved by inclining both wishbones forward at the same angle in side view. This creates a 'ramp' (fig. 287) up which the front of the car slides under braking, just as it would, for example, with Morgan-type **sliding pillar** front suspension, if this were inclined forwards. A similar backward inclination of the rear suspension links contributes to the anti-dive action and creates an anti-squat effect.

Anti-lock brakes

Skidding is a major source of accidents and very often the skid is provoked by panic braking which locks the wheels of the car. As already mentioned, locked wheels lose all ability to steer, and on wet or slippery surfaces generally provide significantly less deceleration than rotating ones.

It is possible, however – though not easy – to retain both steering control and a reason-able measure of deceleration when simultaneously swerving and braking in an emergency. This can be done by adopting a technique known as **cadence braking** which basically means rhythmically pumping the brake pedal rather than maintaining a continuous pressure on it. Each time it is depressed, the wheels lock, providing some braking but losing the ability to steer; each time it is released they no longer slow the car but allow it to be steered again.

The technique, under certain conditions, may also take advantage of the way the deceleration varies with the degree of wheel locking. Experiments have established that the deceleration on a wet or slippery surface rises to a maximum (fig. 288) when there is roughly 15 per cent slip between the tyres and the road, but falls to a minimum at 100 per cent slip which is when the wheel is completely locked. Thus properly timed cadence braking may pass the car through a succession of decelerative peaks to give a higher mean value of deceleration than if the wheels were locked. The difference between this **peak coefficient of friction** and the **locked-wheel coefficient** depends

fig. 287. Dive cancellation can also be achieved by inclining both wishbones forward at the same angle in plan view.

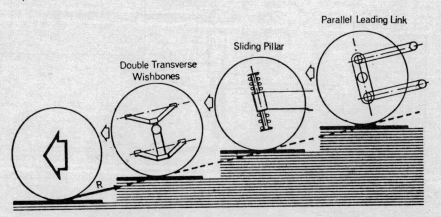

Parallel Leading Link

Sliding Pillar

Double Transverse Wishbones

R

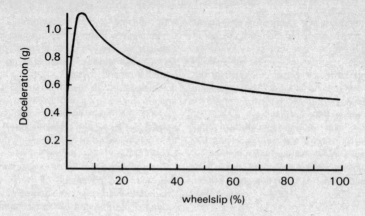

fig. 288. Deceleration on a wet or slippery surface rises to a maximum at around 15 per cent slip.

fig. 289. The antilock brake principle: when the wheel starts to lock its angular deceleration is registered in the electronic computer which causes the brakes to be released; this removes the signal so they are reapplied again. The cycle is repeated several times a second.

upon the tyres and the surface, but it is usually significant except in the dry.

A good deal of effort, therefore, has gone into the development of **antilock braking** systems which are designed to exploit it. The basic purpose of all such systems is to preserve *directional stability and maintain steering control under panic braking*, though in most cases they will also significantly reduce straight-line stopping distances on slippery surfaces.

A modern antilock braking system gen-

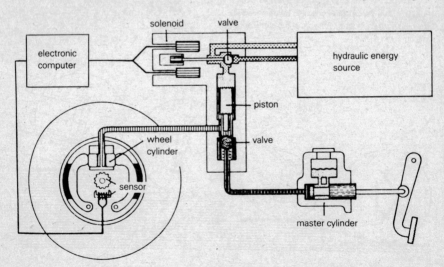

erally incorporates (fig. 289) a toothed wheel sensor which generates an electrical signal proportional to wheel speed. This is passed to an electronic processor which detects the deceleration of the wheel as it begins to lock under heavy braking and generates an output signal controlling a solenoid or other device which reduces the hydraulic pressure in the brake line. The reduction frees the wheel, but it begins to lock again, since the driver is still pressing the brake pedal. Again the system acts to prevent the wheel from locking, and the cycle is repeated several times a second. A well-designed system working on all four wheels will make possible a remarkable combination of hard braking and steering, and will significantly reduce straight-line stopping distances on slippery surfaces.

While the braking pressure is easily relieved, it is not so easily restored. Most antilock systems therefore require for this restoration an external source of energy such as a vacuum servo or small engine-drive hydraulic pump. But in one ingenious, but still experimental, system, devised by Mullard, the brake pressure is restored by the rotation of the wheel itself, which drives a small cam-operated pump integrated into the brake caliper.

Unfortunately, while many such antilock braking systems have been developed, almost all are still experimental and very few are in production. The Jensen FF, built in very small numbers, was at one time the only European production car to be fitted with an antilock device – the Dunlop Maxaret system which worked in conjunction with a central differential. It used a mechanical sensor in the form of a spring-loaded flywheel which overran the wheel as it decelerated.

But the more advanced electronically controlled ABS antilock systems manufactured by Bosch became available for Mercedes cars in 1978 and has since been adopted by BMW and other manufacturers.

twelve **Styling, Structure and Safety**

Styling

Some people believe that a truly 'functional' object – one that is supremely fitted to its purpose – needs no styling or conscious shaping of its own form to make it pleasing to look at, still less any added decoration. The Mini, for example, is often hailed as a highly functional car, which, if not exactly beautiful, has a certain 'rightness' about its appearance.

At the other extreme are those who care nothing about the location of the engine or the nature of the suspension and look only for a pleasing and graceful shape – for which they are sometimes prepared to sacrifice a good deal of vision, interior space and exterior compactness. Sensible motorists take a middle view, but there is no doubt that everyone, consciously or unconsciously, cares about the appearance of their motorcar, and it is to satisfy these feelings that the stylist exists.

Since beauty is a personal thing, so much a matter of opinion, it is impossible to define good or bad styling, but it *is* possible to describe some of the methods and influences and to show how results may interact with the three most important functional or engineering factors: space, vision and aerodynamics. The best way to study the methods is to begin by examining what happens when a large company such as Ford or General Motors decides to launch a new car.

The object is always to meet the demands of a particular group of people who may be the buyers or prospective buyers of an existing model which is to be replaced, or may be an entirely new class of motorist with needs which are not being satisfied by any manufacturer. The first task, therefore, is to define exactly the size and type of car which is to be built, and this is usually done by a product planning committee which includes the company's most senior managers.

Obviously, the first matter to be decided is the size and price class of the car to be introduced – is it to be a large saloon of the Ford Granada type, for instance, or a 'supermini' like the Fiat 127, Volkswagen Polo or BL Metro? This subject in itself is much more complex than the layman might suppose: most manufacturers have their own quite involved classification systems by which they define every conceivable size and type of car – existing or hypothetical.

Next, the product planning committee considers how best to provide the proposed new car with the necessary mechanical assemblies. Here it is nearly always constrained to use existing components, slightly modified at most, due to the immense cost of tooling up for such major assemblies as engines or gearboxes. Thus a company already heavily committed, say, to front-wheel drive for their existing models, will tend to adopt that arrangement for any new one – all-new cars, designed from a clean sheet of paper, are very rare. In this way, the power unit, transmission system and type of suspension to be used for the new car soon become very precisely defined.

The next question to be resolved is the type of body to be chosen. Should the new model be a hatchback, perhaps, or a 'three-box' saloon with a protruding boot? It may be concluded, for example, that although all the existing cars in a certain group are conventional three-box saloons, a new

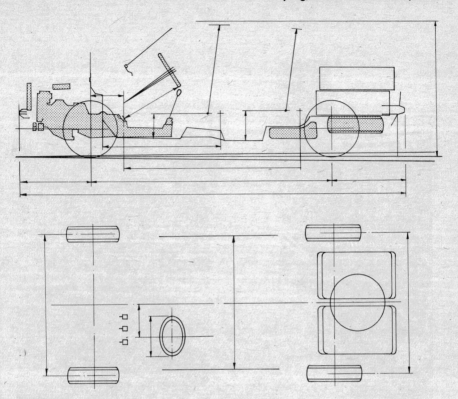

fig. 290. Starting point for the stylist: the general mechanical layout and a set of dimensions that must be adhered to. This is the package drawing of the Alfasud.

hatchback would have a greater chance of success in that class of car than another saloon.

Once this decision has been made, it will generally become a top-level directive, and it will be the job of the engineers and stylists to design the best possible car of the sort the directors of their company have finally decreed shall be built. By that time the length, width, height, number of seats, legroom, headroom, engine-compartment size and luggage space will all have become precisely defined, allowing a detailed 'package' drawing (fig. 290) to be produced.

The chief stylist will have given advice at each of these stages, but until the late seventies, it would not have been until this point that his major task began: to design a pleasing metal suit of clothes, as it were, around the package drawing of the projected new car. But the achievement of a very low wind resistance to help reduce fuel consumption has become so very important that the procedure may now be rather different. Scale models of various proposed cars will probably be subjected to wind-tunnel tests at an early stage, and the shape favoured by the product planners and stylists could well be rejected by the engineers if its drag coefficient (p. 177) proves too high.

When general agreement on a promising approach has been reached, the chief stylist and his staff will then prepare a set of

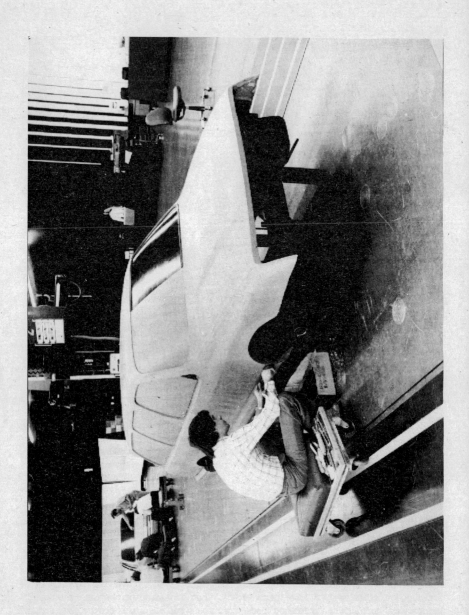

fig. 291. A full-sized clay styling buck.

drawings or paintings of possible designs which are submitted to the product planning committee for their approval. The chosen design is then turned into a three-dimensional model, probably of about 3/8 scale, composed of a wooden or aluminium honeycomb framework covered with clay. This model, known as a **clay styling buck**, is then painstakingly refined, both functionally and aesthetically, by a group of stylists, aerodynamicists, body engineers and other specialists working together.

From the final results of all this work a full-sized styling buck is created (fig 291). Often a model of the interior, called a **seating buck**, is also made, from which legroom, headroom, control location, etc., can be checked. When everything has been agreed, the measurements of the finalized styling buck are taken and recorded – often, these days, using a high-precision computerized measurement 'bridge' with sensitive probes which automatically works out the coordinates of hundreds of datum points on the model's surface. These measurements are used to construct – with the help of highly skilled craftsmen – the hand-built metal bodies of the first running prototypes.

A suitable platform chassis will by then have been developed, which when welded to the body forms a structure of the required rigidity and strength. Anything between four and twelve of these prototypes are built. They are run for tens, often hundreds of thousands of miles of testing, in conditions ranging from the arctic to the tropical, during which time faults are rectified and refinements introduced until the basic design is pronounced fit for the public.

Sometimes at this stage one of the prototypes is shown anonymously to selected members of the public – or perhaps just photographs of it – to gauge their reaction to various styling features. The information gained at these **clinics** is then fed back to the stylists and product planners who may modify the bodywork in consequence.

But there comes a time when the design

of the basic prototype must be 'frozen' so that the tools and dies necessary for mass production can be constructed. When this has been done, anything up to a hundred **pre-production prototypes** are built from the production tools and dies by methods as close as possible to those which are to be used in production. This is an anxious time for the engineer, since all too often a car built on the production tools is not quite the same as the original hand-built prototypes. This is when doors and windows are found to fit poorly and when unwanted vibrations appear. Further last-minute modifications are often required. But when all seems well the car finally goes into production and is put on sale. Unfortunately the general public has a genius for discovering faults which the engineers overlooked.

In smaller companies the process is likely to be much less elaborate: the product planning committee is likely to consist only of the managing director, the chief engineer and the stylist. A full-sized clay model may still be constructed – it can be used to form a mould for a glass-fibre body – but a quarter-scale model may be built instead, or there may be no model at all. Several of Jaguar's masterpieces, for example, were built in prototype form by skilled men under the direction and discerning eye of Sir William Lyons, founder of the company.

Small companies generally depend upon the services of freelance stylists such as William Towns, responsible for the body design of the current Aston Martin and the new Lagonda, or of independent styling firms like Ogle Design, which, led by Tom Karen, shaped the Reliant Scimitar.

In Britain, regrettably, there are few such individuals and companies, but in the Turin area of northern Italy there are several. The biggest of these are the three great styling houses of today, Bertone, Pininfarina and Ital Design, the first two of which have extensive manufacturing facilities, building the bodies of such low-volume cars as the Fiat X1/9 and the Peugeot 504 coupe. In these companies sketches can be converted into chalk lines on the workshop wall, and then into a complete working car, in a matter of weeks — though usually the chassis and running gear are provided.

Influences

Until quite recently, styling was basically a very fashion-conscious business, and was at its most important in the States, where frequent bodywork and trim changes were used to maintain sales rather than the technological improvements more favoured in Europe. The stylists of the big three companies, General Motors, Ford and Chrysler, therefore have a profound influence on automotive body design all over the world. Nor is this necessarily anything to sneer at, for their products are frequently striking and handsome and have usually been purged of the grosser impracticalities.

The influence which the big American companies exerted through their ordinary products in a straightforward way was augmented from time to time by supposedly futuristic **styling exercises**. Generally, though, the styling exercises created by the great Italian designers are considered to have more imagination and audacity. Often these are so wildly impractical as to be virtually undriveable, with minimal legroom, near-horizontal windscreens and no visibility to the rear at all. But some aspect of their proportions or detailing often finds its way into the design of ordinary production cars a few years later. And sometimes the styling exercise itself becomes, with modifications, a road-going car — such as the Bertone Stratos which became a rally winner when taken over by Lancia and the Ital Design Esperit which became the Lotus Esprit.

This last design was the creation of Giorgetto Giugiaro, founder and chief of Ital Design, who was undoubtedly the most influential stylist of the seventies. His crea-

tions include the bodies of the Alfa Romeo Alfasud and Alfetta GTV, the (first) Volkswagen Golf and Scirocco and the Maserati Merak. The clean, angular lines of his shapes in that period were widely admired and copied, but he has since adopted a more rounded style to conform to the aerodynamic requirements of today.

Sometimes it is not a styling exercise or stylist which exerts the influence but a particular car or some feature of it. Porsche's removable Targa Top, for instance, is now accepted as being an intelligent way of providing weather protection but allowing open-air motoring if required. It bridges the gap between the windscreen and the **rollover hoop**, which brings modern standards of safety to the sports car without spoiling its appearance or making it less fun to drive. One of the most influential cars of all was the Renault 16, part saloon, part estate car, which launched the **hatchback** revolution.

Packaging

All too easily, however, a beautiful or flamboyant shape can be extravagant in metal, wasteful of interior space, difficult to see out of and hard to push through the air. Nowadays, therefore, the emphasis is increasingly on the functional aspect of body design, one of the most important of which is the optimum utilization of interior space. This, however, depends not only upon sensible styling but also upon the layout of the mechanical components.

The various ways of **packaging** people and luggage within a car of a given type and size have already been discussed at some length in Chapter 1 (p. 19) so it is only necessary to summarize the main conclusion here: that front-wheel drive with a transverse engine is the most space-saving layout so far evolved. The concept was established by Sir Alec Issigonis with the most compact and space-efficient car of all, the Mini, which will accommodate four adults and a little luggage, yet is only (in its original form) 10 ft (3.05 m) long. Other designers, while admiring the feat, questioned the value of a car so small, and created a new breed of similar but larger models, generally about 11 ft 6 in (3.5 m) long, such as the Fiat 127, the Volkswagen Polo and the Ford Fiesta. But the advantage of a transversely mounted engine forming a compact propulsion unit with a transmission system driving to the front wheels is just as important to these 'Superminis' as they are now being called. A well-designed example such as the Fiat 127 is significantly superior in boot space and rear-seat legroom to rival cars of the same class having front engines driving to live rear axles. As the size of the car increases the value of the Issigonis layout diminishes, but nevertheless the abundance of front and rear legroom in large cars like the Leyland Princess/Ambassador and the Citroën CX, in relation both to their overall length and to the corresponding dimensions of competitive cars with longitudinally aligned engines and rear-wheel drive, is very striking.

The value of a car, though, depends not merely upon the extent of its interior space but also upon the ease with which it can be used and the variety of purposes to which it can be put. From this realization has sprung the popularity of the hatchback body, which if designed well, combines most of the versatility and load-carrying capacity of a good estate car with the appearance of a well-styled saloon. With its rear seat upright and a cover concealing the contents of its boot it should be stylish enough for the most formal of occasions, but with its rear seat folded forward it should be able to carry bulky objects such as refrigerators or chairs which cannot readily be transported in a conventionally styled car. To fulfil such a role properly, the tailgate should reach to the floor so that there is no lip over which luggage must be lifted. Unfortunately the concept is being given a bad name by some poor designs in which the tailgate stops some way short of the floor and the boot space with the rear seat in use is less than that of a car with the same overall length and a conventional **three-box** shape composed of a bonnet, passenger compartment and separate, protruding boot.

Vision

Another important factor is vision. Does, for example, the car have a low waistline? That is, are the bottoms of the windows low in relation to your eyes when you sit in the driver's seat? A car with a high waistline tends to feel dark and claustrophobic inside and is difficult to aim through small gaps when parking or in heavy traffic. If the car is wide and the side furthest from the driver is partially or wholly concealed by a high scuttle, this difficulty is increased. When the waistline is low, on the other hand, the driver is given a commanding view of the road which inspires confidence in the car and reduces fatigue in poor weather.

A low waistline almost inevitably means a generous area of glass, but this does not automatically guarantee good vision. The windscreen pillars should be slender, located well to each side of the car and as far away from the driver as possible – the closer they are the more of his or her view they will obstruct, in a region vital when making turns or approaching roundabouts. Although front quarterlights are still popular in cars without air conditioning, when used in very hot climates their elimination reduces visual clutter to the side in the area immediately behind the windscreen pillars – and well-designed modern fresh-air vents can supply an equally cooling breeze without introducing wind noise. The other pillars should also be as slender as is compatible with adequate roll-over strength (p. 294) to give a clear view directly to the rear – and the interior mirror should be as large as possible and as close to the driver as possible without obstructing the forward view. The three-quarter rear view, important at angled T-junctions, is often a weakness; particularly in mid-engined sports cars. If head restraints are fitted (p. 297) these should be of the skeleton type.

Good vision means not only seeing the road and the other cars around you with ease, but also having a clear view of the extremities of your own car. Bulging, easily scraped sides, or a bonnet that falls out of sight are therefore not to be recommended. Ideally, all four corners of the car should be visible from the driver's seat, a condition most easy to achieve with a three-box body shape and conventional, rectangular styling. But the ability to see the two rear corners is not so important in a **two-box** car (one with a boot that does not protrude) if the tip of its tail extends little beyond the rear window.

Even when all these objectives have been met, there remain some further important factors. The windscreen wipers, for instance, must wipe an area of the screen which is not only generous but comes close to the pillar on the driver's side. The heater must be capable of directing a large volume of warm air on to the screen soon after warm-up for rapid demisting and defrosting – preferably without making the interior of the car intolerably stuffy in the process. Auxiliary vents should demist the side-windows, and an electric heater for the rear screen can no longer be regarded as an extra. Cars prone to accumulate dirt on the rear window should be fitted with a rear wiper and washer as standard. Inside the car there should be few distracting reflections from the glass or glasses of the instruments, or from bright-work on the facia, steering wheel or controls.

Aerodynamics

Wind Resistance

Above 30–40 mph, as already explained, (p. 177) most of the power developed by a car's engine is absorbed in overcoming wind resistance. This is not an effect, as is often implied, of interest mainly of those who habitually exceed speed limits, but is also highly relevant to more sedate and ordinary motoring. A 10 per cent reduction in wind resistance, for example, is estimated to improve overall fuel consumption by about 3 per cent.

The importance of wind resistance lies partly in the fact that the power required to overcome it goes up with the cube of the speed. The exact relationship is given by the formula:

$$P = \frac{C_d A V^3}{146,600}$$

where P = power absorbed in bhp; V = speed in mph; A = frontal area in sq ft and C_d = *drag coefficient*.

When A is in sq m, V in kph and P in metric horsepower (p. 30), then the formula is:

$$P = 17.5 \times 10^{-6} C_d A V^3$$

For a car of a given size and type there is relatively little that can be done, if its occupants are to be accommodated comfortably, about its frontal area. This is the total area, at right angles to its direction of travel, which it presents to the air. But a great deal can be done about its drag coefficient, the number which expresses its aerodynamic efficiency.

A flat plate is a very inefficient object, aerodynamically speaking, with a high inherent wind resistance expressed by a theoretical drag coefficient of 1. In practice the drag coefficient of a flat plate is more like 1.25 (fig. 292) because the energy-wasting eddies which form at its edges increase its effective area. A short cylinder, lying across the air flow, has a drag coefficient of 0.80, but for a fully streamlined object with the

		C_D
Flat plate		1.25
Short cylinder		0.80
Streamline body		0.03
Saloon		0.45
GT coupé		0.33
ARVW		0.15

fig. 292. The drag coefficient of some common objects and different types of car, including the diesel-powered record-breaking Aerodynamic Research Volkswagen car.

classic teardrop shape assumed by a drop of water falling through the air, the drag coefficient is as low as 0.03. Basically this is because the air flows smoothly over a properly streamlined shape without becoming detached from its surface to form the eddies responsible for much of the energy wastage.

While such low drag coefficients are possible for aircraft or parts of aircraft, unhappily they cannot be approached by cars. One reason is that a fully streamlined shape is quite impractical for a road-going car – its extended, tapering tail would have to be around 10 ft long.

The pre-war aerodynamicist, Professor Kamm, argued that for a practical car the best results would be attained by tapering the tail of the car as rapidly as possible without creating flow separation, and then cutting it off sharply at the point of maximum allowable length. In this way the base area over which the energy-consuming eddies are spread is made as small as possible. A

number of modern cars, such as the Citroën GS, have **Kamm tails** of this sort.

But the main reason for a car's high drag factor, compared to the ideally streamlined bodies of the aviation world, is the presence of the ground so close to it, interfering with the flow. Thus the lowest drag coefficient achieved for highly streamlined record-breaking cars lie in the region of 0.15–0.20. A number of experimental road-going cars were built (by Kamm and others) in the thirties with drag coefficients in the 0.20–0.25 range, but generally these suffered from poor visibility, excessive overall length or other drawbacks such as an unacceptably high ground clearance. Nevertheless, in the early sixties one pioneering aerodynamicist, Geoffrey Carr of the Motor Industry Research Association (MIRA), showed that it was perfectly possible for a small car with a practical and modern shape – giving good visibility and allowing a comfortable seating position – to have a drag coefficient as low as 0.25.

Unfortunately the drag coefficient of the modern car is much higher than this – 0.43 was the average in 1982 – because with a few honourable exceptions such as Citroën, the majority of the large motor manufacturers shamefully neglected aerodynamic design until quite recently. But the rising cost of fuel has rapidly changed attitudes with results that confirm what informed engineers have long known: that a very low drag coefficient can be attained without resorting to an exaggeratedly streamlined and bulbous shape. Thus a new generation of aerodynamically superior cars such as the Ford Sierra ($C_d = 0.34$) and the Audi 100 ($C_d = 0.30$) has begun to appear.

The wind-cheating properties of these cars are the result of painstaking attention to detail, aimed at keeping the airflow attracted to the surface of the body to reduce energy-wasting eddies (fig. 293). An obvious first step is to slope the bonnet downwards to a low nose, but not to an unreasonable extent – the front of a BL Metro is about the right

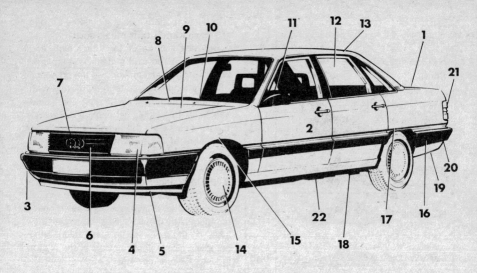

fig. 293. The 1983 Audi 100, with well over twenty different detail aerodynamic features, has a record drag coefficient for a production car of only 0.30. Each feature provides only a few thousandths improvement to the total, but together they make up a significant advance:

1 Optimized wedge-shaped length with high boot lid to 'collect' air flow on tail
2 Distinct barrel section in plan to maintain laminar flow down sides and reduce cross-section of rear wake
3 Smoothly shaped front bumper, closely blended with lower panel and front grille
4 Headlamps and turn indicators smoothly blended into the front panels with specially moulded lenses
5 Small under-bumper spoiler
6 Fully ducted air flow to the radiator, mounted on one side behind the grille
7 Full-width rubber sealing lip between front panel and bonnet lid
8 Heater air intake grille in special low-pressure area at the base of the windscreen in slot created by swept-up trailing edge of the bonnet
9 Heater plenum chamber sealed by lightweight plastic cover

10 Shrouded windscreen wiper pivots
11 Aerodynamic door mirror designed to create minimum disturbance to air flow
12 Flush glass in all windows, bonded for all fixed glass and running on top of the door frames for sliding glass
13 Guttering eliminated by the use of smooth grooves in the roof
14 Flush covers for wheels with controlled air flow over brakes
15 No 'eyebrow' feature mouldings over wheel-arches
16 Wrap-round bumper extensions smoothly moulded into the wheel cutouts
17 Flush interior finish to wheelarches with turned-over edge flanges
18 Contoured section for dead rear axle
19 Smoothly-moulded plastic housing for spare wheel well
20 Small spoiler under the rear bumper
21 Smoothly moulded tail light lenses
22 Complete underside of floor pan pressed in one piece and shaped to provide low underbody drag throughout length of car

sort of shape (though the car as a whole does not have an especially low drag coefficient). The cooling aperture must be as small as possible, and the air that it admits must be carefully ducted to the radiator (or engine if it is aircooled) so that none of it is wasted. A **spoiler** (more about this later) or **air dam** under the cooling aperture can be quite important, as it persuades air to flow round the car rather than underneath it where it tends to form energy-wasting eddies. This front spoiler should approach the ground as closely as possible, but obviously the negotiation of ramps and kerbs imposes a limit – which is why the next generation of aerodynamic bodies will probably have movable front spoilers which will automatically lower at high speed on a motorway. To reduce energy wastage in the air that does flow beneath the car, its undertray should be as smooth as possible with components like the exhaust system recessed into it.

The backward rake of the windscreen must be considerable – but again need not be exaggerated: a slope of about 60° to the horizontal is enough, though a smooth transition between this slope and that of the bonnet is also important. To ensure that the airflow remains smoothly attached to the sides of the car, a gentle rounding of the body in the area of the windscreen pillars is equally important. Other critical areas are the tail of the car and the trailing edge of the roof. Tapering the bodywork in plan towards the rear – if not of the whole car (as for the Citroën DS) then at least the 'greenhouse' or superstructure – is a further way of reducing drag. Details such as flush-fitting glass and covers or **spats** over the rear wheels make additional contributions to a low figure.

But good aerodynamic design is much more than a matter of low drag: stability at high speeds and in side winds is also highly important. A crucial factor here is the location of the **centre of pressure** looking at the car in side view. Roughly speaking, if this lies behind the centre of gravity (fig.294a) the car

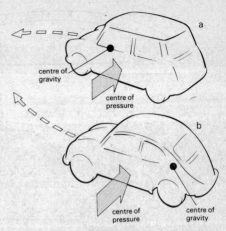

fig. 294. The centre of pressure: a, if this lies behind the centre of gravity the car tends to be stable when deflected by sidewinds: b, but when the centre of pressure lies ahead of the centre of gravity the car tends to be unstable.

will tend to be steered back into a side wind as well as being deflected laterally thus acting in a self-correcting way.

If the centre of pressure lies ahead of the centre of gravity, however, the car will tend to be steered as well as deflected away from any side wind (fig. 294b) and this is inherently unstable behaviour. Since rear-engined cars have rearward-biased centres of gravity, they generally tend to have poorer side-wind stability than front-engined cars.

Another important factor is **lift**, for the body of a car can to some extent act like the wing of an aeroplane. The generation of lift depends upon the same Bernoulli effect (p. 55) that sucks fuel from the jet of a carburetter: when air is speeded up its pressure tends to fall. Thus an aircraft wing is shaped (fig. 295) so that the air flowing above it is forced to travel further, and hence faster than the air flowing beneath it. The resultant reduced pressure above the wing creates the upward force called lift.

It does not take much imagination to look at a car in side view and see it as a very short but very thick (and peculiarly shaped)

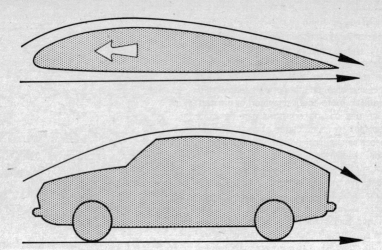

fig. 295. In profile, a motorcar bears some resemblance to an aircraft wing and, like it, generates lift.

wing which forces the air to flow much further and faster above it than below it. Fortunately, too great a resistance is offered by the small gap underneath for much air to flow through. And if air is being withheld from the region beneath the car, the pressure in that region must be reduced. This low pressure or partial vacuum under the car tends to balance the low pressure above the car, cancelling most of the lift.

Some lift is nevertheless often generated, and by reducing the load on the front tyres or rear tyres or both, it can reduce high-speed stability. Minimizing this effect is the purpose of the currently fashionable (fig. 296) front **spoiler** or **air dam**: by forcing more air to flow round the sides of the car the pressure under it is further reduced, and the result is generally a significant reduction in the lift force on the front wheels. Usually the drag coefficient is also slightly reduced – because the air flows more smoothly round the side of the car than beneath it – and the flow to the cooling system is improved, too.

Any wing generating upward lift deflects air downwards, and this **downwash** is the

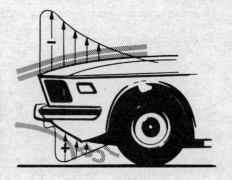

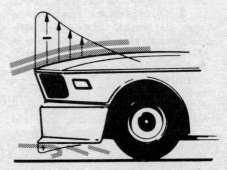

fig. 296. The front spoiler reduces front lift by cutting the flow beneath the car.

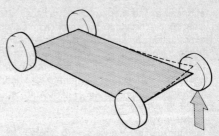

consequence of lift forces acting on the rear of the car (fig. 297). These can be reduced by sharp lips at the rear of the roof or bonnet or by a rear spoiler (fig. 298) which deflects the air so that it flows away from the car more parallel to the ground. In racing cars, of course, this process is carried one stage further with inverted 'wings' which actually force the car towards the ground at high speeds.

fig. 299. The most important loads a car's structure has to withstand are torsional.

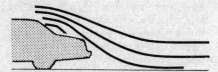

fig. 297. Downwash is the consequence of lift on the rear of the car.

spoiler

fig. 298. A rear spoiler encourages the air to flow parallel to the ground and thus reduces lift.

fig. 300. Bending loads are imposed by the weight the car has to carry – which includes its own sprung weight.

Structure

The structure of a motorcar must be strong in two basic ways: to resist twisting or torsional loads and to withstand bending loads. Torsional loads (fig. 299) are the more important of the two and are imposed whenever one wheel hits a bump, for example, while bending loads are imposed by the weight the car has to carry (fig. 300). Generally speaking, if a car is sufficiently stiff in torsion, it will also be sufficiently stiff in bending.

Just what is meant by 'sufficiently stiff', however, is not easy to define. The structure should certainly be too rigid to act as a 'fifth spring' interacting with the other four springs and spoiling the roadholding with cyclic dis-

turbances such as steering shimmy (p. 239). Such disturbances were common faults in the thirties and forties when the typical chassis was of the torsionally weak girder type (p. 16). The structure should also be stiff enough to ensure that even when it has not been excited into oscillation in this way, its deflections are too small to upset significantly the movements of the wheels on their suspension links.

Both these requirements are probably met by a torsional stiffness of around 2500 lb ft/deg (pounds-feet per degree of deflection) or 350 kg m/deg. But to prevent the structure from creaking on bad surfaces, to stop the doors, bootlid etc from rattling or chafing in their apertures – and to ensure that they can easily be opened and closed when the car is jacked up – the torsional stiffness of the modern car is generally at least double this figure. For a modern integral construction car in which a platform chassis forms a rigid structure with the body, the torsional stiffness is usually at least 6000 lb ft/deg (830 kg m/deg) and sometimes as much as 11,000 lb ft/deg (1520 kg m/deg).

These high figures – many times greater than those of pre-war cars – are achieved by applying two basic principles of construction. The first of these is that a tube is immensely stiffer than an open channel. A square-section tube, for example, is no less than six hundred times stiffer than an open channel of similar dimensions (fig. 301) but weighs only 33 per cent more.

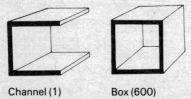

Channel (1)   Box (600)

fig. 301. Closed box sections are immensely stronger in torsion than open channels.

In recognition of a tube's inherently high torsional rigidity, central **backbone chassis** have been used for many cars including the Volkswagen Beetle, the Triumph Herald/Spitfire already described (p. 16) and the Lotus Elan (fig. 302) and current Lotus models including the Elite, Excel and Esprit. Such a chassis consists essentially of a large-diameter tube running down the centre of the car into which the basic torsional and bending loads are fed. Light transverse out-rigger beams are often used to support the body, while the central backbone sometimes houses the gear linkage and other services.

But a tube is not merely much stiffer in torsion than an open channel, it is also far more efficient in its use of material than alternative structures. A square tube, for example, with a cross-section measuring 52 in×52 in and fabricated from 20-gauge steel 0.036 in (0.91 mm) thick, is twenty-four times lighter for the same length than a solid cylindrical bar 15 in (38 cm) thick which has the same torsional stiffness. A tube even larger in cross-section but with correspondingly thinner walls is theoretically even stiffer. But there is a limit to the extent to which

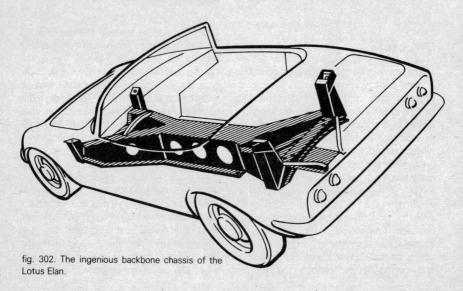

fig. 302. The ingenious backbone chassis of the Lotus Elan.

this concept can be carried, for when the walls of the tube are made very thin they become unstable and liable to buckle.

Nevertheless the principle remains a sound one: the further the structural material is dispersed from the axis about which it is twisted, the stiffer the structure. It is thus easy to understand the high stiffness of the modern unitary chassis, for effectively it constitutes a giant tube, very large in cross-section, formed by the floor, roof and sides of the body.

This is an oversimplification, in fact, for the bulk of the stiffness generally lies in the **floorpan**. This can be thought of as being based on the old-fashioned girder chassis composed of two long side-members connected together by a number of cross-members. But the open channel side-members are boxed in to form the box-section **sills** (fig. 303) which lie under the doors, and the cross-members are boxed in, too. Next these

major members are bridged by steel sheet which is ribbed and corrugated for further rigidity. Rising from this essentially flat structure is the scuttle assembly to which the facia is attached, and which adds materially to the overall stiffness: often the front suspension loads are fed directly into it. At the back of the car there is generally another arched structure to take the rear suspension loads. When the body side-frames and roof are welded to the completed floorpan the result is a structure of great rigidity but lightness. Generally the external body panels form part of the structure, but in a few cars such as the Rover 2000/3500 (Mk 1) and the Citroën DS the body panels are unstressed.

A unitary body is very complex, containing

fig. 303. A typical modern platform chassis – note the number of differently shaped box-section members.

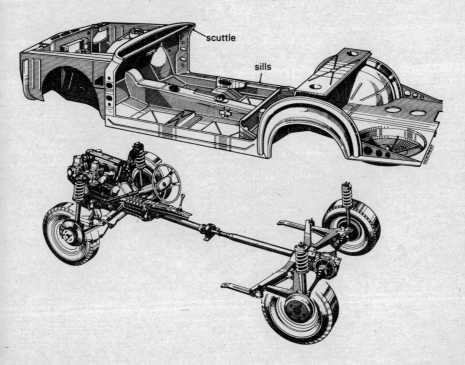

scuttle

sills

at least 1000 structural elements which interact with each other. Until recently, therefore, chassis design involved a good deal of trial and error – and hence waste. To save weight and cost modern designers have been driven to adopt more sophisticated methods using computers, the most common being called **finite element analysis.**

The first stage in this process is to resolve the structure of the car into simple elements – such as struts in tension or compression – with well-understood properties. These (fig. 304) are turned into equations, while further equations define the relationships between each element and its neighbours. This is a lengthy process which generally takes a number of highly qualified engineers

fig. 304. Finite element analysis – each part of the car is broken down into the simplest structural elements which will accurately describe it.

several months to complete, but time is saved as soon as a computer has been programmed and supplied with all the data they have collected. The effect of a given change can then be quickly and easily calculated without going to the trouble of building an experimental bodyshell. In this way the optimum structure with the greatest stiffness for the least weight can be developed.

With the latest and most sophisticated finite element analysis programmes it is even possible to apply a simulated acoustic input to various parts of the structure and to determine the vibrational responses of different panels so that unpleasant resonances can be avoided. Other computer analysis systems also make it possible to investigate how the front and rear of a car crumple and absorb energy in a collision (p. 296).

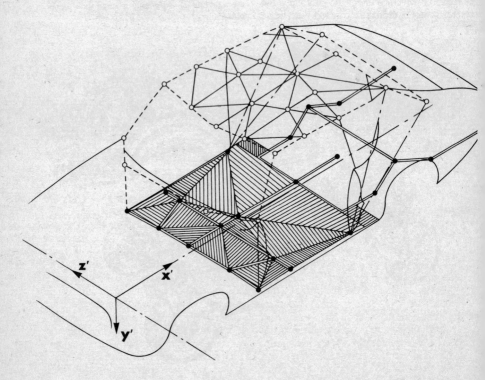

Rust

The chassis of pre-war cars were generally composed of a relatively small area of relatively thick metal which was not especially vulnerable to corrosion – and in any case was usually liberally sprayed with oil from engine, gearbox and back axle leakages. But the integral chassis, first introduced on a large scale in the late thirties, is far more vulnerable to rust, as it is composed of a large area of relatively thin metal. Modern engines, gearboxes and back axles, moreover, are less prone to leak, and the amount of highly corrosive salt laid down on our roads every winter has increased dramatically during the past twenty years. All this has led to a widespread and largely justified outcry against the ease and speed with which the modern car rusts – and to the establishment of a number of rustproofing processes.

But solving the problem is not easy. Merely coating the underside of the car may make matters worse, creating small pockets of mud or water at places were the bond between the metal and the protective coating is weak. At these points the metal will rust faster than if it had not been coated at all.

Only in the seventies were effective methods of combating rust progressively adopted. The first step is to design the structure so that it contains no rust-traps, places where rain, salt, etc, thrown up from the road can be retained in small pockets. Next, fully enclosed structural members must be ventilated and provided with drainage holes so that they are kept clean and dry inside. In certain cars, such as those made by Volvo, for example, the heating system is used to ventilate the sills. Corrosion and erosion by dirt and stones thrown up by the wheels is very difficult to combat, so another important step is to fit plastic wheel-arch liners. The best way of applying the primer or first coat of paint is by the **electrophoretic** process, which is similar in principle to electroplating and ensures that the most inaccessible surfaces of the structure receive a proper coating. After applying several coats of top paint it is usual nowadays to coat the interior surfaces of the sills with a protective wax. If an external undersealant is used, it should be of the permanently plastic and self-healing type so that when penetrated by a stone it gradually spreads to cover the puncture.

Safety

The most profound influence on car design during the past thirty years – equal in importance to the advent of exhaust emission control – has been the drive towards improved safety. This is generally regarded as being of two kinds, the first of which, **active safety**, is concerned with a car's ability to avoid having an accident in the first place: its stability under heavy braking, its ability to swerve suddenly without going out of control and its behaviour in corners when conditions rapidly change. But much of the campaigning for greater safety in cars has come from America where these matters are regarded as less important than **passive safety** which is directed towards protecting the occupants of a car from death or serious injury after a collision with another car or some other solid object has occurred. It is this aspect of safety with which we are primarily concerned here, active safety being covered in Chapter 10 and elsewhere.

The basic principles of passive safety are easily stated, though behind them lie years of study, experiment and research. The first requirement is to ensure that in an accident the occupants of a car are retained within it, which means, among other things, designing doors that will not fly open. It is then vital to prevent the car occupants from being injured by intrusions into the passenger compartment or deformation of it. The steering wheel must not be driven into the driver, for example, and the roof must be strong enough to withstand a rollover with only modest deformation. The next priority is to mitigate the effects of the **second collision** – the one the driver and passengers have with the interior of the car after it has struck something else. Meeting this requirement entails such measures as making the facia control knobs non-aggressive and designing the facia itself to cushion impacts with the human head and face. One of the best ways of coping with the second collision, however – and also of ensuring retention within the car – is to wear a lap-and-diagonal seatbelt. Finally, the safety engineer is required to reduce, as far as is possible, the violence of the decelerations imposed upon the occupants of a car in a collision by providing the car with front and rear sections which deform progressively on impact.

Types of accident

But before the engineer can design for protection, he must first know what he should protect against, that is, he must first know something about the different types of road accident and their relative frequency. In almost every country of the world the majority of serious and fatal accidents take place at *relatively low speeds* – the average closing speed is around 30 mph in Britain – and are of the head-on collision type. For this reason one of the most basic of all safety tests is a 30 mph barrier crash or contrived head-on collision with a solid concrete block – which is roughly equivalent to a collision between two similar cars with a closing speed of 60 mph. The behaviour of a car subjected to an ordeal of this kind is used to define various legal safety requirements. For example the ECE (Economic Commission for Europe) regulations which now govern the safety of British cars lay down that in a 30 mph barrier crash the steering wheel should not be pushed rearwards by more

than 15 cm. This rearward displacement, along with the deformation of the front of the car, the distortion of the doors and many other factors – including the decelerations experienced by belted or unbelted dummies – are carefully monitored during the crash with high-speed cameras and other sophisticated equipment.

In real-life head-on collisions the two cars are rarely exactly aligned with one another. Some safety experts therefore feel that it would be more realistic to crash the car at an angle of about 30° into the concrete barrier or with it offset to one side so that the impact is absorbed by only half of the front of the car. Such tests are in any case carried out by most companies on prototypes or new models.

In Britain, next in importance after the head-on collision is the side impact, followed by accidents involving one or more rollovers, followed in turn by rear-end collisions. Much the same pattern exists in other countries, except that Britain is notable for a higher proportion of accidents involving pedestrians, as might be expected from its high population density and narrow streets. America, on the other hand, differs from the rest of the world in suffering a higher proportion of rear-end collisions.

Retention

Many people believe that the safety movement effectively began with the publication in 1966 of a book by safety campaigner Ralph Nader called *Unsafe at Any Speed – The Designed-in Dangers of the American Automobile*. While his book certainly gave impetus to the safety movement, its roots are at least ten years older. They lie in accident research carried out by a number of institutions and companies such as Cornell University in the States, Volvo in Sweden and what was then the Road Research Laboratory in Britain.

One of the most basic findings of these surveys, collectively based on the study of thousands of accidents, was to explode the fallacy – still popular – that your chances of surviving a crash are increased if you are 'thrown clear' of it. This is more likely to happen in an American car, with its larger door apertures, than a European one, but ejection from either roughly doubles the risk of death or serious injury. When a person is thrown from a car there is a very high probability that he will strike his head on the road or some piece of street furniture such as a lamp-post, be crushed beneath his own car or run over by another one.

This means that retaining the occupants of a car within it during a collision should be given a high priority, and obviously the doors and their locks receive particular attention. A modern burst-proof lock (fig. 305) must not only be able to withstand a lateral force of up to 2000 lb, but also a longitudinal force as great as 2400 lb, since in a violent impact the doors tend to pull away from their doorposts.

Another component that can play a particular part in retaining driver and passengers within a car during an accident is the windscreen. In Britain this can be one of two kinds, the most common being the **toughened windscreen**. A toughened windscreen

fig. 305. A modern burstproof doorlock must be able to withstand very large longitudinal and lateral forces.

consists of a single piece of glass usually 5 mm thick, treated during manufacture by jets of air which cause the surface to cool and contract more quickly than the interior. Thus the surface of the glass is put into compression and the interior into tension. The resultant internal stresses make the glass stronger and more rigid than it otherwise would be, so long as its compressive outer skin is not punctured by a stone or other missile. When it is, the same internal stresses cause the glass to shatter into fragments which do not cut very much.

From a safety point of view a toughened screen has several defects. The fact that it becomes difficult to see through when it shatters is not considered to be a significant cause of accidents, but its skin is easily punctured and it offers little protection against a substantial missile such as a large stone. More important, it is not strong enough to help retain people within the car even when struck at a modest impact speed.

The alternative **laminated windscreen** consists of a piece of flexible transparent plastic, called the **interlayer**, sandwiched between two pieces of glass which are only slightly toughened. When such a screen is struck by a missile, it fractures, forming very sharp fragments like ordinary glass, but these continue to adhere to the plastic interlayer and so are retained in position. The

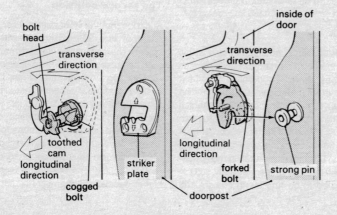

bolt head

transverse direction

toothed cam

longitudinal direction

cogged bolt

striker plate

inside of door

transverse direction

longitudinal direction

forked bolt

strong pin

doorpost

result, generally, is local starring of the screen which has excellent resistance to flying stones, being capable of stopping a brick at high speed.

In the early and middle sixties when windscreens of this type were struck by an unbelted driver or passenger, the plastic interlayer often ruptured, allowing the head to pass through and the fragments of retained glass to inflict horrifying 'horse collar' injuries to the throat. Since 1967, though, a thicker interlayer was adopted by most countries (including Britain) and this has transformed the safety record of the laminated screen. Not only is it an effective means of retention – especially if it is bonded in place with adhesives as is often the case nowadays – but by bowing outwards it cushions the impact well, skull fractures due to windscreen impacts being rare except in very high speed accidents. Unfortunately, though, the forces of the impact are generally such as to draw the head down the screen, inflicting severe lacerations which may call for extensive cosmetic surgery. This risk was greatly reduced with the new Triplex Ten-Twenty glass, the inner layer of which was toughened – and thus when fractured formed small blunt pieces which inflicted little injury. Unfortunately, the cost of the glass was high and, although for a time it was used for the windscreen of the Rover 3500, it had to be taken out of production.

Intrusion

There is little point in retaining people within a car during a collision if it promptly collapses and crushes them, so perhaps the next priority is protection against intrusion. The best-known form of intrusion is that in which the steering column is driven rearwards into the driver's chest. While this is certainly of very real importance, it was always less common in European cars than in the American cars of the late fifties and early sixties, which tended to be fitted with straight and

rigid steering columns running to a steering box right at the front of the car. Rearward displacement is fairly easily avoided in a modern European car by using a rack and pinion mounted behind the wheels in conjunction with a jointed steering column which simply folds up under impact (fig. 306).

Another form of intrusion which must be prevented is rearward movement of the engine or wheels into the front footwell which might crush or trap the driver's or front passenger's legs. Also important is deformation of the roof during a rollover, which is why modern cars now have to pass a **roof crush resistance** test. These requirements, combined with the need to design doors and locks that will not burst open (but are easy to open after the accident) explain why an essential part of safety philosophy is the provision of a strong central passenger compartment (fig. 307).

Additional reinforcement of the doors, however, is needed to minimize **side intrusion**. But it is difficult to protect against side impacts as the distance through which the door of the car can be deflected to absorb energy before striking an occupant is small. A long-term answer might be to standardize sill and bumper heights so that the front of the 'bullet' car nearly always met the strong sill or side member of the 'target' car.

The second collision

Suppose that the front part of a car deforms one foot in a 30 mph impact with a solid object. The passenger compartment would then be subjected to a mean deceleration of roughly 30g – which the human body can easily withstand if properly restrained (by a seatbelt, for instance). The trouble is that as the passenger compartment decelerates, an unrestrained occupant continues forward at 30 mph for 1–2 ft before striking some part of the car and being brought to rest in a matter of inches, sustaining very much higher decelerations on various parts of his

fig. 306. A rack-and-pinion steering system with a jointed column is seldom pushed significantly rearwards in a frontal collision.

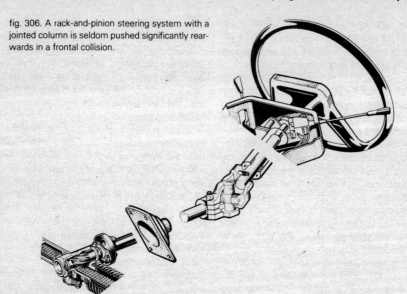

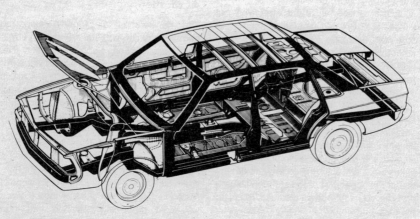

fig. 307. The heavily shaded sections show the safety-related parts of a typical modern car's structure. The beams at front and rear are designed to crumple progressively to absorb energy in an impact, but there is a strong central 'cell' to protect the occupants from intrusion.

body, not to mention point loads which puncture and fracture. It is this second collision of the person with the interior of the car which generally kills or maims.

A number of measures can be taken to mitigate its effects and these depend upon two basic principles. The first is to spread the load over as large an area of the body as possible, the second is to provide the longest possible **ride down** distance to minimize the mean deceleration. If, for example, the driver's head strikes the screen pillar and it deflects less than an inch the deceleration could be 300g and the local pressure immensely high. But if the driver's head were to strike a smooth facia which deformed to fit its shape, the load on the skull could be spread over several square inches instead of one or less, greatly diminishing the risk of fracture. And if, like the front of the car, it deformed for one foot, steadily absorbing energy, it would reduce the decelerations on the delicate tissues of the brain to an acceptable level.

For this sort of protection, what is conventionally understood by padding is virtually useless: it flattens almost instantly, leaving the head or face to withstand an impact against a surface which has effectively not yielded at all. But thin, carefully shaped sheet steel can be made to absorb energy very smoothly and effectively.

Energy-absorbing facias are now a routine feature of modern cars, as are control knobs and instrument surrounds designed to be non-aggressive to the human body. Paradoxically the steering wheel and column are nowadays able to cushion the driver's second collision quite significantly. A suitably shaped and padded boss spreads the load on his body, while controlled forward deflection of the upper part of the steering column provides some ride-down distance, reducing the maximum force.

But all these measures do little more than toy with the basic problem, which is to prevent the second collision from happening at all. And by far the most simple and effective way of doing this is to wear a conventional lap-and-diagonal seatbelt, as is now required by law in Britain for the driver and front passenger, reducing the risk of death and serious injury by at least one half. The rear-seat passengers are a little less at risk, but rear seatbelts are eventually likely to become as commonplace as front ones.

Moreover the seatbelt has virtually no significant disadvantages. The number of *fully authenticated* cases, for instance, in which a seatbelt is actually responsible for injury rather than preventing it, is negligible. Nor are you more likely to be trapped, as is often suggested, if the car catches fire following a collision. On the contrary, without a seatbelt the probability is that you will be knocked unconscious and thus be unable to escape in any case. Similarly, if you drive your car into a river or a canal (often done in places such as Amsterdam) even at the modest speed of 15 mph, the impact is likely to knock you unconscious if you are not wearing a belt. If you are wearing one, you have a good chance of escaping if you do not panic.

Absorption

The deceleration a properly supported human body can withstand without permanent injury depends upon its duration. The limits vary from individual to individual, of course, but roughly speaking the scale is such that 45g can be withstood for 0.04 sec, 40g for 0.1 sec or 15g for 1.0 sec. Thus although the tolerance to deceleration is large, it does have definite limits.

A seatbelt by itself does quite a lot to reduce the deceleration on the wearer's body, since by stretching it provides a ride-down distance of 8 in or so. But this alone is not enough. If the structure of the car were very rigid, deforming only 3 in, say, in a 30 mph barrier crash, the deceleration experienced by a belted occupant would still be above acceptable levels. Thus the front structure of the modern car is designed to collapse progressively to absorb energy, a typical crush distance being 20 in (51 cm).

This controlled deformation, incidentally, has little to do with the massive bumpers mounted on hydraulic dampers which are a feature of many cars sold in the States and a few sold in Britain. These bumpers meet a requirement, made less stringent in 1982, which is quite unconnected with safety and was originally suggested by American insurance companies. It is that a car be capable of withstanding a 5 mph car park impact without damage to the bodyword, lights or fuel system. But the kinetic energy to be absorbed in bringing a car to rest increases with the square of the speed, so the energy absorbed by the 5 mph bumpers is tiny compared to that dissipated in a typical crash – which at 25 mph will be twenty-five times greater. Thus the 5 mph bumpers can be regarded as very weak springs which are compressed almost at once in an accident, before the stiff springs represented by the front structure do the majority of the work – though of course there is nothing springy about the front structure of a car.

There is another factor to be considered in reducing the deceleration on the occupant of a car: belt slackness. For the bodywork deforms through the first half of its crush distance very rapidly indeed, whereas the occupant develops a forward velocity with respect to the interior of the car rather slowly. Thus if the belt is slack by one inch, say, the short time needed to accelerate into contact with it will be enough for the front of the car to deform through a substantial part of its crush distance. Hence the belt wearer will lose the benefit of this crush distance and be subjected to a correspondingly higher deceleration.

The front of the modern car, therefore, is usually designed so that the graph of deceleration against time approximates to a **square wave**.

The very rapid initial rise in deceleration brings the occupants of the car against their seatbelts right at the beginning of the colli-

sion so that they can benefit from the ride-down distance afforded by the stretching of the belt plus a substantial proportion of the crush distance. Inertia reel belts are a help, since they are lightly tensioned against the wearer's body and lock up very rapidly.

The rear part of a modern car is designed to deform progressively in much the same way as the front. The problems, though, are not the same. It is generally necessary, for example, to protect the fuel tank against rupture (and hence fire risk) by mounting it ahead of the rear wheels. It is also important to protect against the **whiplash** injuries associated with severe rear-end impacts: damage to the neck when the head jerks violently backwards. These are reduced by **head restraints** which support the head in such circumstances and bend gently to cushion the impact. A head restraint needs be quite stiff to do this, as the forces involved are surprisingly large, and so it is quite different from a **headrest**, a much more flimsy affair merely intended to provide added comfort. But when a head restraint is adjustable, it must be set at the correct height – otherwise it will do little to reduce whiplash injuries and may actually increase them. Head restraints often impede rearward vision, but by adopting a 'skeleton' design this disadvantage can be minimized.

The future

In 1970, the United States Government, building on earlier work carried out by the Liberty Mutual Assurance Co. of Boston, Mass., and by the State of New York, placed contracts for the construction of some **ESVs** or **Experimental Safety Vehicles**. The resultant programme had an important influence on the development of safety technology.

The original hope of the US Government safety experts was to achieve what they called a 'quantum jump' in safety technology, for the ESVs had to meet requirements far more severe than anything hitherto envisaged. They were called upon, for example, to protect their occupants from significant injury in front or rear barrier collisions at 50 mph, in two successive rollovers at 60 mph and a number of other specified – and very severe – impacts.

Suspicious of motor industry attitudes, the US Government placed these contracts with two companies in technology and engineering but not directly concerned with the motorcar: Fairchild-Hiller and American Machine and Foundry or AMF. Not to be outdone, the major American motor manufacturers General Motors, Ford and Chrysler soon offered to produce – free – their own ESVs, meeting the same requirements. All these vehicles were supposed to be kept within a 4000 lb (1820 kg) weight limit – very heavy by European standards – but the programme became international and was broadened to include ESVs in different weight classes down to 1500 lb. Most of the European companies participated, but Fiat, Mercedes, Volkswagen and Volvo were

major contributors. Less work was done in Britain – partly because it was conducted by the overseas branches of the international companies operating here – but British Leyland produced several interesting vehicles.

Because the level of voluntary seatbelt wearing in most countries was and is low, an essential ingredient of the ESV philosophy was **passive restraint**. (Seatbelt wearing has since become a legal requirement in many countries, including Britain and Australia.) Passive restraint means protecting the occupants of a car without any preliminary action on their part such as buckling on a belt. There are three basic ways of providing this: with a **passive seatbelt** (fig. 308) which automatically wraps itself round the subject as he or she gets into the car and closes the door; by using the **cushioncar** principle (fig. 309) involving large bolsters of padding which bulge out towards the car occupants, almost touching them, or with **airbags**.

An airbag in this context is a large plastic balloon (fig. 310) which, triggered by g-responsive sensors on the front of the car,

fig. 308. A passive seatbelt of the type fitted to the Volkswagen Golf sold in America.

fig. 309. The Cushioncar principle involves padding which is nearly in contact with the passengers at all times in order to all but eliminate the second collision.

inflates during a collision in a tiny fraction of a second in front of the driver or passenger, and by controlled escape of the inflating gases, provides a ride-down which cushions against injury. The subject of bitter controversy, the airbag provoked widespread fears about such possibilities as inadvertent deployment, or of eardrum rupture (inflation occurs with explosive rapidity). Some of these fears have been proved unfounded by extensive and continuing field trials or rendered invalid by improvements in design.

Nevertheless the airbag suffers from two important disadvantages. The first is that it provides little protection in side impacts or rollovers. In fact the recommendation is that it be used in conjunction with a lap strap – which of course largely destroys its reason for existence, though an airbag can provide additional protection for a driver in high-energy impacts. The second is that it is a complex and expensive device, difficult to test without actual deployment, yet which must remain functioning without attention for many years if it is to be of any use at all.

With more elaborate design the first disadvantage could theoretically be removed. One possibility, for example, is a system of shaped bags, each with its own inflation system or chemical charge, which would form a hood over the car occupant retaining

fig. 310. The airbag – a large balloon which inflates in milliseconds to act as a cushion in frontal impacts. The system illustrated is the one designed by Daimler-Benz; to provide the maximum protection in high-energy impacts, both driver and front passenger wear seatbelts, but the driver is given additional protection by the airbag while an automatic belt-tensioning system provides additional safety for the front passenger.

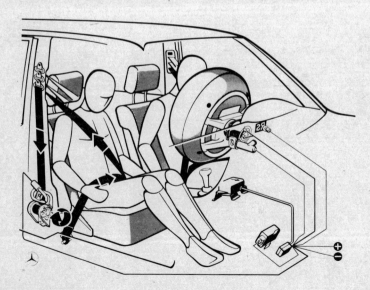

him safely in a wide range of accidents. But the disadvantage of complexity and reliability would remain – or indeed would be reinforced.

For these reasons most safety experts in most parts of the world consider that by far the simplest, cheapest and most effective means of reducing road accident deaths and injuries is to make the wearing of seatbelts compulsory. Despite this, the American legislature decided in 1977 to call for the progressive introduction from 1981 of passive restraint systems for cars sold in the States; this requirement was, however, quashed by the Reagan administration in 1982.

When finally completed the original ESVs proved expensive to construct, immensely ungainly and very heavy – the General Motors vehicle weighed 4700 lb (2136 kg) despite the extensive use of aluminium. Few could afford to buy such cars, even if it were practical to make them, and all the other, smaller ESVs also proved to be grossly overweight. There were some early embar-

rassments, too, such as the failure of the airbags to inflate at one public trial.

Even so, the programme did show that it was at least theoretically possible to protect people in severe impacts and much was learned from it. It also drew attention to various other aspects of road safety, including the reduction of pedestrian injuries. What it also showed, however, was that the requirements were far too extreme to lead to cost-effective safety measures. The kinetic energy to be absorbed in a 50 mph barrier crash, for example, is 2.8 times greater than at 30 mph, yet the equivalent average speed for accidents in most countries in only 30 mph. Accordingly, after a series of annual international conferences, the ESV programme was brought to an end in 1974. It was superseded, however, by the **RSV** or **Research Safety Vehicle** programme, concerned with more rational and cost-effective advanced safety measures, and this led to some far more practical designs, completed in the early eighties.

The perfect motorcar would demand no regular attention whatever beyond the addition of fuel. But since real motorcars are as imperfect as the world we live in, it would be silly to ignore their needs – and the possibility of breakdown or failure.

By far the best way of avoiding trouble is through regular inspection and maintenance.

Regular inspection

Here are some checks that you should carry out *at least each week*.

The first thing most people check under the bonnet is the dipstick, but whereas an engine blow-up through lack of oil will merely cost you money, a brake failure could cost you your life – so start by looking at the fluid reservoir.

Brakes – functioning normally

Check that the master cylinder reservoir is filled to the level indicated. If it is not, top up, first cleaning the area around the cap to avoid contaminating the existing fluid with dirt or grit – and remember that paintwork will be damaged if brake fluid spills on it. Use *only the approved brake fluid* which must be kept in a sealed container to minimize the water it absorbs from the atmosphere. The absorption of a very small amount of water is enough to lower the boiling point of the fluid significantly, making it markedly more prone to vapour lock under heavy braking. Mineral-based fluids such as lubricating oil, petrol, paraffin or trichlorethylene are particularly harmful and should never be used

for flushing or cleaning any part of the braking system.

Clutch

If the clutch is hydraulically operated, it makes sense to check its reservoir in the same way at the same time.

Brakes – low fluid level

Wear of the friction material influences the pedal travel and fluid level of a drum braking system in a different way to that of a disc system. In an all-drum braking system *which has been maintained in a correct state of adjustment* as the linings wear, the play between the hydraulic pistons and the tips of the shoes is mechanically taken up by the adjustment mechanism. Thus the pedal travel should not increase nor should the fluid level decrease.

In a system using disc brakes, however – at the front alone or at the rear as well – the hydraulic pistons gradually move closer to the discs as the pads wear. But the pedal travel does not increase, because each time the pedal is released additional fluid from the reservoir enters the master cylinder to fill the gap between the master cylinder piston and the slave cylinder pistons. The fluid level *does* decrease, though, but always gradually and never further than just below the prescribed level.

If any more sudden or more marked drop in level is discovered, therefore, the system should be immediately checked for leaks. These may be found anywhere in the system but are usually due to faulty slave piston seals. Check for seepage of brake fluid on to the back plates, drums, discs, wheels or tyres. Make sure that the flexible hoses are not chafed, frayed or swollen. Junctions and unions are further possible leakage points, and the master cylinder itself.

If the leakage is heavy, immediate action is required, but if it seems slight, check the travel of the pedal by pressing it as hard as you can for at least 15 seconds. If there is no perceptible increase in travel, it should be safe to drive the car, slowly and with extra anticipation, a short distance to a nearby garage. If there is any noticeable increase in pedal travel the car should not be driven at all until the fault is rectified.

Tyres

A regular inspection of the tyres need last only a couple of minutes and may save your life. Small cuts are not generally important but deep cuts, bulges in the sidewall or separation of the tread from the carcass are all very dangerous – if any of these are discovered, the tyre should be replaced at once. You should also check that the tyres are inflated to the correct pressures which should be measured when they are 'cold', that is, have not been run for an hour or so. Low pressures in the rear tyres are particularly dangerous. Look for any uneven pattern of wear in the tread – a sign of incorrect wheel alignment – and make sure that the tread depth everywhere exceeds the legal 1 mm limit.

Engine oil

Check the oil level at least once a week – more often, obviously, if you cover a high mileage or you know that your engine uses oil. A consumption of more than about 400 miles per pint is generally a sign of wear or trouble in a modern engine. But even if your engine normally needs no oil between changes, its consumption is likely to be increased by the prolonged high-speed cruis-ing in hot weather which is often a feature of touring holidays abroad. In such conditions, check the level at least at every second stop for fuel.

Look at the colour of the oil as well as its position on the dipstick. Oil which is very black and dirty needs changing. A milky colour is a danger sign – it means that the oil has become contaminated with water, probably through a faulty gasket, and this could lead to main bearing failure.

Cooling water

The cooling water (if any) may also need regular inspection if the system is not of the sealed type – but try to avoid checking when the engine has reached its working temperature, since the scalding water tends to spurt violently out when the filler cap is released. If this is unavoidable, cover the filler cap with a large rag and open at arm's length. Never fill above the level indicated in the driver's handbook, as excess water will simply be expelled. If a large amount of water has to be added, let the engine cool down, top up, replace the cap and run the engine for two or three minutes. Repeat until the prescribed level has been reached and all air expelled. Always keep an eye on the water temperature gauge and remember that a sudden loss of warmth from the heater is generally a sign of a leakage or an air lock. When winter approaches, get the antifreeze concentration checked at a garage. The proportion of antifreeze should be at least 25 per cent for adequate protection in Britain – do not gamble on the weather being mild. The antifreeze in a sealed system should have a life of four years.

Battery

Make sure that the level of electrolyte is maintained about a quarter of an inch above the plates. Use *distilled water only* to top up.

Simple maintenance – brakes

Drum brake adjustment

If the brake pedal moves through more than about a third of its travel before a firm resistance is felt and the brakes are fully applied, adjustment is needed. The brakes of most cars these days need no adjustment, though, as they are usually of the disc type at the front and the self-adjusting drum type at the rear. But when drum brakes needing adjustment are fitted, there are generally two adjusters for each front brake and one for each rear brake. These are either screws, accessible through holes in the backplate or drum, or nuts – often square in section, requiring a special tool – which protrude from the backplate (fig. 311).

The adjustment technique is the same in each case. The wheel must be jacked up clear of the ground with the handbrake released (if it works on that wheel) and each adjuster must be turned (in the direction prescribed in the car handbook) until the brake shoe it controls grips the drum and stops the wheel from rotating. The adjuster is then turned back one or two clicks until the wheel is freed again.

Shoe replacement

A few cars have backplates provided with inspection holes through which the linings of drum brakes can be viewed. But in most cases it will be necessary to remove the brake drum – often held on by two screws – to inspect the linings.

The linings must be replaced if worn nearly flush with their retaining rivets or to within 1/16 in (2 mm) of the shoe if they are of the bonded type. Removal and replacement instructions will be found in the workshop manual or a good maintenance manual covering the car in question.

fig. 311. A typical brake adjuster.

fig. 312. The pads of a disc brake are usually readily accessible once the wheel has been removed.

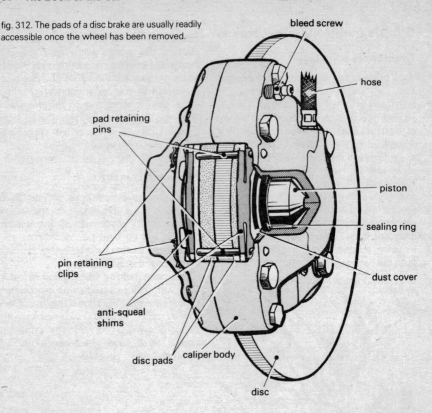

bleed screw

hose

pad retaining pins

piston

sealing ring

pin retaining clips

dust cover

anti-squeal shims

disc pads

caliper body

disc

Pad replacement

On nearly all cars the brake pads (fig. 312) are clearly visible once the wheels have been removed. They should be replaced when the lining material has worn down to within 1/16 in (2 mm) of the backing plates. Never allow metal-to-metal contact to develop. Not only will braking efficiency be greatly reduced, but the disc will very soon become scored and virtually useless, since the scores will cut into the new lining and wear it away with extreme rapidity.

The details vary, but each pad is nearly always retained by split pins, though sometimes retaining plates or anti-rattle springs

are also involved. Remove these pins with a pair of pliers and the pad can generally be pulled out. Then, very *gently* push back the pistons to make room for the new pads. Warning: do not press the brake pedal at this stage – if you do, a piston may be ejected from the cylinder and brake fluid will be lost. The piston will have to be carefully refitted and the complete braking system will need refilling and **bleeding**.

When the pistons have been pushed most of the way into their cylinders, fit the new pads.

Brake testing

When you have completed the adjustment, or replaced the pads or linings, it is worth testing the efficiency of the brakes, though new pads and linings first need a day or two of gentle use to bed-in properly. Find a straight, level, deserted and dry stretch of road with as little camber as possible, then try a succession of stops from 30 mph of gradually increasing severity to make sure the brakes neither pull to one side nor grab.

Brake bleeding

If the first part of the brake pedal's travel feels spongy, there is air in the system which must be removed. The presence of air generally means a leak, so the complete braking system should be thoroughly checked as already described (p. 301).

To purge the system of air or **bleed** the brakes, a piece of rubber or plastic tube approximately 2 ft (60 cm) long is needed – and an assistant. The internal diameter of the tube should be about 1/4 in (6 mm) so that it is a snug push fit on the bleed nipple with which each brake is provided. Top up the master cylinder and start with the bleed nipple furthest from it: push one end of the rubber tube over the nipple (fig. 313) and dip the other in a glass jar containing a small quantity of brake fluid. If a vacuum servo is fitted, the next job is to depress the brake pedal repeatedly with the engine switched off until the servo stops hissing and clicking, showing that the vacuum has been exhausted.

Now unscrew the bleed nipple half a turn with a small spanner and get your assistant to depress and release the brake pedal slowly. Continue pumping in this way until no further bubbles emerge into the fluid in the jar. Keep checking the master cylinder to make sure the level does not fall far, otherwise more air will be drawn into the system. Tighten the nipple. Repeat the process for the other three nipples in turn, ending with the one nearest the master cylinder. The pedal action should now be firm.

Brake fluid condition

As already mentioned, brake fluid absorbs water which creates a risk of vapour lock under heavy braking. The fluid should therefore be changed every eighteen months. Flush the system through with at least a litre of fluid before replenishing with a fresh supply. If in any doubt about the condition of the existing fluid, have it tested at a garage using a Castrol Vapour Lock Indicator or similar instrument.

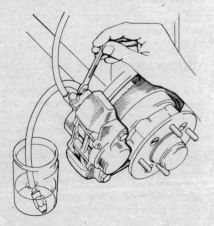

fig. 313. Bleeding the brakes.

Tyre wear and replacement

Most car handbooks still recommend that the wheels and tyres be changed round at regular intervals in a circulation system which brings in the spare. The advice is outdated, however, for two basic reasons. The first is that a tyre acquires a wear pattern determined by the suspension geometry of the particular wheel. For many independent systems the movement on one side is opposite in sense to that on the other – which is why Michelin developed their asymmetrical XAS and XVS tyres. Changing the wheels around not only upsets the handling of the car for a period but also increases the wear rate of the tyres by forcing them to conform to a new profile.

The second objection to this system is that spreading the wear evenly between the tyres means that all of them have to be replaced at once, instead of one or two at a time, creating an unnecessary burden. Consider a front-wheel drive car, for example, the front tyres of which usually wear at about twice the speed of the rear ones. Thus, when the two front tyres have nearly worn down, one can be replaced with the unused spare, the other with a new tyre, while one of the old front tyres will do as a spare. In this way the purchase of a single tyre is enough to keep the car on the road for a further 15–20,000 miles until the rear tyres finally wear out.

Wheel balance

A vibration at a few cycles per second which is felt through the steering and is at its most prominent at some definite speed – usually in the 40–60 mph range – is a sure sign that the front wheels need balancing. Apart from being uncomfortable, out-of-balance wheels are not good for the tyres, suspension system or handling. Choose a balancing specialist with the type of machine that balances the complete wheel, hub and brake assembly. It is a good idea to have the rear wheels balanced as well.

Dampers

When the hydraulic dampers become badly worn, safety is affected as well as comfort. Not only do the slightest bumps set the body into violent and uncontrolled pitching and bouncing movements, but on certain types of bad surface the car may suddenly become virtually uncontrollable. If you are in any doubt as to the condition of the dampers, get them tested.

Unfortunately little is learned from the traditional test: depressing one side of the body and observing the motion after releasing it (though it should certainly execute no more than one complete oscillation before coming to rest). Much more realistic results are obtained from the 'drop' type of test machine which lets one end of the car fall through a certain distance and then monitors the subsequent body movement. Still better is the Boge Shocktester machine which measures the response of the dampers to a range of frequencies and can distinguish the performance of the damper on one side of the car to that of the damper on the other side.

Clutch adjustment

Like the brakes, the clutch has facings of friction material which gradually wear, and this wear brings the pedal's range of movement nearer to the floor unless compensated for by adjustment. Most hydraulic actuation systems are self-adjusting, but very few cable systems are. The location of the clutch operating lever varies, but the important point when making any adjustment is to ensure that a small clearance is maintained

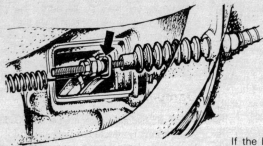

fig. 314. A clearance must be maintained between the operating lever of a mechanically operated clutch and the nipple of its control cable.

between it and the nipple of the control cable (fig. 314) when the pedal is not being depressed. Without clearance – the size of which is usually specified in the driver's handbook – the clutch may slip and wear prematurely.

Electrical system

The battery

In addition to topping up the battery at regular intervals with distilled water, it is worth keeping a check on the condition of the electrolyte with a **hydrometer**. This is simply a density, or specific gravity, measuring device consisting of a weighted float in a tube into which the electrolyte can be drawn with the help of a rubber bulb. When the battery is completely flat or discharged, the specific gravity falls to 1.00–1.15, but rises to 1.27–1.30 when fully charged.

Make sure that the main connectors grip the battery terminals firmly and that both are free of white corrosion products and lightly smeared with vaseline. If the lights go bright as the engine is revved and dim as it slows down, this is often due to poor connections at the battery. Remove the terminal clamps, clean their inner surfaces and the terminal posts with emery paper and replace.

If the battery becomes drained because the lights have been left on for a long period, or some cause of that sort, it can usually be recharged overnight by an inexpensive home charger. If the car can be started, however, the battery will soon become recharged by the generator. If a push-start is not possible, connect the battery of your car to that of another using **jump leads** – heavy-duty cables terminating in crocodile clips. Great care must be taken to connect the positive terminal of one battery to the positive terminal of the other, and similarly to connect negative terminal to negative terminal. On most but not all cars, the negative terminal is earthed to the structure of the car. Connecting the jump leads wrongly will have several consequences, all of them bad: the resultant sparks will create a fire risk; the batteries and their terminals may be damaged and the rectifying diodes on both cars will be burned out if they are fitted with alternators.

Fanbelt

A loose fanbelt or generator drive belt will slip – often emitting a sharp squeal as the engine is revved – and will allow the generator to slow down under load so that the battery eventually becomes discharged. When adjusting the belt, note that it need not be pulled rigidly taut – this will merely strain the generator bearings – but given a moderate tension only. Generally it should be possible to deflect the belt about ¾ in (18 mm) with the index finger at a point midway between the two pulleys.

Alternator care

Alternators are made with a definite polarity which cannot be changed, and they will be damaged if connected to the car's electrical system the wrong way round. Their associated rectifiers, for example, will be burned out, not only if jump leads are incorrectly used as already described, but also if the battery terminals are accidently reversed. Similarly, care is needed to ensure that the leads of a battery charger are connected in the correct sense: positive to positive and negative to negative. The engine may be run if the battery is already disconnected, but it must not be disconnected while the engine is actually running, as this creates surge currents which may also damage the rectifiers. It is advisable to isolate the alternator by removing its main output lead if any electrical welding is to be done to the car, as the stray currents set up are another possible source of trouble.

Conserving fuel

It is important to accept that there is no miracle way of improving fuel consumption. Independent tests have proved virtually all the so-called fuel economy devices to be useless. But quite noticeable economies can be obtained by making sure that every part of your car is functioning properly and is correctly adjusted: a car that is properly tuned can give up to 15 per cent better fuel economy than one which is maladjusted.

Brakes

To get good fuel economy, do not start at the carburetter; you start at the parts of the car most remote from it. Begin by parking on level ground, selecting neutral, releasing the handbrake and trying to push the car. If it will not roll freely, this could be because the handbrake is binding.

Assuming you have slackened the handbrake cables, if necessary, next drive the car around for a few miles using the brakes as little as possible. Then stop and feel the wheel hubs – or better still the drums or discs – to see if any of the shoes or pads are hot – this is a sign of binding; if so, adjust the footbrake as already described (p. 303) or seek skilled help. Touch carefully lest you burn your fingers.

Tyres

The next thing to look at is the tyres: make sure they are inflated to their recommended pressures. Soft tyres waste fuel. But do not over-inflate them. Even if the tyres are merely inflated to the heavy load or high-speed pressures while running lightly loaded or at low speeds, you may well lose more in increased wear at the crown of the tread than you gain in reduced rolling resistance. This is significantly lower for radial-ply tyres, though, than for cross-ply tyres.

The Engine

Cooling system
Within limits, the hotter an engine is, the better it runs. The fuel vaporizes better and the reduction in oil viscosity helps to minimize friction. Therefore, fit the thermostat with the highest temperature setting available for your car – consult a workshop manual or the local dealer. This is unlikely to cause overheating if you have a holiday in a hot country unless you are towing a caravan or the cooling or lubrication systems are of marginal efficiency.

Another good move is to fit one of the proprietory electric cooling fan kits. An engine-driven fan does absorb a bit of power at high revs. One version of the Peugeot 504 engine, for example, developed 97 bhp at 5200 rpm when driving its fan, but 104 bhp when the electromagnetic clutch had disengaged it. But note that the difference is no more than about 7 per cent, and only at maximum power revs used for a very small proportion of the total driving time, so claims of a 10 per cent improvement in overall fuel economy must be viewed with suspicion.

Ignition
The contact-breaker gap is one of the most important factors of all, so setting it correctly may bring you the biggest single improvement. Better still, fit a breakerless electronic ignition system and eliminate entirely the deterioration in performance every few thousand miles caused by erosion and wear of the contact-breaker. Also check that both the centrifugal and vacuum advance systems are working properly – these are very important indeed. In addition make sure that the plugs and their leads are in good condition. By far the best way of doing this is to have your car given an electronic tune-up by a skilled mechanic using equipment of the sort made by Bosch, Crypton, Souriau or Sun.

Carburation
Many cars have two positions for the carburetter air intake pipe: a 'winter' position pointing at the exhaust manifold and a 'summer' position, pointing away from it. Sometimes there is a flap in the air cleaner which achieves the same purpose. If your car has one of these arrangements, set it to the summer position to increase the density of the incoming air a little, and hence weaken the mixture slightly. This may prolong the warm-up period a little, but the hotter thermostat should compensate. The only other adverse possibility is of carburetter icing when the temperature is below 40°F and the humidity is high, but this rarely happens these days, partly because its occurrence is minimized by a standard fuel additive.

Do not remove the air cleaner or its element; *do* make sure that the element itself is clean. If it is a paper cartridge, replace it; if it is of the older type wash it in petrol or paraffin as instructed in the driver's handbook.

If your car has two or more carburetters, make sure that they are properly balanced. There are several devices on the market which will help you to do this.

If your car was made after 20 September 1973 it must conform to European exhaust emission regulations and these simple jobs will be about all that you can usefully carry out. The carburation and ignition settings should not be tampered with by anyone other than the accredited agent. Moreover, it is a myth that carburetter manufacturers stock 'weak' jets or needles which can be fitted to give improved economy. They do make jets and needles for high altitude locations, but if you fit these you could cause serious overheating, piston failure or burning of the exhaust valves during full-throttle running. It would only be safe to fit a weak needle or jet of this sort if at the same time the throttle opening was limited – say to three-quarters of its maximum. Of course, such a combination would amount to a major detuning of the engine.

Some weakening of the mixture may be permissible, however, with the SU and Stromberg constant-depression carburetters, since both of these are fitted with threaded adjustments which allow the jet to be moved with respect to the needle. However, the mixture can only be weakened until the limit of stable idling is reached; any attempt to weaken the mixture until hesitations begin at a steady 40 mph, say, will result in the engine being incapable of idling at all. Even idling adjustment may be difficult or impracticable with the latest emission carburetters.

On no account should the dashpot oil of an SU or Stromberg carburetter be removed in an attempt to reduce the acceleration enrichment normally needed when the throttle is suddenly opened; this is likely to make the economy worse and the car difficult to drive. Many fixed jet carburetters, however, have summer and winter positions for the accelerator pump. Again the summer position should be used all the time for economy, though the car may then be very hesitant after a winter cold start.

Fuel grade

Many people believe – quite wrongly – that even a low-compression, low-output engine runs better on high-octane or high star-rating fuel than on low-octane fuel. This is nonsense: using fuel of too high a grade is simply a waste of money. The correct grade for your car should be specified in the driver's handbook. If you are in any doubt you should consult the local dealer for the make in question, but as a temporary measure you can carry out a rough check for yourself.

With its engine fully warmed, take your car to a level stretch of road, engage top gear, and floor the accelerator. Ignore the various transmission rumblings and vibrations which such an action often provokes, and listen for the sharp tinkling noise in the engine called pinking (p. 27), which means that the fuel is detonating prematurely instead of burning smoothly. If the engine pinks in this way then fuel of a higher grade is needed; if not the grade in use will suffice. Be warned though, that even if the fuel passed this test, it might still allow the very damaging high-speed detonating to occur; also, the test assumes that the ignition tuning is correct.

If fuel of an adequate grade is not available, the engine can to some extent be adapted to it by retarding the ignition – one degree of ignition retard is roughly equivalent to a reduction of a single (Research) octane number. But the total retard should never be more than five degrees, otherwise damage to the engine from the overheating due to the delayed burning will result.

Fuel consumption measurement

Most motorists measure their fuel consumption very carelessly and inaccurately. Subconsciously, moreover, they tend to favour any supposed economy modification with more gentle driving and so are easily persuaded that an improvement has been effected. The only proper way to conduct before-and-after trials, however difficult it may be to arrange, is on a 'blind' basis so that the driver does not know whether the modification has been carried out or not.

If you do decide to monitor the fuel consumption of your car, however, there are a few golden rules to observe. The measurement distance must always be a long one, for instance – preferably at least 1000 miles but certainly more than 500. Never rely on your fuel gauge, but always start by filling the tank to the brim, adding the last gallon or so carefully and slowly, bouncing the car gently to free air bubbles if necessary. Then record all the fuel added, and fill the tank to the brim again to find the total quantity of fuel consumed. If you want to relate your fuel consumption to that of other cars, you should correct for any error in your distance recorder which may be 2–4 per cent inaccurate (usually fast). This can be done using motorway marker posts which are generally spaced at 100-metre and kilometre intervals, 16.1 kilometres being 10 miles true, a convenient measuring distance.

Economy driving

Skilful economy driving is something of an art which is not easily summarized in words. One thing is certain, though, it does not mean pottering along at 25 mph, getting in the way of other people who may have perfectly legitimate cause for haste. Although it is true that the faster you go the more fuel you consume, it is not so much the *speed* at which you drive which counts, but the *way* you drive.

Push the choke in as soon as you can, for example; accelerate gently and smoothly, get into top as quickly as possible and stay in top gear for as long as possible. You will use less fuel, for instance, climbing a hill with the throttle nearly full open in top, than with it partly closed in third – so long as the engine is not labouring or showing signs of distress. Keep it in its most efficient running range which is generally 2000–3000 rpm (you can work it out from the figures given in a road test if you do not have a rev-counter). Do not coast in neutral, but drive as if the brakes had failed, using careful anticipation and looking well ahead so that your car has slowed to a walking pace by the time you have reached the traffic lights. Remember, every time you rush up to the lights, braking hard at the last moment, you have thrown away a few cubic centimetres of fuel merely to heat up the brakes.

Coping with breakdowns

Car will not start

It is difficult to be cool, methodical and systematic when your car will not start, you are late for work and it is pouring with rain. But method and system are your most valuable allies in a crisis of this sort, and the fault-finding chart (fig. 315) helps you to exercise them. A car may not start for many reasons, but if there is enough energy in the battery to turn the starter motor at an adequate speed, the usual causes are lack of spark or lack of fuel. The chart tells you how to investigate both. A few simple tools and aids will vastly improve your chances of getting the car going: a pair of pliers, a couple of screwdrivers (one with Philips or cross-head bits) a hammer, an adjustable spanner, a roll of insulating tape, a length of insulated wire and a short piece of stiff wire.

Breakdowns on the move

Sudden cut

If the engine cuts out suddenly, as if it had been switched off, the trouble is nearly always electrical. Examine the plug leads and connections to the coil; you may be lucky and find the trouble is merely a faulty connection. If not, check the system as described in the ignition section of the fault-finding chart. If the contact-breaker points have worked loose, reset the gap to the thickness of a small nail file – this will be accurate enough to get you home. When checking for a spark, do not hold the plug leads in your bare hand for you may get an electric shock – not dangerous but uncomfortable.

Cough and splutter

A slower loss of engine power, on the other hand, developing in anything up to a minute and accompanied by coughing, spluttering or hesitations is nearly always a fault in the fuel system. Check that the pump is delivering fuel to the carburetter – a transparent pipe or filter bowl may help here, but it may be necessary to undo the connection. Remove the fuel filler cap – if there is a hiss the breather pipe may be blocked, though a hiss is now normal on some modern cars with tanks designed for evaporative loss control systems. You may continue without the cap or with it fitted loosely. If the engine will only run at low rpm even without load, the main jets may be blocked. Try placing your hand over the air intake and removing it suddenly (before the engine dies) for the suction thus created may draw out the dirt.

Power loss

Sometimes the engine will run but with markedly reduced power. Such a power loss can again have many causes, but one of the most common is an air leak into the induction system. Make sure that the carburetter is not loose and that the connecting pipes from

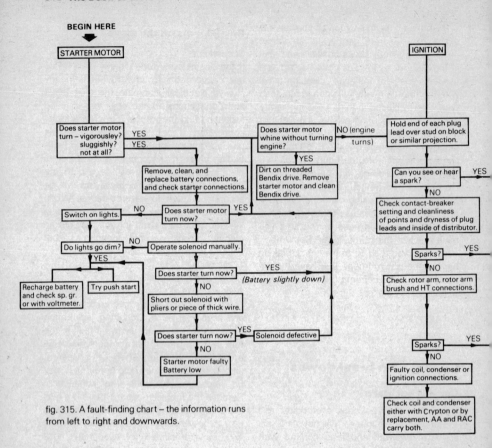

fig. 315. A fault-finding chart – the information runs from left to right and downwards.

the vacuum servo, crankcase breathing system and distributor are in place.

Fanbelt failure
In many cars a breakage of the fanbelt has three effects: it immobilizes the cooling fan, the waterpump and the generator – and a car cannot be safely run with an immobilized water pump. But most cars will run satisfactorily on the open road without the cooling fan, even in quite hot weather. If you cannot avoid some town driving, turn the heater and its booster fan fully on – this will help to dissipate the excess heat – and switch the engine off at each traffic light if the battery is healthy.

The ignition system generally draws 3–5 A, so if the battery is fully charged and you use no other electrical services such as the wipers, heater fan or lights, you can travel a long distance in daylight – perhaps fifty miles – before getting the fault cured. In the dark, of course, the current consumed by the lights will force you to make repairs or seek help as soon as possible.

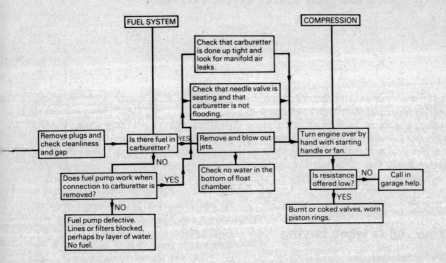

FUEL SYSTEM

Check that carburetter is done up tight and look for manifold air leaks.

Check that needle valve is seating and that carburetter is not flooding.

Remove plugs and check cleanliness and gap

Is there fuel in carburetter? — YES

NO

Does fuel pump work when connection to carburetter is removed? — YES

NO

Fuel pump defective. Lines or filters blocked, perhaps by layer of water. No fuel.

Remove and blow out jets.

Check no water in the bottom of float chamber.

COMPRESSION

Turn engine over by hand with starting handle or fan.

Is resistance offered low? — NO — Call in garage help.

YES

Burnt or coked valves, worn piston rings.

fourteen **Legal and Insurance**

As soon as you set out to buy or drive a car you come into contact with the immense, highly complicated – and continually growing – body of law which governs every aspect of the motorcar and its use. There is space to sketch only a few of the simpler and more basic points in this chapter.

Your rights when buying

One of the basic laws governing the purchase of a motorcar (and other objects for that matter) is the Sale of Goods Act 1893 which lays down that when someone sells something to a buyer a contract is in force which implies certain terms such as that the object sold be of 'merchantable quality' and 'fit for the purpose for which it is intended'. This applies to the sale of secondhand cars as well as new ones.

Unhappily the courts interpreted the 1893 Act to mean that these implied terms are in force only if they had not been specifically excluded or changed. Until quite recently, therefore, sellers of goods were able to take advantage of this loophole by listing on their guarantee or warranty forms a number of exclusion clauses which greatly limited their responsibility. Most buyers were obliged to sign agreement to these terms when purchasing a car, and in doing so they signed away their legal rights.

All this changed with the Supply of Goods (Implied Terms) Act of 1973 which made such exclusions void and strengthened the position of the buyer. If the car needs repair during what the court regards as a 'reason-able' period after purchase, for example, then it may be the seller's responsibility to provide a replacement car of similar type and calibre for the buyer's use while the repair is being carried out. In certain cases the buyer is even entitled to hire a car elsewhere and to require the seller to pay the bill – and to claim for loss of earnings due to the fault, if he can prove that his livelihood depends upon a car. Alternatively, if the buyer acts quickly and has done nothing to confirm the contract, he has the legal right to give the car back and apply to the courts for the return of his money.

There are, however, some exceptions to these rules. One is when the buyer examines the car and should have discovered the defect or defects about which he subsequently complains. Ironically this means that it may be better not to lift the bonnet of the car you buy. You should certainly not sign any form or invoice which says 'As seen, tried and approved' or carries any similar formula, even though it is of dubious legal force.

Another exception is sales between businesses, which may involve 'reasonable' exclusion clauses, because businessmen are held to be capable of looking after themselves. Finally, the sales of cars between private citizens are not in general bound by either of the two acts mentioned, though both are modified by the Unfair Contract Terms Act of 1977, and there is some doubt as to its influence on the position. But the buyer has grounds for a claim if the seller specifically promised that the car was in good condition, and it can be proved that it was not. It is the seller's legal responsibility to ensure that the car conforms with the construction and use regulations and is roadworthy in every respect. An unroadworthy car may be sold, so long as it can be proved that the sale proceeded on the understanding that the car was not to be used on the road.

A car dealer is also bound by the Trades Descriptions Act which makes misstatements about the condition of the car a potential criminal offence. He is allowed to extol his wares with a vague and generalized 'trade puff', but will be liable under the Act if he makes specific claims which are proved to be untrue. He will put himself in danger of prosecution, for instance, if the milometer reading of a car that he sells is claimed to be evidence of its condition but proves to be incorrect – for this reason many dealers now disclaim liability for the accuracy of the speedometer.

Hire purchase

The majority of cars are bought with the help of a hire purchase or consumer credit agreement. The buyer pays an initial cash deposit – or instead offers his existing car in part-exchange – and pays the remainder of the price in monthly instalments which include the interest charged by the hire purchase company. The agreement is that the dealer sells the car to the hire purchase company who then hire it to you with an option to buy at the end of the hire period if the instalments have been maintained.

Here again the buyer has been given much improved legal protection, in recent years. You are under no legal obligation to the hire purchase company unless you have signed an agreement form, for example. This must specify a number of vital factors such as the cash price, the interest rate, the total interest to be paid and the size and number of the monthly repayments. A copy of this document must be supplied to you after signature. The hire purchase company must then send to you *through the post* (*not* by hand) a second copy. You may cancel the contract at any time up to five days after receiving this second copy but you must do so in writing.

If you fall behind in the instalments and have paid, including the deposit, less than a third of the total cash price, the hire purchase company has the right to take back the car or **repossess** it without a court order. If you have paid more than a third, the hire purchase company does not have that right and before applying for a court order must first serve a **Notice of Default** specifying the amount of the arrears and requiring its repayment within seven days. When the hire purchase company obtains a court order it usually asks for the return of the car, but will very often allow the hire arrangement to continue if the payments are resumed – and at the same time increased to make up the arrears. If the hirer again defaults on the payments, or continues to do so in the first instance, the hire purchase company has the right, through the courts, to enforce the return of the car and to sue for damages to pay for any losses they may have incurred. The law defining the rights of the parties involved is in these circumstances too complex to describe further.

Registration

If you buy a new car the dealer generally arranges for its **registration** with the proper authorities for taxation and identification purposes. This can be done through any one of fifty-three Local Vehicle Licensing Offices. These allocate the identifying sequences of letters and numbers which every vehicle using the public roads is obliged to carry on flat, vertical plates at front and rear. If you want a particular unallocated number you need not deal with the Local Vehicle

Licensing Office nearest to you, but may obtain it from another one. The information you must supply includes the car's engine and chassis numbers as well as its make, model and engine capacity. This information is placed on record (using a computer storage system) at the Department of Transport's Driver and Vehicle Licensing Centre at Swansea which issues the motorcar's title deed or Registration Slip now used in place of the former logbook document.

If you buy a secondhand car which is already registered – as is nearly always the case – then the seller must hand the Registration Slip over to you when the sale is completed and you must inform the licensing authorities of the change of ownership.

If you build a car of your own which is a **special**, not substantially based on an existing model, it must be certified roadworthy by a Department of Transport vehicle examiner before registration is allowed.

Construction and use regulations

To ensure that cars are both roadworthy and used in a safe and considerate way, they and their drivers are governed by an elaborate code of **Construction and Use Regulations**. These are far too complex even to summarize in this book, but here are a few of the basic provisions:

Construction

Brakes

All cars except those first used before 1 January 1915 (to which special regulations apply) must be equipped with an efficient braking system having two means of operation or with two efficient systems each with its own means of operation. But a single braking system with a single means of operation will suffice if it is divided (p. 266). Whatever the system, if any part fails, except a

fixed member or brake shoe anchor pin, the system must still be capable of braking on not less than half the vehicle's wheels with enough efficiency to bring the vehicle to rest in a 'reasonable' distance under the most adverse conditions. For cars first used after 1 January 1915 and before 1 January 1968 the footbrake must be capable of achieving a deceleration of 0.45g on a dry surface and the secondary brake of 0.20g. For cars first used after 1 January 1968 the corresponding figures are 0.50g and 0.25g. The handbrake is often the secondary brake, but a split-circuit footbrake giving the required efficiency when one circuit fails, is permissible. With a few minor exceptions, cars and trailers first used after 1 January 1936 must be fitted at the rear with a pair of red stoplamps.

Lights

During the hours of darkness cars must in general carry a minimum of two sidelights showing to the front a white light visible from a reasonable distance, two tail lamps showing to the rear, a red light visible from a reasonable distance, a numberplate light and two red rear reflectors. Cars first used after 1931 must in general also have a matched pair of headlamps with a minimum power consumption of 30 W each, and capable of emitting main and dipped beams. Additional fog or driving lights may be fitted one each side of the car but must be simultaneously illuminated if used as an alternative to the headlamps. The locations of all these lamps must conform to various height and width limitations.

Belts

The seats of the driver and front passenger of cars first registered on or after 1 April 1967 must be fitted with anchorages marked BS AU 48:1965 or BS AU 48a, and with seatbelts marked BS 3254:1960 or BS AU 160a together with the British Standard Kite mark. Cars first registered between 1 January 1965 and 31 March 1967 must also comply, except that the anchorages do not have to meet the

British Standard. Similar requirements apply to three-wheelers first used from 1 September 1970, but all cars built before 30 June 1964 are exempt.

Since 31 January 1983, it has been a legal requirement for drivers and front passengers to wear seatbelts, except when reversing, in all vehicles to which they are fitted in accordance with the foregoing regulations. Medical exemption certificates may be granted by qualified doctors in rare cases, and a few special categories of motorist – such as milkmen and firemen – are also exempt.

Silencers

Cars must not emit excessive noise, and for those first registered after 1931 there is a specified limit measured with a sound level meter in a specified way. Cars travelling to and from a place, by previous arrangement, where either the sound level is to be measured or the silencer system improved to meet the legal requirements, are exempt.

Exhaust pollution

Cars first used from 1 January 1973 and fitted with a four-stroke spark ignition engine must be fitted with a system which recycles the crankcase fumes. A spark-ignition engined car first used after 10 November 1973 must bear an approval mark indicating compliance with exhaust emission requirements.

Use

Engine

If a driver leaves a car which is on the public roads he must switch off the engine and engage the handbrake.

Lights

Headlamps as well as sidelamps *must* be kept illuminated during the hours of darkness on roads without street lighting.

Tyres

Tyres must be free of major cuts and faults as already described (p. 302) and their treads must have a depth of at least 1 mm across their complete breadth and around the complete circumference of the tyre. The tyres of a given 'axle' must be of the same size and construction; i.e. be both radial or both crossplies. Crossplies may be fitted to the front wheels with radials at the rear, but not the other way round.

Horn

A private car may not be fitted with a gong, bell, siren or horn emitting two consecutive tones, while musical and multi-tone horns must not be fitted to cars first used from 1 August 1973. The horn must not be sounded between 11.30 pm and 7.00 am or when the car is stationary except in an emergency or as an anti-theft device.

The MoT test

In 1960 the so-called compulsory annual MoT (Ministry of Transport) test was introduced to improve standards of roadworthiness and reduce accidents due to mechanical failure. It is mostly applied by appointed garages whose standards tend to be inconsistent, so, if possible, use one of the few well-run and impartial government-run testing stations. Originally the test applied only to cars ten or more years old, but it now applies to cars three or more years old.

The test involves simple checks of the condition and efficiency of the parts of the car affecting safety and is divided into six parts covering brakes, steering and suspension, lights, tyres and wheels, seatbelts and other areas influencing safety. In 1977 the requirements were tightened to include such matters as the condition of the structure in the region of the mounting points of the brakes, suspension and steering.

If your car passes the test, you will be supplied, on payment of the appropriate fee, with a test certificate valid for one year. If it fails, and is considered by the examiner to be suffering from one or more defects which seriously prejudice its safety, you must have these defects repaired before you may legally drive the car from the testing station. So long as the defects constitute no immediate danger to safety, however, you may legally drive the car without a test certificate to a place of repair and back again to the testing station for a retest, though it is essential to do this by prior arrangement so that you can prove your intentions if stopped by the police, and of course the car must still be roadworthy.

If you feel that the grounds for the refusal of a test certificate are invalid, by far the best plan is to get the car tested at another garage, though you do have the right of appeal. This must be done within fourteen days and in writing to the office of any local Area Traffic Commissioners.

Insurance

So far we have seen that before you may legally drive your car on the public roads it must be properly registered with the authorities, must comply with the Construction and Use Regulations and must be roadworthy and must have an MoT certificate if it is more than three years old. But there is another very important requirement: that you take out insurance in at least the legally permitted minimum form. This is known as **third party** insurance because there may be three parties to the contract involved: yourself, the insurance company and the injured party.

Third party insurance insures you against claims which might be made against you as the result of death, injury, or damage to other vehicles or property caused by, or arising out of, the use of your car on the road. It also provides insurance cover against liabilities to any passengers carried in your car. Note that 'use' in this context includes leaving the car parked and unattended, and that the courts have been known to award very large sums in damages, so this is one legal requirement which it is particularly foolhardy and selfish to ignore. To prove that you are legally covered you must possess a certificate of insurance (usually valid for one year) which you must be prepared to produce at a police station within five days if requested. Additional protection can be obtained at extra expense (usually modest) by taking out a third party, fire and theft insurance policy which, as its name suggests, covers you against fire and theft as well as third parties.

Even a policy of this kind, however, gives no cover against injury to yourself or damage to your own car. The majority of motorists, therefore, take out a **fully comprehensive** policy which covers against these risks to varying carefully defined degrees – it pays to read the small print very carefully.

Most insurance companies run **no-claims bonus** schemes by which they progressively reduce the annual premiums to a certain minimum if you make no claims against them. The amount saved is usually considerable but if you make a claim as the result of an accident you will generally lose your accumulated no-claims bonus – very often whether the accident was your fault or not – and the next premium may well be increased in addition.

Vehicle excise licence

A further legal requirement is that you obtain a valid vehicle excise licence for your car, and that the circular licence disc be displayed on the windscreen. You are unlikely to be prosecuted if the licence disc has been removed for renewal, or if the new licence is not received or displayed for a period of up to fourteen days after the expiry of the old one, though strictly speaking you will be acting illegally in both cases.

Licences are valid for a year from the date of application or (at higher cost) for a period of six months. Existing licences may be renewed at a post office, but when there has been a change of ownership, a change in the specification of the vehicle or a break in the licensing period, a new licence may only b⌐ obtained from your Local Vehicle Licensing Office or from the Driver and Vehicle Licensing Centre at Swansea. In all cases you will be required to produce a valid certificate of insurance and MoT certificate (where relevant) and for the first excise licence of new vehicles registered after 1 April 1978 a Tyre Approval Certificate will also be required.

Driving licence

If you wish to drive your own car by yourself on the public roads yet another requirement is that you be the possessor of a current driving licence for the class of vehicle you intend to drive. To qualify for this you must be at least seventeen years old, suffer from no relevant prescribed or prospective disability such as uncontrolled epilepsy and be capable of reading (with glasses or contact lenses if worn) a numberplate with large symbols at 75 feet or one with small symbols at 67 feet in good daylight. Disabled drivers in receipt of a mobility allowance are eligible for a driving licence from the age of sixteen.

You must also, of course, have passed the Department of Transport driving test. While you are preparing for this you may drive with a provisional licence provided that you are accompanied by a qualified driver with a current licence, and displaying L-plates, are not towing a trailer and do not venture on to motorways. To pass the test these days, it is almost essential to have at least a few lessons with a qualified instructor (who must by law be registered), though there is no reason why you should not practise with a friend or relative who holds a current driving licence.

On the road

To summarize, then, before you can legally drive a car by yourself on the public roads you must comply with the following requirements. You must hold a current driving licence and have taken out at least the minimum third party insurance, while the car you drive must be roadworthy, have an MoT certificate if more than three years old, and must carry a valid vehicle excise licence.

Trailers and caravans

A trailer or caravan must display to the rear a numberplate, illuminated at night and carrying the same letters and numbers as the towing vehicle's. In general two red rear lamps and direction indicator repeater lamps must also be carried. In general, too, passengers must not be carried in a moving trailer or caravan.

A car may tow at up to 50 mph provided that the laden weight of the trailer, if load carrying, or gross weight of the caravan does not exceed the kerbside weight of the car; that it is fitted with brakes; that the towing vehicle is marked with its kerbside weight; and that a '50' sign is displayed at the rear of the trailer.

Going abroad

Passports

Before you may travel abroad with your car, you and your companions must first of all possess valid passports, though children under sixteen may be entered on the passports of their fathers, mothers or guardians. Passports are normally valid for ten years (five for children under sixteen) and application forms are available at main post offices. It is advisable to apply at least two months in advance of your visit, especially in spring or early summer. If you have little time, however, a temporary or British Visitor's passport may be obtained at once from a main post office if you apply in person. Evidence of British nationality (such as a birth certificate) is required for a full passport, evidence of identity for a temporary one, while for both, two passport-sized photographs of yourself are needed. To visit some countries, notably the East European ones, you may need in addition to obtain a visa from their consulate in Britain.

Driving licence

An ordinary full driving licence is sufficient for most countries providing that you are above a certain minimum age which varies for different countries but is usually eighteen. For certain countries such as Spain, though, you need an International Driving Permit, obtainable on the spot from main AA and RAC offices if you have a full driving licence and bring a passport photograph.

Registration

You should also carry your car's registration document – either the obsolescent logbook, if still in force, or the new Regislation Slip. If the car does not belong to you, a letter authorizing its use abroad, signed by the owner, should be carried.

Insurance

Nowadays the third party insurance which is the legal minimum in Britain automatically gives you the legal minimum cover in all EEC countries – Belgium, Denmark, Eire, France, West Germany, Greece, Italy, Luxembourg and the Netherlands – plus Austria, Finland, Norway, Sweden, Hungary, Czechoslovakia, East Germany and Switzerland provided that you *inform your insurance company of your journey beforehand.* However, you would be most ill-advised to rely on this alone, as the minimum legal requirements in other countries are in many cases lower than in Britain and may not, for example, provide compensation for the passengers. Instead you should obtain an international insurance certificate or Green Card, which in any case is a legal requirement in some other countries, such as Spain. Your insurance company will supply you with one on payment of a small additional premium. It gives you additional protection, but only in proportion to your UK cover. Thus if you have comprehensive cover in Britain, it will give you this abroad, but if you have third party cover only, it will not give you more than that abroad. Make sure that the Green Card covers your caravan if you are towing one – you may need special insurance for it.

For travel in Spain an additional document known as a bail bond is needed. For a small sum it provides a guarantee that the insurance company will pay a cash deposit of up to £500 to a Spanish court as bail, if necessary. This is because a driver may be arrested in Spain after an accident, and have his car and property impounded.

Health insurance

Free medical treatment can now be obtained in an emergency in the EEC countries if you produce Form E111, issued by the Department of Health, and in Bulgaria, Poland, Norway, Sweden, Austria and Yugoslavia if you produce your passport. The treatment available will not cover every contingency, however, so you would be well advised to take out health insurance for the trip.

Motoring offences

Speeding

One of the most common of all motoring offences is exceeding the speed limit – which these days can be 30 mph, 40 mph, 50 mph, 60 mph or 70 mph, depending upon the locality. You may be convicted on the evidence of one policeman alone, especially if he has a speedometer, radar meter or VASCAR (Visual Average Speed Computer And Recorder) system to refer to. However, if the evidence is purely subjective, two witnesses are required. If found guilty the penalty is a fine and three penalty points will be imposed.

Careless driving

More serious than speeding is driving 'without due care and attention or without reasonable consideration for other persons using the road'. This means what it says and is difficult to define more precisely, especially since what one court regards as being without due care and attention another may regard as something more serious still. A fine is again the penalty; two to five penalty points will be imposed.

Reckless driving

Still more serious than careless driving is 'driving recklessly or at a speed or in a manner which is dangerous to the public having regard to all the circumstances of the case including the nature, condition and use of the road, and the amount of traffic which is actually or which might reasonably be expected to be on the road'. Failure to observe traffic lights might be construed by a court as reckless driving, as might passing on the inside on a motorway. The usual penalty is endorsement and a fine, but the magistrate has the power to disqualify and to impose a prison sentence; ten penalty points will be imposed.

Notice of prosecution

You cannot be convicted of any of these three offences unless (a) you were warned at the time, (b) you are served with a summons within fourteen days, or (c) you are served with a Notice of Intended Prosecution within fourteen days specifying the nature of the alleged offence and the time and place at which it was supposed to have been committed. You may be regarded as having been served with the notice if it is sent by registered post or recorded delivery, even if you do not receive it.

Drink and drug offences

Short of causing death by reckless driving, the most serious motoring offence of all is driving or attempting to drive while unfit to do so through drink or drugs. Nowadays charges of this nature are nearly always linked to a breathalyser check and subsequent tests at the nearest police station. The legal limit is 80 mg of alcohol per 100 ml of blood or 107 mg of alcohol per 100 ml of urine. Disqualification is virtually automatic.

Penalty points system

Until quite recently, a driver who received three endorsements in three years was liable for disqualification for six months, but since the endorsements could be for minor offences, this system was considered to be harsh and arbitrary. It was replaced, with effect from 1 November 1982, with a more flexible penalty points system, under which the driver faces disqualification if he or she accumulates twelve penalty points in three years (the magistrates have the power to waive disqualification if there are mitigating circumstances); reckless driving, for example, carries a penalty of ten points, but the score is lower for minor offences, being only three for speeding.

Appearing in court

It is possible to plead guilty by post to minor offences which do not involve disqualification. If you do this, the prosecution will be obliged to confine their plea to the Statement of Facts sent to you with the summons, and the court will hear any mitigating circumstances you set down on the form provided.

If you appear in court, however, it will almost certainly be a magistrates' court, which is where the majority of motoring offences are heard. Only a limited number of offences may now be heard in a higher court. You also have the right of appeal against a magistrate's decision if you have pleaded not guilty, and against sentence if you plead guilty.

If you are quick-witted, not easily flustered and absolutely convinced that you were in the right, it may be worth taking the risk of defending yourself. The golden rules are to be scrupulously polite to everyone involved, including hostile witnesses, and, while trying to expose any inconsistencies in the evidence against you, to avoid humiliating people. The magistrates are seldom impressed by an overbearing attitude.

Generally, though, the most sensible plan is to find a really good solicitor with experience of motoring cases to defend you. Solicitors – like everyone else – vary quite a bit in their competence, so make careful inquiries before choosing one. As legal defence can be an expensive business, and as free legal aid is available to relatively few people, the legal services offered by the AA and RAC are well worth while.

What to do after an accident

Reporting it

If you are driving a car involved in an accident in which there is damage or injury to another car, any property on the road or its vicinity, an animal or any person or persons, you are required by law to stop – it is a criminal offence not to do so unless you can show that you could not reasonably have known that an accident occurred. An animal in this context basically means any animal of domestic value and includes horses, mules, cattle, pigs, sheep, goats or dogs, but does not include some other animals such as rabbits and cats.

Having stopped, it is then your duty to give your name and address to anyone with reasonable grounds for requiring it. If you are unable to do this, you must report the accident to the police *as soon as reasonably practicable* and whatever happens within twenty-four hours. If the accident involves personal injury to one or more persons, you are further required to produce your certificate of insurance to anyone reasonably requiring it – and this is almost always the police. If you cannot produce the certificate at the time of the accident or the time of reporting it, you are allowed five days (altogether) in which to do so at any police station you care to designate.

Further action

So much for the letter of the law, but there are other matters to be considered. Do not move your car, for instance, from its final position at the end of the accident, if it is possible to leave it there without obstructing the traffic. This will allow the police to take measurements, and may help you later on.

After this, your next priority must be to care for any injured. Administer first aid if you know how, and make sure that an ambulance is called as soon as possible. At the same time, though, *make sure you get the names and addresses of as many witnesses as possible.*

What you do next – or more important, what you say next – should be constrained by a good deal of care and caution. Unfortunately the rules of behaviour which serve us best in normal situations are not appropriate to accidents. Natural courtesy may make you want to apologize if you feel you were even partially to blame; natural honesty may make you feel you have nothing to fear by making on-the-spot statements. But even if you are not injured yourself, you will almost certainly be in a state of shock and thus less capable of describing the accident accurately than you think you are. Moreover, other people may not be as honest as yourself: they may bend the facts to suit their own interests or even deny any responsibility when they were clearly to blame.

By far the best plan, therefore, is to make no immediate statement at all. Wait until you have consulted a solicitor, or at least until you have considered the matter carefully. Certainly you should never apologize or admit liability. Some insurance policies specifically warn you not to, and there is no law which requires you to make statements against yourself. Only if your involvement was solely as an observer, or if you are convinced you were entirely blameless (and can prove it) should you be prepared to make a statement to the police without taking advice from a solicitor.

As soon as possible after the accident you should make careful notes about it, drawing a plan. If the accident is to be the subject of legal proceedings, the case will probably not come to court for some weeks, perhaps months, by which time your memories of the accident will have dimmed. At the same time you should obtain an accident report form from your broker or insurance company and then complete and return it. A summons or Notice of Intended Prosecution should be reported to your insurance company and your solicitor.

Index